System-on-Chip Architecture

ARM System-on-Chip Architecture

Steve Furber

Pearson

Authorized adaptation from the United Kingdom edition, entitled *ARM System-on-Chip Architecture*, ISBN: 9780201675191 by Furber, Steve, published by Pearson Education Limited, Copyright © Pearson Education Limited 2000.

Indian Subcontinent Adaptation

ISBN 978-93-325-5557-0

First Impression 2016
Third Impression 2017
Fourth Impression 2017

Published by Pearson India Education Services Pvt. Ltd, CIN: U72200TN2005PTC057128, formerly known as TutorVista Global Pvt. Ltd, licensee of Pearson Education in South Asia.

Head Office: 15th Floor, Tower-B, World Trade Tower, Plot No. 1, Block-C, Sector 16, Noida 201301, Uttar Pradesh, India.

Registered Office: 4th floor, Software Block, Elnet Software City, TS -140, Block 2 & 9 Rajiv Gandhi Salai, Taramani, Chennai 600 113, Tamil Nadu, India.
Fax: 080-30461003, Phone: 080-30461060
www.pearson.co.in, Email: companysecretary.india@pearson.com

Printed in India by Saurabh Printers Pvt. Ltd., Noida

Contents

Preface

Aims

This book in [illegible] based around [illegible] microprocessor [illegible]

The aim [illegible] designed and [illegible] to know only [illegible] which can otherwise [illegible] the ARM sho[illegible]

Other [illegible] a comparative [illegible] elsewhere fo[illegible]

Audience

The book is [illegible]

- Professional [illegible] which [illegible] find the book [illegible] nical [illegible] subsequ[illegible] be useful [illegible]
- Students of [illegible] the [illegible] course [illegible] from a [illegible]

Prerequisite Knowledge

This book is [illegible] design. Readers are [illegible] a second year [illegible] material is pre[illegible]

No prior fa[illegible] ARM processor is [illegible]

The ARM

On 26 April 19[illegible] the first ARM prototypes [illegible] England, having been fabricated by VLSI Technology [illegible] they were running [illegible] of the 1980s the ARM was [illegible] basis of educational computers [illegible]

Preface

Aims

This book introduces the concepts and methodologies employed in designing a system-on-chip (SoC) based around a microprocessor core and in designing the microprocessor core itself. The principles of microprocessor design are made concrete by extensive illustrations based upon the ARM.

The aim of the book is to assist the reader in understanding how SoCs and microprocessors are designed and used, and why a modern processor is designed the way that it is. The reader who wishes to know only the general principles should find that the ARM illustrations add substance to issues which can otherwise appear somewhat ethereal; the reader who wishes to understand the design of the ARM should find that the general principles illuminate the rationale for the ARM being as it is.

Other microprocessor architectures are not described in this book. The reader who wishes to make a comparative study of architectures will find the required information on the ARM here but must look elsewhere for information on other designs.

Audience

The book is intended to be of use to two distinct groups of readers:

- Professional hardware and software engineers who are tasked with designing an SoC product which incorporates an ARM processor, or who are evaluating the ARM for a product, should find the book helpful in their duties. Although there is considerable overlap with ARM technical publications, this book provides a broader context with more background. It is not a substitute for the manufacturer's data, since much detail has had to be omitted, but it should be useful as an introductory overview and adjunct to that data.
- Students of computer science, computer engineering and electrical engineering should find the material of value at several stages in their courses. Some chapters are closely based on course material previously used in undergraduate teaching; some other material is drawn from a postgraduate course.

Prerequisite Knowledge

This book is not intended to be an introductory text on computer architecture or computer logic design. Readers are assumed to have a level of familiarity with these subjects equivalent to that of a second year undergraduate student in computer science or computer engineering. Some first year material is presented, but this is more by way of a refresher than as a first introduction to this material.

No prior familiarity with the ARM processor is assumed.

The ARM

On 26 April 1985, the first ARM prototypes arrived at Acorn Computers Limited in Cambridge, England, having been fabricated by VLSI Technology, Inc., in San Jose, California. A few hours later they were running code, and a bottle of *Moët & Chandon* was opened in celebration. For the remainder of the 1980s the ARM was quietly developed to underpin Acorn's desktop products which form the basis of educational computing in the UK; over the 1990s, in the care of ARM Limited, the ARM has sprung onto the world stage and has established a market-leading position in high-performance low-power and low-cost embedded applications.

This prominent market position has increased ARM's resources and accelerated the rate at which new ARM-based developments appear.

The highlights of the last decade of ARM development include:

- the introduction of the novel compressed instruction format called 'Thumb' which reduces cost and power dissipation in small systems;
- significant steps upwards in performance with the ARM9, ARM10 and 'Strong-ARM' processor families;
- a state-of-the-art software development and debugging environment;
- a very wide range of embedded applications based around ARM processor cores.

Most of the principles of modern SoC and processor design are illustrated somewhere in the ARM family, and ARM has led the way in the introduction of some concepts (such as dynamically decompressing the instruction stream). The inherent simplicity of the basic 3-stage pipeline ARM core makes it a good pedagogical introductory example to real processor design, whereas the debugging of a system based around an ARM core deeply embedded into a complex system chip represents the cutting-edge of technological development today.

Book Structure

Chapter 1 starts with a refresher on first year undergraduate processor design material. It illustrates the principle of abstraction in hardware design by reviewing the roles of logic and gate-level representations. It then introduces the important concept of the *Reduced Instruction Set Computer* (RISC) as background for what follows, and closes with some comments on design for low power.

Chapter 2 describes the ARM processor architecture in terms of the concepts introduced in the previous chapter, and Chapter 3 is a gentle introduction to user-level assembly language programming and could be used in first year undergraduate teaching for this purpose.

Chapter 4 describes the organization and implementation of the 3- and 5-stage pipeline ARM processor cores at a level suitable for second year undergraduate teaching, and covers some implementation issues.

Chapters 5 and 6 go into the ARM instruction set architecture in increasing depth. Chapter 5 goes back over the instruction set in more detail than was presented in Chapter 3, including the binary representation of each instruction, and it penetrates more deeply into the corners of the instruction set. It is probably best read once and then used for reference. Chapter 6 backs off a bit to consider what a high-level language (in this case, C) really needs and how those needs are met by the ARM instruction set. This chapter is based on second year undergraduate material.

Chapter 7 introduces the 'Thumb' instruction set which is an ARM innovation to address the code density and power requirements of small embedded systems. It is of peripheral interest to a generic study of computer science, but adds an interesting lateral perspective to a postgraduate course.

Chapter 8 raises the issues involved in debugging systems which use embedded processor cores and in the production testing of board-level systems. These issues are background to Chapter 9 which introduces a number of different ARM integer cores, broadening the theme introduced in Chapter 4 to include cores with 'Thumb', debug hardware, and more sophisticated pipeline operation.

Chapter 10 introduces the concept of memory hierarchy, discussing the principles of memory management and caches. Chapter 11 reviews the requirements of a modern operating system at a second year undergraduate level and describes the approach adopted by the ARM to address these requirements. Chapter 12 introduces the integrated ARM CPU cores (including StrongARM) that incorporate full support for memory management.

Chapter 13 covers the issues of designing SoCs with embedded processor cores. Here, the ARM is at the leading edge of technology. Several examples are presented of production embedded system chips to show the solutions that have been developed to the many problems inherent in committing a complex application-specific system to silicon.

Chapter 14 moves away from mainstream ARM developments to describe the asynchronous ARM-compatible processors and systems developed at the University of Manchester, England, during the 1990s. After a decade of research the AMULET technology is, at the time of writing, about to take its first step into the commercial domain. Chapter 14 concludes with a description of the DRACO SoC design, the first commercial application of a 32-bit asynchronous microprocessor.

A short appendix presents the fundamentals of computer logic design and the terminology which is used in Chapter 1.

A glossary of the terms used in the book and a bibliography for further reading are appended at the end of the book, followed by a detailed index.

Course Relevance

The chapters are at an appropriate level for use on undergraduate courses as follows:

Year 1: Chapter 1 (basic processor design); Chapter 3 (assembly language programming); Chapter 5 (instruction binaries and reference for assembly language programming).

Year 2: Chapter 4 (simple pipeline processor design); Chapter 6 (architectural support for high-level languages); Chapters 10 and 11 (memory hierarchy and architectural support for operating systems).

Year 3: Chapter 8 (embedded system debug and test); Chapter 9 (advanced pipelined processor design); Chapter 12 (advanced CPUs); Chapter 13 (example embedded systems).

A postgraduate course could follow a theme across several chapters, such as processor design (Chapters 1, 2, 4, 9, 10 and 12), instruction set design (Chapters 2, 3, 5, 6, 7 and 11) or embedded systems (Chapters 2, 4, 5, 8, 9 and 13).

Chapter 14 contains material relevant to a third year undergraduate or advanced postgraduate course on asynchronous design, but a great deal of additional background material (not presented in this book) is also necessary.

Support Material

Many of the figures and tables will be made freely available over the Internet for non-commercial use. The only constraint on such use is that this book should be a recommended text for any course which makes use of such material. Information about this and other support material may be found on the World Wide Web at:

http://www.cs.man.ac.uk/amulet/publications/books/ARMsysArch

Any enquiries relating to commercial use must be referred to the publishers. The assertion of the copyright for this book outlined on page iv remains unaffected.

Feedback

The author welcomes feedback on the style and content of this book, and details of any errors that are found. Please email any such information to:

sfurber@cs.man.ac.uk

Steve Furber

Acknowledgements

Many people have contributed to the success of the ARM over the past decade. As a policy decision I have not named in the text the individuals with principal responsibilities for the developments described therein since the lists would be long and attempts to abridge them invidious. History has a habit of focusing credit on one or two high-profile individuals, often at the expense of those who keep their heads down to get the job done on time. However, it is not possible to write a book on the ARM without mentioning Sophie Wilson whose original instruction set architecture survives, extended but otherwise largely unscathed to this day.

I would also like to acknowledge the support received from ARM Limited in giving access to their staff and design documentation, and I am grateful for the help I have received from ARM's semiconductor partners, particularly VLSI Technology, Inc., which is now wholly owned by Philips Semiconductors.

The book has been considerably enhanced by helpful comments from reviewers of draft versions. I am grateful for the sympathetic reception the drafts received and the direct suggestions for improvement that were returned. The publishers, Addison Wesley Longman Limited, have been very helpful in guiding my responses to these suggestions and in other aspects of authorship.

Lastly I would like to thank my wife, Valerie, and my daughters, Alison and Catherine, who allowed me time off from family duties to write this book.

Steve Furber

The publishers would like to thank Lyla B. Das, Department of Electronics and Communication, National Institute of Technology Calicut, for her valuable inputs for enhancing the content of this book to suit the requirements of Indian universities.

Trademark Notice

Acorn™, Risc PC™, Acorn Archimedes™ and Online Media™ are trademarks of Acorn Computer Ltd.

ARM®, StrongARM® and Thumb® are registered trademarks and AMBA™, Angel™, ARMulator™, EmbeddedICE™, ARM7TDMI™, ARM7TDMI-S™, ARM9TDMI™, Piccolo™ and STRONG™ are trademarks of ARM Ltd.

Apple™ and Newton™ are trademarks of Apple Computer, Inc.

Digital™, Digital Semiconductor™, PDP-8™ and Alpha™ are trademarks of Digital Equipment Corporation.

TimeMill™, Piccolo™ is a trademark of EPIC Design Technology, Inc.

Hagenuk® is a registered trademark of Hagenuk GmbH.

IBM® is a registered trademark of International Business Machines Corporation.

Inmos® is a registered trademark and transputer™ is a trademark of Inmos Group of Companies.

Intel® is a registered trademark of Intel Corporation.

MS-DOS®, Microsoft® and Windows® are registered trademarks of Microsoft Corporation.

MC68000™ is a trademark of Motorola Corporation.

UNIX® is a registered trademark of Novell, Inc.

I²C Bus® is a registered trademark and JumpStart™, N-Trace™, OneC™, Rapid Silicon Prototyping™, Ruby II™ and VLSI ISDN Subscriber Processor™ are trademarks of Philips Semiconductors.

Psion Series 5MX™ is a trademark of Psion plc.

Samsung SGH2400™ is a trademark of Samsung.

SPARC® is a registered trademark of SPARC International, Inc.

SUN™ is a trademark of Sun Microsystems, Inc.

Bluetooth™ is a technology trademark owned by Telefonaktiebolaget LM Ericsson.

Within this publication, the term BBC is used as an abbreviation for British Broadcasting Corporation.

1

An Introduction to Processor Design

SUMMARY OF CHAPTER CONTENTS

The design of a general-purpose processor, in common with most engineering endeavours, requires the careful consideration of many trade-offs and compromises. In this chapter we will look at the basic principles of processor instruction set and logic design and the techniques available to the designer to help achieve the design objectives.

Abstraction is fundamental to understanding complex computers. This chapter introduces the abstractions which are employed by computer hardware designers, of which the most important is the logic gate. The design of a simple processor is presented, from the instruction set, through a register transfer level description, down to logic gates.

The ideas behind the *Reduced Instruction Set Computer* (RISC) originated in processor research programmes at Stanford and Berkeley universities around 1980, though some of the central ideas can be traced back to earlier machines. In this chapter we look at the thinking that led to the RISC movement and consequently influenced the design of the ARM processor which is the subject of the following chapters.

With the rapid development of markets for portable computer-based products, the power consumption of digital circuits is of increasing importance. At the end of the chapter we will look at the principles of low-power high-performance design.

1.1 | Processor Architecture and Organization

All modern general-purpose computers employ the principles of the *stored-program digital computer*. The stored-program concept originated from the Princeton Institute of Advanced Studies in the 1940s and was first implemented in the 'Baby' machine which first ran in June 1948 at the University of Manchester in England.

Fifty years of development have resulted in a spectacular increase in the performance of processors and an equally spectacular reduction in their cost. Over this period of relentless progress in the cost-effectiveness of computers, the principles of operation have changed remarkably little. Most of the improvements have resulted from advances in the technology of electronics, moving from valves (vacuum tubes) to individual transistors, to integrated circuits **(ICs)** incorporating several bipolar transistors and then through generations of IC technology leading to today's very large scale integrated **(VLSI)** circuits delivering millions of field-effect transistors on a single chip. As transistors get smaller they get cheaper, faster, and consume less power. This win-win scenario has carried the computer industry forward for the past three decades, and will continue to do so at least for the next few years.

However, not all of the progress over the past 50 years has come from advances in electronics technology. There have also been occasions when a new insight into the way that technology is employed has made a significant contribution. These insights are described under the headings of computer architecture and computer organization, where we will work with the following interpretations of these terms:

1.1.1 | Computer Architecture

- Computer architecture describes the user's view of the computer. The instruction set, visible registers, memory management table structures and exception handling model are all part of the architecture.

1.1.2 | Computer Organization

- Computer organization describes the user-invisible implementation of the architecture. The pipeline structure, transparent cache, table-walking hardware and translation look-aside buffer are all aspects of the organization.

Amongst the advances in these aspects of the design of computers, the introduction of virtual memory in the early 1960s, of transparent cache memories, of pipelining and so on, have all been milestones in the evolution of computers. The RISC idea ranks amongst these advances, offering a significant shift in the balance of forces which determines the cost-effectiveness of computer technology.

1.1.3 | What is a Processor?

A general-purpose processor is a finite-state automaton that executes instructions held in a memory. The state of the system is defined by the values held in the memory locations together with the values held in certain registers within the processor itself (see Figure 1.1; the hexadecimal notation for the memory addresses is explained in Section 6.2 on page 134). Each instruction defines a particular way the total state should change and it also defines which instruction should be executed next.

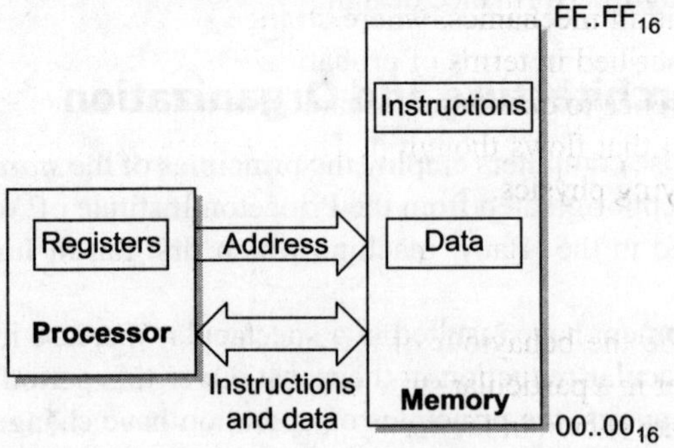

Figure 1.1 The state in a stored-program digital computer

1.1.4 | The Stored-program Computer

The **stored-program** digital computer keeps its instructions and data in the same memory system, allowing the instructions to be treated as data when necessary. This enables the processor itself to generate instructions which it can subsequently execute. Although programs that do this at a fine granularity **(self-modifying** code) are generally considered bad form these days since they are very difficult to debug, use at a coarser granularity is fundamental to the way most computers operate. Whenever a computer loads in a new program from disk (overwriting an old program) and then executes it the computer is employing this ability to change its own program.

1.1.5 | Computer Applications

Because of its programmability a stored-program digital computer is **universal**, which means that it can undertake any task that can be described by a suitable algorithm. Sometimes this is reflected by its configuration as a desktop machine where the user runs different programs at different times, but sometimes it is reflected by the same processor being used in a range of different applications, each with a fixed program. Such applications are characteristically embedded into products such as mobile telephones, automotive engine-management systems, and so on.

1.2 | Abstraction in Hardware Design

Computers are very complex pieces of equipment that operate at very high speeds. A modern microprocessor may be built from several million transistors each of which can switch a hundred million times a second. Watch a document scroll up the screen on a desktop PC or workstation and try to imagine how a hundred million million transistor switching actions are used in each second of that movement. Now consider that every one of those switching actions is, in some sense, the consequence of a deliberate design decision. None of them is random or uncontrolled; indeed a single error amongst those transitions is likely to cause the machine to collapse into a useless state. How can such complex systems be designed to operate so reliably?

1.2.1 | Transistors

A clue to the answer may be found in the question itself. We have described the operation of the computer in terms of transistors, but what is a transistor? It is a curious structure composed from carefully chosen chemical substances with complex electrical properties that can only be understood by reference to the theory of quantum mechanics, where strange subatomic particles sometimes behave like waves and can only be described in terms of probabilities. Yet the gross behaviour of a transistor can be described, without reference to quantum mechanics, as a set of equations that relate the voltages on its terminals to the current that flows though it. These equations **abstract** the essential behaviour of the device from its underlying physics.

1.2.2 | Logic Gates

The equations that describe the behaviour of a transistor are still fairly complex. When a group of transistors is wired together in a particular structure, such as the CMOS (Complementary Metal Oxide Semiconductor) NAND gate shown in Figure 1.2, the behaviour of the group has a particularly simple description.

If each of the input wires (*A* and *B*) is held at a voltage which is either near to *Vdd* or near to *Vss*, the output will also be near to *Vdd* or *Vss* according to the following rules:

- If *A* and *B* are both near to *Vdd*, the output will be near to *Vss*.
- If either *A* or *B* (or both) is near to *Vss*, the output will be near to *Vdd*.

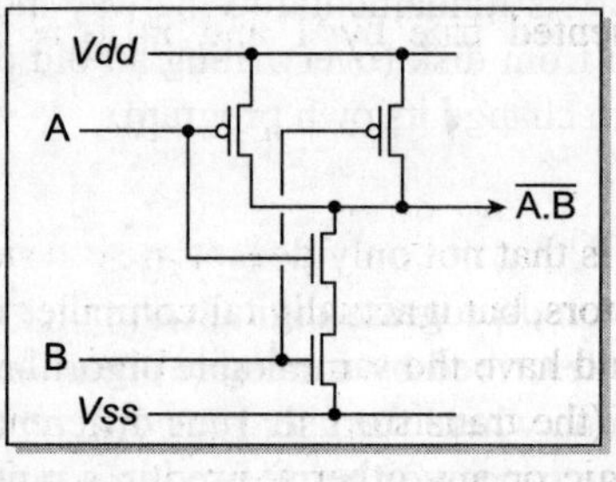

Figure 1.2 The transistor circuit of a static 2-input CMOS NAND gate

With a bit of care we can define what is meant by 'near to' in these rules, and then associate the meaning **true** with a value near to *Vdd* and **false** with a value near to *Vss*. The circuit is then an implementation of the NAND Boolean logic function:

$$output = \neg(A \wedge B) \qquad \text{Equation 1}$$

Although there is a lot of engineering design involved in turning four transistors into a reliable implementation of this equation, it can be done with sufficient reliability that the logic designer can think almost exclusively in terms of logic gates. The concepts that the logic designer works with are illustrated in Figure 1.3, and consist of the following 'views' of the logic gate:

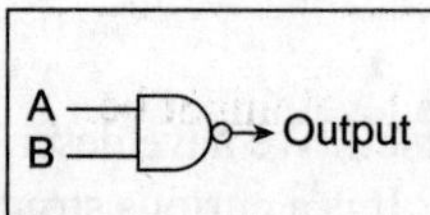

A	B	Output
0	0	1
0	1	1
1	0	1
1	1	0

Truth table

Figure 1.3 The logic symbol and truth table for a NAND gate

1.2.3 | Logic Symbol

- A logic symbol.

This is a symbol that represents a NAND gate function in a circuit schematic; there are similar symbols for other logic gates (for instance, removing the bubble from the output leaves an AND gate which generates the opposite output function; further examples are given in 'Appendix: Computer Logic' on page 343).

1.2.4 | Truth Table

- A truth table.

This describes the logic function of the gate, and encompasses everything that the logic designer needs to know about the gate for most purposes. The significance here is that it is a lot simpler than four sets of transistor equations.

(In this truth table we have represented 'true' by '1' and 'false' by '0', as is common practice when dealing with Boolean variables.)

1.2.5 | The Gate Abstraction

The point about the gate abstraction is that not only does it greatly simplify the process of designing circuits with great numbers of transistors, but it actually removes the need to know that the gate is built from transistors. A logic circuit should have the same logical behaviour whether the gates are implemented using field-effect transistors (the transistors that are available on a CMOS process), bipolar transistors, electrical relays, fluid logic or any other form of logic. The implementation technology will affect the *performance* of the circuit, but it should have no effect on its *function*. It is the duty of the transistor-level circuit designer to support the gate abstraction as near perfectly as is possible in order to isolate the logic circuit designer from the need to understand the transistor equations.

1.2.6 | Levels of Abstraction

It may appear that this point is being somewhat laboured particularly to those readers who have worked with logic gates for many years. However, the principle that is illustrated in the gate level abstraction is repeated many times at different levels in computer science and is absolutely fundamental to the process which we began considering at the start of this section, which is the management of complexity.

The process of gathering together a few components at one level to extract their essential joint behaviour and hide all the unnecessary detail at the next level enables us to scale orders of complexity in a few steps. For instance, if each level encompasses four components of the next lower level as our gate model does, we can get from a transistor to a microprocessor comprising a million transistors in just ten steps. In many cases we work with more than four components, so the number of steps is greatly reduced.

A typical hierarchy of abstraction at the hardware level might be:

1. transistors;
2. logic gates, memory cells, special circuits;
3. single-bit adders, multiplexers, decoders, flip-flops;
4. word-wide adders, multiplexers, decoders, registers, buses;
5. ALUs (Arithmetic-Logic Units), barrel shifters, register banks, memory blocks;
6. processor, cache and memory management organizations;
7. processors, peripheral cells, cache memories, memory management units;
8. integrated system chips;
9. printed circuit boards;
10. mobile telephones, PCs, engine controllers.

The process of understanding a design in terms of levels of abstraction is reasonably concrete when the design is expressed in hardware. But the process doesn't stop with the hardware; if anything, it is even more fundamental to the understanding of software and we will return to look at abstraction in software design in due course.

1.2.7 | Gate-level Design

The next step up from the logic gate is to assemble a library of useful functions each composed of several gates. Typical functions are, as listed above, adders, multiplexers, decoders and flip-flops, each 1-bit wide. This book is not intended to be a general introduction to logic design since its principal subject material relates to the design and use of processor cores and any reader who is considering applying this information should already be familiar with conventional logic design.

For those who are not so familiar with logic design or who need their knowledge refreshing, 'Appendix: Computer Logic' on page 343 describes the essentials which will be assumed in the next section. It includes brief details on:

- Boolean algebra and notation;
- binary numbers;
- binary addition;
- multiplexers;
- clocks;
- sequential circuits;
- latches and flip-flops;
- registers.

If any of these terms is unfamiliar, a brief look at the appendix may yield sufficient information for what follows.

Note that although the appendix describes these circuit functions in terms of simple logic gates, there are often more efficient CMOS implementations based on alternative transistor circuits. There are many ways to satisfy the basic requirements of logic design using the complementary transistors available on a CMOS chip, and new transistor circuits are published regularly.

For further information consult a text on logic design; a suitable reference is suggested in the 'Bibliography' on page 355.

1.3 | MU0 - a Simple Processor

A simple form of processor can be built from a few basic components:

- a **program counter** (PC) register that is used to hold the address of the current instruction;
- a single register called an **accumulator** (ACC) that holds a data value while it is worked upon;
- an **arithmetic-logic unit** (ALU) that can perform a number of operations on binary operands, such as add, subtract, increment, and so on;
- an **instruction register** (IR) that holds the current instruction while it is executed;
- instruction decode and control logic that employs the above components to achieve the desired results from each instruction.

This limited set of components allows a restricted set of instructions to be implemented. Such a design has been employed at the University of Manchester for many years to illustrate the principles of processor design. Manchester-designed machines are often referred to by the names MU*n* for $1 \le n \le 6$, so this simple machine is known as MU0. It is a design developed only for teaching and was not one of the large-scale machines built at the university as research vehicles, though it is similar to the very first Manchester machine and has been implemented in various forms by undergraduate students.

1.3.1 | The MU0 Instruction Set

MU0 is a 16-bit machine with a 12-bit address space, so it can address up to 8 Kbytes of memory arranged as 4,096 individually addressable 16-bit locations. Instructions are 16 bits long, with a 4-bit operation code (or **opcode**) and a 12-bit address field (S) as shown in Figure 1.4. The simplest instruction set uses only eight of the 16 available opcodes and is summarized in Table 1.1.

An instruction such as 'ACC := ACC + mem_{16}[S]' means 'add the contents of the (16-bit wide) memory location whose address is S to the accumulator'. Instructions are fetched from consecutive memory addresses, starting from address zero, until an instruction which modifies the PC is executed, whereupon fetching starts from the new address given in the 'jump' instruction.

4 bits	12 bits
Opcode	S

Figure 1.4 The MU0 instruction format

Table 1.1 The MU0 instruction set

Instruction	Opcode	Effect
LDA S	0000	ACC := mem_{16}[S]
STO S	0001	mem_{16}[S] := ACC
ADD S	0010	ACC := ACC + mem_{16}[S]
SUB S	0011	ACC := ACC − mem_{16}[S]
JMP S	0100	PC := S
JGE S	0101	if ACC $\geq$ 0 PC := S
JNE S	0110	if ACC $\neq$ 0 PC := S
STP	0111	stop

1.3.2 | MU0 Logic Design

To understand how this instruction set might be implemented we will go through the design process in a logical order. The approach taken here will be to separate the design into two components:

- The datapath.
  All the components carrying, storing or processing many bits in parallel will be considered part of the datapath, including the accumulator, program counter, ALU and instruction register. For these components we will use a register transfer level **(RTL)** design style based on registers, multiplexers, and so on.
- The control logic.
  Everything that does not fit comfortably into the datapath will be considered part of the control logic and will be designed using a finite state machine **(FSM)** approach.

1.3.3 | Datapath Design

There are many ways to connect the basic components needed to implement the MU0 instruction set. Where there are choices to be made we need a guiding principle to help us make the right choices.

Here we will follow the principle that the memory will be the limiting factor in our design, and a memory access will always take a clock cycle. Hence we will aim for an implementation where:

- Each instruction takes exactly the number of clock cycles defined by the number of memory accesses it must make.

Referring back to Table 1.1 we can see that the first four instructions each require two memory accesses (one to fetch the instruction itself and one to fetch or store the operand) whereas the last four instructions can execute in one cycle since they do not require an operand. (In practice we would probably not worry about the efficiency of the STP instruction since it halts the processor for ever.) Therefore we need a datapath design which has sufficient resource to allow these instructions to complete in two or one clock cycles. A suitable datapath is shown in Figure 1.5.

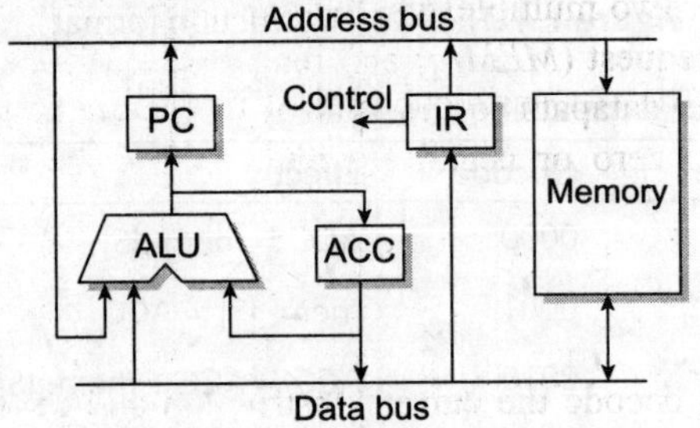

Figure 1.5 MU0 datapath example

(Readers who might expect to see a dedicated PC incrementer in this datapath should note that all instructions that do not change the PC take two cycles, so the main ALU is available during one of these cycles to increment the PC.)

1.3.4 | Datapath Operation

The design we will develop assumes that each instruction starts when it has arrived in the instruction register. After all, until it is in the instruction register we cannot know which instruction we are dealing with. Therefore an instruction executes in two stages, possibly omitting the first of these:

1. Access the memory operand and perform the desired operation.
   The address in the instruction register is issued and either an operand is read from memory, combined with the accumulator in the ALU and written back into the accumulator, or the accumulator is stored out to memory.
2. Fetch the next instruction to be executed.
   Either the PC or the address in the instruction register is issued to fetch the next instruction, and in either case the address is incremented in the ALU and the incremented value saved into the PC.

1.3.5 | Initialization

The processor must start in a known state. Usually this requires a *reset* input to cause it to start executing instructions from a known address. We will design MU0 to start executing from address 000_{16}.

There are several ways to achieve this, one of which is to use the reset signal to zero the ALU output and then clock this into the PC register.

1.3.6 | Register Transfer Level Design

The next step is to determine exactly the control signals that are required to cause the datapath to carry out the full set of operations. We assume that all the registers change state on the falling edge of the input clock, and where necessary have control signals that may be used to prevent them from changing on a particular clock edge. The PC, for example, will change at the end of a clock cycle where *PCce* is '1' but will not change when *PCce* is '0'.

A suitable register organization is shown in Figure 1.6. This shows enables on all of the registers, function select lines to the ALU (the precise number and interpretation to be determined later), the select control lines for two multiplexers, the control for a tri-state driver to send the ACC value to memory and memory request (*MEMrq*) and read/write (*RnW*) control lines. The other signals shown are outputs from the datapath to the control logic, including the opcode bits and signals indicating whether ACC is zero or negative which control the respective conditional jump instructions.

1.3.7 | Control Logic

The control logic simply has to decode the current instruction and generate the appropriate levels on the datapath control signals, using the control inputs from the datapath where necessary. Although the control logic is a finite state machine, and therefore in principle the design should start from a state transition diagram, in this case the FSM is trivial and the diagram not worth drawing. The implementation requires only two states, 'fetch' and 'execute', and one bit of state (*Ex/ft*) is therefore sufficient.

The control logic can be presented in tabular form as shown in Table 1.2. In this table an 'x' indicates a *don't care* condition. Once the ALU function select codes have been assigned the table may be implemented directly as a **PLA** (programmable logic array) or translated into combinatorial logic and implemented using standard gates.

A quick scrutiny of Table 1.2 reveals a few easy simplifications. The program counter and instruction register clock enables (*PCce* and *IRce*) are always the same. This makes sense, since whenever a new instruction is being fetched the ALU is computing the next program counter value, and this should be latched too. Therefore these control signals may be merged into one. Similarly, whenever the accumulator is driving the data bus (*ACCoe* is high) the memory should perform a write operation (*RnW* is low), so one of these signals can be generated from the other using an inverter.

After these simplifications the control logic design is almost complete. It only remains to determine the encodings of the ALU functions.

1.3.8 | ALU Design

Most of the register transfer level functions in Figure 1.6 have straightforward logic implementations (readers who are in doubt should refer to 'Appendix: Computer Logic' on page 345). The MU0 ALU is a little more complex than the simple adder described in the appendix, however.

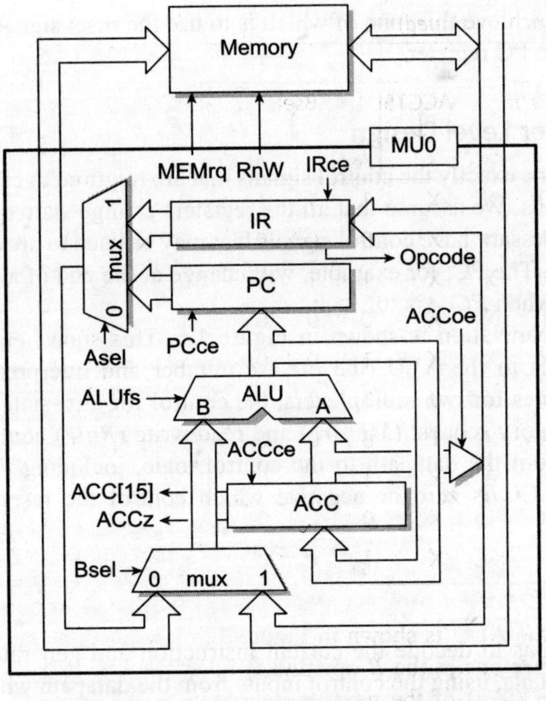

Figure 1.6 MU0 register transfer level organization

The ALU functions that are required are listed in Table 1.2. There are five of them ($A + B$, $A - B$, B, $B + 1$, 0), the last of which is only used while reset is active. Therefore the reset signal can control this function directly and the control logic need only generate a 2-bit function select code to choose between the other four. If the principal ALU inputs are the A and B operands, all the functions may be produced by augmenting a conventional binary adder:

- $A + B$ is the normal adder output (assuming that the carry-in is zero).
- $A - B$ may be implemented as $A + \overline{B} + 1$, requiring the B inputs to be inverted and the carry-in to be forced to a one.
- B is implemented by forcing the A inputs and the carry-in to zero.
- $B + 1$ is implemented by forcing A to zero and the carry-in to one.

Table 1.2 MU0 control logic

	Inputs					Outputs									
Instruction	Opcode	Reset	Ex/ft	ACCz	ACC15	Asel	Bsel	ACCce	PCce	IRce	ACCoe	ALUfs	MEMrq	RnW	Ex/ft
Reset	xxxx	1	X	X	X	0	0	1	1	1	0	= 0	1	1	0
LDA S	0000	0	0	X	X	1	1	1	0	0	0	= B	1	1	1
	0000	0	1	X	X	0	0	0	1	1	0	B+1	1	1	0
STO S	0001	0	0	X	X	1	X	0	0	0	1	X	1	0	1
	0001	0	1	X	X	0	0	0	1	1	0	B+1	1	1	0

(Continued)

Table 1.2 MU0 control logic (*Continued*)

	Inputs					Outputs									
Instruction	Opcode	Reset	Ex/ft	ACCz	ACC15	Asel	Bsel	ACCce	PCce	IRce	ACCoe	ALUfs	MEMrq	RnW	Ex/ft
ADD S	0010	0	0	X	X	1	1	1	0	0	0	A+B	1	1	1
	0010	0	1	X	X	0	0	1	1	0	0	B+I	1	1	0
SUB S	0011	0	0	X	X	1	1	1	0	0	0	A–B	1	1	1
	0011	0	1	X	X	0	0	0	1	1	0	B+I	1	1	0
JMP S	0100	0	X	X	X	1	0	0	1	1	0	B+I	1	1	0
JGE S	0101	0	X	X	0	1	0	0	1	1	0	B+I	1	1	0
	0101	0	X	X	1	0	0	0	1	1	0	B+I	1	1	0
JNE S	0110	0	X	0	X	1	0	0	1	1	0	B+I	1	1	0
	0110	0	X	1	X	0	0	0	1	1	0	B+I	1	1	0
STP	0111	0	X	X	X	1	X	0	0	0	0	X	0	1	0

The gate-level logic for the ALU is shown in Figure 1.7. *Aen* enables the *A* operand or forces it to zero; *Binv* controls whether or not the *B* operand is inverted. The carry-out (*Cout*) from one bit is connected to the carry-in (*Cin*) of the next; the carry-in to the first bit is controlled by the ALU function selects (as are *Aen* and *Binv*), and the carry-out from the last bit is unused. Together with the multiplexers, registers, control logic and a bus buffer (which is used to put the accumulator value onto the data bus), the processor is complete. Add a standard memory and you have a workable computer.

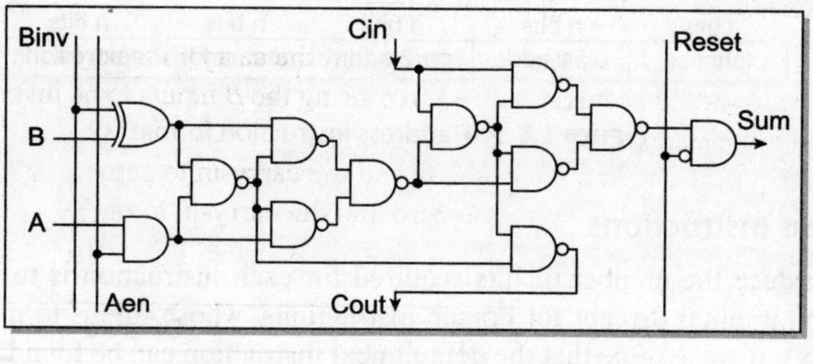

Figure 1.7 MU0 ALU logic for one bit

1.3.9 | MU0 Extensions

Although MU0 is a very simple processor and would not make a good target for a high-level language compiler, it serves to illustrate the basic principles of processor design. The design process used to develop the first ARM processors differed mainly in complexity and not in principle. MU0 designs based on microcoded control logic have also been developed, as have extensions to incorporate indexed addressing. Like any good processor, MU0 has spaces left in the instruction space which allow future expansion of the instruction set.

To turn MU0 into a useful processor takes quite a lot of work. The following extensions seem most important:

- Extending the address space.
- Adding more addressing modes.
- Allowing the PC to be saved in order to support a subroutine mechanism.
- Adding more registers, supporting interrupts, and so on…

Overall, this doesn't seem to be the place to start from if the objective is to design a high-performance processor which is a good compiler target.

1.4 | Instruction Set Design

If the MU0 instruction set is not a good choice for a high-performance processor, what other choices are there?

Starting from first principles, let us look at a basic machine operation such as an instruction to add two numbers to produce a result.

1.4.1 | 4-address Instructions

In its most general form, this instruction requires some bits to differentiate it from other instructions, some bits to specify the operand addresses, some bits to specify where the result should be placed (the **destination**), and some bits to specify the address of the next instruction to be executed. An assembly language format for such an instruction might be:

ADD d, s1, s2, next_i; d := s1 + s2

Such an instruction might be represented in memory by a binary format such as that shown in Figure 1.8. This format requires 4n + *f* bits per instruction where each operand requires *n* bits and the opcode that specifies 'ADD' requires *f* bits.

f bits	n bits	n bits	n bits	n bits
function	op 1 addr.	op 2 addr.	dest. addr.	next_i addr.

Figure 1.8 A 4-address instruction format

1.4.2 | 3-address Instructions

The first way to reduce the number of bits required for each instruction is to make the address of the next instruction implicit (except for branch instructions, whose role is to modify the instruction sequence explicitly). If we assume that the default next instruction can be found by adding the size of the instruction to the PC, we get a 3-address instruction with an assembly language format like this:

ADD d, s1, s2 ;d := s1 + s2

A binary representation of such an instruction is shown in Figure 1.9.

f bits	n bits	n bits	n bits
function	op 1 addr.	op 2 addr.	dest. addr.

Figure 1.9 A 3-address instruction format

1.4.3 | 2-address Instructions

A further saving in the number of bits required to store an instruction can be achieved by making the destination register the same as one of the source registers. The assembly language format could be:

```
ADD    d, s1         ;d := d + s1
```

The binary representation now reduces to that shown in Figure 1.10.

f bits	n bits	n bits
function	op 1 addr.	dest. addr.

Figure 1.10 A 2-address instruction format

1.4.4 | 1-address Instructions

If the destination register is made implicit it is often called the **accumulator** (see, for example, MU0 in the previous section); an instruction need only specify one operand:

```
ADD    s1            ; accumulator := accumulator + s1
```

The binary representation simplifies further to that shown in Figure 1.11.

f bits	n bits
function	op 1 addr.

Figure 1.11 A 1-address (accumulator) instruction format

1.4.5 | 0-address Instructions

Finally, an architecture may make all operand references implicit by using an evaluation stack. The assembly language format is:

```
ADD          ; top_of_stack := top_of_stack + next_on_stack
```

The binary representation is as shown in Figure 1.12.

f bits
function

Figure 1.12 A 0-address instruction format

1.4.6 | Examples of n-address Use

All these forms of instruction have been used in processor instruction sets apart from the 4-address form which, although it is used internally in some microcode designs, is unnecessarily expensive for a machine-level instruction set. For example:

- The Inmos transputer uses a 0-address evaluation stack architecture.
- The MU0 example in the previous section illustrates a simple 1-address architecture.
- The Thumb instruction set used for high code density on some ARM processors uses an architecture which is predominantly of the 2-address form (see Chapter 7).
- The standard ARM instruction set uses a 3-address architecture.

1.4.7 | Addresses

An address in the MU0 architecture is the straightforward 'absolute' address of the memory location which contains the desired operand. However, the three addresses in the ARM 3-address instruction format are register specifiers, not memory addresses. In general, the term '3-address architecture' refers to an instruction set where the two source operands and the destination can be specified independently of each other, but often only within a restricted set of possible values.

1.4.8 | Instruction Types

We have just looked at a number of ways of specifying an 'ADD' instruction. A complete instruction set needs to do more than perform arithmetic operations on operands in memory. A general-purpose instruction set can be expected to include instructions in the following categories:

- Data processing instructions such as add, subtract and multiply.
- Data movement instructions that copy data from one place in memory to another, or from memory to the processor's registers, and so on.
- Control flow instructions that switch execution from one part of the program to another, possibly depending on data values.
- Special instructions to control the processor's execution state, for instance to switch into a privileged mode to carry out an operating system function.

Sometimes an instruction will fit into more than one of these categories. For example, a 'decrement and branch if non-zero' instruction, which is useful for controlling program loops, does some data processing on the loop variable and also performs a control flow function. Similarly, a data processing instruction which fetches an operand from an address in memory and places its result in a register can be viewed as performing a data movement function.

1.4.9 | Orthogonal Instructions

An instruction set is said to be **orthogonal** if each choice in the building of an instruction is independent of the other choices. Since add and subtract are similar operations, one would expect to be able to use them in similar contexts. If add uses a 3-address format with register addresses, so should subtract, and in neither case should there be any peculiar restrictions on the registers which may be used.

An orthogonal instruction set is easier for the assembly language programmer to learn and easier for the compiler writer to target. The hardware implementation will usually be more efficient too.

1.4.10 | Addressing Modes

When accessing an operand for a data processing or movement instruction, there are several standard techniques used to specify the desired location. Most processors support several of these **addressing modes** (though few support all of them):

1. Immediate addressing: the desired value is presented as a binary value in the instruction.
2. Absolute addressing: the instruction contains the full binary address of the desired value in memory.
3. Indirect addressing: the instruction contains the binary address of a memory location that contains the binary address of desired value.

4. Register addressing: the desired value is in a register, and the instruction contains the register number.
5. Register indirect addressing: the instruction contains the number of a register which contains the address of the value in memory.
6. Base plus offset addressing: the instruction specifies a register (the **base**) and a binary offset to be added to the base to form the memory address.
7. Base plus index addressing: the instruction specifies a base register and another register (the **index**) which is added to the base to form the memory address.
8. Base plus scaled index addressing: as above, but the index is multiplied by a constant (usually the size of the data item, and usually a power of two) before being added to the base.
9. Stack addressing: an implicit or specified register (the **stack pointer**) points to an area of memory (the **stack**) where data items are written (**pushed**) or read (**popped**) on a last-in-first-out basis.

Note that the naming conventions used for these modes by different processor manufacturers are not necessarily as above. The list can be extended almost indefinitely by adding more levels of indirection, adding base plus index plus offset, and so on. However, most of the common addressing modes are covered in the list above.

1.4.11 | Control Flow Instructions

Where the program must deviate from the default (normally sequential) instruction sequence, a control flow instruction is used to modify the program counter (PC) explicitly. The simplest such instructions are usually called 'branches' or 'jumps'. Since most branches require a relatively short range, a common form is the 'PC-relative' branch. A typical assembly language format is:

```
        B      LABEL
               ..
LABEL          ..
```

Here the assembler works out the displacement which must be added to the value the PC has when the branch is executed in order to force the PC to point to LABEL. The maximum range of the branch is determined by the number of bits allocated to the displacement in the binary format; the assembler should report an error if the required branch is out of range.

1.4.12 | Conditional Branches

A Digital Signal Processing (DSP) program may execute a fixed instruction sequence for ever, but a general-purpose processor is usually required to vary its program in response to data values. Some processors (including MU0) allow the values in the general registers to control whether or not a branch is taken through instructions such as:

- Branch if a particular register is zero (or not zero, or negative, and so on).
- Branch if two specified registers are equal (or not equal).

1.4.13 | Condition Code Register

However, the most frequently used mechanism is based on a condition code register, which is a special-purpose register within the processor. Whenever a data processing instruction is executed (or possibly only for special instructions, or instructions that specifically enable the condition code register), the condition code register records whether the result was zero, negative, overflowed, produced a carry output, and so on. The conditional branch instructions are then controlled by the state of the condition code register when they execute.

1.4.14 | Subroutine Calls

Sometimes a branch is executed to call a subprogram where the instruction sequence should **return** to the calling sequence when the subprogram terminates. Since the subprogram may be called from many different places, a record of the calling address must be kept. There are many different ways to achieve this:

- The calling routine could compute a suitable return address and put it in a standard memory location for use by the subprogram as a return address before executing the branch.
- The return address could be pushed onto a stack.
- The return address could be placed in a register.

Subprogram calls are sufficiently common that most architectures include specific instructions to make them efficient. They typically require to jump further across memory than simple branches, so it makes sense to treat them separately. Often they are not conditional; a conditional subprogram call is programmed, when required, by inserting an unconditional call and branching around it with the opposite condition.

1.4.15 | Subprogram Return

The return instruction moves the return address from wherever it was stored (in memory, possibly on a stack, or in a register) back into the PC.

1.4.16 | System Calls

Another category of control flow instruction is the system call. This is a branch to an operating system routine, often associated with a change in the **privilege** level of the executing program. Some functions in the processor, possibly including all the input and output peripherals, are protected from access by user code. Therefore a user program that needs to access these functions must make a system call.

System calls pass through protection barriers in a controlled way. A well-designed processor will ensure that it is possible to write a multi-user operating system where one user's program is protected from assaults from other, possibly malicious, users. This requires that a malicious user cannot change the system code and, when access to protected functions is required, the system code must make thorough checks that the requested function is authorized.

This is a complex area of hardware and software design. Most embedded systems (and many desktop systems) do not use the full protection capabilities of the hardware, but a processor which does not support a protected system mode will be excluded from consideration for those applications that demand this facility, so most microprocessors now include such support. Whilst it is not necessary to understand the full implications of supporting a secure operating system to appreciate the basic design of an instruction set, even the less well-informed reader should have an awareness of the issues since some features of commercial processor architectures make little sense unless this objective of potentially secure protection is borne in mind.

1.4.17 | Exceptions

The final category of control flow instruction comprises cases where the change in the flow of control is not the primary intent of the programmer but is a consequence of some unexpected (and possibly unwanted) side-effect of the program. An attempt to access a memory location may fail, for instance, because a fault is detected in the memory subsystem. The program must therefore deviate from its planned course in order to attempt to recover from the problem.

These unplanned changes in the flow of control are termed **exceptions**.

1.5 | Processor Design Trade-offs

The art of processor design is to define an instruction set that supports the functions that are useful to the programmer whilst allowing an implementation that is as efficient as possible. Preferably, the same instruction set should also allow future, more sophisticated implementations to be equally efficient.

The programmer generally wants to express his or her program in as abstract a way as possible, using a high-level language which supports ways of handling concepts that are appropriate to the problem. Modern trends towards functional and object-oriented languages move the level of abstraction higher than older imperative languages such as C, and even the older languages were quite a long way removed from typical machine instructions.

The **semantic gap** between a high-level language construct and a machine instruction is bridged by a **compiler**, which is a (usually complex) computer program that translates a high-level language program into a sequence of machine instructions. Therefore the processor designer should define his or her instruction set to be a good compiler target rather than something that the programmer will use directly to solve the problem by hand. So, what sort of instruction set makes a good compiler target?

1.5.1 | Complex Instruction Set Computers

Prior to 1980, the principal trend in instruction set design was towards increasing complexity in an attempt to reduce the semantic gap that the compiler had to bridge. Single instruction procedure entries and exits were incorporated into the instruction set, each performing a complex sequence of operations over many clock cycles. Processors were sold on the sophistication and number of their addressing modes, data types, and so on.

The origins of this trend were in the minicomputers developed during the 1970s. These computers had relatively slow main memories coupled to processors built using many simple integrated circuits. The processors were controlled by microcode ROMs (Read Only Memories) that were faster than main memory, so it made sense to implement frequently used operations as microcode sequences rather than them requiring several instructions to be fetched from main memory.

Throughout the 1970s microprocessors were advancing in their capabilities. These single chip processors were dependent on state-of-the-art semiconductor technology to achieve the highest possible number of transistors on a single chip, so their development took place within the semiconductor industry rather than within the computer industry. As a result, microprocessor designs displayed a lack of original thought at the architectural level, particularly with respect to the demands of the technology that was used in their implementation. Their designers, at best, took ideas from the minicomputer industry where the implementation technology was very different. In particular, the microcode ROM which was needed for all the complex routines absorbed an unreasonable proportion of the area of a single chip, leaving little room for other performance-enhancing features.

This approach led to the single-chip Complex Instruction Set Computers **(CISCs)** of the late 1970s, which were microprocessors with minicomputer instruction sets that were severely compromised by the limited available silicon resource.

1.5.2 | The RISC Revolution

Into this world of increasingly complex instruction sets the Reduced Instruction Set Computer (**RISC**) was born. The RISC concept was a major influence on the design of the ARM processor; indeed, RISC was the ARM's middle name. But before we look at either RISC or the ARM in more detail we need a bit more background on what processors do and how they can be designed to do it quickly.

If reducing the semantic gap between the processor instruction set and the high-level language is not the right way to make an efficient computer, what other options are open to the designer?

1.5.3 | What Processors Do

If we want to make a processor go fast, we must first understand what it spends its time doing. It is a common misconception that computers spend their time computing, that is, carrying out arithmetic operations on user data. In practice they spend very little time 'computing' in this sense. Although they do a fair amount of arithmetic, most of this is with addresses in order to locate the relevant data items and program routines. Then, having found the user's data, most of the work is in moving it around rather than processing it in any transformational sense.

At the instruction set level, it is possible to measure the frequency of use of the various different instructions. It is very important to obtain **dynamic** measurements, that is, to measure the frequency of instructions that are executed, rather than the **static** frequency, which is just a count of the various instruction types in the binary image. A typical set of statistics is shown in Table 1.3; these statistics were gathered running a print preview program on an ARM instruction emulator, but are broadly typical of what may be expected from other programs and instruction sets.

Table 1.3 Typical dynamic instruction usage

Instruction type	Dynamic usage
Data movement	43%
Control flow	23%
Arithmetic operations	15%
Comparisons	13%
Logical operations	5%
Other	1%

These sample statistics suggest that the most important instructions to optimise are those concerned with data movement, either between the processor registers and memory or from register to register. These account for almost half of all instructions executed. Second most frequent are the control flow instructions such as branches and procedure calls, which account for another quarter. Arithmetic operations are down at 15%, as are comparisons.

Now we have a feel for what processors spend their time doing, we can look at ways of making them go faster. The most important of these is pipelining. Another important technique is the use of a cache memory, which will be covered in Section 10.3 on page 233. A third technique, super-scalar instruction execution, is very complex, has not been used on ARM processors and is not covered in this book.

1.5.4 | Pipelines

A processor executes an individual instruction in a sequence of steps. A typical sequence might be:

1. Fetch the instruction from memory (fetch).
2. Decode it to see what sort of instruction it is (dec).
3. Access any operands that may be required from the register bank (reg).
4. Combine the operands to form the result or a memory address (ALU).
5. Access memory for a data operand, if necessary (mem).
6. Write the result back to the register bank (res).

Not all instructions will require every step, but most instructions will require most of them. These steps tend to use different hardware functions, for instance the ALU is probably only used in step 4. Therefore, if an instruction does not start before its predecessor has finished, only a small proportion of the processor hardware will be in use in any step.

An obvious way to improve the utilization of the hardware resources, and also the processor throughput, would be to start the next instruction before the current one has finished. This technique is called **pipelining**, and is a very effective way of exploiting concurrency in a general-purpose processor.

Taking the above sequence of operations, the processor is organized so that as soon as one instruction has completed step 1 and moved on to step 2, the next instruction begins step 1. This is illustrated in Figure 1.13. In principle such a pipeline should deliver a six times speed-up compared with non-overlapped instruction execution; in practice things do not work out quite so well for reasons we will see below.

1.5.5 | Pipeline Hazards

It is relatively frequent in typical computer programs that the result from one instruction is used as an operand by the next instruction. When this occurs the pipeline operation shown in Figure 1.13 breaks down, since the result of instruction 1 is not available at the time that instruction 2 collects its operands. Instruction 2 must therefore stall until the result is available, giving the behaviour shown in Figure 1.14. This is a **read-after-write** pipeline hazard.

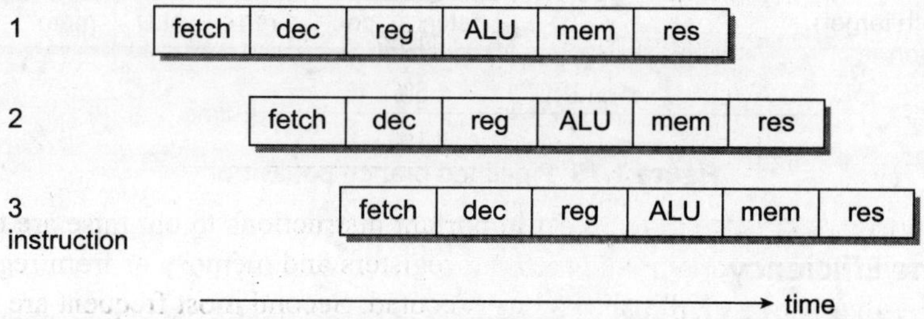

Figure 1.13 Pipelined instruction execution

Branch instructions result in even worse pipeline behaviour since the fetch step of the following instruction is affected by the branch target computation and must therefore be deferred. Unfortunately, subsequent fetches will be taking place while the branch is being decoded and before it has been recognized as a branch, so the fetched instructions may have to be discarded. If, for example, the branch target calculation is performed in the ALU stage of the pipeline in Figure 1.13, three instructions will have been fetched from the old stream before the branch target is available (see Figure 1.15). It is better to compute the branch target earlier in the pipeline if possible, even though this will probably require dedicated hardware. If branch instructions have a fixed format, the target may be computed **speculatively** (that is, before it has been determined that the instruction is a branch) during the 'dec' stage, thereby reducing the branch latency to a single cycle, though note that in this pipeline there may still be hazards on a conditional branch due to dependencies on the condition code result of the instruction preceding the branch. Some RISC architectures (though not the ARM) define that the instruction following the branch is executed whether or not the branch is taken. This technique is known as the **delayed branch**.

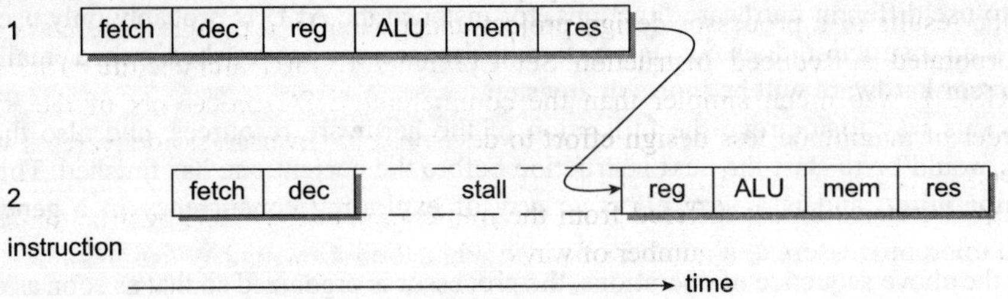

Figure 1.14 Read-after-write pipeline hazard

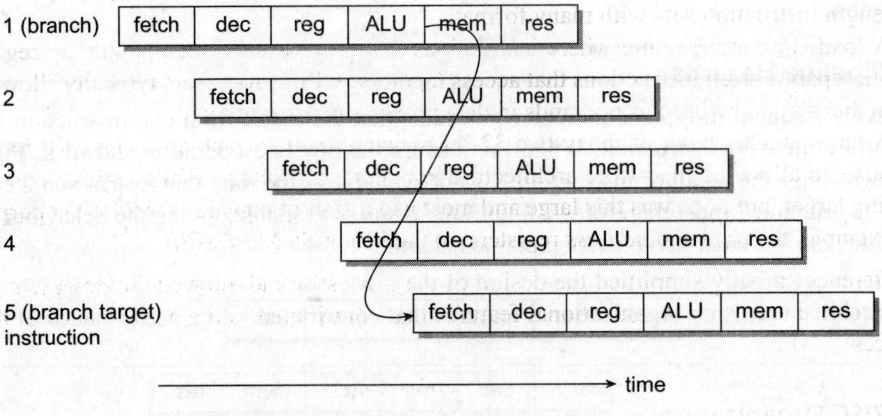

Figure 1.15 Pipelined branch behaviour

1.5.6 | Pipeline Efficiency

Though there are techniques which reduce the impact of these pipeline problems, they cannot remove the difficulties altogether. The deeper the pipeline (that is, the more pipeline stages there are), the worse the problems get. For reasonably simple processors, there are significant benefits in introducing pipelines from three to five stages long, but beyond this the law of diminishing returns begins to apply and the added costs and complexity outweigh the benefits.

Pipelines clearly benefit from all instructions going through a similar sequence of steps. Processors with very complex instructions where every instruction behaves differently from the next are hard to pipeline. In 1980 the complex instruction set microprocessor of the day was not pipelined due to the limited silicon resource, the limited design resource and the high complexity of designing a pipeline for a complex instruction set.

1.6 | The Reduced Instruction Set Computer

In 1980 Patterson and Ditzel published a paper entitled 'The Case for the Reduced Instruction Set Computer' (a full reference is given in the bibliography on page 355). In this seminal work they expounded the view that the optimal architecture for a single-chip processor need not be the same as the optimal architecture for a multi-chip processor. Their argument was subsequently supported by the results of a processor design project undertaken by a postgraduate class at Berkeley which incorporated a Reduced Instruction Set Computer (RISC) architecture. This design, the Berkeley RISC I, was much simpler than the commercial CISC processors of the day and had taken an order of magnitude less design effort to develop, but nevertheless delivered a very similar performance.

The RISC I instruction set differed from the minicomputer-like CISC instruction sets used on commercial microprocessors in a number of ways. It had the following key features:

1.6.1 | RISC Architecture

- A fixed (32-bit) instruction size with few formats; CISC processors typically had variable length instruction sets with many formats.
- A load-store architecture where instructions that process data operate only on registers and are separate from instructions that access memory; CISC processors typically allowed values in memory to be used as operands in data processing instructions.
- A large register bank of thirty-two 32-bit registers, all of which could be used for any purpose, to allow the load-store architecture to operate efficiently; CISC register sets were getting larger, but none was this large and most had different registers for different purposes (for example, the *data* and *address* registers on the Motorola MC68000).

These differences greatly simplified the design of the processor and allowed the designers to implement the architecture using organizational features that contributed to the performance of the prototype devices:

1.6.2 | RISC Organization

- Hard-wired instruction decode logic; CISC processors used large microcode ROMs to decode their instructions.
- Pipelined execution; CISC processors allowed little, if any, overlap between consecutive instructions (though they do now).
- Single-cycle execution; CISC processors typically took many clock cycles to complete a single instruction.

By incorporating all these architectural and organizational changes at once, the Berkeley RISC microprocessor effectively escaped from the problem that haunts progress by incremental improvement, which is the risk of getting stuck in a local maximum of the performance function.

1.6.3 | RISC Advantages

Patterson and Ditzel argued that RISC offered three principal advantages:

- A smaller die size.
  A simple processor should require fewer transistors and less silicon area. Therefore a whole CPU will fit on a chip at an earlier stage in process technology development, and once the technology has developed beyond the point where either CPU will fit on a chip, a RISC CPU leaves more die area free for performance-enhancing features such as cache memory, memory management functions, floating-point hardware, and so on.
- A shorter development time.
  A simple processor should take less design effort and therefore have a lower design cost and be better matched to the process technology when it is launched (since process technology developments need be predicted over a shorter development period).
- A higher performance.
  This is the tricky one! The previous two advantages are easy to accept, but in a world where higher performance had been sought through ever-increasing complexity, this was a bit hard to swallow.

The argument goes something like this: smaller things have higher natural frequencies (insects flap their wings faster than small birds, small birds faster than large birds, and so on) so a simple processor ought to allow a high clock rate. So let's design our complex processor by starting with a simple one, then add complex instructions one at a time. When we add a complex instruction it will make some high-level function more efficient, but it will also slow the clock down a bit for all instructions. We can measure the overall benefit on typical programs, and when we do, all complex instructions make the program run slower. Hence we stick to the simple processor we started with.

These arguments were backed up by experimental results and the prototype processors (the Berkeley RISC II came shortly after RISC I). The commercial processor companies were sceptical at first, but most new companies designing processors for their own purposes saw an opportunity to reduce development costs and get ahead of the game. These commercial RISC designs, of which the ARM was the first, showed that the idea worked and since 1980 all new general-purpose processor architectures have embraced the concepts of the RISC to a greater or lesser degree.

1.6.4 | RISC in Retrospect

Since the RISC is now well established in commercial use it is possible to look back and see more clearly what its contribution to the evolution of the microprocessor really was.

Early RISCs achieved their performance through:

- Pipelining.
  Pipelining is the simplest form of concurrency to implement in a processor and delivers around two to three times speed-up. A simple instruction set greatly simplifies the design of the pipeline.
- A high clock rate with single-cycle execution.
  In 1980 standard semiconductor memories (DRAMs - Dynamic Random Access Memories) could operate at around 3 MHz for random accesses and at 6 MHz for sequential (page mode)

accesses. The CISC microprocessors of the time could access memory at most at 2 MHz, so memory bandwidth was not being exploited to the full. RISC processors, being rather simpler, could be designed to operate at clock rates that would use all the available memory bandwidth.

Neither of these properties is a feature of the architecture, but both depend on the architecture being simple enough to allow the implementation to incorporate it. RISC architectures succeeded because they were simple enough to enable the designers to exploit these organizational techniques. It was entirely feasible to implement a fixed-length instruction load-store architecture using microcode, multi-cycle execution and no pipeline, but such an implementation would exhibit no advantage over an off-the-shelf CISC. It was not possible, at that time, to implement a hard-wired, single-cycle execution pipelined CISC. But it is now!

1.6.5 | Clock Rates

As footnotes to the above analysis, there are two aspects of the clock rate discussion that require further explanation:

- 1980s CISC processors often had higher clock rates than the early RISCs, but they took several clock cycles to perform a single memory access, so they had a lower memory access rate. Beware of evaluating processors on their clock rate alone!
- The mismatch between the CISC memory access rate and the available bandwidth appears to conflict with the comments in 'Complex Instruction Set Computers' on page 17 where microcode is justified in an early 1970s minicomputer on the grounds of the slow main memory speed relative to the processor speed. The resolution of the conflict lies in observing that in the intervening decade memory technology had become significantly faster while early CISC microprocessors were slower than typical minicomputer processors. This loss of processor speed was due to the necessity to switch from fast bipolar technologies to much slower NMOS technologies to achieve the logic density required to fit the complete processor onto a single chip.

1.6.6 | RISC Drawbacks

RISC processors have clearly won the performance battle and should cost less to design, so is a RISC all good news? With the passage of time, two drawbacks have come to light:

- RISCs generally have poor code density compared with CISCs.
- RISCs don't execute x86 code.

The second of these is hard to fix, though PC emulation software is available for many RISC platforms. It is only a problem, however, if you want to build an IBM PC compatible; for other applications it can safely be ignored.

The poor code density is a consequence of the fixed-length instruction set and is rather more serious for a wide range of applications. In the absence of a cache, poor code density leads to more main memory bandwidth being used for instruction fetching, resulting in a higher memory power consumption. When the processor incorporates an on-chip cache of a particular size, poor code density results in a smaller proportion of the working set being held in the cache at any time, increasing the cache miss rate, resulting in an even greater increase in the main memory bandwidth requirement and consequent power consumption.

1.6.7 | ARM Code Density and Thumb

The ARM processor design is based on RISC principles, but for various reasons suffers less from poor code density than most other RISCs. Its code density is still, however, not as good as some CISC processors. Where code density is of prime importance, ARM Limited has incorporated a novel mechanism, called the **Thumb** architecture, into some versions of the ARM processor. The Thumb instruction set is a 16-bit compressed form of the original 32-bit ARM instruction set, and employs dynamic decompression hardware in the instruction pipeline. Thumb code density is better than that achieved by most CISC processors.

The Thumb architecture is described in Chapter 7.

1.6.8 | Beyond RISC

It seems unlikely that RISC represents the last word on computer architecture, so is there any sign of another breakthrough which will render the RISC approach obsolete?

There is no development visible at the time of writing which suggests a change on the same scale as RISC, but instruction sets continue to evolve to give better support for efficient implementations and for new applications such as multimedia.

1.7 | Design for Low Power Consumption

Since the introduction of digital computers 50 years ago there has been sustained improvement in their cost-effectiveness at a rate unparalleled in any other technical endeavour. As a side-effect of the route taken to increased performance, the power consumption of the machines has reduced equally dramatically. Only very recently, however, has the drive for minimum power consumption become as important as, and in some application areas more important than, the drive for increased performance. This change has come about as a result of the growing market for battery-powered portable equipment, such as digital mobile telephones and lap-top computers, which incorporate high-performance computing components.

Following the introduction of the integrated circuit the computer business has been driven by the win-win scenario whereby smaller transistors yield lower cost, higher performance and lower power consumption. Now, though, designers are beginning to design specifically for low power, even, in some cases, sacrificing performance to achieve it.

The ARM processor is at the centre of this drive for power-efficient processing. It therefore seems appropriate to consider the issues around design for low power.

1.7.1 | Where does the Power Go?

The starting point for low-power design is to understand where the power goes in existing circuits. CMOS is the dominant technology for modern high-performance digital electronics, and has itself some good properties for low-power design, so we start by looking at where the power goes in a CMOS circuit.

A typical CMOS circuit is the static NAND gate, illustrated in Figure 1.2. All signals swing between the voltages of the power and ground rails, *Vdd* and *Vss*. Until recently a 5 volt supply was standard, but many modern CMOS processes require a lower supply voltage of around 3 volts and the latest technologies operate with supplies of between 1 and 2 volts, and this will reduce further in the future.

The gate operates by connecting the output either to *Vdd* through a pull-up network of p-type transistors, or to *Vss* through a pull-down network of n-type transistors. When the inputs are both close to one rail or the other, then one of these networks is conducting and the other is effectively not conducting, so there is no path through the gate from *Vdd* to *Vss*. Furthermore, the output is normally connected to the inputs of similar gates and therefore sees only capacitive load. Once the output has been driven close to either rail, it takes no current to hold it there. Therefore a short time after the gate has switched the circuit reaches a stable condition and no further current is taken from the supply.

This characteristic of consuming power only when switching is not shared by many other logic technologies and has been a major factor in making CMOS the technology of choice for high-density integrated circuits.

1.7.2 | CMOS Power Components

The total power consumption of a CMOS circuit comprises three components:

- Switching power.
  This is the power dissipated by charging and discharging the gate output capacitance C_L, and represents the useful work performed by the gate.
  The energy per output transition is:

$$E_t = \frac{1}{2} \cdot C_L \cdot Vdd^2 \qquad \text{Equation 2}$$

$$\approx 1 \text{ picojoule}$$

- Short-circuit power.
  When the gate inputs are at an intermediate level both the p- and n-type networks can conduct. This results in a transitory conducting path from *Vdd* to *Vss*. With a correctly designed circuit (which generally means one that avoids slow signal transitions) the short-circuit power should be a small fraction of the switching power.
- Leakage current.
  The transistor networks do conduct a very small current when they are in their 'off' state; though on a conventional process this current is very small (a small fraction of a nanoamp per gate), it is the only dissipation in a circuit that is powered but inactive, and can drain a supply battery over a long period of time. It is generally negligible in an active circuit.

In a well-designed active circuit the switching power dominates, with the short-circuit power adding perhaps 10% to 20% to the total power, and the leakage current being significant only when the circuit is inactive. However, the trend to lower voltage operation does lead to a trade-off between performance and leakage current as discussed further below, and leakage is an increasing concern for future low-power high-performance designs.

1.7.3 | CMOS Circuit Power

The total power dissipation, P_C, of a CMOS circuit, neglecting the short-circuit and leakage components, is therefore given by summing the dissipation of every gate g in the circuit *C*:

$$P_C = \frac{1}{2} f \cdot Vdd^2 \cdot \sum_{g \in C} A_g \cdot C_L^g \qquad \text{Equation 3}$$

where *f* is the clock frequency, A_g is the gate **activity factor** (reflecting the fact that not all gates switch every clock cycle) and C_L^g is the gate load capacitance. Note that within this summation clock lines, which make two transitions per clock cycle, have an activity factor of 2.

1.7.4 | Low-power Circuit Design

The typical gate load capacitance is a function of the process technology and therefore not under the direct control of the designer. The remaining parameters in Equation 3 suggest various approaches to low-power design. These are listed below with the most important first:

1. Minimize the power supply voltage, *Vdd*.
   The quadratic contribution of the supply voltage to the power dissipation makes this an obvious target. This is discussed further below.
2. Minimize the circuit activity, *A*.
   Techniques such as clock gating fall under this heading. Whenever a circuit function is not needed, activity should be eliminated.
3. Minimize the number of gates.
   Simple circuits use less power than complex ones, all other things being equal, since the sum is over a smaller number of gate contributions.
4. Minimize the clock frequency, *f*.
   Avoiding unnecessarily high clock rates is clearly desirable, but although a lower clock rate reduces the power consumption it also reduces performance, having a neutral effect on power-efficiency (measured, for example, in MIPS - Millions of Instructions Per Second - per watt). If, however, a reduced clock frequency allows operation at a reduced *Vdd*, this will be highly beneficial to the power-efficiency.

1.7.5 | Reducing *Vdd*

As the feature size on CMOS processes gets smaller, there is pressure to reduce the supply voltage. This is because the materials used to form the transistors cannot withstand an electric field of unlimited strength, and as transistors get smaller the field strength increases if the supply voltage is held constant.

However, with increasing interest in design specifically for low power, it may be desirable for the supply voltage to be reduced faster than is necessary solely to prevent electrical breakdown. What prevents very low supply voltages from being used now?

The problem with reducing *Vdd* is that this also reduces the performance of the circuit. The saturated transistor current is given by:

$$I_{sat} \propto (Vdd - V_t)^2 \qquad \text{Equation 4}$$

where V_t is the transistor threshold. The charge on a circuit node is proportional to *Vdd*, so the maximum operating frequency is given by:

$$f_{max} \propto \frac{(Vdd - V_t)^2}{Vdd} \qquad \text{Equation 5}$$

Therefore the maximum operating frequency is reduced as *Vdd* is reduced. The performance loss on a sub-micron process may not be as severe as Equation 5 suggests since the current at high voltage may be limited by velocity saturation effects, but performance will be lost to some extent. Equation 5 suggests that an obvious way to ameliorate the performance loss would be to reduce V_t. However the leakage current depends strongly on V_t:

$$I_{leak} \propto \exp\left(-\frac{V_t}{35\,\text{mV}}\right) \qquad \text{Equation 6}$$

Even a small reduction in V_t can significantly increase the leakage current, increasing the battery drain through an inactive circuit. There is therefore a trade-off to be struck between maximizing performance and minimizing standby power, and this issue must be considered carefully by designers of systems where both characteristics are important.

Even where standby power is not important designers must be aware that maximizing performance by using very low threshold transistors can increase the leakage power to the point where is becomes comparable with the dynamic power, and therefore leakage power must be taken into consideration when selecting packaging and cooling systems.

1.7.6 | Low-power Strategies

To conclude this introduction to design techniques for low power consumption, here are some suggested strategies for low-power applications.

- Minimize *Vdd*.
  Choose the lowest clock frequency that delivers the required performance, then set the power supply voltage as low as is practical given the clock frequency and the requirements of the various system components. Be wary of reducing the supply voltage so far that leakage compromises standby power.
- Minimize off-chip activity.
  Off-chip capacitances are much higher than on-chip loads, so always minimize off-chip activity. Avoid allowing transients to drive off-chip loads and use caches to minimize accesses to off-chip memories.
- Minimize on-chip activity.
  Lower priority than minimizing off-chip activity, it is still important to avoid clocking unnecessary circuit functions (for example, by using gated clocks) and to employ sleep modes where possible.
- Exploit parallelism.
  Where the power supply voltage is a free variable parallelism can be exploited to improve power-efficiency. Duplicating a circuit allows the two circuits to sustain the same performance at half the clock frequency of the original circuit, which allows the required performance to be delivered with a lower supply voltage.

Design for low power is an active research area and one where new ideas are being generated at a high rate. It is expected that a combination of process and design technology improvements will yield considerable further improvement in the power-efficiency of high-speed digital circuits over the next decade.

1.8 | Examples and Exercises

(The more practical exercises will require you to have access to some form of hardware simulation environment.)

EXAMPLE 1.1

Design a 4-bit binary counter using logic gates and a 4-bit register.

If the register inputs are denoted by $D[0]$ to $D[3]$ and its outputs are denoted by $Q[0]$ to $Q[3]$, the counter may be implemented by building combinatorial logic that generates $D[3{:}0] = Q[3{:}0] + 1$.

The logic equations for a binary adder are given in the Appendix (Equation 20 on page 345 gives the sum and Equation 21 the carry). When the second operand is a constant these equations simplify to:

$$D[0] = \overline{Q[0]} \qquad \text{Equation 7}$$

$$D[i] = Q[i] \cdot \overline{C[i-1]} + \overline{Q[i]} \cdot C[i-1] \qquad \text{Equation 8}$$

$$C[i] = Q[i] \cdot C[i-1] \qquad \text{Equation 9}$$

for $1 \leq i \leq 3$, and $C[0] = 1$. ($C[3]$ is not needed.). These equations may be drawn as the logic circuit shown on page 28, which also includes the register.

Exercise 1.1.1
Design a counter which counts from 0 to 7. This makes it a counter with just three bits as output.

Exercise 1.1.2
Design a decade counter using synchronous logic. All changes must occur simultaneously when the clock changes from 0 to 1.

Exercise 1.1.3
Use two decade counters to make a two digit BCD counter. This counter has two 4 bit outputs, one for each of the two digits.

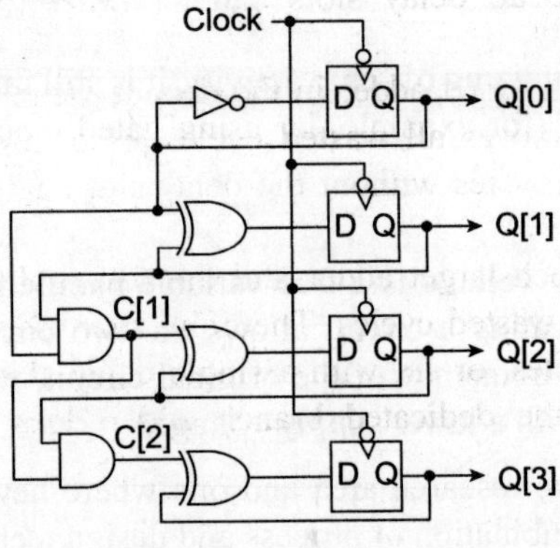

EXAMPLE 1.2
Add indexed addressing to the MU0 instruction set.
The minimum extension that is useful here is to introduce a new 12-bit index register (X) and some new instructions that allow it to be initialized and used in load and store instructions. Referring to Table 1.1, there are eight unused opcodes in the original design, so we could add up to eight new instructions before we run out of space. The basic set of indexing operations is:

LDX S	; X := mem_{16}[S]
LDA S, X	; ACC := mem_{16}[S + X]
STA S, X	; mem_{16}[S + X] := ACC

An index register is much more useful if there is some way to modify it, for instance to step through a table:

```
INX    ; X := X + 1
DEX    ; X := X – 1
```

This gives the basic functionality of an index register. It would increase the usefulness of X to include a way to store it in memory, then it could be used as a temporary register, but for simplicity we will stop here.

Exercise 1.2.1

Modify the RTL organization shown in Figure 1.6 to include the X register, indicating the new control signals required.

Exercise 1.2.2

Modify the control logic in Table 1.2 to support indexed addressing. If you have access to a hardware simulator, test your design. (This is non-trivial!)

EXAMPLE 1.3

Estimate the performance benefit of a single-cycle delayed branch.

A delayed branch allows the instruction following the branch to be executed whether or not the branch is taken. The instruction after the branch is in the 'delay slot'. Assume the dynamic instruction frequencies shown in Table 1.3 and the pipeline structure shown in Figure 1.13; ignore register hazards; assume all delay slots can be filled (most single delay slots can be filled).

If there is a dedicated branch target adder in the decode stage, a branch has a 1-cycle delayed effect, so a single delay slot removes all wasted cycles. One instruction in four is a branch, so four instructions take five clock cycles without the delay slot and four with it, giving 25% higher performance.

If there is no dedicated branch target adder and the main ALU stage is used to compute the target, a branch will incur three wasted cycles. Therefore four instructions on average include one branch and take seven clock cycles, or six with a single delay slot. The delay slot therefore gives 17% higher performance (but the dedicated branch adder does better even without the delay slot).

Exercise 1.3.1

Estimate the performance benefit of a 2-cycle delayed branch assuming that all the first delay slots can be filled, but only 50% of the second delay slots can be filled.

Why is the 2-cycle delayed branch only relevant if there is no dedicated branch target adder?

Exercise 1.3.2

What is the effect on code size of the 1- and 2-cycle delayed branches suggested above? (All unfilled branch delay slots must be filled with no-ops.)

2

The ARM Architecture

SUMMARY OF CHAPTER CONTENTS

The ARM processor is a *Reduced Instruction Set Computer* (RISC). The RISC concept, as we saw in the previous chapter, originated in processor research programmes at Stanford and Berkeley universities around 1980.

In this chapter we see how the RISC ideas helped shape the ARM processors. The ARM was originally developed at Acorn Computers Limited of Cambridge, England, between 1983 and 1985. It was the first RISC microprocessor developed for commercial use and has some significant differences from subsequent RISC architectures. The principal features of the ARM architecture are presented here in overview form; the details are postponed to subsequent chapters.

In 1990 ARM Limited was established as a separate company specifically to widen the exploitation of ARM technology, since when the ARM has been licensed to many semiconductor manufacturers around the world. It has become established as a market-leader for low-power and cost-sensitive embedded applications.

No processor is particularly useful without the support of hardware and software development tools. The ARM is supported by a toolkit which includes an instruction set emulator for hardware modelling and software testing and benchmarking, an assembler, C and C++ compilers, a linker and a symbolic debugger.

2.1 | The Acorn RISC Machine

The first ARM processor was developed at Acorn Computers Limited, of Cambridge, England, between October 1983 and April 1985. At that time, and until the formation of Advanced RISC Machines Limited (which later was renamed simply ARM Limited) in 1990, ARM stood for **Acorn RISC Machine**.

Acorn had developed a strong position in the UK personal computer market due to the success of the BBC (British Broadcasting Corporation) microcomputer. The BBC micro was a machine powered by the 8-bit 6502 microprocessor and rapidly became established as the dominant machine in UK schools following its introduction in January 1982 in support of a series of television programmes broadcast by the BBC. It also enjoyed enthusiastic support in the hobbyist market and found its way into a number of research laboratories and higher education establishments.

Following the success of the BBC micro, Acorn's engineers looked at various microprocessors to build a successor machine around, but found all the commercial offerings lacking. The 16-bit CISC microprocessors that were available in 1983 were slower than standard memory parts. They also had instructions that took many clock cycles to complete (in some cases, many hundreds of clock cycles), giving them very long interrupt latencies. The BBC micro benefited greatly from the 6502's rapid interrupt response, so Acorn's designers were unwilling to accept a retrograde step in this aspect of the processor's performance.

As a result of these frustrations with the commercial microprocessor offerings, the design of a proprietary microprocessor was considered. The major stumbling block was that the Acorn team knew that commercial microprocessor projects had absorbed hundreds of man-years of design effort. Acorn could not contemplate an investment on that scale since it was a company of only just over 400 employees in total. It had to produce a better design with a fraction of the design effort, and with no experience in custom chip design beyond a few small gate arrays designed for the BBC micro.

Into this apparently impossible scenario, the papers on the Berkeley RISC I fell like a bolt from the blue. Here was a processor which had been designed by a few postgraduate students in under a year, yet was competitive with the leading commercial offerings. It was inherently simple, so there were no complex instructions to ruin the interrupt latency. It also came with supporting arguments that suggested it could point the way to the future, though technical merit, however well supported by academic argument, is no guarantee of commercial success.

The ARM, then, was born through a serendipitous combination of factors, and became the core component in Acorn's product line. Later, after a judicious modification of the acronym expansion to **Advanced RISC Machine**, it lent its name to the company formed to broaden its market beyond Acorn's product range. Despite the change of name, the architecture still remains close to the original Acorn design.

2.2 | Architectural Inheritance

At the time the first ARM chip was designed, the only examples of RISC architectures were the Berkeley RISC I and II and the Stanford MIPS (which stands for **Microprocessor without Interlocking Pipeline Stages**), although some earlier machines such as the Digital PDP-8, the Cray-1 and the IBM 801, which predated the RISC concept, shared many of the characteristics which later came to be associated with RISCs.

2.2.1 | Features Used

The ARM architecture incorporated a number of features from the Berkeley RISC design, but a number of other features were rejected. Those that were used were:

- a load-store architecture;
- fixed-length 32-bit instructions;
- 3-address instruction formats.

2.2.2 | Features Rejected

The features that were employed on the Berkeley RISC designs which were rejected by the ARM designers were:

- Register windows.

  The register banks on the Berkeley RISC processors incorporated a large number of registers, 32 of which were visible at any time. Procedure entry and exit instructions moved the visible 'window' to give each procedure access to new registers, thereby reducing the data traffic between the processor and memory resulting from register saving and restoring.

The principal problem with register windows is the large chip area occupied by the large number of registers. This feature was therefore rejected on cost grounds, although the shadow registers used to handle exceptions on the ARM are not too different in concept.

In the early days of RISC the register window mechanism was strongly associated with the RISC idea due to its inclusion in the Berkeley prototypes, but subsequently only the Sun SPARC architecture has adopted it in its original form.

- Delayed branches.

  Branches cause pipelines problems since they interrupt the smooth flow of instructions. Most RISC processors ameliorate the problem by using delayed branches where the branch takes effect *after* the following instruction has executed.

  The problem with delayed branches is that they remove the atomicity of individual instructions. They work well on single issue pipelined processors, but they do not scale well to super-scalar implementations and can interact badly with branch prediction mechanisms.

  On the original ARM delayed branches were not used because they made exception handling more complex; in the long run this has turned out to be a good decision since it simplifies re-implementing the architecture with a different pipeline.

- Single-cycle execution of all instructions.

  Although the ARM executes most data processing instructions in a single clock cycle, many other instructions take multiple clock cycles.

  The rationale here was based on the observation that with a single memory for both data and instructions, even a simple load or store instruction requires at least two memory accesses (one for the instruction and one for the data). Therefore single cycle operation of all instructions is only possible with separate data and instruction memories, which were considered too expensive for the intended ARM application areas.

  Instead of single-cycle execution of all instructions, the ARM was designed to use the minimum number of cycles required for memory accesses. Where this was greater than one, the extra cycles were used, where possible, to do something useful, such as support auto-indexing addressing modes. This reduces the total number of ARM instructions required to perform any sequence of operations, improving performance and code density.

2.2.3 | Simplicity

An overriding concern of the original ARM design team was the need to keep the design simple. Before the first ARM chips, Acorn designers had experience only of gate arrays with complexities up to around 2,000 gates, so the full-custom CMOS design medium was approached with some respect. When venturing into unknown territory it is advisable to minimize those risks which are under your control, since this still leaves significant risks from those factors which are not well understood or are fundamentally not controllable.

The simplicity of the ARM may be more apparent in the hardware organization and implementation (described in Chapter 4) than it is in the instruction set architecture. From the programmer's perspective it is perhaps more visible as a conservatism in the ARM instruction set design which, while accepting the fundamental precepts of the RISC approach, is less radical than many subsequent RISC designs.

The combination of the simple hardware with an instruction set that is grounded in RISC ideas but retains a few key CISC features, and thereby achieves a significantly better code density than a pure RISC, has given the ARM its power-efficiency and its small core size.

2.3 | The ARM Programmer's Model

A processor's instruction set defines the operations that the programmer can use to change the state of the system incorporating the processor. This state usually comprises the values of the data items in the processor's visible registers and the system's memory. Each instruction can be viewed as performing a defined transformation from the state before the instruction is executed to the state after it has completed. Note that although a processor will typically have many invisible registers involved in executing an instruction, the values of these registers before and after the instruction is executed are not significant; only the values in the visible registers have any significance. The visible registers in an ARM processor are shown in Figure 2.1.

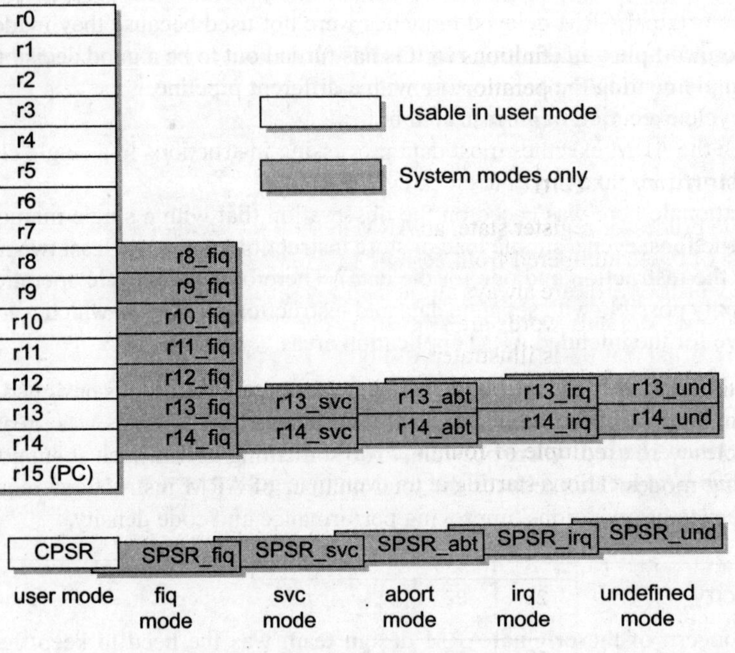

Figure 2.1 ARM's visible registers

When writing user-level programs, only the 15 general-purpose 32-bit registers (r0 to r14), the program counter (r15) and the current program status register (CPSR) need be considered. The remaining registers are used only for system-level programming and for handling exceptions (for example, interrupts).

2.3.1 | The Current Program Status Register (CPSR)

The CPSR is used in user-level programs to store the condition code bits. These bits are used, for example, to record the result of a comparison operation and to control whether or not a conditional branch is taken. The user-level programmer need not usually be concerned with how this register is configured, but for completeness the register is illustrated in Figure 2.2. The bits at the bottom of the register control

Figure 2.2 ARM CPSR format

the processor mode (see Section 5.1 on page 91), instruction set ('T', see Section 7.1 on page 163) and interrupt enables ('I' and 'F', see Section 5.2 on page 94) and are protected from change by the user-level program. The condition code flags are in the top four bits of the register and have the following meanings:

- N: Negative; the last ALU operation which changed the flags produced a negative result (the top bit of the 32-bit result was a one).
- Z: Zero; the last ALU operation which changed the flags produced a zero result (every bit of the 32-bit result was zero).
- C: Carry; the last ALU operation which changed the flags generated a carry-out, either as a result of an arithmetic operation in the ALU or from the shifter.
- V: Overflow; the last arithmetic ALU operation which changed the flags generated an overflow into the sign bit.

Note that although the above definitions for C and V look quite complex, their use does not require a detailed understanding of their operation. In most cases there is a simple condition test which gives the desired result without the programmer having to work out the precise values of the condition code bits.

2.3.2 | The Memory System

In addition to the processor register state, an ARM system has memory state. Memory may be viewed as a linear array of bytes numbered from zero up to $2^{32}-1$. Data items may be 8-bit bytes, 16-bit half-words or 32-bit words. Words are always aligned on 4-byte boundaries (that is, the two least significant address bits are zero) and half-words are aligned on even byte boundaries.

The memory organization is illustrated in Figure 2.3. This shows a small area of memory where each byte location has a unique number. A byte may occupy any of these locations, and a few examples are shown in the figure. A word-sized data item must occupy a group of four byte locations starting at a byte address which is a multiple of four, and again the figure contains a couple of examples. Half-words occupy two byte locations starting at an even byte address.

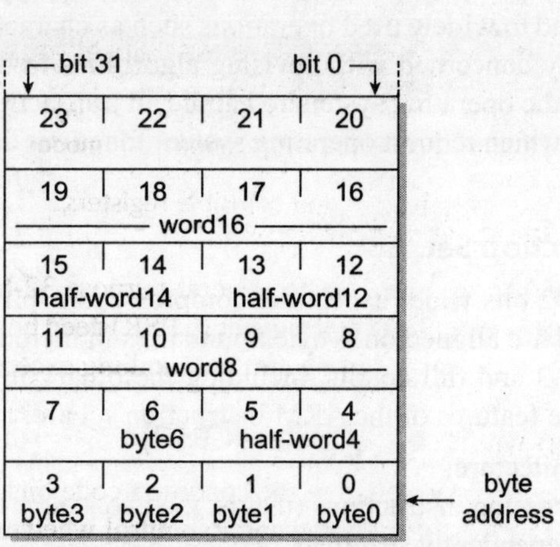

Figure 2.3 ARM memory organization

(This is the standard, 'little-endian', memory organization used by the ARM. ARM can also be configured to work with a 'big-endian' memory organization; we will return to this issue in Chapter 5.)

2.3.3 | Load-store Architecture

In common with most RISC processors, ARM employs a load-store architecture. This means that the instruction set will only process (add subtract, and so on) values which are in registers (or specified directly within the instruction itself), and will always place the results of such processing into a register. The only operations which apply to memory state are ones which copy memory values into registers (load instructions) or copy register values into memory (store instructions).

CISC processors typically allow a value from memory to be added to a value in a register, and sometimes allow a value in a register to be added to a value in memory. ARM does not support such 'memory-to-memory' operations. Therefore all ARM instructions fall into one of the following three categories:

1. Data processing instructions. These use and change only register values. For example, an instruction can add two registers and place the result in a register.
2. Data transfer instructions. These copy memory values into registers (load instructions) or copy register values into memory (store instructions). An additional form, useful only in systems code, exchanges a memory value with a register value.
3. Control flow instructions. Normal instruction execution uses instructions stored at consecutive memory addresses. Control flow instructions cause execution to switch to a different address, either permanently (branch instructions) or saving a return address to resume the original sequence (branch and link instructions) or trapping into system code (supervisor calls).

2.3.4 | Supervisor Mode

The ARM processor supports a protected supervisor mode. The protection mechanism ensures that user code cannot gain supervisor privileges without appropriate checks being carried out to ensure that the code is not attempting illegal operations.

The upshot of this for the user-level programmer is that system-level functions can only be accessed through specified supervisor calls. These functions generally include any accesses to hardware peripheral registers, and to widely used operations such as character input and output. User-level programmers are principally concerned with devising algorithms to operate on the data 'owned' by their programs, and rely on the operating system to handle all transactions with the world outside their programs. The instructions which request operating system functions are covered in 'Supervisor calls' on page 58.

2.3.5 | The ARM Instruction Set

All ARM instructions are 32 bits wide (except the compressed 16-bit Thumb instructions which are described in Chapter 7) and are aligned on 4-byte boundaries in memory. Basic use of the instruction set is described in Chapter 3 and full details, including the binary instruction formats, are given in Chapter 5. The most notable features of the ARM instruction set are:

- The load-store architecture;
- 3-address data processing instructions (that is, the two source operand registers and the result register are all independently specified);

- conditional execution of every instruction;
- the inclusion of very powerful load and store multiple register instructions;
- the ability to perform a general shift operation and a general ALU operation in a single instruction that executes in a single clock cycle;
- open instruction set extension through the coprocessor instruction set, including adding new registers and data types to the programmer's model;
- a very dense 16-bit compressed representation of the instruction set in the Thumb architecture.

To those readers familiar with modern RISC instruction sets, the ARM instruction set may appear to have rather more formats than other commercial RISC processors. While this is certainly the case and it does lead to more complex instruction decoding, it also leads to higher code density. For the small embedded systems that most ARM processors are used in, this code density advantage outweighs the small performance penalty incurred by the decode complexity. Thumb code extends this advantage to give ARM better code density than most CISC processors.

2.3.6 | The I/O System

The ARM handles **I/O** (input/output) peripherals (such as disk controllers, network interfaces, and so on) as memory-mapped devices with interrupt support. The internal registers in these devices appear as addressable locations within the ARM's memory map and may be read and written using the same (load-store) instructions as any other memory locations.

Peripherals may attract the processor's attention by making an interrupt request using either the normal interrupt (*IRQ*) or the fast interrupt (*FIQ*) input. Both interrupt inputs are level-sensitive and maskable. Normally most interrupt sources share the IRQ input, with just one or two time-critical sources connected to the higher-priority FIQ input.

Some systems may include direct memory access **(DMA)** hardware external to the processor to handle high-bandwidth I/O traffic. This is discussed further in Section 11.9 on page 266.

Interrupts are a form of *exception* and are handled as outlined below.

2.3.7 | ARM Exceptions

The ARM architecture supports a range of interrupts, traps and supervisor calls, all grouped under the general heading of exceptions. The general way these are handled is the same in all cases:

1. The current state is saved by copying the PC into r14_*exc* and the CPSR into SPSR_*exc* (where *exc* stands for the exception type).
2. The processor operating mode is changed to the appropriate exception mode.
3. The PC is forced to a value between 00_{16} and $1C_{16}$, the particular value depending on the type of exception.

The instruction at the location the PC is forced to (the *vector address)* will usually contain a branch to the exception handler. The exception handler will use r13_*exc*, which will normally have been initialized to point to a dedicated stack in memory, to save some user registers for use as work registers.

The return to the user program is achieved by restoring the user registers and then using an instruction to restore the PC and the CPSR atomically. This may involve some adjustment of the PC value saved in r14_*exc* to compensate for the state of the pipeline when the exception arose. This is described in more detail in Section 5.2 on page 94.

2.4 | ARM Development Tools

Software development for the ARM is supported by a coherent range of tools developed by ARM Limited, and there are also many third party and public domain tools available, such as an ARM back-end for the *gcc* C compiler.

Since the ARM is widely used as an embedded controller where the target hardware will not make a good environment for software development, the tools are intended for **cross-development** (that is, they run on a different architecture from the one for which they produce code) from a platform such as a PC running Windows or a suitable UNIX workstation. The overall structure of the ARM cross-development toolkit is shown in Figure 2.4. C or assembler source files are compiled or assembled into ARM object format (*.aof*) files, which are then linked into ARM image format (*.aif*) files. The image format files can be built to include the debug tables required by the ARM symbolic debugger (**ARMsd** which can load, run and debug programs either on hardware such as the **ARM Development Board** or using a software emulation of the ARM (the **ARMulator**). The ARMulator has been designed to allow easy extension of the software model to include system features such as caches, particular memory timing characteristics, and so on.

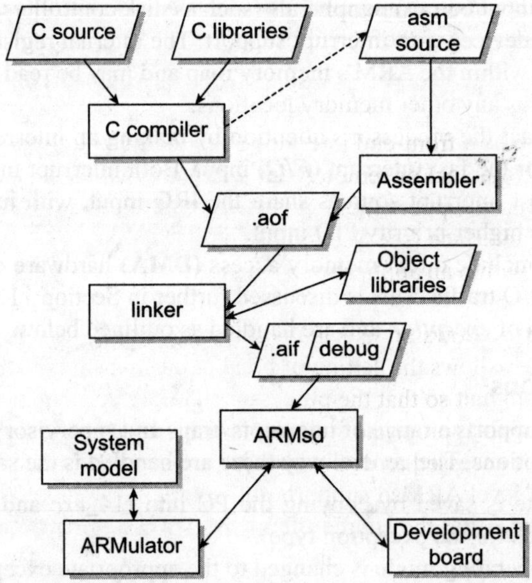

Figure 2.4 The structure of the ARM cross-development toolkit

2.4.1 | The ARM C Compiler

The ARM C compiler is compliant with the **ANSI** (American National Standards Institute) standard for C and is supported by the appropriate library of standard functions. It uses the ARM Procedure Call Standard (see Section 6.8 on page 151) for all externally available functions. It can be told to produce assembly source output instead of ARM object format, so the code can be inspected, or even hand optimized, and then assembled subsequently.

The compiler can also produce Thumb code.

2.4.2 | The ARM Assembler

The ARM assembler is a full macro assembler which produces ARM object format output that can be linked with output from the C compiler.

Assembly source language is near machine-level, with most assembly instructions translating into single ARM (or Thumb) instructions. ARM assembly language programming is introduced in the next chapter, and the full details of the ARM instruction set, including assembly language formats, are given in Chapter 5. The Thumb instruction set and assembly language formats are given in Chapter 7.

2.4.3 | The Linker

The linker takes one or more object files and combines them into an executable program. It resolves symbolic references between the object files and extracts object modules from libraries as needed by the program. It can assemble the various components of the program in a number of different ways, depending on whether the code is to run in RAM (Random Access Memory, which can be read and written) or ROM (Read Only Memory), whether overlays are required, and so on.

Normally the linker includes debug tables in the output file. If the object files were compiled with full debug information, this will include full symbolic debug tables (so the program can be debugged using the variable names in the source program). The linker can also produce object library modules that are not executable but are ready for efficient linking with object files in the future.

2.4.4 | ARMsd

The ARM symbolic debugger is a front-end interface to assist in debugging programs running either under emulation (on the ARMulator) or remotely on a target system such as the ARM development board. The remote system must support the appropriate remote debug protocols either via a serial line or through a JTAG test interface (see Section 8.6 on page 194). Debugging a system where the processor core is embedded within an application-specific system chip is a complex issue that we will return to in Chapter 8.

At its most basic, ARMsd allows an executable program to be loaded into the ARMulator or a development board and run. It allows the setting of breakpoints, which are addresses in the code that, if executed, cause execution to halt so that the processor state can be examined. In the ARMulator, or when running on hardware with appropriate support, it also allows the setting of watchpoints. These are memory addresses that, if accessed as data addresses, cause execution to halt in a similar way.

At a more sophisticated level ARMsd supports full source level debugging, allowing the C programmer to debug a program using the source file to specify breakpoints and using variable names from the original program.

2.4.5 | ARMulator

The ARMulator (*ARM emulator*) is a suite of programs that models the behaviour of various ARM processor cores in software on a host system. It can operate at various levels of accuracy:

- *Instruction-accurate* modelling gives the exact behaviour of the system state without regard to the precise timing characteristics of the processor.
- *Cycle-accurate* modelling gives the exact behaviour of the processor on a cycle-by-cycle basis, allowing the exact number of clock cycles that a program requires to be established.
- *Timing-accurate* modelling presents signals at the correct time within a cycle, allowing logic delays to be accounted for.

All these approaches run considerably slower than the real hardware, but the first incurs the smallest speed penalty and is best suited to software development.

At its simplest, the ARMulator allows an ARM program developed using the C compiler or assembler to be tested and debugged on a host machine with no ARM processor connected. It allows the number of clock cycles the program takes to execute to be measured exactly, so the performance of the target system can be evaluated.

At its most complex, the ARMulator can be used as the centre of a complete, timing-accurate, C model of the target system, with full details of the cache and memory management functions added, running an operating system.

In between these two extremes the ARMulator comes with a set of model prototyping modules including a rapid prototype memory model and coprocessor interfacing support. (There is more detail on this in Section 8.5 on page 193.)

The ARMulator can also be used as the core of a timing-accurate ARM behavioural model in a hardware simulation environment based around a language such as VHDL. (VHDL is a standard widely supported hardware description language.) A VHDL 'wrapper' must be generated to interface the ARMulator C code to the VHDL environment.

2.4.6 | ARM Development Board

The ARM Development Board is a circuit board incorporating a range of components and interfaces to support the development of ARM-based systems. It includes an ARM core (for example, an ARM7TDMI), memory components which can be configured to match the performance and bus-width of the memory in the target system, and electrically programmable devices which can be configured to emulate application-specific peripherals. It can support both hardware and software development before the final application-specific hardware is available.

2.4.7 | Software Toolkit

ARM Limited supplies the complete set of tools described above, with some support utility programs and documentation, as the 'ARM Software Development Toolkit'. The Toolkit CD-ROM includes a PC version of the toolset that runs under most versions of the Windows operating system and includes a full Windows-based project manager. The toolkit is updated as new versions of the ARM become available.

The ARM Project Manager is a graphical front-end for the tools described above. It supports the building of a single library or executable image from a list of files that make up a particular project. These files may be:

- source files (C, assembler, and so on);
- object files;
- library files.

The source files may be edited within the Project Manager, a dependency list created and the output library or executable image built. There are many options which may be chosen for the build, such as:

- Whether the output should be optimized for code size or execution time.
- Whether the output should be in debug or release form.
  (Code compiled for source-level debugging cannot be fully optimized since the mapping from the source to fully optimized output is too obscure for debugging purposes.)
- Which ARM processor is the target (and, particularly, whether it supports the Thumb instruction set).

The CD-ROM also contains versions of the tools that run on a Sun or HP UNIX host, where a command-line interface is used. All versions have on-line help available.

2.4.8 | JumpStart

The JumpStart tools from VLSI Technology, Inc., include the same basic set of development tools but present a full X-windows interface on a suitable workstation rather than the command-line interface of the standard ARM toolkit.

There are many other suppliers of tools that support ARM development.

2.5 | Example and Exercises

EXAMPLE 2.1

Describe the principal features of the ARM architecture.

The main features of the ARM architecture are:

- a large set of registers, all of which can be used for most purposes;
- a load-store architecture;
- 3-address instructions (that is, the two source operand registers and the result register are all independently specified);
- conditional execution of every instruction;
- the inclusion of very powerful load and store multiple register instructions;
- the ability to perform a general shift operation and a general ALU operation in a single instruction that executes in a single clock cycle;
- open instruction set extension through the coprocessor instruction set, including adding new registers and data types to the programmer's model.

If the Thumb instruction set is considered part of the ARM architecture, we could also add:

- a very dense 16-bit compressed representation of the instruction set in the Thumb architecture.

Exercise 2.1.1

Which features does ARM have in common with many other RISC architectures?

Exercise 2.1.2

Which features of the ARM architecture are not shared by most other RISCs?

Exercise 2.1.3

What is the function of the SPSR register?

3

ARM Assembly Language Programming

SUMMARY OF CHAPTER CONTENTS

The ARM processor is very easy to program at the assembly level, though for most applications it is more appropriate to program in a high-level language such as C or C++.

Assembly language programming requires the programmer to think at the level of the individual machine instruction. An ARM instruction is 32 bits long, so there are around 4 billion different binary machine instructions. Fortunately there is considerable structure within the instruction space, so the programmer does not have to be familiar with each of the 4 billion binary encodings on an individual basis. Even so, there is a considerable amount of detail to be got right in each instruction. The assembler is a computer program which handles most of this detail for the programmer.

In this chapter we will look at ARM assembly language programming at the user level and see how to write simple programs which will run on an ARM development board or an ARM emulator (for example, the ARMulator which comes as part of the ARM development toolkit). Once the basic instruction set is familiar we will move on, in Chapter 5, to look at system-level programming and at some of the finer details of the ARM instruction set, including the binary-level instruction encoding.

Some ARM processors support a form of the instruction set that has been compressed into 16-bit 'Thumb' instructions. These are discussed in Chapter 7.

3.1 | Data Processing Instructions

ARM data processing instructions enable the programmer to perform arithmetic and logical operations on data values in registers. All other instructions just move data around and control the sequence of program execution, so the data processing instructions are the only instructions which modify data values. These instructions typically require two operands and produce a single result, though there are exceptions to both of these rules. A characteristic operation is to add two values together to produce a single result which is the sum.

Here are some rules which apply to ARM data processing instructions:

- All operands are 32 bits wide and come from registers or are specified as literals in the instruction itself.

- The result, if there is one, is 32 bits wide and is placed in a register. (There is an exception here: long multiply instructions produce a 64-bit result; they are discussed in Section 5.8 on page 106.)
- Each of the operand registers and the result register are independently specified in the instruction. That is, the ARM uses a '3-address' format for these instructions.

3.1.1 | Simple Register Operands

A typical ARM data processing instruction is written in assembly language as shown below:

```
ADD     r0, r1, r2        ; r0 : = r1 + r2
```

The semicolon in this line indicates that everything to the right of it is a comment and should be ignored by the assembler. Comments are put into the assembly source code to make reading and understanding it easier.

This example simply takes the values in two registers (r1 and r2), adds them together, and places the result in a third register (r0). The values in the source registers are 32 bits wide and may be considered to be either unsigned integers or signed 2's-complement integers. The addition may produce a carry-out or, in the case of signed 2's-complement values, an internal overflow into the sign bit, but in either case this is ignored.

Note that in writing the assembly language source code, care must be taken to write the operands in the correct order, which is result register first, then the first operand and lastly the second operand (though for **commutative** operations the order of the first and second operands is not significant when they are both registers). When this instruction is executed the only change to the system state is the value of the destination register r0 (and, optionally, the N, Z, C and V flags in the CPSR, as we shall see later).

The different instructions available in this form are listed below in their classes:

- Arithmetic operations.
  These instructions perform binary arithmetic (addition, subtraction and reverse subtraction, which is subtraction with the operand order reversed) on two 32-bit operands. The operands may be unsigned or 2's-complement signed integers; the carry-in, when used, is the current value of the C bit in the CPSR.

```
ADD     r0, r1, r2        ; r0 := r1 + r2
ADC     r0, r1, r2        ; r0 := r1 + r2 + C
SUB     r0, r1, r2        ; r0 := r1 – r2
SBC     r0, r1, r2        ; r0 := r1 – r2 + C – 1
RSB     r0, r1, r2        ; r0 := r2 – r1
RSC     r0, r1, r2        ; r0 := r2 – r1 + C – 1
```

  'ADD' is simple addition, 'ADC' is add with carry, 'SUB' is subtract, 'SBC' is subtract with carry, 'RSB' is reverse subtraction and 'RSC' reverse subtract with carry.
- Bit-wise logical operations.
  These instructions perform the specified Boolean logic operation on each bit pair of the input operands, so in the first case *r0[i]*: = *r1[i]* AND *r2[i]* for each value of *i* from 0 to 31 inclusive, where *r0[i]* is the *i*'th bit of r0.

```
AND     r0, r1, r2        ; r0 := r1 and r2
ORR     r0, r1, r2        ; r0 := r1 or r2
```

```
EOR     r0, rl, r2      ; r0 := rl xor r2
BIC     r0, rl, r2      ; r0 := rl and not r2
```

We have met AND, OR and XOR (here called EOR) logical operations at the hardware gate level in Section 1.2 on page 3; the final mnemonic, BIC, stands for 'bit clear' where every '1' in the second operand clears the corresponding bit in the first. (The 'not' operation in the assembly language comment inverts each bit of the following operand.)

- Register movement operations.
  These instructions ignore the first operand which is omitted from the assembly language format, and simply move the second operand (possibly bit-wise inverted) to the destination.

```
MOV     r0, r2          ; r0 := r2
MVN     r0, r2          ; r0 := not r2
```

The 'MVN' mnemonic stands for 'move negated'; it leaves the result register set to the value obtained by inverting every bit in the source operand.

- Comparison operations.
  These instructions do not produce a result (which is therefore omitted from the assembly language format) but just set the condition code bits (N, Z, C and V) in the CPSR according to the selected operation.

```
CMP     rl, r2          ; set cc on rl − r2
CMN     rl, r2          ; set cc on rl + r2
TST     rl, r2          ; set cc on rl and r2
TEQ     rl, r2          ; set cc on rl xor r2
```

The mnemonics stand for 'compare' (CMP), 'compare negated' (CMN), '(bit) test' (TST) and 'test equal' (TEQ).

3.1.2 | Immediate Operands

If, instead of adding two registers, we simply wish to add a constant to a register we can replace the second source operand with an immediate value, which is a literal constant, preceded by '#':

```
ADD     r3, r3, #1      ; r3 := r3 + 1
AND     r8, r7, #&ff    ; r8 := r7[7:0]
```

The first example also illustrates that although the 3-address format allows source and destination operands to be specified separately, they are not required to be distinct registers. The second example shows that the immediate value may be specified in hexadecimal (base 16) notation by putting '&' after the '#'.

Since the immediate value is coded within the 32 bits of the instruction, it is not possible to enter every possible 32-bit value as an immediate. The values which can be entered correspond to any 32-bit binary number where all the binary ones fall within a group of eight adjacent bit positions on a 2-bit boundary. Most valid immediate values are given by:

$$immediate = (0 \rightarrow 255) \times 2^{2n} \quad \text{Equation 10}$$

where $0 \le n \le 12$. The assembler will also replace MOV with MVN, ADD with SUB, and so on, where this can bring the immediate within range.

This may appear a complex constraint on the immediate values, but it does, in practice, cover all the most common cases such as a byte value at any of the four byte positions within a 32-bit word, any power of 2, and so on. In any case the assembler will report any value which is requested that it cannot encode.

(The reason for the constraint on immediate values is the way they are specified at the binary instruction level. This is described in the Chapter 5, and the reader who wishes to understand this issue fully should look there for the complete explanation.)

3.1.3 | Shifted Register Operands

A third way to specify a data operation is similar to the first, but allows the second register operand to be subject to a shift operation before it is combined with the first operand. For example:

```
ADD     r3, r2, rl, LSL #3;          r3:= r2 + 8 × rl
```

Note that this is still a single ARM instruction, executed in a single clock cycle. Most processors offer shift operations as separate instructions, but the ARM combines them with a general ALU operation in a single instruction.

Here 'LSL' indicates 'logical shift left by the specified number of bits', which in this example is 3. Any number from 0 to 31 may be specified though using 0 is equivalent to omitting the shift altogether. As before, '#' indicates an immediate quantity. The available shift operations are:

- LSL: logical shift left by 0 to 31 places; fill the vacated bits at the least significant end of the word with zeros.
- LSR: logical shift right by 0 to 32 places; fill the vacated bits at the most significant end of the word with zeros.
- ASL: arithmetic shift left; this is a synonym for LSL.
- ASR: arithmetic shift right by 0 to 32 places; fill the vacated bits at the most significant end of the word with zeros if the source operand was positive, or with ones if the source operand was negative.
- ROR: rotate right by 0 to 32 places; the bits which fall off the least significant end of the word are used in order, to fill the vacated bits at the most significant end of the word.
- RRX: rotate right extended by 1 place; the vacated bit (bit 31) is filled with the old value of the C flag and the operand is shifted one place to the right. With appropriate use of the condition codes (see below) a 33-bit rotate of the operand and the C flag is performed.

These shift operations are illustrated in Figure 3.1.

It is also possible to use a register value to specify the number of bits the second operand should be shifted by:

```
ADD     r5, r5, r3, LSL r2;          r5 := r5 + r3 × 2^r2
```

This is a 4-address instruction. Only the bottom eight bits of r2 are significant, but since shifts by more than 32 bits are not very useful this limitation is not important for most purposes.

3.1.4 | Setting the Condition Codes

Any data processing instruction can set the condition codes (N, Z, C and V) if the programmer wishes it to. The comparison operations only set the condition codes, so there is no option with them, but for all other data processing instructions a specific request must be made. At the assembly language level this request is indicated by adding an 's' to the opcode, standing for 'Set condition codes'. As an example, the following code performs a 64-bit addition of two numbers held in r0-rl and r2-r3, using the C condition code flag to store the intermediate carry:

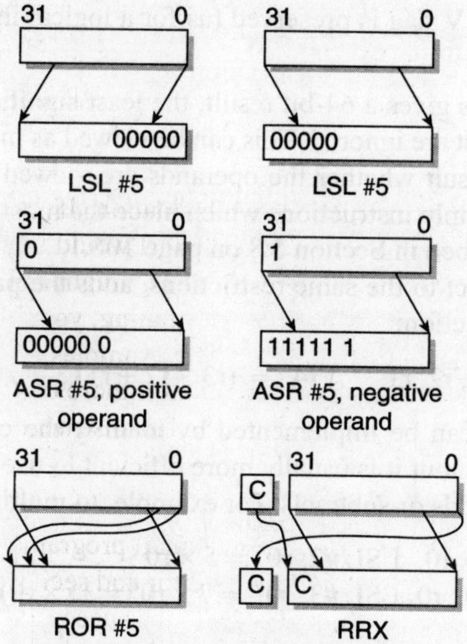

Figure 3.1 ARM shift operations

```
ADDS    r2, r2, r0;     32-bit carry out -> C..
ADC     r3, r3, rl;     .. and added into high word
```

Since the S opcode extension gives the programmer control over whether or not an instruction modifies the condition codes, the codes can be preserved over long instruction sequences when it is appropriate to do so.

An arithmetic operation (which here includes CMP and CMN) sets all the flags according to the arithmetic result. A logical or move operation does not produce a meaningful value for C or V, so these operations set N and Z according to the result but preserve V, and either preserve C when there is no shift operation, or set C to the value of the last bit to fall off the end of the shift. This detail is not often significant.

3.1.5 | Use of the Condition Codes

We have already seen the C flag used as an input to an arithmetic data processing instruction. However we have not yet seen the most important use of the condition codes, which is to control the program flow through the conditional branch instructions. These will be described in Section 3.3.

3.1.6 | Multiplies

A special form of the data processing instruction supports multiplication:

MUL   r4, r3, r2   ; $r4 := (r3 \times r2)_{[31:0]}$

There are some important differences from the other arithmetic instructions:

- Immediate second operands are not supported.
- The result register must not be the same as the first source register.
- If the 'S' bit is set the V flag is preserved (as for a logical instruction) and the C flag is rendered meaningless.

Multiplying two 32-bit integers gives a 64-bit result, the least significant 32 bits of which are placed in the result register and the rest are ignored. This can be viewed as multiplication in modulo 2^{32} arithmetic and gives the correct result whether the operands are viewed as signed or unsigned integers. (ARMs also support long multiply instructions which place the most significant 32 bits into a second result register; these are described in Section 5.8 on page 106.)

An alternative form, subject to the same restrictions, adds the product to a running total. This is the multiply-accumulate instruction:

```
MLA    r4, r3, r2, r1    ; r4 := (r3 × r2 + r1)[31:0]
```

Multiplication by a constant can be implemented by loading the constant into a register and then using one of these instructions, but it is usually more efficient to use a short series of data processing instructions using shifts and adds or subtracts. For example, to multiply r0 by 35:

```
ADD    r0, r0, r0, LSL #2; r0′ := 5 × r0
RSB    r0, r0, r0, LSL #3; r0″ := 7 × r0′(= 35 × r0)
```

3.2 | Data Transfer Instructions

Data transfer instructions move data between ARM registers and memory. There are three basic forms of data transfer instruction in the ARM instruction set:

- Single register load and store instructions.
  These instructions provide the most flexible way to transfer single data items between an ARM register and memory. The data item may be a byte, a 32-bit word, or a 16-bit half-word. (Older ARM chips may not support half-words.)
- Multiple register load and store instructions.
  These instructions are less flexible than single register transfer instructions, but enable large quantities of data to be transferred more efficiently. They are used for procedure entry and exit, to save and restore workspace registers, and to copy blocks of data around memory.
- Single register swap instructions.
  These instructions allow a value in a register to be exchanged with a value in memory, effectively doing both a load and a store operation in one instruction. They are little used in user-level programs, so they will not be discussed further in this section. Their principal use is to implement semaphores to ensure mutual exclusion on accesses to shared data structures in multi-processor systems, but don't worry if this explanation has little meaning for you at the moment.

It is quite possible to write any program for the ARM using only the single register load and store instructions, but there are situations where the multiple register transfers are much more efficient, so the programmer should be familiar with them.

3.2.1 | Register-indirect Addressing

Towards the end of Section 1.4 on page 12 there was a discussion of memory addressing mechanisms that are available to the processor instruction set designer. The ARM data transfer instructions are all based around register-indirect addressing, with modes that include base-plus-offset and base-plus-index addressing.

Register-indirect addressing uses a value in one register (the **base** register) as a memory address and either **loads** the value from that address into another register or **stores** the value from another register into that memory address.

These instructions are written in assembly language as follows:

LDR r0, [r1] ; r0:= mem_{32} [r1]
STR r0, [r1] ; mem_{32} [r1] := r0

Other forms of addressing all build on this form, adding immediate or register offsets to the base address. In all cases it is necessary to have an ARM register loaded with an address which is near to the desired transfer address, so we will begin by looking at ways of getting memory addresses into a register.

3.2.2 | Initializing an Address Pointer

To load or store from or to a particular memory location, an ARM register must be initialized to contain the address of that location, or, in the case of single register transfer instructions, an address within 4 Kbytes of that location (the 4 Kbyte range will be explained later).

If the location is close to the code being executed it is often possible to exploit the fact that the program counter, r15, is close to the desired address. A data processing instruction can be employed to add a small offset to r15, but calculating the appropriate offset may not be that straightforward. However, this is the sort of tricky calculation that assemblers are good at, and ARM assemblers have an inbuilt 'pseudo instruction', ADR, which makes this easy. A pseudo instruction looks like a normal instruction in the assembly source code but does not correspond directly to a particular ARM instruction. Instead the assembler has a set of rules which enable it to select the most appropriate ARM instruction or short instruction sequence for the situation in which the pseudo instruction is used. (In fact, ADR is always assembled into a single ADD or SUB instruction.)

As an example, consider a program which must copy data from TABLE1 to TABLE2, both of which are near to the code:

```
COPY    ADR     r1, TABLE1      ; r1 points to TABLE1
        ADR     r2, TABLE2      ; r2 points to TABLE2
        ..
TABLE1                          ; < source of data >
        ..
TABLE2                          ; < destination >
        ..
```

Here we have introduced **labels** (COPY, TABLE1 and TABLE2) which are simply names given to particular points in the assembly code. The first ADR pseudo instruction causes r1 to contain the address of the data that follows TABLE1; the second ADR likewise causes r2 to hold the address of the memory starting at TABLE2.

Of course any ARM instruction can be used to compute the address of a data item in memory, but for the purposes of small programs the ADR pseudo instruction will do what we require.

3.2.3 | Single Register Load and Store Instructions

These instructions compute an address for the transfer using a base register, which should contain an address near to the target address, and an offset which may be another register or an immediate value.

We have just seen the simplest form of these instructions, which does not use an offset:

```
        LDR     r0, [r1]        ; r0:= mem32 [r1]
        STR     r0, [r1]        ; mem32 [r1]:= r0
```

The notation used here indicates that the data quantity is the 32-bit memory word addressed by r1. The word address in r1 should be aligned on a 4-byte boundary, so the two least significant bits of r1 should be zero. We can now copy the first word from one table to the other:

```
COPY    ADR     r1, TABLE1      ; r1 points to TABLE1
        ADR     r2, TABLE2      ; r2 points to TABLE2
        LDR     r0, [r1]        ; load first value...
        STR     r0, [r2]        ; and store it in TABLE2
        ..
TABLE1                          ; < source of data >
        ..
TABLE2                          ; < destination >
        ..
```

We could now use data processing instructions to modify both base registers ready for the next transfer:

```
COPY    ADR     r1, TABLE1      ; r1 points to TABLE1
        ADR     r2, TABLE2      ; r2 points to TABLE2
LOOP    LDR     r0, [r1]        ; get TABLE1 1st word
        STR     r0, [r2]        ; copy into TABLE2
        ADD     r1, r1,#4       ; step r1 on 1 word
        ADD     r2, r2,#4       ; step r2 on 1 word
        ???                     ; if more go back to LOOP
        ..
TABLE1                          ; < source of data >
        ..
TABLE2                          ; < destination >
        ..
```

Note that the base registers are incremented by 4 (bytes), since this is the size of a word. If the base register was word-aligned before the increment, it will be word-aligned afterwards too.

All load and store instructions could use just this simple form of register-indirect addressing. However, the ARM instruction set includes more addressing modes that can make the code more efficient.

3.2.4 | Base Plus Offset Addressing

If the base register does not contain exactly the right address, an offset of up to 4 Kbytes may be added (or subtracted) to the base to compute the transfer address:

```
        LDR     r0, [r1, #4]    ; r0 := mem32[r1 + 4]
```

This is a **pre-indexed** addressing mode. It allows one base register to be used to access a number of memory locations which are in the same area of memory.

Sometimes it is useful to modify the base register to point to the transfer address. This can be achieved by using pre-indexed addressing with **auto-indexing**, and allows the program to walk through a table of values:

```
LDR     r0, [r1, #4]!     ; r0 := mem32 [r1 + 4]
                          ; r1 := r1 + 4
```

The exclamation mark indicates that the instruction should update the base register after initiating the data transfer. On the ARM this auto-indexing costs no extra time since it is performed on the processor's datapath while the data is being fetched from memory. It is exactly equivalent to preceding a simple register-indirect load with a data processing instruction that adds the offset (4 bytes in this example) to the base register, but the time and code space cost of the extra instruction are avoided.

Another useful form of the instruction, called **post-indexed** addressing, allows the base to be used without an offset as the transfer address, after which it is auto-indexed:

```
LDR     r0, [r1], #4      ; r0 : = mem32[r1]
                          ; r1 : = r1 + 4
```

Here the exclamation mark is not needed since the only use of the immediate offset is as a base register modifier. Again, this form of the instruction is exactly equivalent to a simple register-indirect load followed by a data processing instruction, but it is faster and occupies less code space.

Using the last of these forms we can now improve on the table copying program example introduced earlier:

```
COPY      ADR     r1, TABLE1       ; r1 points to TABLE1
          ADR     r2, TABLE2       ; r2 points to TABLE2
LOOP      LDR     r0, [r1], #4     ; get TABLE1 1st word
          STR     r0, [r2], #4     ; copy into TABLE2
          ???                      ; if more go back to LOOP

TABLE1                             ; < source of data >
          ..
TABLE2                             ; < destination >
          ..
```

The load and store instructions are repeated until the required number of values has been copied into TABLE2, then the loop is exited. Control flow instructions are required to determine the loop exit; they will be introduced shortly.

In the above examples the address offset from the base register was always an immediate value. It can equally be another register, optionally subject to a shift operation before being added to the base, but such forms of the instruction are less useful than the immediate offset form. They are described fully in Section 5.10 on page 108.

As a final variation, the size of the data item which is transferred may be a single unsigned 8-bit byte instead of a 32-bit word. This option is selected by adding a letter B onto the opcode:

```
LDRB    r0, [r1]          ; r0 := mem8[r1]
```

In this case the transfer address can have any alignment and is not restricted to a 4-byte boundary, since bytes may be stored at any byte address. The loaded byte is placed in the bottom byte of r0 and the remaining bytes in r0 are filled with zeros.

(All but the oldest ARM processors also support **signed** bytes, where the top bit of the byte indicates whether the value should be treated as positive or negative, and signed and unsigned 16-bit half-words; these variants will be described when we return to look at the instruction set in more detail in Section 5.11 on page 111.)

3.2.5 | Multiple Register Data Transfers

Where considerable quantities of data are to be transferred, it is preferable to move several registers at a time. These instructions allow any subset (or all) of the 16 registers to be transferred with a single instruction. The trade-off is that the available addressing modes are more restricted than with a single register transfer instruction.

A simple example of this instruction class is:

```
LDMIA    r1, {r0, r2, r5}    ; r0 := mem32[r1]
                             ; r2 := mem32[r1 + 4]
                             ; r5 := mem32[ r1 + 8]
```

Since the transferred data items are always 32-bit words, the base address (r1) should be word-aligned.

The transfer list, within the curly brackets, may contain any or all of r0 to r15. The order of the registers within the list is insignificant and does not affect the order of transfer or the values in the registers after the instruction has executed. It is normal practice, however, to specify the registers in increasing order within the list.

Note that including r15 in the list will cause a change in the control flow, since r15 is the PC. We will return to this case when we discuss control flow instructions and will not consider it further until then.

The above example illustrates a common feature of all forms of these instructions: the lowest register is transferred to or from the lowest address, and then the other registers are transferred in order of register number to or from consecutive word addresses above the first. However there are several variations on how the first address is formed, and auto-indexing is also available (again by adding a '!' after the base register).

3.2.6 | Stack Addressing

The addressing variations stem from the fact that one use of these instructions is to implement stacks within memory. A stack is a form of last-in-first-out store which supports simple dynamic memory allocation, that is, memory allocation where the address to be used to store a data value is not known at the time the program is compiled or assembled. An example would be a recursive function, where the depth of recursion depends on the value of the argument. A stack is usually implemented as a linear data structure which grows up (an **ascending** stack) or down (a **descending** stack) memory as data is added to it and shrinks back as data is removed. A **stack pointer** holds the address of the current top of the stack, either by pointing to the last valid data item pushed onto the stack (a **full** stack), or by pointing to the vacant slot where the next data item will be placed (an **empty** stack).

The above description suggests that there are four variations on a stack, representing all the combinations of ascending and descending full and empty stacks. The ARM multiple register transfer instructions support all four forms of stack:

- Full ascending: the stack grows up through increasing memory addresses and the base register points to the highest address containing a valid item.
- Empty ascending: the stack grows up through increasing memory addresses and the base register points to the first empty location above the stack.
- Full descending: the stack grows down through decreasing memory addresses and the base register points to the lowest address containing a valid item.
- Empty descending: the stack grows down through decreasing memory addresses and the base register points to the first empty location below the stack.

3.2.7 | Block Copy Addressing

Although the stack view of multiple register transfer instructions is useful, there are occasions when a different view is easier to understand. For example, when these instructions are used to copy a block of data from one place in memory to another a mechanistic view of the addressing process is more useful. Therefore the ARM assembler supports two different views of the addressing mechanism, both of which map onto the same basic instructions, and which can be used interchangeably. The block copy view is based on whether the data is to be stored above or below the address held in the base register and whether the address incrementing or decrementing begins before or after storing the first value. The mapping between the two views depends on whether the operation is a load or a store, and is detailed in Table 3.1.

Table 3.1 The mapping between the stack and block copy views of the load and store multiple instructions

		Ascending		Descending	
		Full	Empty	Full	Empty
Increment	Before	STMIB STMFA			LDMIB LDMED
	After		STMIA STMEA	LDMIA LDMFD	
Decrement	Before		LDMDB LDMEA	STMDB STMFD	
	After	LDMDA LDMFA			STMDA STMED

The block copy views are illustrated in Figure 3.2, which shows how each variant stores three registers into memory and how the base register is modified if auto-indexing is enabled. The base register value before the instruction is r9, and after the auto-indexing it is r9'.

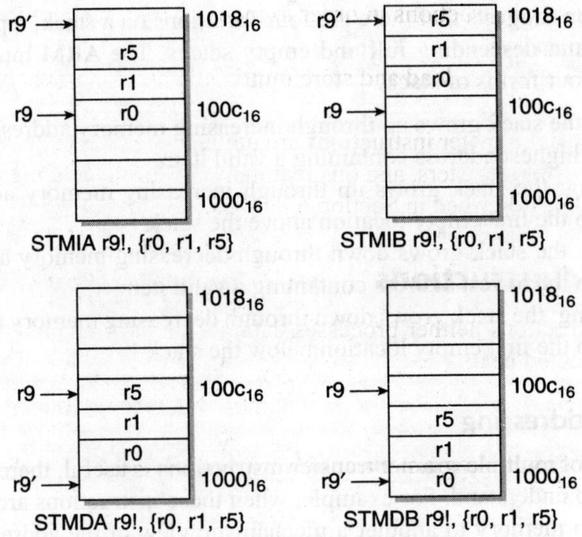

Figure 3.2 Multiple register transfer addressing modes

To illustrate the use of these instructions, here are two instructions which copy eight words from the location r0 points to to the location r1 points to:

```
LDMIA    r0!, {r2 – r9}
STMIA    r1, {r2 – r9}
```

After executing these instructions r0 has increased by 32 since the '!' causes it to auto-index across eight words, whereas r1 is unchanged. If r2 to r9 contained useful values, we could preserve them across this operation by pushing them onto a stack:

```
STMFD    r13!, {r2 – r9}     ; save regs onto stack
LDMIA    r0!, {r2 – r9}
STMIA    r1, {r2 – r9}
LDMFD    r13!, {r2 – r9}     ; restore from stack
```

Here the 'FD' postfix on the first and last instructions signifies the full descending stack address mode as described earlier. Note that auto-indexing is almost always specified for stack operations in order to ensure that the stack pointer has a consistent behaviour.

The load and store multiple register instructions are an efficient way to save and restore processor state and to move blocks of data around in memory. They save code space and operate up to four times faster than the equivalent sequence of single register load or store instructions (a factor of two due to improved sequential behaviour and another factor of nearly two due to the reduced instruction count). This significant advantage suggests that it is worth thinking carefully about how data is organized in memory in order to maximize the potential for using multiple register data transfer instructions to access it.

These instructions are, perhaps, not pure 'RISC' since they cannot be executed in a single clock cycle even with separate instruction and data caches, but other RISC architectures are beginning to adopt multiple register transfer instructions in order to increase the data bandwidth between the processor's registers and the memory.

On the other side of the equation, load and store multiple instructions are complex to implement, as we shall see later.

The ARM multiple register transfer instructions are uniquely flexible in being able to transfer any subset of the 16 currently visible registers, and this feature is powerfully exploited by the ARM procedure call mechanism which is described in Section 6.8 on page 151.

3.3 | Control Flow Instructions

This third category of instructions neither processes data nor moves it around; it simply determines which instructions get executed next.

3.3.1 | Branch Instructions

The most common way to switch program execution from one place to another is to use the branch instruction:

```
        B       LABEL
        ..
LABEL   ..
```

The processor normally executes instructions sequentially, but when it reaches the branch instruction it proceeds directly to the instruction at LABEL instead of executing the instruction immediately after the branch. In this example LABEL comes after the branch instruction in the program, so the instructions in between are skipped. However, label could equally well come before the branch, in which case the processor goes back to it and possibly repeats some instructions it has already executed.

3.3.2 | Conditional Branches

Sometimes you will want the processor to take a decision whether or not to branch. For example, to implement a loop a branch back to the start of the loop is required, but this branch should only be taken until the loop has been executed the required number of times, then the branch should be skipped.

The mechanism used to control loop exit is conditional branching. Here the branch has a condition associated with it and it is only executed if the condition codes have the correct value. A typical loop control sequence might be:

```
        MOV     r0, #0          ; initialize counter
LOOP    ..
        ADD     r0, r0, #1      ; increment loop counter
        CMP     r0, #10         ; compare with limit
        BNE     LOOP            ; repeat if not equal
        ..                      ; else fall throuh
```

This example shows one sort of conditional branch, BNE, or 'branch if not equal'. There are many forms of the condition. All the forms are listed in Table 3.2, along with their normal interpretations. The pairs of conditions which are listed in the same row of the table (for instance BCC and BLO) are synonyms which result in identical binary code, but both are available because each makes the interpretation of the assembly source code easier in particular circumstances. Where the table refers to signed or unsigned comparisons this does not reflect a choice in the comparison instruction itself but supports alternative interpretations of the operands.

Table 3.2 Branch conditions

Branch	Interpretation	Normal uses
B BAL	Unconditional Always	Always take this branch Always take this branch
BEQ	Equal	Comparison equal or zero result
BNE	Not equal	Comparison not equal or non-zero result
BPL	Plus	Result positive or zero
BMI	Minus	Result minus or negative
BCC BLO	Carry clear Lower	Arithmetic operation did not give carry-out Unsigned comparison gave lower
BCS BHS	Carry set Higher or same	Arithmetic operation gave carry-out Unsigned comparison gave higher or same
BVC	Overflow clear	Signed integer operation; no overflow occurred
BVS	Overflow set	Signed integer operation; overflow occurred
BGT	Greater than	Signed integer comparison gave greater than
BGE	Greater or equal	Signed integer comparison gave greater or equal
BLT	Less than	Signed integer comparison gave less than
BLE	Less or equal	Signed integer comparison gave less than or equal
BHI	Higher	Unsigned comparison gave higher
BLS	Lower or same	Unsigned comparison gave lower or same

3.3.3 | Conditional Execution

An unusual feature of the ARM instruction set is that conditional execution applies not only to branches but to all ARM instructions. A branch which is used to skip a small number of following instructions may be omitted altogether by giving those instructions the opposite condition. For example, consider the following sequence:

```
            CMP     r0, #5
            BEQ     BYPASS      ; if (r0 != 5) {
            ADD     rl, rl, r0  ; rl := rl + r0 – r2
            SUB     rl, rl, r2  ; }
BYPASS      ..
```

This may be replaced by:

```
CMP         r0, #5      ; if (r0 != 5) {
ADDNE       rl, rl, r0  ; rl := rl + r0 – r2
SUBNE       rl, rl, r2  ; }
..
```

The new sequence is both smaller and faster than the old one. Whenever the conditional sequence is three instructions or fewer it is better to exploit conditional execution than to use a branch, provided that the skipped sequence is not doing anything complicated with the condition codes within itself.

(The three instruction guideline is based on the fact that ARM branch instructions typically take three cycles to execute, and it is only a guideline. If the code is to be fully optimized then the decision on whether to use conditional execution or a branch must be based on measurements of the dynamic code behaviour.)

Conditional execution is invoked by adding the 2-letter condition after the 3-letter opcode (and before any other instruction modifier letter such as the 'S' that controls setting the condition codes in a data processing instruction or the 'B' that specifies a byte load or store).

Just to emphasize the scope of this technique, note that every ARM instruction, including supervisor calls and coprocessor instructions, may have a condition appended which causes it to be skipped if the condition is not met.

It is sometimes possible to write very compact code by cunning use of conditionals, for example:

```
        ; if ((a==b) && (c==d)) e++;
        CMP             r0, rl
        CMPEQ           r2, r3
        ADDEQ           r4, r4, #1
```

Note how if the first comparison finds unequal operands the second is skipped, causing the increment to be skipped also. The logical 'and' in the if clause is implemented by making the second comparison conditional.

3.3.4 | Branch and Link Instructions

A common requirement in a program is to be able to branch to a subroutine in a way which makes it possible to resume the original code sequence when the subroutine has completed. This requires that a record is kept of the value of the program counter just before the branch is taken.

ARM offers this functionality through the branch and link instruction which, as well as performing a branch in exactly the same way as the branch instruction, also saves the address of the instruction following the branch in the link register, rl4:

```
            BL          SUBR            ;branch to SUBR
            ..                          ;return to here
    SUBR    ..                          ;subroutine entry point
            MOV         pc, rl4         ;return
```

Note that since the return address is held in a register, the subroutine should not call a further, nested, subroutine without first saving rl4, otherwise the new return address will overwrite the old one and it will not be possible to find the way back to the original caller. The normal mechanism used here is to push r14 onto a stack in memory. Since the subroutine will often also require some work registers, the old values in these registers can be saved at the same time using a store multiple instruction:

```
            BL          SUBl
            ..
    SUB1    STMFD       rl3!, {r0–r2, rl4}          ; save work & link regs
```

```
        BL      SUB2
        ..
SUB2    ..
```

A subroutine that does not call another subroutine (a **leaf** subroutine) need not save r14 since it will not be overwritten.

3.3.5 | Subroutine Return Instructions

To get back to the calling routine, the value saved by the branch and link instruction in r14 must be copied back into the program counter. In the simplest case of a leaf subroutine (a subroutine that does not call another subroutine) a MOV instruction suffices, exploiting the visibility of the program counter as rl5:

```
SUB2    ..
        MOV   pc, r14 ; copy rl4 into rl5 to return
```

In fact the availability of the program counter as rl5 means that any of the data processing instructions can be used to compute a return address, though the 'MOV' form is by far the most commonly used.

Where the return address has been pushed onto a stack, it can be restored along with any saved work registers using a load multiple instruction:

```
SUB1    STMFD   r13!, {r0 – r2, r14};  save work regs & link
        BL          SUB2
        ..
        LDMFD       r13!,       {r0 – r2, pc}   ; restore work regs & return
```

Note here how the return address is restored directly to the program counter, not to the link register. This single restore and return instruction is very powerful. Note also the use of the stack view of the multiple register transfer addressing modes. The same stack model (in this case 'full descending', which is the most common stack type for ARM code) is used for both the store and the load, ensuring that the correct values will be collected. It is important that for any particular stack the same addressing mode is used for every use of the stack, unless you really know what you are doing.

3.3.6 | Supervisor Calls

Whenever a program requires input or output, for instance to send some text to the display, it is normal to call a supervisor routine. The supervisor is a program which operates at a privileged level, which means that it can do things that a user-level program cannot do directly. The limitations on the capabilities of a user-level program vary from system to system, but in many systems the user cannot access hardware facilities directly.

The supervisor provides trusted ways to access system resources which appear to the user-level program rather like special subroutine accesses. The instruction set includes a special instruction, SWI, to call these functions, (SWI stands for 'Software Interrupt', but is usually pronounced 'Supervisor Call'.)

Although the supervisor calls are implemented in system software, and could therefore be totally different from one ARM system to another, most ARM systems implement a common subset of calls in addition to any specific calls required by the particular application. The most useful of these is a routine which sends the character in the bottom byte of r0 to the user display device:

```
        SWI       SWI_WriteC    ; output r0[7:0]
```

Another useful call returns control from a user program back to the monitor program:

```
        SWI       SWI_Exit      ; return to monitor
```

The operation of SWIS is described in more detail in Section 5.6 on page 101.

3.3.7 | Jump Tables

Jump tables are not normally used by less experienced programmers, so you can ignore this section if you are relatively new to programming at the assembly level.

The idea of a jump table is that a programmer sometimes wants to call one of a set of subroutines, the choice depending on a value computed by the program. It is clearly possible to do this with the instructions we have seen already. Suppose the value is in r0. We can then write:

```
                BL      JUMPTAB
                ..
JUMPTAB         CMP     r0, #0
                BEQ     SUB0
                CMP     r0, #1
                BEQ     SUB1
                CMP     r0, #2
                BEQ     SUB2
                ..
```

However, this solution becomes very slow when the list of subroutines is long unless there is some reason to think that the later choices will rarely be used. A solution which is more efficient in this case exploits the visibility of the program counter in the general register file:

```
                BL      JUMPTAB
                ..
JUMPTAB         ADR     r1, SUBTAB              ; r1 -> SUBTAB
                CMP     r0, #SUBMAX             ; check for overrun..
                LDRLS   pc, [r1, r0, LSL #2]    ;   .. if OK, table jump
                B       ERROR                   ;  .. otherwise signal error
SUBTAB          DCD     SUB0                    ; table of subroutine
                DCD     SUB1                    ; entry points
                DCD     SUB2
                ..
```

The 'DCD' directive instructs the assembler to reserve a word of store and to initialize it to the value of the expression to the right, which in these cases is just the address of the label.

This approach has a constant performance however many subroutines are in the table and independent of the distribution of frequency of use. Note, however, that the consequences of reading beyond the end of the table are likely to be dire, so checking for overrun is essential! Here, note how the overrun check is implemented by making the load into the PC conditional, so the overrun case skips the load and falls into the branch to the error handler. The only performance cost of checking for overrun is the comparison with the maximum value. More obvious code might have been:

```
        ..
        CMP     r0, #SUBMAX             ; check for overrun..
        BHI     ERROR                   ; .. if overrun call error
        LDR     pc,  [rl, r0, LSL #2]   ; .. else table jump
        ..
```

but note that here the cost of conditionally skipping the branch is borne every time the jump table is used. The original version is more efficient except when overrun is detected, which should be infrequent and, since it represents an error, performance in that case is not of great concern.

An alternative, less obvious way to implement a jump table is discussed in 'switches' on page 148.

3.4 | Writing Simple Assembly Language Programs

We now have all the basic tools for writing simply assembly language programs. As with any programming task, it is important to have a clear idea of your algorithm before beginning to type instructions into the computer. Large programs are almost certainly better written in C or C++, so we will only look at small examples of assembly language programs.

Even the most experienced programmers begin by checking that they can get a very simple program to run before moving on to whatever their real task is. There are so many complexities to do with learning to use a text editor, working out how to get the assembler to run, how to load the program into the machine, how to get it to start executing and so on. This sort of simple test program is often referred to as a *Hello World* program because all it does is print 'Hello World' on the display before terminating. Here is an ARM assembly language version:

```
            AREA    HelloW, CODE, READONLY    ; declare code area
SWI_WriteC          EQU  &0                   ; output character in r0
SWI_Exit            EQU  &11                  ; finish program
            ENTRY                             ; code entry point
START       ADR     rl, TEXT                  ; rl -> "Hello World"
LOOP        LDRB    r0, [r1], #1              ; get the next byte
            CMP     r0, #0                    ; check for text end
            SWINE   SWI_WriteC                ; if not end print ..
            BNE     LOOP                      ; .. and loop back
            SWI     SWI_Exit                  ; end of execution
TEXT        =       "Hello World", &0a, &0d, 0
            END                               ; end of program source
```

This program illustrates a number of the features of the ARM assembly language and instruction set:

- The declaration of the code 'AREA', with appropriate attributes.
- The definitions of the system calls which will be used in the routine. (In a larger program these would be defined in a file which other code files would reference.)
- The use of the ADR pseudo instruction to get an address into a base register.
- The use of auto-indexed addressing to move through a list of bytes.
- Conditional execution of the SWI instruction to avoid an extra branch.

Note also the use of a zero byte to mark the end of the string (following the linefeed and carriage return special characters). Whenever you use a looping structure, make sure it has a terminating condition.

In order to run this program you will need the following tools, all of which are available within the ARM software development toolkit:

- A text editor to type the program into.
- An assembler to turn the program into ARM binary code.
- An ARM system or emulator to execute the binary on. The ARM system must have some text output capability. (The ARM development board, for example, sends text output back up to the host for output onto the host's display.)

Once you have this program running you are ready to try something more useful. From now on, the only thing that changes is the program text. The use of the editor, the assembler, and the test system or emulator will remain pretty similar to what you have done already, at least up to the point where your program refuses to do what you want and you can't see why it refuses. Then you will need to use a debugger to see what is happening inside your program. This means learning how to use another complex tool, so we will put off that moment for as long as possible.

For the next example, we can now complete the block copy program developed partially earlier in the text. To ensure that we know it has worked properly, we will use a text source string so that we can output it from the destination address, and we will initialize the destination area to something different:

```
            AREA    BlkCpy, CODE, READONLY
SWI_WriteC  EQU &0                          ; output character in r0
SWI_Exit    EQU &11                         ; finish program
            ENTRY                           ; code entry point
            ADR     r1, TABLE1              ; r1 -> TABLE1
            ADR     r2, TABLE2              ; r2 -> TABLE2
            ADR     r3, T1END               ; r3 -> T1END
LOOP1       LDR     r0, [r1], #4            ; get TABLE1 1st word
            STR     r0 , [r2], #4           ; copy into TABLE2
            CMP     r1, r3                  ; finished?
            BLT     LOOP1                   ; if not, do more
            ADR     r1, TABLE2              ; r1 -> TABLE2
LOOP2       LDRB    r0, [r1], #1            ; get next byte
            CMP     r0, #0                  ; check for text end
            SWINE   SWI_WriteC              ; if not end, print ..
            BNE     LOOP2                   ; .. and loop back
            SWI     SWI_ Exit               ; finish
TABLE1 =    "This is the right string!", &0a, &0d, 0
T1END
            ALIGN                           ; ensure word alignment
TABLE2 =    "This is the wrong string!", 0
            END
```

This program uses word loads and stores to copy the table, which is why the tables must be word-aligned. It then uses byte loads to print out the result using a routine which is the same as that used in the 'Hello World' program.

Note the use of 'BLT' to control the loop termination. If TABLE1 contains a number of bytes which is not a multiple of four, there is a danger that rl would step past T1END without ever exactly equalling it, so a termination condition based on 'BNE' might fail.

If you have succeeded in getting this program running, you are well on the way to understanding the basic operation of the ARM instruction set. The examples and exercises which follow should be studied to reinforce this understanding. As you attempt more complex programming tasks, questions of detail will arise. These should be answered by the full instruction set description given in Chapter 5.

3.4.1 | Program Design

With a basic understanding of the instruction set, small programs can be written and debugged without too much trouble by just typing them into an editor and seeing if they work. However, it is dangerous to assume that this simple approach will scale to the successful development of complex programs which may be expected to work for many years, which may be changed by other programmers in the future, and which may end up in the hands of customers who will use them in unexpected ways.

This book is not a text on program design, but having offered an introduction to programming it would be a serious omission not to point out that there is a lot more to writing a useful program than just sitting down and typing code.

Serious programming should start not with coding, but with careful design. The first step of the development process is to understand the requirements; it is surprising how often programs do not behave as expected because the requirements were not well understood by the programmer! Then the (often informal) requirements should be translated into an unambiguous specification. Now the design can begin, defining a program structure, the data structures that the program works with and the algorithms that are used to perform the required operations on the data. The algorithms may be expressed in **pseudo-code**, a program-like notation which does not follow the syntax of a particular programming language but which makes the meaning clear.

Only when the design is developed should the coding begin. Individual modules should be coded, tested thoroughly (which may require special programs to be designed as 'test-harnesses') and documented and the program built piece by piece.

Today nearly all programming is based on high-level languages, so it is rare for large programs to be built using assembly programming as described here. Sometimes, however, it may be necessary to develop small software components in assembly language to get the best performance for a critical application, so it is useful to know how to write assembly code for these purposes.

3.5 | Examples and Exercises

Once you have the basic flavour of an instruction set the easiest way to learn to write programs is to look at some examples, then attempt to write your own program to do something slightly different. To see whether or not your program works you will need an ARM assembler and either an ARM emulator or hardware with an ARM processor in it. The following sections contain example ARM programs and suggestions for modifications to them. You should get the original program working first, then see if you can edit it to perform the modified function suggested in the exercises.

EXAMPLE 3.1

Print out r1 in hexadecimal.

This is a useful little routine which dumps a register to the display in hexadecimal (base 16) notation; it can be used to help debug a program by writing out register values and checking that algorithms are producing the expected results, though in most cases using a debugger is a better way of seeing what is going on inside a program.

```
            AREA    Hex_Out, CODE, READONLY
SWI_WriteC          EQU &0              ; output character in r0
SWI_Exit            EQU &11             ; finish program
            ENTRY                       ; code entry point
            LDR     rl, VALUE           ; get value to print
            BL      HexOut              ; call hexadecimal output
            SWI     SWI_Exit            ; finish
VALUE       DCD     &12345678           ; test value
HexOut      MOV     r2, #8              ; nibble count = 8
LOOP        MOV     r0, r1, LSR #28     ; get top nibble
            CMP     r0, #9              ; 0–9 or A–F?
            ADDGT   r0, r0, #"A"–10     ; ASCII alphabetic
            ADDLE   r0, r0, #"0"        ; ASCII numeric
            SWI     SWI_WriteC          ; print character
            MOV     rl, rl, LSL #4      ; shift left one nibble
            SUBS    r2, r2, #1          ; decrement nibble count
            BNE     LOOP                ; if more do next nibble
            MOV     pc, rl4             ; return
            END
```

Exercise 3.1.1

Why does ARM have a 'link register'? Which is the branch instruction that takes advantage of the link register?

Exercise 3.1.2

Write a program which compares three numbers and finds out the largest among the three.

EXAMPLE 3.2

Write a subroutine to output a text string immediately following the call.

It is often useful to be able to output a text string without having to set up a separate data area for the text (though this is inefficient if the processor has separate data and instruction caches, as does the StrongARM; in this case it is better to set up a separate data area). A call should look like:

```
BL      TextOut
=       "Test string", &0a, &0d, 0
ALIGN
..                                  ; return to here
```

The issue here is that the return from the subroutine must not go directly to the value put in the link register by the call, since this would land the program in the text string. Here is a suitable subroutine and test harness:

```
            AREA    Text_Out, CODE, READONLY
SWI_WriteC          EQU &0              ; output character in r0
SWI_Exit            EQU &11             ; finish program
```

```
            ENTRY                               ; code entry point
            BL      TextOut                     ; print following string
            =       "Test string", &0a, &0d, 0
            ALIGN
            SWI     SWI_Exit                    ; finish
TextOut     LDRB    r0, [rl4], #1               ; get next character
            CMP     r0, #0                      ; test for end mark
            SWINE   SWI_WriteC                  ; if not end, print..
            BNE     TextOut                     ; .. and loop
            ADD     rl4, rl4, #3                ; pass next word boundary
            BIC     rl4, rl4, #3                ; round back to boundary
            MOV     pc, r14                     ; return
            END
```

This example shows rl4 incrementing along the text string and then being adjusted to the next word boundary prior to the return. If the adjustment (add 3, then clear the bottom two bits) looks like slight of hand, check it; there are only four cases.

Exercise 3.2.1
Using code from this and the previous examples, write a program to dump the ARM registers in hexadecimal with formatting such as:

r0 = 12345678
rl = 9ABCDEF0

Exercise 3.2.2
Now try to save the registers you need to work with before they are changed, for instance by saving them near the code using PC-relative addressing.

4

ARM Organization and Implementation

SUMMARY OF CHAPTER CONTENTS

The organization of the ARM integer processor core changed very little from the first 3 micron devices developed at Acorn Computers between 1983 and 1985 to the ARM6 and ARM7 developed by ARM Limited between 1990 and 1995. The 3-stage pipeline used by these processors was steadily tightened up, and CMOS process technology reduced in feature size by almost an order of magnitude over this period, so the performance of the cores improved dramatically, but the basic principles of operation remained largely the same.

Since 1995 several new ARM cores have been introduced which deliver significantly higher performance through the use of 5-stage pipelines and separate instruction and data memories (usually in the form of separate caches which are connected to a shared instruction and data main memory system).

This chapter includes descriptions of the internal structures of these two basic styles of processor core and covers the general principles of operation of the 3-stage and 5-stage pipelines and a number of implementation details. Details on particular cores are presented in Chapter 9.

4.1 | 3-stage Pipeline ARM Organization

The organization of an ARM with a 3-stage pipeline is illustrated in Figure 4.1. The principal components are:

- The register bank, which stores the processor state. It has two read ports and one write port which can each be used to access any register, plus an additional read port and an additional write port that give special access to r15, the program counter. (The additional write port on r15 allows it to be updated as the instruction fetch address is incremented and the read port allows instruction fetch to resume after a data address has been issued.)
- The barrel shifter, which can shift or rotate one operand by any number of bits.
- The ALU, which performs the arithmetic and logic functions required by the instruction set.
- The address register and incrementer, which select and hold all memory addresses and generate sequential addresses when required.
- The data registers, which hold data passing to and from memory.
- The instruction decoder and associated control logic.

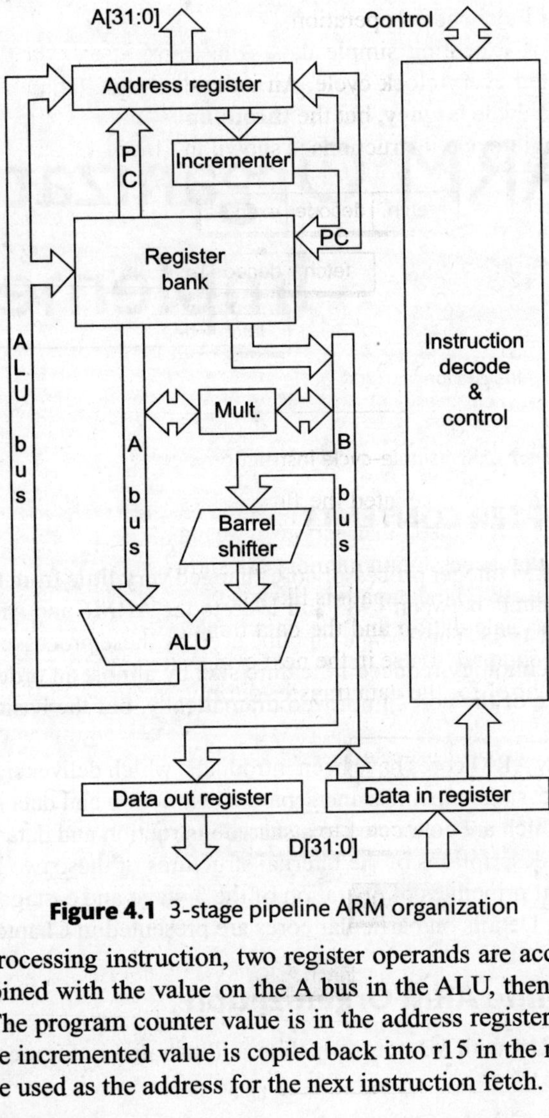

Figure 4.1 3-stage pipeline ARM organization

In a single-cycle data processing instruction, two register operands are accessed, the value on the B bus is shifted and combined with the value on the A bus in the ALU, then the result is written back into the register bank. The program counter value is in the address register, from where it is fed into the incrementer, then the incremented value is copied back into r15 in the register bank and also into the address register to be used as the address for the next instruction fetch.

4.1.1 | The 3-Stage Pipeline

ARM processors up to the ARM7 employ a simple 3-stage pipeline with the following pipeline stages:

- Fetch;
  the instruction is fetched from memory and placed in the instruction pipeline.
- Decode;
  the instruction is decoded and the datapath control signals prepared for the next cycle. In this stage the instruction 'owns' the decode logic but not the datapath.
- Execute;
  the instruction 'owns' the datapath; the register bank is read, an operand shifted, the ALU result generated and written back into a destination register.

At any one time, three different instructions may occupy each of these stages, so the hardware in each stage has to be capable of independent operation.

When the processor is executing simple data processing instructions the pipeline enables one instruction to be completed every clock cycle. An individual instruction takes three clock cycles to complete, so it has a three-cycle **latency**, but the **throughput** is one instruction per cycle. The 3-stage pipeline operation for single-cycle instructions is shown in Figure 4.2.

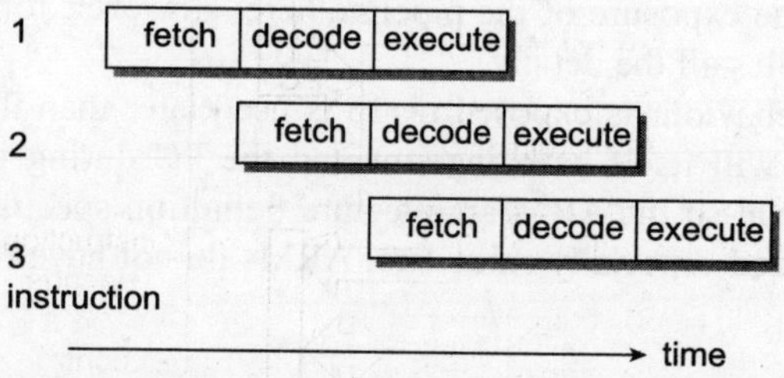

Figure 4.2 ARM single-cycle instruction 3-stage pipeline operation

When a multi-cycle instruction is executed the flow is less regular, as illustrated in Figure 4.3. This shows a sequence of single-cycle ADD instructions with a data store instruction, STR, occurring after the first ADD. The cycles that access main memory are shown with light shading so it can be seen that memory is used in every cycle. The datapath is likewise used in every cycle, being involved in all the execute cycles, the address calculation and the data transfer. The decode logic is always generating the control signals for the datapath to use in the next cycle, so in addition to the explicit decode cycles it is also generating the control for the data transfer during the address calculation cycle of the STR.

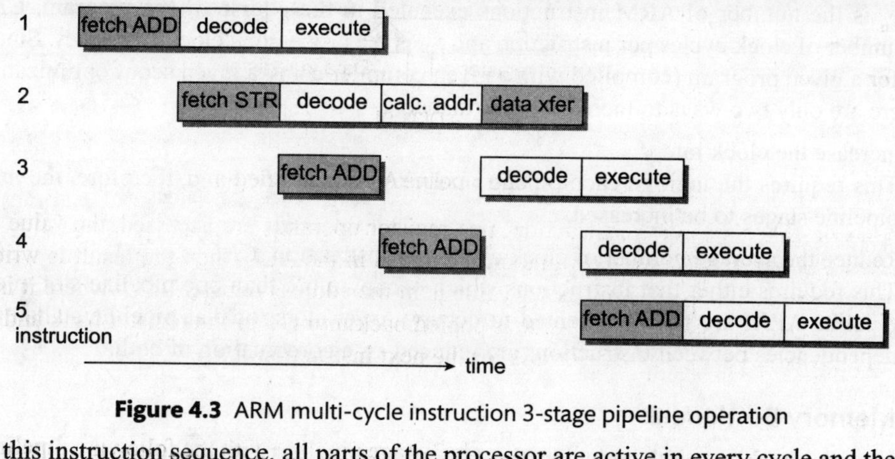

Figure 4.3 ARM multi-cycle instruction 3-stage pipeline operation

Thus, in this instruction sequence, all parts of the processor are active in every cycle and the memory is the limiting factor, defining the number of cycles the sequence must take.

The simplest way to view breaks in the ARM pipeline is to observe that:

- All instructions occupy the datapath for one or more adjacent cycles.
- For each cycle that an instruction occupies the datapath, it occupies the decode logic in the immediately preceding cycle.
- During the first datapath cycle each instruction issues a fetch for the next instruction but one.
- Branch instructions flush and refill the instruction pipeline.

4.1.2 | PC Behaviour

One consequence of the pipelined execution model used on the ARM is that the program counter, which is visible to the user as r15, must run ahead of the current instruction. If, as noted above, instructions fetch the next instruction but one during their first cycle, this suggests that the PC must point eight bytes (two instructions) ahead of the current instruction.

This is, indeed what happens, and the programmer who attempts to access the PC directly through r15 must take account of the exposure of the pipeline here. However, for most normal purposes the assembler or compiler handles all the details.

Even more complex behaviour is exposed if r15 is used later than the first cycle of an instruction, since the instruction will itself have incremented the PC during its first cycle. Such use of the PC is not often beneficial so the ARM architecture definition specifies the result as 'unpredictable' and it should be avoided especially since later ARMs do not have the same behaviour in these cases.

4.2 | 5-stage Pipeline ARM Organization

All processors have to develop to meet the demand for higher performance. The 3-stage pipeline used in the ARM cores up to the ARM7 is very cost-effective, but higher performance requires the processor organization to be rethought. The time, T_{prog}, required to execute a given program is given by:

$$T_{prog} = \frac{N_{inst} \times CPI}{f_{clk}}, \quad \text{Equation 11}$$

where N_{inst} is the number of ARM instructions executed in the course of the program, CPI is the average number of clock cycles per instruction and f_{clk} is the processor's clock frequency. Since N_{inst} is constant for a given program (compiled with a given compiler using a given set of optimizations, and so on) there are only two ways to increase performance:

- Increase the clock rate, f_{clk}.
  This requires the logic in each pipeline stage to be simplified and, therefore, the number of pipeline stages to be increased.
- Reduce the average number of clock cycles per instruction, *CPI*.
  This requires either that instructions which occupy more than one pipeline slot in a 3-stage pipeline ARM are re-implemented to occupy fewer slots, or that pipeline stalls caused by dependencies between instructions are reduced, or a combination of both.

4.2.1 | Memory Bottleneck

The fundamental problem with reducing the CPI relative to a 3-stage core is related to the von Neumann bottleneck – any stored-program computer with a single instruction and data memory will have its performance limited by the available memory bandwidth. A 3-stage ARM core accesses memory on (almost) every clock cycle either to fetch an instruction or to transfer data. Simply tightening up on the few cycles where the memory is not used will yield only a small performance gain. To get a significantly better CPI the memory system must deliver more than one value in each clock cycle either by delivering more than 32 bits per cycle from a single memory or by having separate memories for instruction and data accesses.

As a result of the above issues, higher performance ARM cores employ a 5-stage pipeline and have separate instruction and data memories. Breaking instruction execution down into five components rather than three reduces the maximum work which must be completed in a clock cycle, and hence allows a higher clock frequency to be used (provided that other system components, and particularly the instruction memory, are also redesigned to operate at this higher clock rate). The separate instruction and data memories (which may be separate caches connected to a unified instruction and data main memory) allow a significant reduction in the core's CPI.

A typical 5-stage ARM pipeline is that employed in the ARM9TDMI. The organization of the ARM9TDMI is illustrated in Figure 4.4.

4.2.2 | The 5-stage Pipeline

The ARM processors which use a 5-stage pipeline have the following pipeline stages:

- Fetch;
  the instruction is fetched from memory and placed in the instruction pipeline.
- Decode;
  the instruction is decoded and register operands read from the register file. There are three operand read ports in the register file, so most ARM instructions can source all their operands in one cycle.
- Execute;
  an operand is shifted and the ALU result generated. If the instruction is a load or store the memory address is computed in the ALU.
- Buffer/data;
  data memory is accessed if required. Otherwise the ALU result is simply buffered for one clock cycle to give the same pipeline flow for all instructions.
- Write-back;
  the results generated by the instruction are written back to the register file, including any data loaded from memory.

This 5-stage pipeline has been used for many RISC processors and is considered to be the 'classic' way to design such a processor. Although the ARM instruction set was not designed with such a pipeline in mind, it maps onto it relatively simply. The principal concessions to the ARM instruction set architecture in the organization shown in Figure 4.4 are the three source operand read ports and two write ports in the register file (where a 'classic' RISC has two read ports and one write port), and the inclusion of address incrementing hardware in the execute stage to support load and store multiple instructions.

4.2.3 | Data Forwarding

A major source of complexity in the 5-stage pipeline (compared to the 3-stage pipeline) is that, because instruction execution is spread across three pipeline stages, the only way to resolve data dependencies without stalling the pipeline is to introduce *forwarding* paths.

Data dependencies arise when an instruction needs to use the result of one of its predecessors before that result has returned to the register file. (This issue was discussed previously under 'Pipeline hazards' on page 19.) Forwarding paths allow results to be passed between stages as soon as they are available, and the 5-stage ARM pipeline requires each of the three source operands to be forwarded from any of three intermediate result registers as shown in Figure 4.4.

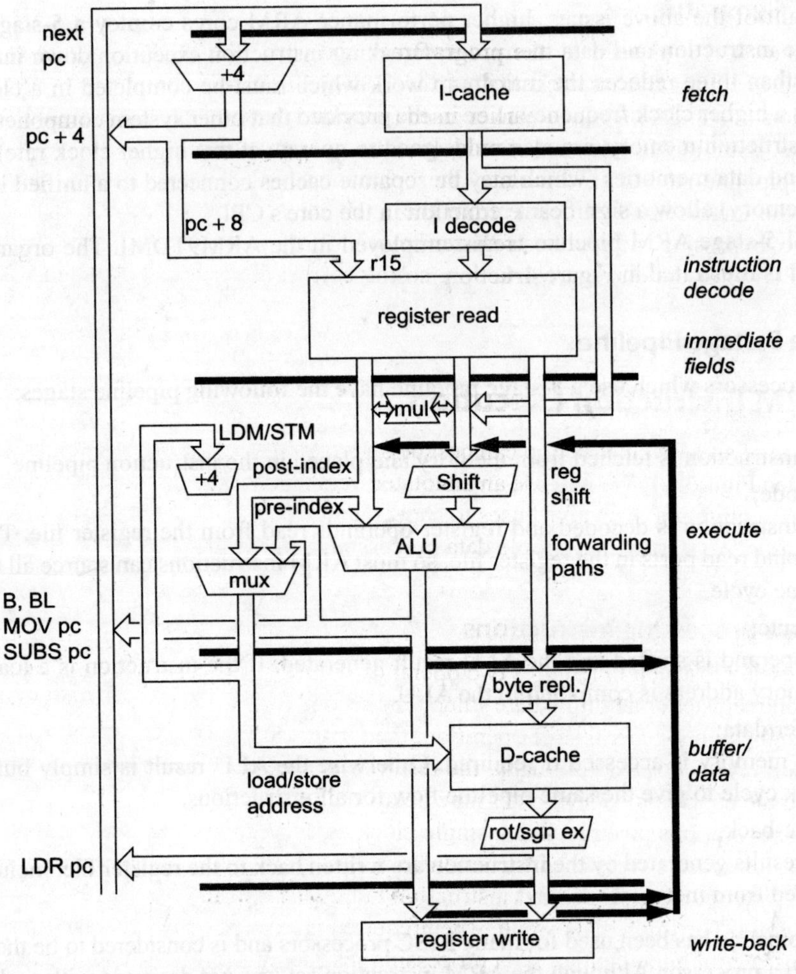

Figure 4.4 ARM9TDMI 5-stage pipeline organization

There is one case where, even with forwarding, it is not possible to avoid a pipeline stall. Consider the following code sequence:

```
LDR    rN,    [..]      ;load rN from somewhere
ADD    r2,    r1, rN    ;and use it immediately
```

The processor cannot avoid a one-cycle stall as the value loaded into rN only enters the processor at the end of the buffer/data stage and it is needed by the following instruction at the start of the execute stage. The only way to avoid this stall is to encourage the compiler (or assembly language programmer) not to put a dependent instruction immediately after a load instruction.

Since the 3-stage pipeline ARM cores are not adversely affected by this code sequence, existing ARM programs will often use it. Such programs will run correctly on 5-stage ARM cores, but could probably be rewritten to run faster by simply reordering the instructions to remove these dependencies.

4.2.4 | PC Generation

The behaviour of r15, as seen by the programmer and described in 'PC behaviour' on page 68, is based on the operational characteristics of the 3-stage ARM pipeline. The 5-stage pipeline reads the instruction operands one stage earlier in the pipeline, and would naturally get a different value (PC+4 rather than PC+8). As this would lead to unacceptable code incompatibilities, however, the 5-stage pipeline ARMs all 'emulate' the behaviour of the older 3-stage designs. Referring to Figure 4.4, the incremented PC value from the fetch stage is fed directly to the register file in the decode stage, bypassing the pipeline register between the two stages. PC+4 for the next instruction is equal to PC+8 for the current instruction, so the correct r15 value is obtained without additional hardware.

4.3 | ARM Instruction Execution

The execution of an ARM instruction can best be understood by reference to the datapath organization as presented in Figure 4.1. We will use an annotated version of this diagram, omitting the control logic section, and highlighting the active buses to show the movement of operands around the various units in the processor. We start with a simple data processing instruction.

4.3.1 | Data Processing Instructions

A data processing instruction requires two operands, one of which is always a register and the other is either a second register or an immediate value. The second operand is passed through the barrel shifter where it is subject to a general shift operation, then it is combined with the first operand in the ALU using a general ALU operation. Finally, the result from the ALU is written back into the destination register (and the condition code register may be updated).

All these operations take place in a single clock cycle as shown in Figure 4.5. Note also how the PC value in the address register is incremented and copied back into both the address register and r15 in the register bank, and the next instruction but one is loaded into the bottom of the instruction pipeline (*i. pipe*). The immediate value, when required is extracted from the current instruction at the top of the instruction pipeline. For data processing instructions only the bottom eight bits (bits [7:0]) of the instruction are used in the immediate value.

4.3.2 | Data Transfer Instructions

A data transfer (load or store) instruction computes a memory address in a manner very similar to the way a data processing instruction computes its result. A register is used as the base address, to which is added (or from which is subtracted) an offset which again may be another register or an immediate value. This time, however, a 12-bit immediate value is used without a shift operation rather than a shifted 8-bit value. The address is sent to the address register, and in a second cycle the data transfer takes place. Rather than leave the datapath largely idle during the data transfer cycle, the ALU holds the address components from the first cycle and is available to compute an auto-indexing modification to the base register if this is required. (If auto-indexing is not required the computed value is not written back to the base register in the second cycle.)

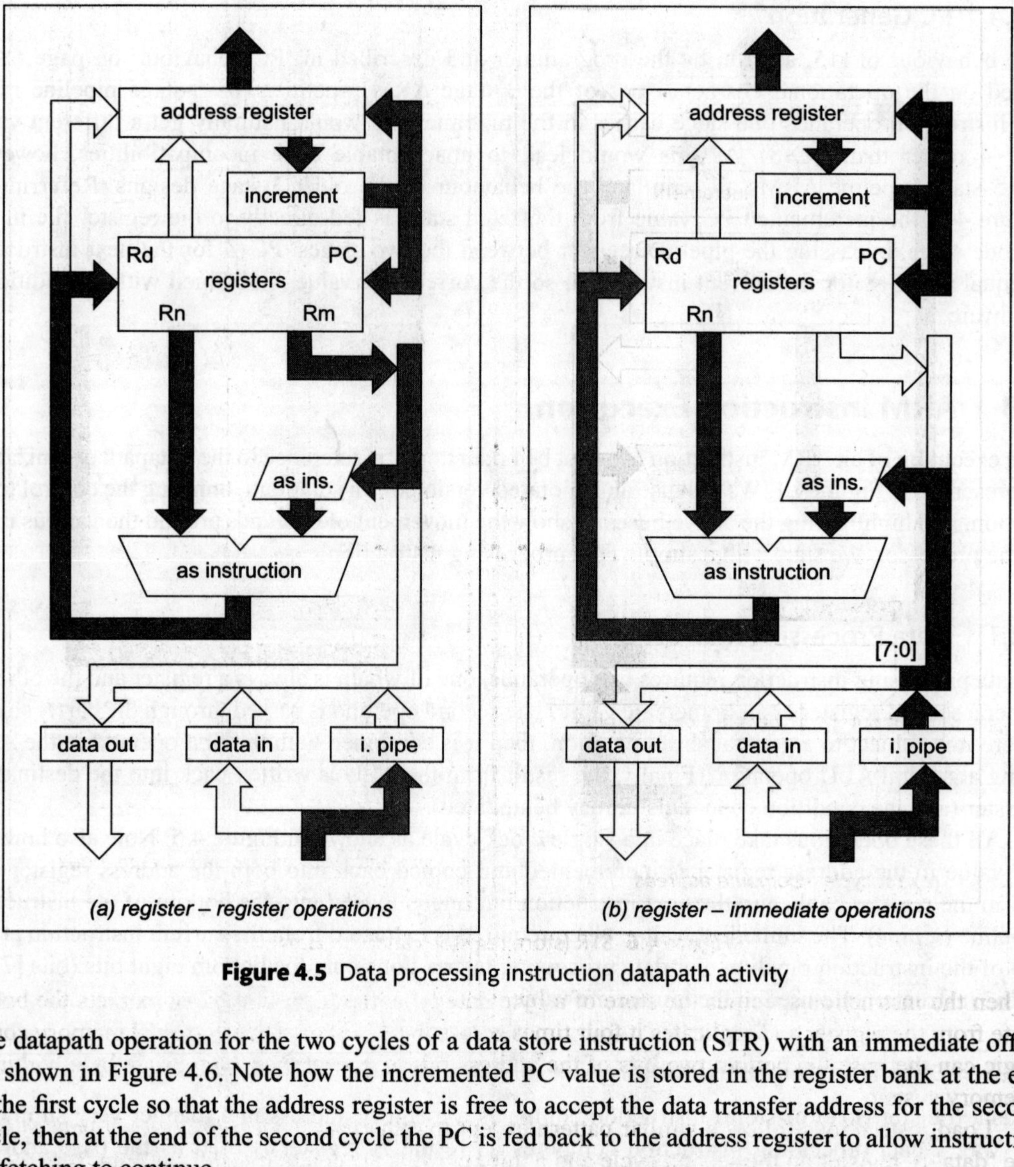

Figure 4.5 Data processing instruction datapath activity

The datapath operation for the two cycles of a data store instruction (STR) with an immediate offset are shown in Figure 4.6. Note how the incremented PC value is stored in the register bank at the end of the first cycle so that the address register is free to accept the data transfer address for the second cycle, then at the end of the second cycle the PC is fed back to the address register to allow instruction prefetching to continue.

It should, perhaps, be noted at this stage that the value sent to the address register in a cycle is the value used for the memory access in the *following* cycle. The address register is, in effect, a pipeline register between the processor datapath and the external memory.

(The address register can produce the memory address for the next cycle a little before the end of the current cycle, moving responsibility for the pipeline delay out into the memory when this is desired. This can enable some memory devices to operate at higher performance, but this detail can be postponed for the time being. For now we will view the address register as a pipeline register to memory.)

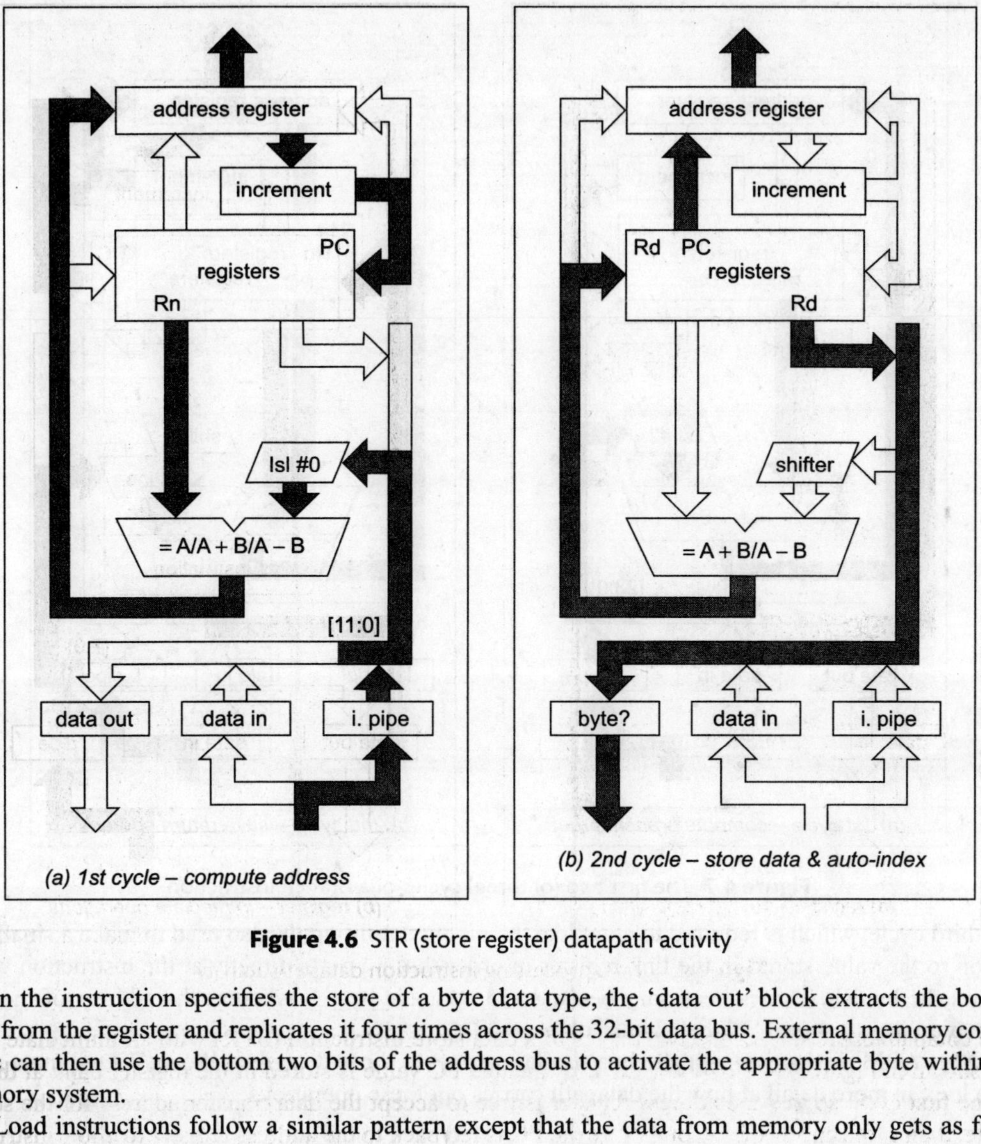

Figure 4.6 STR (store register) datapath activity

When the instruction specifies the store of a byte data type, the 'data out' block extracts the bottom byte from the register and replicates it four times across the 32-bit data bus. External memory control logic can then use the bottom two bits of the address bus to activate the appropriate byte within the memory system.

Load instructions follow a similar pattern except that the data from memory only gets as far as the 'data in' register on the second cycle and a third cycle is needed to transfer the data from there to the destination register.

4.3.3 | Branch Instructions

Branch instructions compute the target address in the first cycle as shown in Figure 4.7. A 24-bit immediate field is extracted from the instruction and then shifted left two bit positions to give a word-aligned offset which is added to the PC. The result is issued as an instruction fetch address, and while the instruction pipeline refills the return address is copied into the link register (r14) if this is required (that is, if the instruction is a 'branch with link').

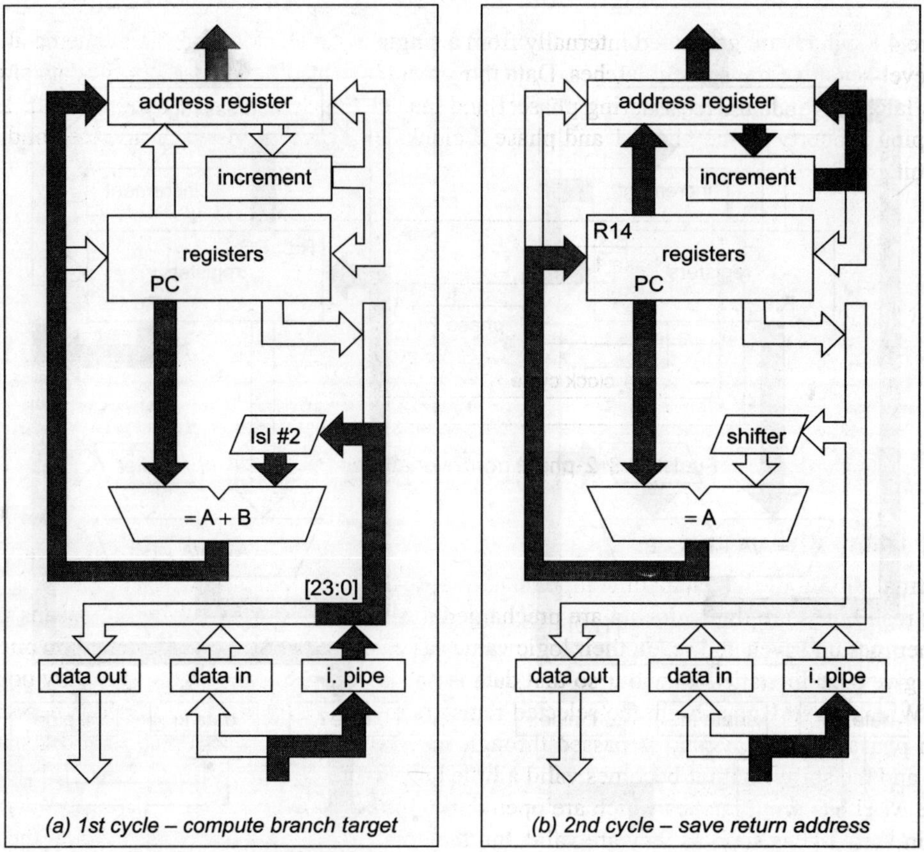

Figure 4.7 The first two (of three) cycles of a branch instruction

The third cycle, which is required to complete the pipeline refilling, is also used to make a small correction to the value stored in the link register in order that it points directly at the instruction which follows the branch. This is necessary because r15 contains pc + 8 whereas the address of the next instruction is pc + 4 (see 'PC behaviour' on page 68).

Other ARM instructions operate in a similar manner to those described above. We will now move on to look in more detail at how the datapath carries out these operations.

4.4 | ARM Implementation

The ARM implementation follows a similar approach to that outlined in Chapter 1 for MU0; the design is divided into a datapath section that is described in *register transfer level* (RTL) notation and a control section that is viewed as a *finite state machine* (FSM).

4.4.1 | Clocking Scheme

Unlike the MU0 example presented in Section 1.3 on page 6, most ARMs do not operate with edge-sensitive registers; instead the design is based around 2-phase non-overlapping clocks, as shown in Figure 4.8, which are generated internally from a single input clock signal. This scheme allows the use of level-sensitive transparent latches. Data movement is controlled by passing the data alternately through latches which are open during phase 1 and latches which are open during phase 2. The non-overlapping property of the phase 1 and phase 2 clocks ensures that there are no race conditions in the circuit.

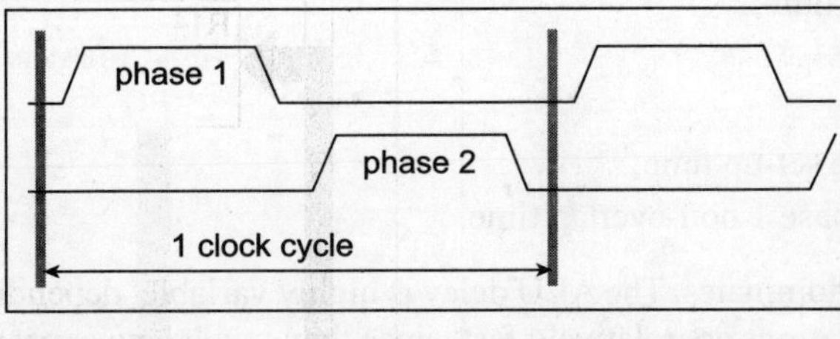

Figure 4.8 2-phase non-overlapping clock scheme

4.4.2 | Datapath Timing

The normal timing of the datapath components in a 3-stage pipeline is illustrated in Figure 4.9. The register read buses are dynamic and are precharged during phase 2 (here 'dynamic' means that they are sometimes undriven and retain their logic values as electrical charge; charge-retention circuits are used to give pseudo-static behaviour so that data is not lost if the clock is stopped at any point in its cycle). When phase 1 goes high, the selected registers discharge the read buses which become valid early in phase 1. One operand is passed through the barrel shifter, which also uses dynamic techniques, and the shifter output becomes valid a little later in phase 1.

The ALU has input latches which are open during phase 1, allowing the operands to begin combining in the ALU as soon as they are valid, but they close at the end of phase 1 so that the phase 2 precharge does not get through to the ALU. The ALU then continues to process the operands through phase 2, producing a valid output towards the end of the phase which is latched in the destination register at the end of phase 2.

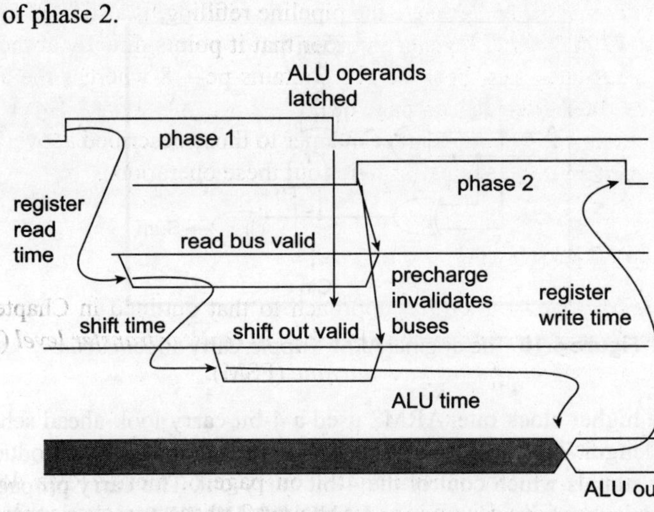

Figure 4.9 ARM datapath timing (3-stage pipeline)

Note how, though the data passes through the ALU input latches, these do not affect the datapath timing since they are open when valid data arrives. This property of transparent latches is exploited in many places in the design of the ARM to ensure that clocks do not slow critical signals.

The minimum datapath cycle time is therefore the sum of:

- the register read time;
- the shifter delay;
- the ALU delay;
- the register write set-up time;
- the phase 2 to phase 1 non-overlap time.

Of these, the ALU delay dominates. The ALU delay is highly variable, depending on the operation it is performing. Logical operations are relatively fast, since they involve no carry propagation. Arithmetic operations (addition, subtraction and comparisons) involve longer logic paths as the carry can propagate across the word width.

4.4.3 | Adder Design

Since the 32-bit addition time has a significant effect on the datapath cycle time, and hence the maximum clock rate and the processor's performance, it has been the focus of considerable attention during the development of successive versions of the ARM processor.

The first ARM processor prototype used a simple ripple-carry adder as shown in Figure 4.10. Using a CMOS AND-OR-INVERT gate for the carry logic and alternating AND/OR logic so that even bits use the circuit shown and odd bits use the dual circuit with inverted inputs and outputs and AND and OR gates swapped around the worst-case carry path is 32 gates long.

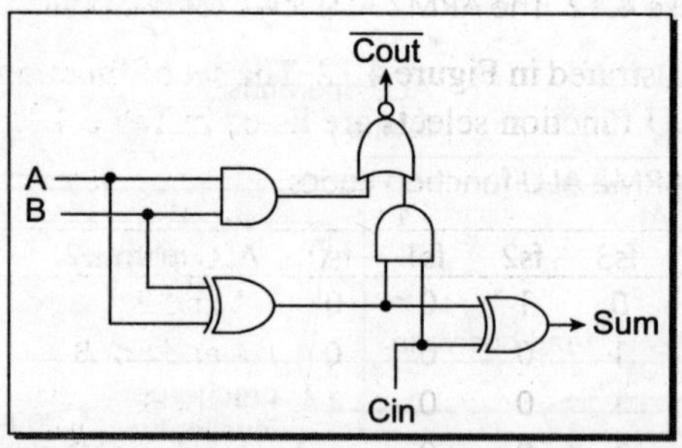

Figure 4.10 The original ARM 1 ripple-carry adder circuit

In order to allow a higher clock rate, ARM2 used a 4-bit carry look-ahead scheme to reduce the worst-case carry path length. The circuit is shown in Figure 4.11. The logic produces carry generate (G) and propagate (P) signals which control the 4-bit carry-out. The carry propagate path length is reduced to eight gate delays, again using merged AND-OR-INVERT gates and alternating AND/OR logic.

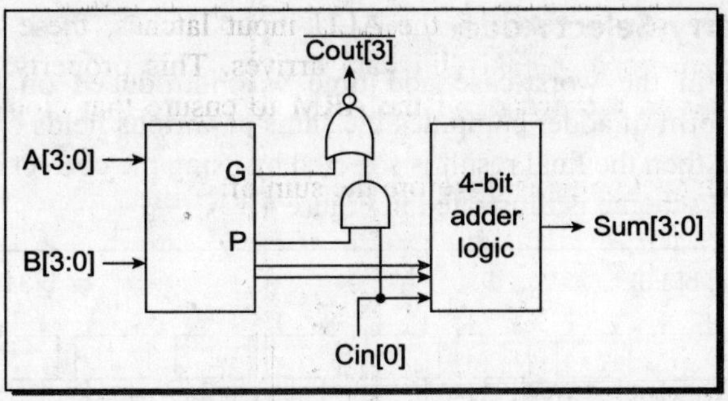

Figure 4.11 The ARM2 4-bit carry look-ahead scheme

4.4.4 | ALU Functions

The ALU does not only add its two inputs. It must perform the full set of data operations defined by the instruction set, including address computations for memory transfers, branch calculations, bit-wise logical functions, and so on.

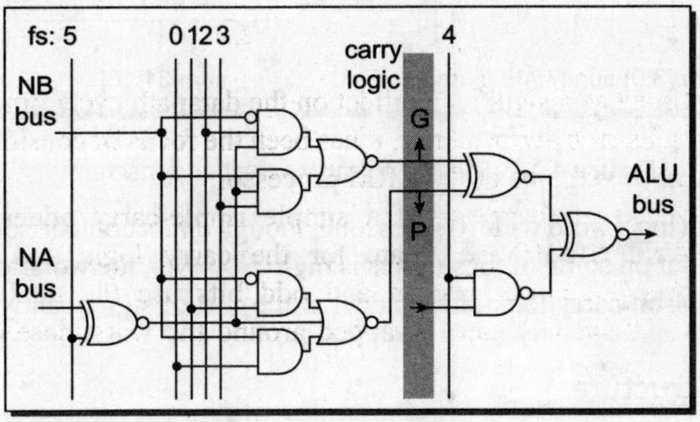

Figure 4.12 The ARM2 ALU logic for one result bit

The full ARM2 ALU logic is illustrated in Figure 4.12. The set of functions generated by this ALU and the associated values of the ALU function selects are listed in Table 4.1.

Table 4.1 ARM2 ALU function codes

fs5	fs4	fs3	fs2	fs1	fs0	ALU output
0	0	0	1	0	0	A and B
0	0	1	0	0	0	A and not B
0	0	1	0	0	1	A xor B
0	1	1	0	0	1	A plus not B plus carry
0	1	0	0	1	0	A plus B plus carry
1	1	0	1	1	0	not A plus B plus carry
0	0	0	0	0	0	A
0	0	0	0	0	1	A or B
0	0	0	1	0	1	B
0	0	1	0	1	0	not B
0	0	1	1	0	0	zero

4.4.5 | The ARM6 Carry-Select Adder

A further improvement in the worst-case add time was introduced on the ARM6 by using a carry-select adder. This form of adder computes the sums of various fields of the word for a carry-in of both zero and one, and then the final result is selected by using the correct carry-in value to control a multiplexer. The overall scheme is illustrated in Figure 4.13.

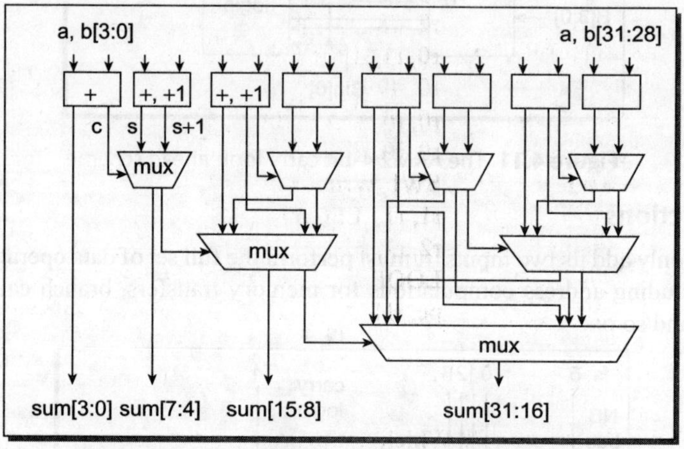

Figure 4.13 The ARM6 carry-select adder scheme

The critical path is now O($\log_2$ [word width]) gates long, though direct comparison with previous schemes is difficult since the fan-out on some of these gates is high. However, the worst-case addition time is significantly faster than the 4-bit carry look-ahead adder at the cost of significantly increased silicon area.

4.4.6 | ARM6 ALU Structure

The ARM6 carry-select adder does not easily lead to a merging of the arithmetic and logic functions into a single structure as was used on ARM2. Instead, a separate logic unit runs in parallel with the adder, and a multiplexer selects the output from the adder or from the logic unit as required.

The overall ALU structure is shown in Figure 4.14. The input operands are each selectively inverted, then added and combined in the logic unit, and finally the required result is selected and issued on the ALU result bus.

The *C* and *V* flags are generated in the adder (they have no meaning for logical operations), the *N* flag is copied from bit 31 of the result and the *Z* flag is evaluated from the whole result bus. Note that producing the *Z* flag requires a 32-input NOR gate and this can easily become a critical path signal.

4.4.7 | Carry Arbitration Adder

The adder logic was further improved on the ARM9TDMI, where a 'carry arbitration' adder is used. This adder computes all intermediate carry values using a 'parallel-prefix' tree, which is a very fast parallel logic structure.

The carry arbitration scheme recodes the conventional propagate-generate information in terms of two new variables, *u* and *v*. Consider the computation of the carry out, C, from a particular bit position in the adder with inputs A and B. Before the carry in is known, the information available is as shown

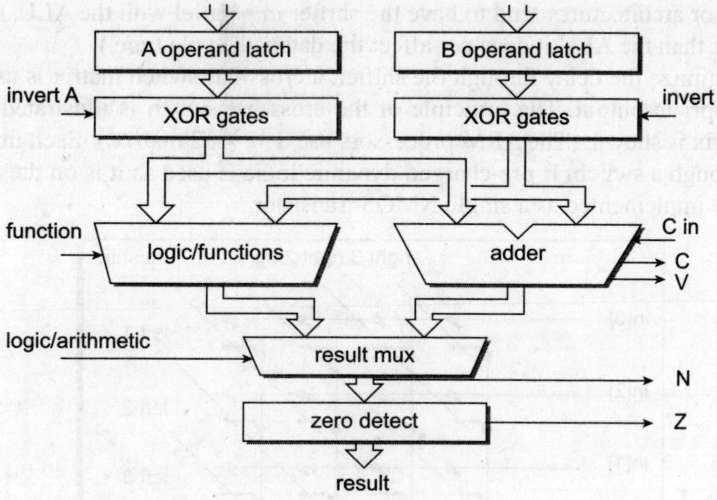

Figure 4.14 The ARM6 ALU organization

Table 4.2 ARM9 carry arbitration encoding.

A	B	C	u	V
0	0	0	0	0
0	1	unknown	1	0
1	0	unknown	1	0
1	1	1	1	1

in Table 4.2, which also shows how this information is encoded by *u* and *v*. This information can be combined with that from a neighbouring bit position using the formula:

$$(u, v) \bullet (u', v') = (v + u \cdot u', v + u \cdot v') \qquad \text{Equation 12}$$

It can be shown that this combinational operator is associative and hence *u* and v can be computed for all the bits in the sum using a regular parallel prefix tree. The logic required to implement Equation 12 can combine up to 4 pairs of inputs in a single CMOS gate, producing the new *u* and v outputs from a single transistor structure.

Furthermore, it can be seen that *u* gives the carry-out if the carry-in is one, and *v* gives the carry-out if the carry-in is zero. *u* and *v* can therefore be used to generate the (*Sum*, *Sum*+1) values required for a hybrid carry arbitration/carry select adder, resulting in a number of possible designs which allow a trade-off between performance, area and power consumption.

4.4.8 | The Barrel Shifter

The ARM architecture supports instructions which perform a shift operation in series with an ALU operation, leading to the organization shown in Figure 4.1. The shifter performance is therefore critical since the shift time contributes directly to the datapath cycle time as shown in the datapath timing diagram in Figure 4.9.

(Other processor architectures tend to have the shifter in parallel with the ALU, so as long as the shifter is no slower than the ALU it does not affect the datapath cycle time.)

In order to minimize the delay through the shifter, a cross-bar switch matrix is used to steer each input to the appropriate output. The principle of the cross-bar switch is illustrated in Figure 4.15, where a 4 × 4 matrix is shown. (The ARM processors use a 32 × 32 matrix.) Each input is connected to each output through a switch. If pre-charged dynamic logic is used as it is on the ARM datapaths, each switch can be implemented as a single NMOS transistor.

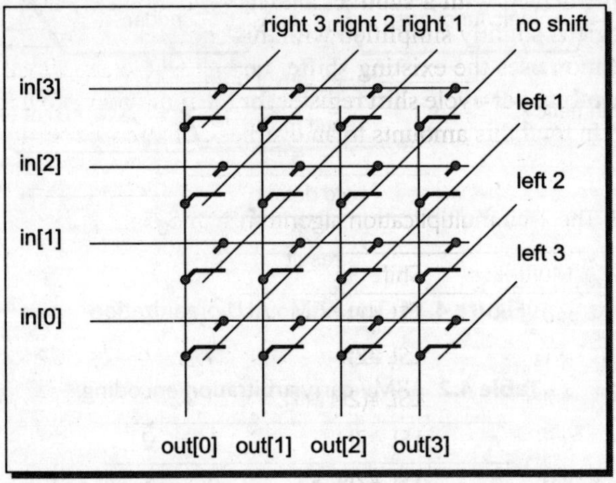

Figure 4.15 The cross-bar switch barrel shifter principle

The shifting functions are implemented by wiring switches along diagonals to a common control input:

- For a left or right shift function, one diagonal is turned on. This connects all the input bits to their respective outputs where they are used. (Not all are used since some bits 'fall off the end'.) In the ARM the barrel shifter operates in negative logic where a '1' is represented as a potential near ground and a '0' by a potential near the supply. Precharging sets all the outputs to a logic '0', so those outputs that are not connected to any input during a particular switching operation remain at '0' giving the zero filling required by the shift semantics.
- For a rotate right function, the right shift diagonal is enabled together with the complementary left shift diagonal. For example, on the 4-bit matrix rotate right one bit is implemented using the 'right 1' and the 'left 3' (3 = 4 – 1) diagonals.
- Arithmetic shift right uses sign-extension rather than zero-fill for the unconnected output bits. Separate logic is used to decode the shift amount and discharge those outputs appropriately.

4.4.9 | Multiplier Design

All ARM processors apart from the first prototype have included hardware support for integer multiplication. Two styles of multiplier have been used:

- Older ARM cores include low-cost multiplication hardware that supports only the 32-bit result multiply and multiply-accumulate instructions.
- Recent ARM cores have high-performance multiplication hardware and support the 64-bit result multiply and multiply-accumulate instructions.

The low-cost support uses the main datapath iteratively, employing the barrel shifter and ALU to generate a 2-bit product in each clock cycle. Early-termination logic stops the iterations when there are no more ones in the multiply register.

The multiplier employs a modified Booth's algorithm to produce the 2-bit product, exploiting the fact that × 3 can be implemented as × (–1) + × 4. This allows all four values of the 2-bit multiplier to be implemented by a simple shift and add or subtract, possibly carrying the × 4 over to the next cycle.

The control settings for the Nth cycle of the multiplication are shown in Table 4.3. (Note that the × 2 case is also implemented with a subtract and carry; it could equally well use an add with no carry, but the control logic is slightly simplified with this choice.)

Since this multiplication uses the existing shifter and ALU, the additional hardware it requires is limited to a dedicated two-bits-per-cycle shift register for the multiplier and a few gates for the Booth's algorithm control logic. In total this amounts to an overhead of a few per cent on the area of the ARM core.

Table 4.3 The 2-bit multiplication algorithm, Nth cycle

Carry-in	Multiplier	Shift	ALU	Carry-out
0	×0	LSL #2N	A + 0	0
	×1	LSL #2N	A + B	0
	×2	LSL #(2N + 1)	A – B	1
	×3	LSL #2N	A – B	1
1	×0	LSL #2N	A + B	0
	×1	LSL #(2N + 1)	A + B	0
	×2	LSL #2N	A – B	1
	×3	LSL #2N	A + 0	1

4.4.10 | High-speed Multiplier

Where multiplication performance is very important, more hardware resource must be dedicated to it. In some embedded systems the ARM core is used to perform real-time digital signal processing (DSP) in addition to general control functions. DSP programs are typically multiplication intensive and the performance of the multiplication hardware can be critical to meeting the real-time constraints.

The high-performance multiplication used in some ARM cores employs a widely-used redundant binary representation to avoid the carry-propagate delays associated with adding partial products together. Intermediate results are held as partial sums and partial carries where the true binary result is obtained by adding these two together in a carry-propagate adder such as the adder in the main ALU, but this is only done once at the end of the multiplication. During the multiplication the partial sums and carries are combined in **carry-save** adders where the carries only propagate across one bit per addition stage. This gives the carry-save adder a much shorter logic path than the carry-propagate adder, which may have to propagate a carry across all 32 bits. Therefore several carry-save operations may be performed in a single clock cycle which can only accommodate one carry-propagate operation.

There are many ways to construct carry-save adders, but the simplest is the 3-input 2-output form. This accepts as inputs a partial sum, a partial carry and a partial product, all of the same binary weight, and produces as outputs a new partial sum and a new partial carry where the carry has twice the weight of the sum. The logic function for each bit is identical to a conventional full adder as used in a ripple-carry carry-propagate adder (see Figure 4.10), but the structure is different. Figure 4.16 illustrates the two structures. The carry-propagate adder takes two conventional (irredundant) binary numbers as inputs and produces a binary sum; the carry-save adder takes one binary and one redundant (partial sum and partial carry) input and produces a sum in redundant binary representation.

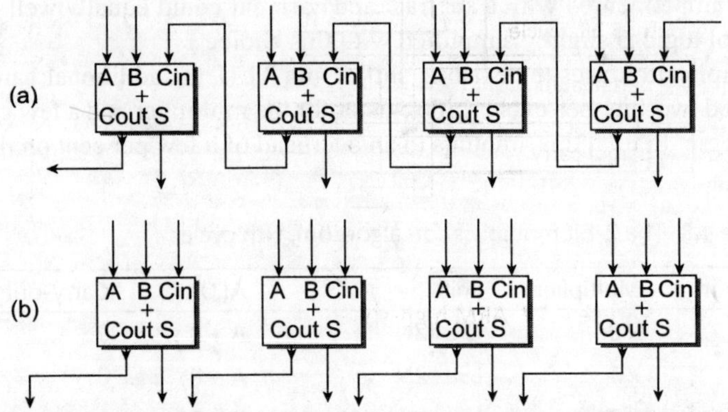

Figure 4.16 Carry-propagate (a) and carry-save (b) adder structures

During the iterative multiplication stages, the sum is fed back and combined with one new partial product in each iteration. When all the partial products have been added the redundant representation is converted into a conventional binary number by adding the partial sum and partial carry in the carry-propagate adder in the ALU.

High-speed multipliers have several layers of carry-save adder in series, each handling one partial product. If the partial product is produced following a modified Booth's algorithm similar to the one described in Table 4.3, each stage of carry-save adder handles two bits of the multiplier in each cycle.

The overall structure of the high-performance multiplier used on some ARM cores is shown in Figure 4.17. The register names refer to the instruction fields described in Section 5.8 on page 106. The carry-save array has four layers of adders, each handling two multiplier bits, so the array can multiply eight bits per clock cycle. The partial sum and carry registers are cleared at the start of the instruction, or the partial sum register may be initialized to the accumulate value. As the multiplier is shifted right eight bits per cycle in the 'Rs' register, the partial sum and carry are rotated right eight bits per cycle. The array is cycled up to four times, using early termination to complete the instruction in fewer cycles where the multiplier has sufficient zeros in the top bits, and the partial sum and carry are combined 32 bits at a time and written back into the register bank. (When the multiply terminates early some realignment of the partial sum and carry is required; this is not shown in Figure 4.17.)

The high-speed multiplier requires considerably more dedicated hardware than the low-cost solution employed on other ARM cores. There are 160 bits of shift register and 128 bits of carry-save adder logic. The incremental area cost is around 10% of the simpler processor cores, though a rather smaller proportion of the higher-performance cores such as ARM8 and Strong ARM. Its benefits are that it speeds up multiplication by a factor of around 3 and it supports the added functionality of the 64-bit result forms of the multiply instruction.

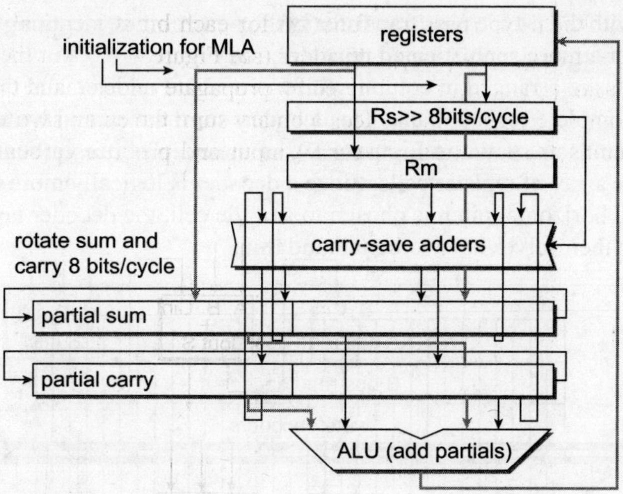

Figure 4.17 ARM high-speed multiplier organization

4.4.11 | The Register Bank

The last major block on the ARM datapath is the register bank. This is where all the user-visible state is stored in 31 general-purpose 32-bit registers, amounting to around 1 Kbits of data altogether. Since the basic 1-bit register cell is repeated so many times in the design, it is worth putting considerable effort into minimizing its size.

The transistor circuit of the register cell used in ARM cores up to the ARM6 is shown in Figure 4.18. The storage cell is an asymmetric cross-coupled pair of CMOS inverters which is overdriven by a strong signal from the ALU bus when the register contents are changed. The feedback inverter is made weak in order to minimize the cell's resistance to the new value. The *A* and *B* read buses are precharged to *Vdd* during phase 2 of the clock cycle, so the register cell need only discharge the read buses, which it does through n-type pass transistors when the read-lines are enabled.

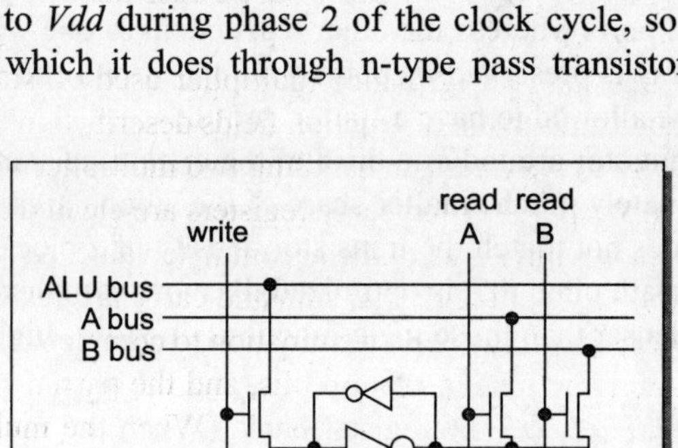

Figure 4.18 ARM6 register cell circuit

This register cell design works well with a 5 volt supply, but writing a '1' through the n-type pass transistor becomes difficult at lower supply voltages. Since a low supply voltage gives good power-efficiency, ARM cores since the ARM6 have either used a full CMOS transmission gate (with a p-type transistor in parallel with the n-type pass transistor in the write circuit, requiring complementary write enable control lines) or a more sophisticated register circuit.

These register cells are arranged in columns to form a 32-bit register, and the columns are packed together to form the complete register bank. The decoders for the read and write enable lines are then packed above the columns as shown in Figure 4.19, so the enables run vertically and the data buses horizontally across the array of register cells. Since a decoder is logically more complex than the register cell itself, but the horizontal pitch is chosen to suit the cell, the decoder layout can become very tight and the decoders themselves have to be tall and thin.

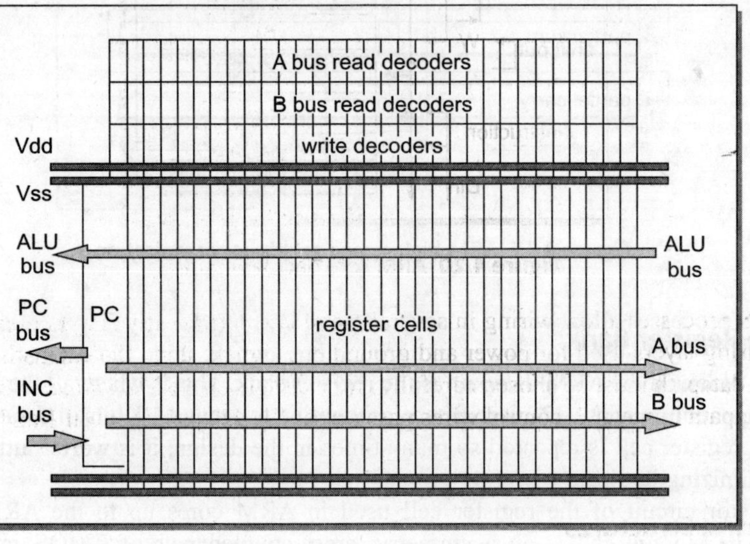

Figure 4.19 ARM register bank floorplan

The ARM program counter register is physically part of the register bank in the simpler cores, but it has two write and three read ports whereas the other registers have one write and two read ports. The symmetry of the register array is preserved by putting the PC at one end where it is accessible to the additional ports and it can be allowed to have a 'fatter' profile.

The register bank accounts for around one-third of the total transistor count of the simpler ARM cores, but takes a proportionately much smaller share of the silicon area by virtue of its very dense, memory-like structure. It does not match the transistor density of a block of SRAM since it has two read ports and fits on a datapath pitch that is optimized for more complex logic functions such as the ALU. However, it is much denser than those logic functions due to its higher regularity.

4.4.12 | Datapath Layout

The ARM datapath is laid out to a constant pitch per bit. The pitch will be a compromise between the optimum for the complex functions (such as the ALU) which are best suited to a wide pitch and the simple functions (such as the barrel shifter) which are most efficient when laid out on a narrow pitch.

Each function is then laid out to this pitch, remembering that there may also be buses passing over a function (for example the B bus passes through the ALU but is not used by it); space must be allowed for these. It is a good idea to produce a floor-plan for the datapath noting the 'passenger' buses through each block, as illustrated in Figure 4.20. The order of the function blocks is chosen to minimize the number of additional buses passing over the more complex functions.

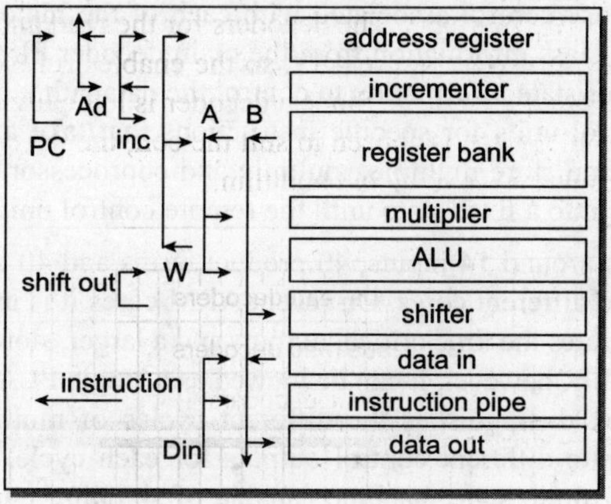

Figure 4.20 ARM core datapath buses

Modern CMOS processes allow wiring in several metal layers (the early ARM cores used two metal layers). The wiring layers used for power and ground bus signals along the datapath and control signals across the datapath must be chosen carefully (for example on ARM2 *Vdd* and *Vss* run along both sides of the datapath in metal 2, control wires pass across the datapath in metal 1 and buses run along it in metal 2).

4.4.13 | Control Structures

The control logic on the simpler ARM cores has three structural components which relate to each other as shown in Figure 4.21.

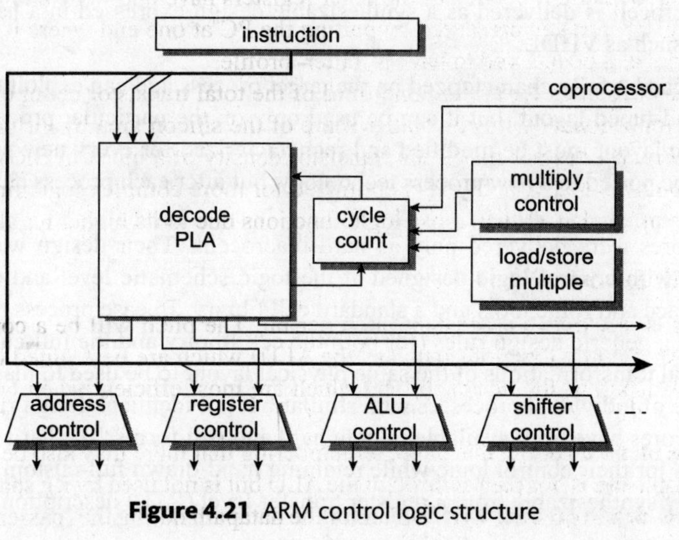

Figure 4.21 ARM control logic structure

1. An instruction decoder **PLA** (programmable logic array). This unit uses some of the instruction bits and an internal cycle counter to define the class of operation to be performed on the datapath in the next cycle.
2. Distributed secondary control associated with each of the major datapath function blocks. This logic uses the class information from the main decoder PLA to select other instruction bits and/or processor state information to control the datapath.
3. Decentralized control units for specific instructions that take a variable number of cycles to complete (load and store multiple, multiply and coprocessor operations). Here the main decoder PLA locks into a fixed state until the remote control unit indicates completion.

The main decoder PLA has around 14 inputs, 40 product terms and 40 outputs, the precise number varying slightly between the different cores. On recent ARM cores it is implemented as two PLAs: a small, fast PLA which generates the time critical outputs and a larger, slower PLA which generates all the other outputs. Functionally, however, it can be viewed as a single PLA unit.

The 'cycle count' block distinguishes the different cycles of multi-cycle instructions so that the decode PLA can generate different control outputs for each cycle. It is, in fact, not simply a counter but a more general finite state machine capable of skipping unneeded cycles and of locking into a fixed state. It determines when the current instruction is about to complete and initiates the transfer of the next instruction from the instruction pipeline, including aborting instructions at the end of their first cycle if they fail their condition test. However, much of the time its behaviour is like that of a simple counter so it is not *too* misleading to think of it as an instruction cycle counter.

4.4.14 | Physical Design

So far we have been concerned principally with the logic design of an ARM core and said little about its physical implementation on a particular CMOS process.

There are two principal mechanisms used to implement an ARM processor core (or any other core, for than matter) on a particular process:

- a hard macrocell is delivered as physical layout ready to be incorporated into the final design;
- a soft macrocell is delivered as a synthesizable design expressed in a hardware description language such as VHDL.

A hard macrocell can be fully characterized on the target process and can exploit the area advantages of full-custom hand-tuned layout, but it can be used only on the particular process for which it has been designed. The layout must be modified and recharacterized for every new process. A soft macrocell can readily be ported to a new process technology, but after each process change it must still be recharacterized.

Early ARM cores were delivered only as hard macrocells. Their design was based upon full-custom datapaths, with control logic designed at the logic schematic level and converted to layout using automatic place and route tools and a standard cell library. To ease process portability the cores were designed using generic design rules (for both the cell library and the full-custom datapath) that allowed geometrical transformations of the same physical layout to be used to map the same physical layout onto a range of individual processes with similar but not identical design rules.

Recent ARM cores have been available in both hard and soft forms. The hard macrocells increasingly use synthesis for their control logic while retaining hand-drawn full-custom datapaths. The soft macrocells are fully synthesizable from a register transfer level (RTL) description.

Some ARM partners have adopted a middle course, using a gate-level netlist description of an ARM core as their basis for porting to new processes. The porting procedure no longer involves resynthesis, but simply mapping the same netlist (using automatic place and route tools) onto a standard cell library implemented on the new process.

The choice between hard and soft macrocells (or gate-level netlists) is a complex decision. Hard macrocells can clearly give the best area, performance and power-efficiency on a process, but it takes significant time, effort and cost to port them to each process. Soft macrocells and portable netlists are more flexible, and automated tools are now of a quality that means that they come close to hand layout in performance. The portablility of the soft macrocell may mean that the choice is between a soft macrocell on the latest process or a hard macrocell on an older process, and the process technology advantage could easily outweigh the slight loss of optimization.

4.5 | The ARM Coprocessor Interface

The ARM supports a general-purpose extension of its instruction set through the addition of hardware coprocessors, and it also supports the software emulation of these coprocessors through the undefined instruction trap.

4.5.1 | Coprocessor Architecture

The coprocessor architecture is described in Section 5.16 on page 117. Its most important features are:

- Support for up to 16 logical coprocessors.
- Each coprocessor can have up to 16 private registers of any reasonable size; they are not limited to 32 bits.
- Coprocessors use a load-store architecture, with instructions to perform internal operations on registers, instructions to load and save registers from and to memory, and instructions to move data to or from an ARM register.

The simpler ARM cores offer the coprocessor interface at board level, so a coprocessor may be introduced as a separate component. High clock speeds make board-level interfacing very difficult, so the higher-performance ARMs restrict the coprocessor interface to on-chip use, in particular for cache and memory management control functions, but other on-chip coprocessors may also be supported.

4.5.2 | ARM7TDMI Coprocessor Interface

The ARM7TDMI coprocessor interface is based on 'bus watching' (other ARM cores use different techniques). The coprocessor is attached to a bus where the ARM instruction stream flows into the ARM, and the coprocessor copies the instructions into an internal pipeline that mimics the behaviour of the ARM instruction pipeline.

As each coprocessor instruction begins execution there is a 'hand-shake' between the ARM and the coprocessor to confirm that they are both ready to execute it. The handshake uses three signals:

1. $\overline{cpi}$ (from ARM to all coprocessors).

   This signal, which stands for 'CoProcessor Instruction', indicates that the ARM has identified a coprocessor instruction and wishes to execute it.

2. *cpa* (from the coprocessors to ARM).

   This is the 'CoProcessor Absent' signal which tells the ARM that there is no coprocessor present that is able to execute the current instruction.

3. *cpb* (from the coprocessors to ARM).
   This is the 'CoProcessor Busy' signal which tells the ARM that the coprocessor cannot begin executing the instruction yet.

The timing is such that both the ARM and the coprocessor must generate their respective signals autonomously. The coprocessor cannot wait until it sees $\overline{cpi}$ before generating *cpa* and *cpb*.

4.5.3 | Handshake Outcomes

Once a coprocessor instruction has entered the ARM7TDMI and coprocessor pipelines, there are four possible ways it may be handled depending on the handshake signals:

1. The ARM may decide not to execute it, either because it falls in a branch shadow or because it fails its condition code test. (All ARM instructions are conditionally executed, including coprocessor instructions.) ARM will not assert $\overline{cpi}$, and the instruction will be discarded by all parties.
2. The ARM may decide to execute it (and signal this by asserting $\overline{cpi}$), but no present coprocessor can take it so *cpa* stays active. ARM will take the undefined instruction trap and use software to recover, possibly by emulating the trapped instruction.
3. ARM decides to execute the instruction and a coprocessor accepts it, but cannot execute it yet. The coprocessor takes *cpa* low but leaves *cpb* high. The ARM will 'busy-wait' until the coprocessor takes *cpb* low, stalling the instruction stream at this point. If an enabled interrupt request arrives while the coprocessor is busy, ARM will break off to handle the interrupt, probably returning to retry the coprocessor instruction later.
4. ARM decides to execute the instruction and a coprocessor accepts it for immediate execution. $\overline{cpi}$, *cpa* and *cpb* are all taken low and both sides commit to complete the instruction.

4.5.4 | Data Transfers

If the instruction is a coprocessor data transfer instruction the ARM is responsible for generating an initial memory address (the coprocessor does not require any connection to the address bus) but the coprocessor determines the length of the transfer; ARM will continue incrementing the address until the coprocessor signals completion. The *cpa* and *cpb* handshake signals are also used for this purpose.

Since the data transfer is not interruptible once it has started, coprocessors should limit the maximum transfer length to 16 words (the same as a maximum length load or store multiple instruction) so as not to compromise the ARM's interrupt response.

4.5.5 | Pre-emptive Execution

A coprocessor may begin executing an instruction as soon as it enters its pipeline so long as it can recover its state if the handshake does not ultimately complete. All activity must be **idempotent** (repeatable with identical results) up to the point of commitment.

4.6 | Examples and Exercises

EXAMPLE 4.1

Why does r15 give pc + 8 in the first cycle of an instruction and pc + 12 in subsequent cycles on an ARM7?

This is the ARM pipeline being exposed to the programmer. Referring back to Figure 4.2, we can see that the pc value was incremented once when the current instruction ('1' in the figure below) was fetched and once when its successor ('2') was fetched giving pc + 8 at the start of the first execute cycle. During the first execute cycle a third instruction ('3') is fetched, giving pc + 12 in all subsequent execute cycles.

While multi-cycle instructions interrupt the pipeline flow they do not affect this aspect of the behaviour. An instruction always fetches the next-instruction-but-one during its first execute cycle, so r15 always progresses from pc + 8 at the start of the first execute cycle to pc + 12 at the start of the second (and subsequent) execute cycle(s).

(Note that other ARM processors do not share this behaviour, so it should never be relied upon when writing ARM programs.)

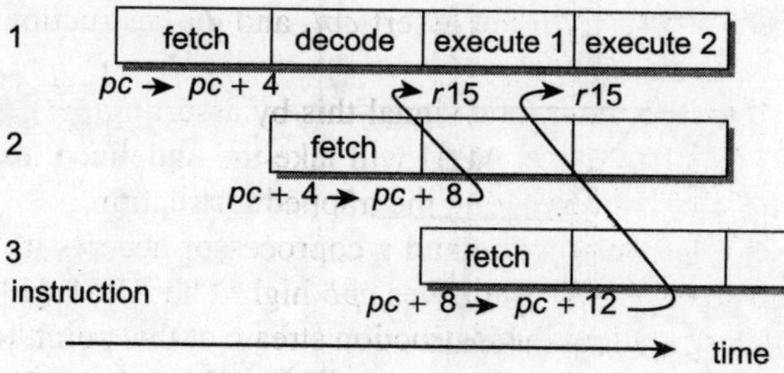

Exercise 4.1.1
Draw a pipeline flow diagram along the lines of the one above to illustrate the timing of an ARM branch instruction. (The branch target is computed in the first execute cycle of the instruction and issued to memory in the following cycle.)

Exercise 4.1.2
In ARM's five stage pipeline, loading data into the register file is done in the 'write back' stage.

When data is to be stored into memory, which stage is utilised ?

EXAMPLE 4.2
Complete the ARM2 4-bit carry logic circuit outlined in Figures 4.11 and 4.12.
The 4-bit carry look-ahead scheme uses the individual bit carry generate and propagate signals produced by the logic shown in Figure 4.12. Denoting these by G[3:0] and P[3:0], the carry-out from the top bit of a 4-bit group is given by:

$$Cout = G[3] + P[3].(G[2] + P[2].(G[1] + P[1].(G[0] + P[0].Cin)))$$

Therefore the group generate and propagate signals, G4 and P4, as used in Figure 4.11 are given by:

$$G4 = G[3] + P[3].(G[2] + P[2].(G[1] + P[1].G[0]))$$

$$P4 = P[3].P[2].P[1].P[0]$$

These two signals are independent of the carry-in signal and therefore can be set up ready for its arrival, allowing the carry to propagate across the 4-bit group in just one AND-OR-INVERT gate delay.

Exercise 4.2.1

The figure below shows the way the barrel shifter is included in the series path of the ALU.

State at least one reason to justify such a design (most other processors have the barrel shifter in parallel with the ALU).

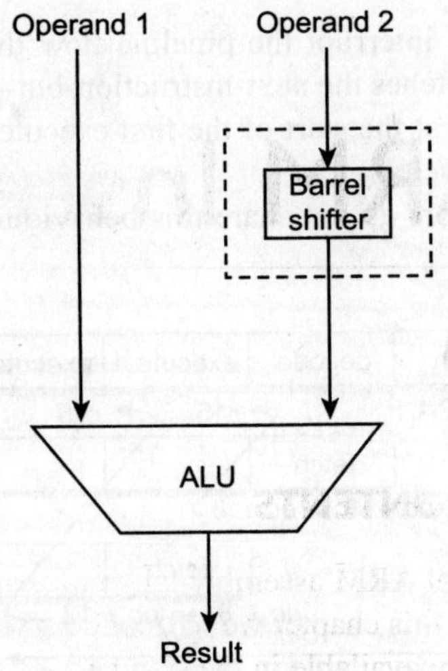

Exercise 4.2.2

Estimate the gate count for the ripple-carry adder and for the 4-bit carry look-ahead adder, basing both designs on the circuit in Figure 4.12 and varying only the carry scheme.

How much does the extra speed of the carry look-ahead scheme cost in terms of gate count? How does it affect the regularity, and hence the design cost, of the adder?

5

The ARM Instruction Set

SUMMARY OF CHAPTER CONTENTS

In Chapter 3 we looked at user-level ARM assembly language programming and got the general flavour of the ARM instruction set. In this chapter we will look in finer detail at the instruction set to see the full range of instructions that are available in the standard ARM instruction set.

Some ARM cores will also execute a compressed form of the instruction set where a subset of the full ARM instruction set is encoded into 16-bit instructions. These instructions are 'Thumb' instructions, and are discussed in Chapter 7. The only aspects of the Thumb architecture we will see in this chapter are the instructions available in the ARM instruction set which cause the processor to switch to executing Thumb instructions. Likewise, some ARM cores support instruction set extensions to enhance their signal processing capabilities, discussion of which is deferred to Section 8.9 on page 206.

As with any processor's full instruction set, the ARM instruction set has corners which conceal complex behaviour. Often these corners are not at all useful to programmers, in which case ARM Limited does not define the behaviour of the processor in the corner cases and the corresponding instructions should not be used. The fact that a particular implementation of the ARM behaves in a particular way in such a case should not be taken as meaning that future implementations will behave the same way. Programs should only use instructions with defined semantics!

Some ARM instructions are not available on all ARM chips; these will be highlighted as they arise.

5.1 | Introduction

The ARM programmers' model was introduced in Figure 2.1 on page 34. In this chapter we will consider the supervisor and exception modes, so now the shaded registers will also come into play.

5.1.1 | Data Types

ARM processors support six data types:

- 8-bit signed and unsigned bytes.
- 16-bit signed and unsigned half-words; these are aligned on 2-byte boundaries.
- 32-bit signed and unsigned words; these are aligned on 4-byte boundaries.

(Some older ARM processors do not have half-word and signed byte support.)

ARM instructions are all 32-bit words and must be word-aligned. Thumb instructions are half-words and must be aligned on 2-byte boundaries.

Internally all ARM operations are on 32-bit operands; the shorter data types are only supported by data transfer instructions. When a byte is loaded from memory it is zero- or sign-extended to 32 bits and then treated as a 32-bit value for internal processing.

ARM coprocessors may support other data types, and in particular there is a defined set of types to represent floating-point values. There is no explicit support for these types within the ARM core, however, and in the absence of a floating-point coprocessor these types are interpreted by software which uses the standard types listed above.

5.1.2 | Memory Organization

There are two ways to store words in a byte-addressed memory, depending on whether the least significant byte is stored at a lower or higher address than the next most significant byte. Since there is no good reason for choosing one approach over the other the argument as to which is better is more a matter of religion than reason.

The two schemes are illustrated in Figure 5.1, which shows how an assortment of data types would be stored under the two schemes. ('half-wordl2' is found at address 12, and so on.)

The 'little-endian' and 'big-endian' terminology which is used to denote the two approaches is derived from Swift's *Gulliver's Travels.* The inhabitants of Lilliput, who are well known for being rather small are, in addition, constrained by law to break their eggs only at the little end. When this law is imposed, those of their fellow citizens who prefer to break their eggs at the big end take exception to the new rule and civil war breaks out. The big-endians eventually take refuge on a nearby island, which is the kingdom of Blefuscu. The civil war results in many casualties.

The application of the 'big-endian' and 'little-endian' terms to the two ways to organize computer memory comes from 'On Holy Wars and a Plea for Peace' by Danny Cohen in the October 1981 issue of *Computer*.

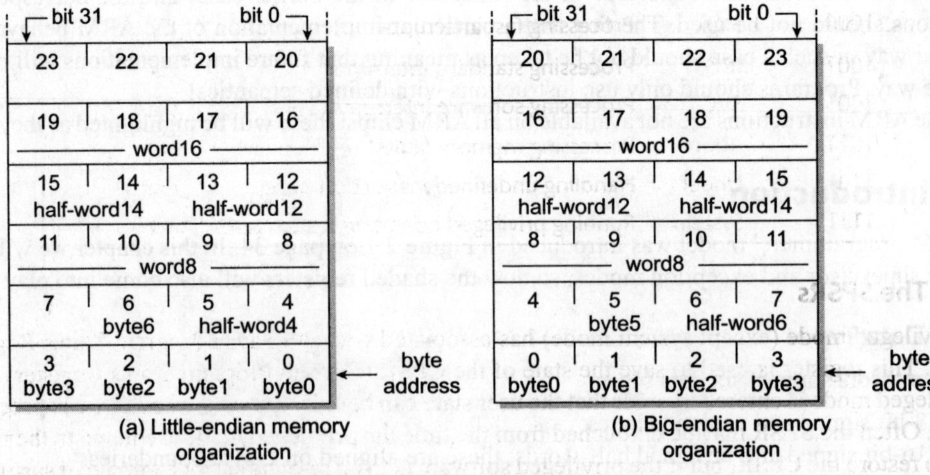

Figure 5.1 Little- and big-endian memory organizations

To my knowledge, no one has yet been mortally wounded in an argument over byte ordering. However the issue causes significant practical difficulties when datasets are transferred between machines of opposite orderings.

Most ARM chips remain strictly neutral in the dispute and can be configured to work with either memory arrangement, though they default to little-endian. Throughout this book we will assume a little-endian ordering, where bytes of increasing significance are stored at increasing addresses in memory. ARM may be neutral, but I am not!

5.1.3 | Privileged Modes

Most programs operate in user mode as described in Chapter 3. However, ARM has other **privileged** operating modes which are used to handle exceptions and supervisor calls (which are sometimes called **software interrupts**).

The current operating mode is defined by the bottom five bits of the CPSR (see Figure 2.2 on page 35). The interpretation of these bits is summarized in Table 5.1. Where the register set is not the user registers, the relevant shaded registers shown in Figure 2.1 on page 34 replace the corresponding user registers and the current SPSR (**Saved Program Status Register**; see below) also becomes accessible.

Some ARM processors do not support all of the above operating modes, and some also support '26-bit' modes for backwards compatibility with older ARMs; these will be discussed further in Section 5.23.

The privileged modes can only be entered through controlled mechanisms; with suitable memory protection they allow a fully protected operating system to be built. This issue will be discussed further in Chapter 11.

Most ARMs are used in embedded systems where such protection is inappropriate, but the privileged modes can still be used to give a weaker level of protection that is useful for trapping errant software.

Table 5.1 ARM operating modes and register usage

CPSR[4:0]	Mode	Use	Registers
10000	User	Normal user code	user
10001	FIQ	Processing fast interrupts	_fiq
10010	IRQ	Processing standard interrupts	_irq
10011	SVC	Processing software interrupts (SWIs)	_svc
10111	Abort	Processing memory faults	_abt
11011	Undef	Handling undefined instruction traps	_und
11111	System	Running privileged operating system tasks	user

5.1.4 | The SPSRs

Each privileged mode (except system mode) has associated with it a Saved Program Status Register, or SPSR. This register is used to save the state of the CPSR (Current Program Status Register) when the privileged mode is entered in order that the user state can be fully restored when the user process is resumed. Often the SPSR may be untouched from the time the privileged mode is entered to the time it is used to restore the CPSR, but if the privileged software is to be re-entrant (for example, if supervisor code makes supervisor calls to itself) then the SPSR must be copied into a general register and saved.

5.2 | Exceptions

Exceptions are usually used to handle unexpected events which arise during the execution of a program, such as interrupts or memory faults. In the ARM architecture the term is also used to cover software interrupts and undefined instruction traps (which do not really qualify as 'unexpected') and the system reset function which logically arises before rather than during the execution of a program (although the processor may be reset again while running). These events are all grouped under the 'exception' heading because they all use the same basic mechanism within the processor.

ARM exceptions may be considered in three groups:

1. Exceptions generated as the direct effect of executing an instruction.
   Software interrupts, undefined instructions (including coprocessor instructions where the requested coprocessor is absent) and prefetch aborts (instructions that are invalid due to a memory fault occurring during fetch) come under this heading.
2. Exceptions generated as a side-effect of an instruction.
   Data aborts (a memory fault during a load or store data access) are in this class.
3. Exceptions generated externally, unrelated to the instruction flow.
   Reset, IRQ and FIQ fall into this category.

5.2.1 | Exception Entry

When an exception arises, ARM completes the current instruction as best it can (except that *reset* exceptions terminate the current instruction immediately) and then departs from the current instruction sequence to handle the exception. Exception entry caused by a side-effect or an external event usurps the next instruction in the current sequence; direct-effect exceptions are handled in sequence as they arise. The processor performs the following sequence of actions:

- It changes to the operating mode corresponding to the particular exception.
- It saves the address of the instruction following the exception entry instruction in rl4 of the new mode.
- It saves the old value of the CPSR in the SPSR of the new mode.
- It disables IRQs by setting bit 7 of the CPSR and, if the exception is a fast interrupt, disables further fast interrupts by setting bit 6 of the CPSR.
- It forces the PC to begin executing at the relevant vector address given in Table 5.2.

Table 5.2 Exception vector addresses

Exception	Mode	Vector address
Reset	SVC	0x00000000
Undefined instruction	UND	0x00000004
Software interrupt (SWI)	SVC	0x00000008
Prefetch abort (instruction fetch memory fault)	Abort	0x0000000C
Data abort (data access memory fault)	Abort	0x00000010
IRQ (normal interrupt)	IRQ	0x00000018
FIQ (fast interrupt)	FIQ	0x0000001C

Normally the vector address will contain a branch to the relevant routine, though the FIQ code can start immediately since it occupies the highest vector address.

The two banked registers in each of the privileged modes are used to hold the return address and a stack pointer; the stack pointer may be used to save other user registers so that they can be used by the exception handler. FIQ mode has additional private registers to give better performance by avoiding the need to save user registers in most cases where it is used.

5.2.2 | Exception Return

Once the exception has been handled the user task is normally resumed. This requires the handler code to restore the user state exactly as it was when the exception first arose:

- Any modified user registers must be restored from the handler's stack.
- The CPSR must be restored from the appropriate SPSR.
- The PC must be changed back to the relevant instruction address in the user instruction stream.

Note that the last two of these steps cannot be carried out independently. If the CPSR is restored first, the banked r14 holding the return address is no longer accessible; if the PC is restored first, the exception handler loses control of the instruction stream and cannot cause the restoration of the CPSR to take place. There are also more subtle difficulties to do with ensuring that instructions are always fetched in the correct operating mode to ensure that memory protection schemes are not bypassed. Therefore ARM provides two mechanisms which cause both steps to happen atomically as part of a single instruction. One of these is used when the return address has been kept in the banked r14 and the other when the return address has been saved onto a stack. First we look at the case where the return address is in r14.

- To return from a SWI or undefined instruction trap use:
```
MOVS    pc, r14
```
- To return from an IRQ, FIQ or prefetch abort use:
```
SUBS    pc, r14, #4
```
- To return from a data abort to retry the data access use:
```
SUBS    pc, r14, #8
```

The 's' modifier after the opcode signifies the special form of the instruction when the destination register is the PC. Note how the return instruction incorporates an adjustment to the return address where necessary:

- IRQ and FIQ must return one instruction early in order to execute the instruction that was 'usurped' for the exception entry.
- Prefetch abort must return one instruction early to execute the instruction that had caused a memory fault when first requested.
- Data abort must return two instructions early to retry the data transfer instruction, which was the instruction *before* the one usurped for exception entry.

If the handler has copied the return address out onto a stack (in order, for example, to allow re-entrant behaviour, though note that in this case the SPSR must be saved as well as the PC) the restoration of the user registers and the return may be implemented with a single multiple register transfer instruction such as:

```
LDMFD    r13!, {r0 – r3, pc}^  ; restore and return
```

Here the '^' after the register list (which must include the PC) indicates that this is a special form of the instruction. The CPSR is restored at the same time that the PC is loaded from memory, which will always be the last item transferred from memory since the registers are loaded in increasing order.

The stack pointer (r13) used here is the banked register belonging to the privileged operating mode; each privileged mode can have its own stack pointer which must be initialized during system start-up.

Clearly the stack return mechanism can only be employed if the value in rl4 was adjusted, where necessary, before being saved onto the stack.

5.2.3 | Exception Priorities

Since multiple exceptions can arise at the same time it is necessary to define a priority order to determine the order in which the exceptions are handled. On ARM this is:

1. reset (highest priority);
2. data abort;
3. FIQ;
4. IRQ;
5. prefetch abort;
6. SWI, undefined instruction (including absent coprocessor). These are mutually exclusive instruction encodings and therefore cannot occur simultaneously.

Reset starts the processor from a known state and renders all other pending exceptions irrelevant.

The most complex exception scenario is where an FIQ, an IRQ and a third exception (which is not Reset) happen simultaneously. FIQ has higher priority than IRQ and also masks it out, so the IRQ will be ignored until the FIQ handler explicitly enables IRQ or returns to the user code.

If the third exception is a data abort, the processor will enter the data abort handler and then immediately enter the FIQ handler, since data abort entry does not mask FIQs out. The data abort is 'remembered' in the return path and will be processed when the FIQ handler returns.

If the third exception is not a data abort, the FIQ handler will be entered immediately. When FIQ and IRQ have both completed, the program returns to the instruction which generated the third exception, and in all the remaining cases the exception will recur and be handled accordingly.

5.2.4 | Address Exceptions

The observant reader will have noticed that Table 5.2 shows the use of all of the first eight word locations in memory as exception vector addresses apart from address 0x00000014. This location was used on earlier ARM processors which operated within a 26-bit address space to trap load or store addresses which fell outside the address space. These traps were referred to as 'address exceptions'.

Since 32-bit ARMs are unable to generate addresses which fall outside their 32-bit address space, address exceptions have no role in the current architecture and the vector address at 0x00000014 is unused.

5.3 | Conditional Execution

An unusual feature of the ARM instruction set is that every instruction (with the exception of certain v5T instructions) is conditionally executed. Conditional branches are a standard feature of most instruction sets, but ARM extends the conditional execution to all of its instructions, including supervisor calls and coprocessor instructions. The condition field occupies the top four bits of the 32-bit instruction field:

Figure 5.2 The ARM condition code field

Each of the 16 values of the condition field causes the instruction to be executed or skipped according to the values of the N, Z, C and V flags in the CPSR. The conditions are given in Table 5.3. Every ARM instruction mnemonic may be extended by appending the two letters defined in this table, though the 'always' condition (AL) may be omitted since it is the default condition that is assumed if no other condition is specified.

Table 5.3 ARM condition codes

Opcode [31:28]	Mnemonic extension	Interpretation	Status flag state for execution
0000	EQ	Equal/equals zero	Z set
0001	NE	Not equal	Z clear
0010	CS/HS	Carry set/unsigned higher or same	C set
0011	CC/LO	Carry clear/unsigned lower	C clear
0100	MI	Minus/negative	N set
0101	PL	Plus/positive or zero	N clear
0110	VS	Overflow	V set
0111	VC	No overflow	V clear
1000	HI	Unsigned higher	C set and Z clear
1001	LS	Unsigned lower or same	C clear or Z set
1010	GE	Signed greater than or equal	N equals V
1011	LT	Signed less than	N is not equal to V
1100	GT	Signed greater than	Z clear and N equals V
1101	LE	Signed less than or equal	Z set or N is not equal to V
1110	AL	Always	any
1111	NV	Never (do not use!)	None

5.3.1 | The 'never' Condition

The 'never' condition (NV) should not be used – there are plenty of other ways to write no-ops (instructions that have no effect on the processor state) in ARM code. The reason to avoid the 'never' condition is that ARM Limited have indicated that they may use this area of the instruction space for other purposes in the future (and have done so in architecture v5T), so although current ARMs may behave as expected, there is no guarantee that future variants will behave the same way.

5.3.2 | Alternative mnemonics

Where alternative mnemonics are shown in the same row in the condition table this indicates that there is more than one way to interpret the condition field. For instance, in row 3 the same condition field value can be invoked by the mnemonic extension CS or HS. Both cause the instruction to be executed only if the C bit in the CPSR is set. The alternatives are available because the same test is used in different circumstances. If you have previously added two unsigned integers and want to test whether there was a carry-out from the addition, you should use CS. If you have compared two unsigned integers and want to test whether the first was higher or the same as the second, use HS. The alternative mnemonic removes the need for the programmer to remember that an unsigned comparison sets the carry on higher or the same.

The observant reader will note that the conditions are in pairs where the second condition is the inverse of the first, so for any condition the opposite condition is also available (with the exception of 'always', since 'never' should not be used). Therefore whenever *if...then...* can be implemented with conditional instructions, *...else...* can be added using instructions with the opposite condition.

5.4 | Branch and Branch with Link (B, BL)

Branch and Branch with Link instructions are the standard way to cause a switch in the sequence of instruction execution. The ARM normally executes instructions from sequential word addresses in memory, using conditional execution to skip over individual instructions where required. Whenever the program must deviate from sequential execution a control flow instruction is used to modify the program counter. Although there are several ways to achieve this in special circumstances, Branch and Branch with Link instructions are the standard way.

5.4.1 | Binary Encoding

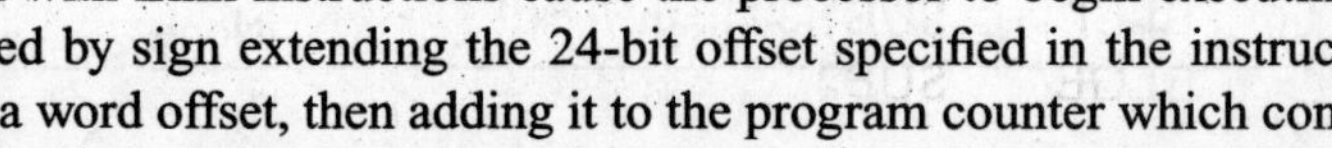

Figure 5.3 Branch and Branch with Link binary encoding

5.4.2 | Description

Branch and Branch with Link instructions cause the processor to begin executing instructions from an address computed by sign extending the 24-bit offset specified in the instruction, shifting it left two places to form a word offset, then adding it to the program counter which contains the address of the branch instruction plus eight bytes. (See 'PC behaviour' on page 68 for an explanation of the PC offset.) The assembler will compute the correct offset under normal circumstances.

The range of the branch instruction is +/– 32 Mbytes.

The Branch with Link variant, which has the L bit (bit 24) set, also moves the address of the instruction following the branch into the link register (rl4) of the current processor mode. This is normally used to perform a subroutine call, with the return being caused by copying the link register back into the PC.

Both forms of the instruction may be executed conditionally or unconditionally.

5.4.3 | Assembler Format

```
B{L}{<cond>}    <target address>
```

'L' specifies the branch and link variant; if 'L' is not included a branch without link is generated. '<cond>' should be one of the mnemonic extensions given in Table 5.3 or, if omitted 'AL' is assumed. '<target address>' is normally a label in the assembler code; the assembler will generate the offset (which will be the difference between the address of the target and the address of the branch instruction plus 8).

EXAMPLES

An unconditional jump:

```
            B       LABEL   ; unconditional jump ..
            ..
LABEL       ..              ; .. to here
```

To execute a loop ten times:

```
            MOV     r0, #10 ; initialize loop counter
LOOP        ..
            SUBS    r0, #1  ; decrement counter setting CCs
            BNE     LOOP    ; if counter <> 0 repeat loop ..
            ..              ; .. else drop through
```

To call a subroutine:

```
            ..
            BL      SUB     ; branch and link to subroutine SUB
            ..              ; return to here
SUB         ..
            ..              ; subroutine entry point
            MOV     PC, rl4 ; return
```

Conditional subroutine call:

```
            ..
            CMP     r0, #5  ; if r0 < 5
            BLLT    SUB1    ; then call SUB1
            BLGE    SUB2    ; else call SUB2
            ..
```

(Note that this example will only work correctly if SUB1 does not change the condition codes, since if the BLLT is taken it will return to the BLGE. If the condition codes are changed by SUB1, SUB2 may be executed as well.)

Notes

1. If you are familiar with other RISC processors you might expect ARM to execute the instruction after the branch before moving to LABEL in the first example above, following the *delayed branch* model employed by many other RISCs. This expectation will not be fulfilled, however, since ARM does not employ a delayed branch mechanism.

2. Branches which attempt to go past the beginning or the end of the 32-bit address space should be avoided since they may have unpredictable results.

5.5 | Branch, Branch with Link and exchange (BX, BLX)

These instructions are available on ARM chips which support the Thumb (16-bit) instruction set, and are a mechanism for switching the processor to execute Thumb instructions or for returning symmetrically to ARM and Thumb calling routines. A similar Thumb instruction causes the processor to switch back to 32-bit ARM instructions. The Thumb instruction set is described in Chapter 7.

BLX is available only on ARM processors that support architecture v5T.

5.5.1 | Binary Encoding

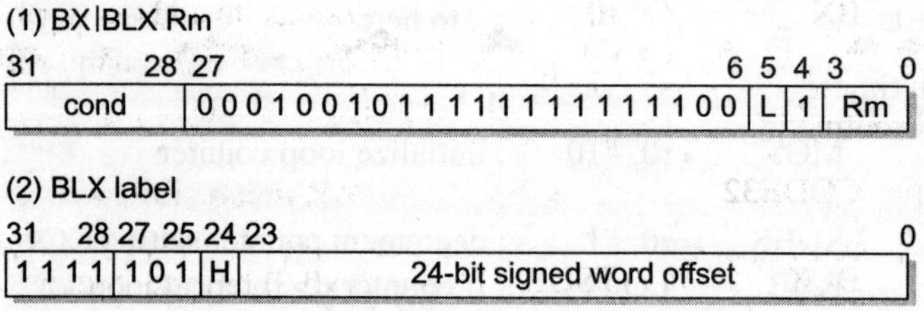

Figure 5.4 Branch (with optional link) and exchange instruction binary encodings

5.5.2 | Description

In the first format the branch target is specified in a register, Rm. Bit[0] of Rm is copied into the T bit in the CPSR and bits[31:1] are moved into the PC:

- If Rm[0] is 1, the processor switches to execute Thumb instructions and begins executing at the address in Rm aligned to a half-word boundary by clearing the bottom bit.
- If Rm[0] is 0, the processor continues executing ARM instructions and begins executing at the address in Rm aligned to a word boundary by clearing Rm[1].

In the second format the branch target is an address computed by sign extending the 24-bit offset specified in the instruction, shifting it left two places to form a word offset, then adding it to the program counter which contains the address of the BX instruction plus eight bytes. (See 'PC behaviour' on page 68 for an explanation of the PC offset.) The H bit (bit 24) is also added into bit 1 of the resulting address, allowing an odd half-word address to be selected for the target instruction which will always be a Thumb instruction (BL is used to target an ARM instruction). The assembler will compute the correct offset under normal circumstances. The range of the branch instruction is +/− 32 Mbytes.

The Branch with Link variants (BLX, available only on v5T processors) of both formats, which have the L bit (bit 5) set in the first format, also move the address of the instruction following the branch into the link register (rl4) of the current processor mode. This is normally used to save the return address when calling a Thumb subroutine. If BX is used as the subroutine return mechanism the instruction set of the calling routine can be saved along with the return address, so the same return mechanism can be used to return symmetrically to either an ARM or a Thumb caller from an ARM or Thumb subroutine.

Format (1) instructions may be executed conditionally or unconditionally, but format (2) instructions are executed unconditionally.

5.5.3 | Assembler Format

```
1:      B{L}X{<cond>} Rm
2:      BLX <target address>
```

'<target address>' is normally a label in the assembler code; the assembler will generate the offset (which will be the difference between the word address of the target and the address of the branch instruction plus 8) and set the H bit if appropriate.

EXAMPLES

An unconditional jump:

```
        BX      r0          ; branch to address in r0,
                            ; enter Thumb state if r0[0]  = 1
```

A call to a Thumb subroutine:

```
        CODE32              ; ARM code follows
        ..
        BLX     TSUB        ; call Thumb subroutine
        ..
        C0DE16              ; start of Thumb code
TSUB    ..                  ; Thumb subroutine
        BX      r14         ; return to ARM code
```

Notes

1. Some ARM processors which do not support the Thumb instruction set will trap these instructions, allowing software emulation of Thumb.
2. Only processors that implement ARM architecture v5T support either format of the BLX instruction (see Section 5.23).

5.6 | Software Interrupt (SWI)

The software interrupt instruction is used for calls to the operating system and is often called a 'supervisor call'. It puts the processor into supervisor mode and begins executing instructions from address 0x08.

If this area of memory is suitably protected it is possible to build an operating system on the ARM that is fully protected from a malicious user, though since ARM is rarely used in multi-user applications this level of protection is not often sought.

5.6.1 | Binary Encoding

31 28	27 24	23 0
cond	1 1 1 1	24-bit (interpreted) immediate

Figure 5.5 Software interrupt binary encoding

5.6.2 | Description

The 24-bit immediate field does not influence the operation of the instruction but may be interpreted by the system code.

If the condition is passed the instruction enters supervisor mode using the standard ARM exception entry sequence. In detail, the processor actions are:

1. Save the address of the instruction after the SWI in r14_svc.
2. Save the CPSR in SPSR_svc.
3. Enter supervisor mode and disable IRQs (but not FIQs) by setting CPSR[4:0] to 10011_2 and CPSR[7] to 1.
4. Set the PC to 08_{16} and begin executing the instructions there.

To return to the instruction after the SWI the system routine must not only copy r14_svc back into the PC, but it must also restore the CPSR from SPSR_svc. This requires the use of one of the special forms of the data processing instruction described in the next section.

5.6.3 | Assembler Format

```
SWI{<cond>}    <24-bit immediate>
```

EXAMPLES

To output the character 'A':

```
        MOV     r0, #'A'        ; get 'A' into r0..
        SWI     SWI_WriteC      ; .. and print it
```

A subroutine to output a text string following the call:

```
        ..
        BL      STROUT          ; output following message
        =       "Hello World",&0a,&0d, 0
        ..                      ; return to here
        ..
STROUT  LDRB    r0, [r14], #1   ; get character
        CMP     r0, #0          ; check for end marker
        SWINE   SWI_WriteC      ; if not end, print..
        BNE     STROUT          ; .. and loop
        ADD     r14, #3         ; align to next word
        BIC     r14, #3
        MOV     pc, r14         ; return
```

To finish executing the user program and return to the monitor program:

```
        SWI     SWI_Exit        ; return to monitor
```

Notes

1. An SWI may be executed when the processor is already in supervisor mode provided the original return address (in r14_svc) and SPSR_svc have been saved; otherwise these registers will be overwritten when the SWI is executed.

2. The interpretation of the 24-bit immediate is system dependent, but most systems support a standard subset for character I/O and similar basic functions.
   The immediates can be specified as constant expressions, but it is usually better to declare names for the required calls (and set their values) at the start of the program (or import a file which declares their values for the local operating system) and then use these names in the code.
   To see how to declare names and give them values look at the 'Examples and exercises' on page 62.
3. The first instruction executed in supervisor mode, which is at 08_{16}, is normally a branch to the SWI handler which resides somewhere nearby in memory. Writing the SWI handler to start at 08_{16} is not possible because the next memory word, at $0C_{16}$, is the entry point for the prefetch abort handler.

5.7 | Data Processing Instructions

The ARM data processing instructions are used to modify data values in registers. The operations that are supported include arithmetic and bit-wise logical combinations of 32-bit data types. One operand may be shifted or rotated *en route* to the ALU, allowing, for example, shift and add in a single instruction.

Multiply instructions use different formats, so these are considered separately in the next section.

5.7.1 | Binary Encoding

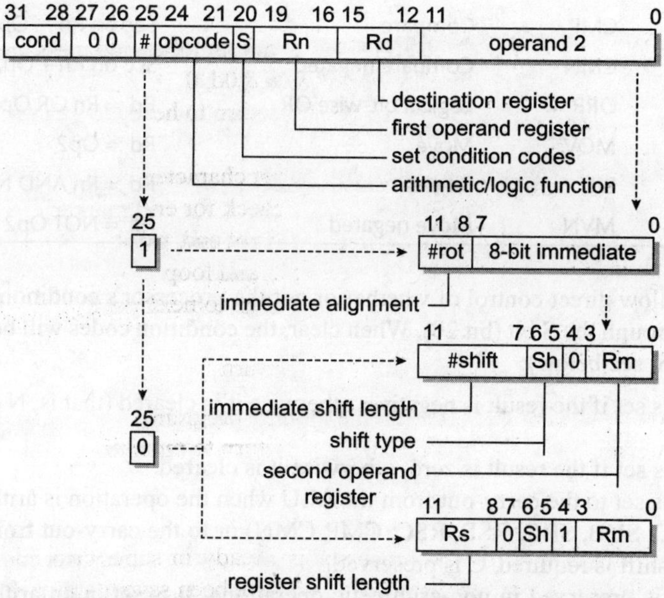

Figure 5.6 Data processing instruction binary encoding

5.7.2 | Description

The ARM data processing instructions employ a 3-address format, which means that the two source operands and the destination register are specified independently. One source operand is always a register; the second may be a register, a shifted register or an immediate value. The shift applied to the second operand, if it is a register, may be a logical or arithmetic shift or a rotate (see Figure 3.1 on page 47), and it may be by an amount specified either as an immediate quantity or by a fourth register.

The operations that may be specified are listed in Table 5.4.

When the instruction does not require all the available operands (for instance MOV ignores Rn and CMP ignores Rd) the unused register field should be set to zero. The assembler will do this automatically.

Table 5.4 ARM data processing instructions

Opcode [24:21]	Mnemonic	Meaning	Effect
0000	AND	Logical bit-wise AND	Rd := Rn AND Op2
0001	EOR	Logical bit-wise exclusive OR	Rd := Rn EOR Op2
0010	SUB	Subtract	Rd := Rn – Op2
0011	RSB	Reverse subtract	Rd := Op2 – Rn
0100	ADD	Add	Rd := Rn + Op2
0101	ADC	Add with carry	Rd := Rn + Op2 + C
0110	SBC	Subtract with carry	Rd := Rn – Op2 + C – 1
0111	RSC	Reverse subtract with carry	Rd := Op2 – Rn + C – 1
1000	TST	Test	Scc on Rn AND Op2
1001	TEQ	Test equivalence	Scc on Rn EOR Op2
1010	CMP	Compare	Scc on Rn – Op2
1011	CMN	Compare negated	Scc on Rn + Op2
1100	ORR	Logical bit-wise OR	Rd := Rn OR Op2
1101	MOV	Move	Rd := Op2
1110	BIC	Bit clear	Rd := Rn AND NOT Op2
1111	MVN	Move negated	Rd := NOT Op2

These instructions allow direct control of whether or not the processor's condition codes are affected by their execution through the S bit (bit 20). When clear, the condition codes will be unchanged; when set (and Rd is not rl5; see below):

- The N flag is set if the result is negative, otherwise it is cleared (that is, N equals bit 31 of the result).
- The Z flag is set if the result is zero, otherwise it is cleared.
- The C flag is set to the carry-out from the ALU when the operation is arithmetic (ADD, ADC, SUB, SBC, RSB, RSC, CMP, CMN) or to the carry-out from the shifter otherwise. If no shift is required, C is preserved.
- The V flag is preserved in non-arithmetic operations. It is set in an arithmetic operation if there is an overflow from bit 30 to bit 31 and cleared if no overflow occurs. It has significance

only when an arithmetic operation has operands that are viewed as 2's complement signed values, and indicates a result that is out of range.

5.7.3 | Multiply by a Constant

These instructions may be used to multiply a register by a small constant much more efficiently than can be achieved using the multiply instructions described in the next section. Examples are given below.

5.7.4 | Use of r15

The PC may be used as a source operand except when a register-specified shift amount is used, in which case none of the three source registers should be r15. When r15 is used as a source operand, the value supplied is the address of the instruction plus eight bytes. (The 8-byte offset exposes the pipelined operation of the processor; see 'PC behaviour' on page 68.)

The PC may also be specified as the destination for the result, in which case the instruction is a form of branch. This is exploited as a standard way to return from a subroutine.

When the PC is specified as the destination register Rd, the S bit still controls the effect of the instruction on the CPSR, but in a rather different way. Instead of updating the flags according to the ALU output as described above, when the S bit is set the SPSR of the current mode is copied into the CPSR, possibly affecting the interrupt enable flags and the processor operating mode. This mechanism restores the PC and the CPSR atomically, and is the standard way to return from an exception. Since there is no SPSR in user and system modes, this form of the instruction should not be used in those modes.

5.7.5 | Assembler Format

The assembler representation is one of the following, omitting Rn when the instruction is monadic (MOV, MVN) or Rd when the instruction is a comparison producing only condition code outputs (CMP, CMN, TST, TEQ):

```
<op> {<cond>} {s}   Rd, Rn,  #<32-bit immediate>
<op> {<cond>} {s}   Rd, Rn,  Rm, {<shift>}
```

where <shift> specifies the shift type (LSL, LSR, ASL, ASR, ROR or RRX) and, in all cases but RRX, the shift amount which may be a 5-bit immediate (#<#shift>) or a register (Rs).

EXAMPLES

To add r1 to r3 and place the result in r5:

```
ADD     r5,  r1, r3
```

To decrement r2 and check for zero:

```
SUBS    r2, r2,  #1        ; dec r2 and set cc
BEQ     LABEL              ; branch if r2 zero
..                         ; .. else fall through
```

To multiply r0 by 5:

```
ADD     r0,  r0,  r0,  LSL #2
```

A subroutine to multiply r0 by 10:

```
            MOV     r0, #3
            BL      TIMES10
            ..
TIMES10     MOV     r0, r0, LSL #1          ; ×2
            ADD     r0, r0, r0, LSL #2      ; ×5
            MOV     pc, r14                 ; return
```

To add a 64-bit integer in r0, r1 to one in r2, r3:

```
            ADDS    r2, r2, r0              ; add lower, save carry
            ADC     r3, r3, r1              ; add higher and carry
```

Note

1. Since the immediate field must be encoded within a subset of a 32-bit instruction, not all 32-bit immediate values can be represented. The binary encoding shown in Figure 5.6 shows how the immediate values are encoded. The immediate value is generated by rotating an 8-bit immediate field through an even number of bit positions.

5.8 | Multiply Instructions

ARM multiply instructions produce the product of two 32-bit binary numbers held in registers. The result of multiplying two 32-bit binary numbers is a 64-bit product. Some forms of the instruction, available only on certain versions of the processor, store the full result into two independently specified registers; other forms store only the least significant 32 bits into a single register.

In all cases there is a multiply-accumulate variant that adds the product to a running total and both signed and unsigned operands may be used. The least significant 32 bits of the result are the same for signed and unsigned operands, so there is no need for separate signed and unsigned versions of the 32-bit result instructions.

5.8.1 | Binary Encoding

31 28	27 24	23 21	20	19 16	15 12	11 8	7 4	3 0
cond	0 0 0 0	mul	S	Rd/RdHi	Rn/RdLo	Rs	1 0 0 1	Rm

Figure 5.7 Multiply instruction binary encoding

5.8.2 | Description

The functions of the various forms of multiply are listed in Table 5.5. The notation used in the table is as follows:

- 'RdHi:RdLo' is the 64-bit number formed by concatenating RdHi (the most significant 32 bits) and RdLo (the least significant 32 bits). '[31:0]' selects only the least significant 32 bits of the result.
- Simple assignment is denoted by ':='.
- Accumulation (adding the right-hand side to the left) is denoted by '+='.

Table 5.5 Multiply instructions

Opcode [23:21]	Mnemonic	Meaning	Effect
000	MUL	Multiply (32-bit result)	Rd := (Rm *Rs) [31:0]
001	MLA	Multiply-accumulate (32-bit result)	Rd := (Rm *Rs + Rn) [31:0]
100	UMULL	Unsigned multiply long	RdHi:RdLo := Rm * Rs
101	UMLAL	Unsigned multiply-accumulate long	RdHi:RdLo += Rm * Rs
110	SMULL	Signed multiply long	RdHi:RdLo := Rm * Rs
111	SMLAL	Signed multiply-accumulate long	RdHi:RdLo += Rm * Rs

The S bit controls the setting of the condition codes as with the other data processing instructions. When it is set in the instruction:

- The N flag is set to the value of bit 31 of Rd for the variants which produce a 32-bit result, and bit 31 of RdHi for the long forms.
- The Z flag is set if Rd or RdHi and RdLo are zero.
- The C flag is set to a meaningless value.
- The V flag is unchanged.

5.8.3 | Assembler Formats

Instructions that produce the least significant 32 bits of the product:

```
MUL{<cond>}{s}   Rd,   Rm, Rs
MLA{<cond>}{s}   Rd,   Rm, Rs, Rn
```

The following instructions produce the full 64-bit result:

```
<mul>{<cond>}{s}RdHi, RdLo, Rm, Rs
```

where <mul> is one of the 64-bit multiply types (UMULL, UMLAL, SMULL, SMLAL).

EXAMPLES

To form a scalar product of two vectors:

```
        MOV    r11, #20          ; initialize loop counter
        MOV    r10, #0           ; initialize total
LOOP    LDR    r0, [r8], #4      ; get first component ..
        LDR    r1, [r9], #4      ; ..and second
        MLA    r10, r0, r1, r10  ; accumulate product
        SUBS   r11, r11, #1      ; decrement loop counter
        BNE    LOOP
```

Notes

1. Specifying r15 for any of the operand or result registers should be avoided as it produces unpredictable results.
2. Rd, RdHi and RdLo should be distinct from Rm, and RdHi and RdLo should not be the same register.
3. Early ARM processors only supported the 32-bit multiply instructions (MUL and MLA). The 64-bit multiplies are available only on ARM7 versions with an 'M' in their name (ARM7DM, ARM7TM, and so on) and subsequent processors.

5.9 | Count Leading Zeros (CLZ – architecture v5T only)

This instruction is only available on ARM processors that support architecture v5T. It is useful for renormalizing numbers, and performs its functions far more efficiently than can be achieved using other ARM instructions.

5.9.1 | Binary Encoding

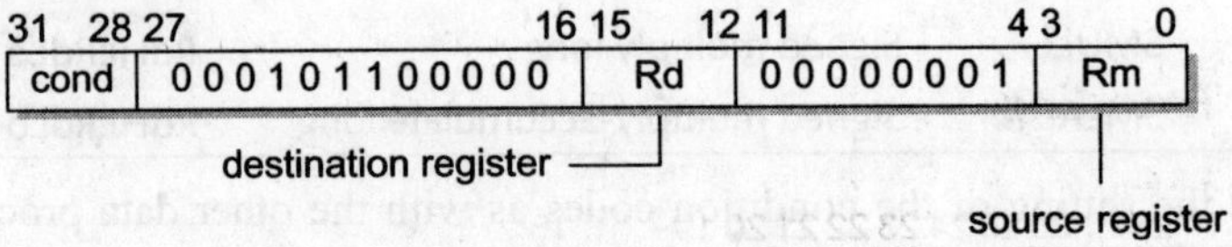

Figure 5.8 Count leading zeros instruction binary encoding

5.9.2 | Description

The instruction sets Rd to the number of zeros at more significant bit positions than the most significant 1 in Rm. If Rm is zero Rd will be set to 32.

5.9.3 | Assembler Format

```
CLZ{<cond>} Rd, Rm
```

EXAMPLE

```
MOV     r0, #&100
CLZ r1, r0          ; r1 := 23
```

Note

1. Only processors that implement ARM architecture v5T support the CLZ instruction (see Section 5.23).

5.10 | Single Word and Unsigned Byte Data Transfer Instructions

These instructions are the most flexible way to transfer single bytes or words of data between ARM's registers and memory. Transferring large blocks of data is usually better done using the multiple register transfer instructions, and recent ARM processors also support instructions for transferring half-words and signed bytes.

Provided that a register has been initialized to point somewhere near (usually within 4 Kbytes of) the required memory address, these instructions provide an efficient load and store mechanism with a relatively rich set of addressing modes which includes immediate and register offsets, auto-indexing and PC-relative.

5.10.1 | Description

These instructions construct an address starting from a base register (Rn), then adding (U = 1) or subtracting (U = 0) an unsigned immediate or (possibly scaled) register offset. The base or computed address is used to load (L = 1) or store (L = 0) an unsigned byte (B = 1) or word (B = 0) quantity to or from a register (Rd), from or to memory. When a byte is loaded into a register it is zero extended to 32 bits. When a byte is stored into memory, the bottom eight bits of the register are stored into the addressed location.

A pre-indexed (P = 1) addressing mode uses the computed address for the load or store operation, and then, when write-back is requested (W = 1), updates the base register to the computed value.

5.10.2 | Binary Encoding

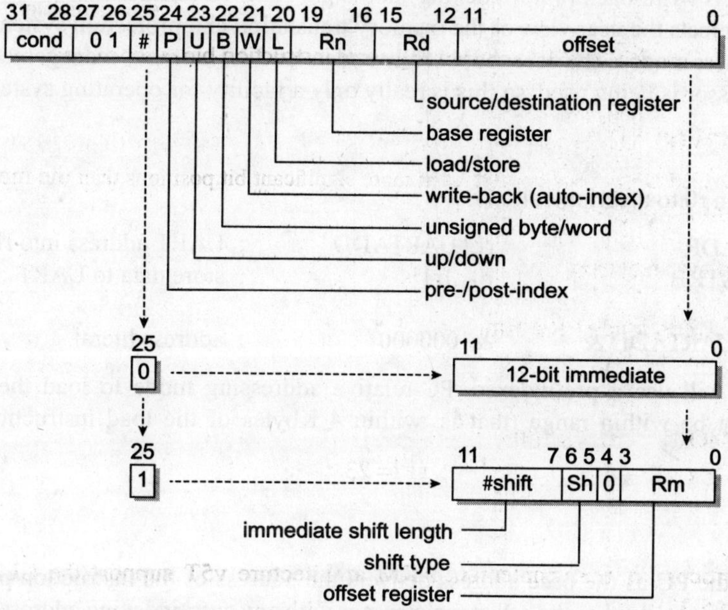

Figure 5.9 Single word and unsigned byte data transfer instruction binary encoding

A post-indexed (P = 0) addressing mode uses the unmodified base register for the transfer and then updates the base register to the computed address irrespective of the W bit (since the offset has no significance other than as a base register modifier, and can always be set to immediate zero if no change is desired). Since the W bit is unused in this case, it has an alternative function which is only relevant in code which is not running in user mode: setting W = 1 causes the processor to request a user mode access to memory, allowing the operating system to adopt a user view of the memory translation and protection scheme.

5.10.3 | Assembler Format

The pre-indexed form of the instruction:

LDR | STR{<cond>}{B} Rd, [Rn, <offset>]{!}

The post-indexed form:

```
LDR | STR{<cond>}{B}{T} Rd, [Rn], <offset>
```

A useful PC-relative form that leaves the assembler to do all the work:

```
LDR | STR{<cond>}{B} Rd, LABEL
```

LDR is 'load register', STR is 'store register'; the optional 'B' selects an unsigned byte transfer, the default is word; <offset> may be #+/–<12-bit immediate> or + /–Rm {, shift} where the shift specifier is the same as for data processing instructions except that register specified shift amounts are not available; ! selects write-back (auto-indexing) in the pre-indexed form.

The T flag selects the user view of the memory translation and protection system and should only be used in non-user modes. The user should fully understand the memory management environment in which the processor is being used, so this is really only a facility for operating system experts.

EXAMPLES

To store a byte in r0 to a peripheral:

```
        LDR         rl, UARTADD     ; UART address into rl
        STRB        r0, [r1]        ; store data to UART
        ..
        UARTADD &   &1000000        ; address literal
```

The assembler will use a pre-indexed, PC-relative addressing mode to load the address into r1. The literal must be within range (that is, within 4 Kbytes of the load instruction) for this to be possible.

Notes

1. Using the PC as the base address delivers the address of the instruction plus eight bytes; it should not be used as the offset register, nor with any auto-indexing addressing mode (including any post-indexed mode).
2. Loading a word into the PC causes a branch to the loaded address and is a recognized way of implementing jump tables. Loading a byte into the PC should be avoided.
3. Storing the PC to memory gives different results on different implementations of the processor and should therefore be avoided if possible.
4. In general Rd, Rn and Rm should be distinct registers, though loading into the base register (Rd = Rn) is acceptable provided auto-indexing is not used in the same instruction.
5. When a word is loaded from a non-word-aligned address the loaded data is the word-aligned word containing the addressed byte, rotated so that the addressed byte is in the least significant byte of the destination register. Some ARM systems may raise an exception under these circumstances (controlled by the A flag in bit 1 of CP15 register 1, described in Section 11.2 on page 252).
6. When a word is stored to a non-word-aligned address the bottom two bits of the address are ignored and the word is stored as though they had been zero. Some ARM systems may raise an exception under these circumstances (again controlled by the A flag in CP15 register 1).

5.11 | Half-word and Signed Byte Data Transfer Instructions

These instructions are not supported by some early ARM processors. As a result of their late addition to the architecture they are somewhat 'shoe-horned' into the instruction space as indicated by the split immediate field.

The addressing modes available with these instructions are a subset of those available with the unsigned byte and word forms.

5.11.1 | Binary Encoding

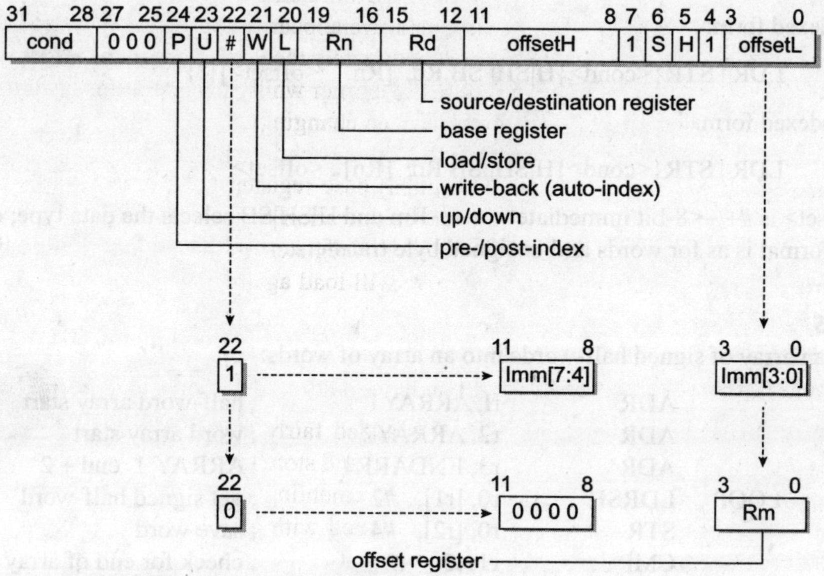

Figure 5.10 Half-word and signed byte data transfer instruction binary encoding

5.11.2 | Description

These instructions are very similar to the word and unsigned byte forms described in the previous section, but here the immediate offset is limited to eight bits and the scaled register offset is no longer available.

Table 5.6 Data type encoding

S	H	Data type
1	0	Signed byte
0	1	Unsigned half-word
1	1	Signed half-word

The S and H bits define the type of the operand to be transferred as listed in Table 5.6. Note that the fourth combination of these bits, corresponding to an unsigned byte type, is not available in this format. The format described in the previous section should be used instead. Since there is no difference between storing signed and unsigned data, the only relevant forms of this instruction format are;

- Load signed byte, signed half-word or unsigned half-word.
- Store half-word.

An unsigned value is zero-extended to 32 bits when loaded; a signed value is extended to 32 bits by replicating the most significant bit of the data.

5.11.3 | Assembler Formats

The pre-indexed form:

```
LDR | STR{<cond>}H|SH| SB Rd, [Rn, <offset>]{!}
```

The post-indexed form:

```
LDR | STR{<cond>}H|SH| SB Rd, [Rn] , <offset>
```

where <offset> is #+/–<8-bit immediate> or +/–Rm and H|SH|SB selects the data type; otherwise the assembler format is as for words and unsigned byte transfers.

EXAMPLES

To expand an array of signed half-words into an array of words:

```
        ADR     rl, ARRAY1      ; half-word array start
        ADR     r2, ARRAY2      ; word array start
        ADR     r3, ENDARR1     ; ARRAY 1 end + 2
LOOP    LDRSH   r0, [r1], #2    ; get signed half-word
        STR     r0, [r2], #4    ; save word
        CMP     r1, r3          ; check for end of array
        BLT     LOOP            ; if not finished, loop
```

Notes

1. Similar limitations to those on the word and unsigned byte transfers described in the previous section apply on the use of r15 and the register operands.
2. All half-word transfers should use half-word aligned addresses.

5.12 | Multiple Register Transfer Instructions

The ARM multiple register transfer instructions allow any subset (or all) of the 16 registers visible in the current operating mode to be loaded from or stored to memory. A form of the instruction also allows the operating system to load or store the user-mode registers to save or restore the user process state, and another form allows the CPSR to be restored from the SPSR as part of a return from an exception handler.

These instructions are used on procedure entry and return to save and restore workspace registers and are useful for high-bandwidth memory block copy routines.

5.12.1 | Binary Encoding

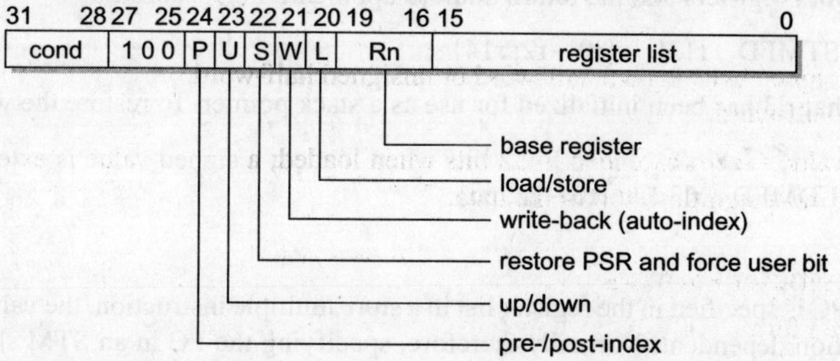

Figure 5.11 Multiple register data transfer instruction binary encoding

5.12.2 | Description

The register list in the bottom 16 bits of the instruction includes a bit for each visible register, with bit 0 controlling whether or not r0 is transferred, bit 1 controls r1, and so on up to bit 15 which controls the transfer of the PC.

The registers are loaded from or stored to a contiguous block of memory words defined by the base register and the addressing mode. The base address will be incremented (U = 1) or decremented (U = 0) before (P = 1) or after (P = 0) each word transfer. Auto-indexing is supported; if W = 1 the base register will be increased (U = 1) or decreased (U = 0) by the number of bytes transferred when the instruction completes.

Special forms of the instruction allow it to be used to restore the CPSR: if the PC is in the register list of a load multiple and the S bit is set, the SPSR of the current mode will be copied into the CPSR, giving an atomic return and restore state instruction. This form should not be used in user mode code since there is no SPSR in user mode.

If the PC is not in the register list and the S bit is set, both load and store multiple instructions executed in non-user modes will transfer the user mode registers (while using the current mode base register). This allows an operating system to save and restore user process state.

5.12.3 | Assembler Format

The normal form of the instruction is:

LDM | STM{<cond>}<add mode> Rn{!}, <registers>

where <add mode> specifies one of the addressing modes detailed in Table 3.1 on page 53. The instruction bits correspond closely to the mechanistic view described in this table, with 'increment' corresponding to U = 1 and 'before' corresponding to P = 1. '!' specifies auto-indexing (W = 1), and <registers> is a list of registers and register ranges enclosed in curly brackets, for example: {r0, r3 – r7, pc}.

In a non-user mode, the CPSR may be restored by:

LDM{<cond>}<add mode> Rn{!}, <registers + pc>^

The register list must contain the PC. In a non-user mode, the user registers may be saved or restored by:

LDM | STM{<cond>}<add mode> Rn, <registers – pc>^

Here the register list must not contain the PC and write-back is not allowed.

EXAMPLES

To save three work registers and the return address upon entering a subroutine:

STMFD r13!, {r0 – r2, r14}

This assumes that r13 has been initialized for use as a stack pointer. To restore the work registers and return:

LDMFD r13 !, {r0 – r2, pc}

Notes

1. If the PC is specified in the register list in a store multiple instruction, the value saved is implementation dependent. Normally therefore, specifying the PC in an STM should be avoided. (Loading the PC has the expected result and is a standard way of returning from a procedure.)
2. The base register may be specified in the transfer list of either a load or store multiple, but write-back should not be specified in the same instruction since the result of doing so is unpredictable.
3. If the base register contains an address that is not word-aligned, the bottom two bits will be ignored. Some ARM systems may generate an exception.
4. In architecture v5T only, the bottom bit of a loaded PC updates the Thumb bit.

5.13 | Swap Memory and Register Instructions (SWP)

Swap instructions combine a load and a store of a word or an unsigned byte in a single instruction. Normally the two transfers are combined into an atomic memory operation that cannot be split by an external memory access (for instance from a DMA controller), and therefore the instruction can be used as the basis of a semaphore mechanism to give mutually exclusive access to data structures that are shared between multiple processes, processors, or a processor and a DMA controller. These instructions are little used outside their role in the construction of semaphores.

5.13.1 | Binary Encoding

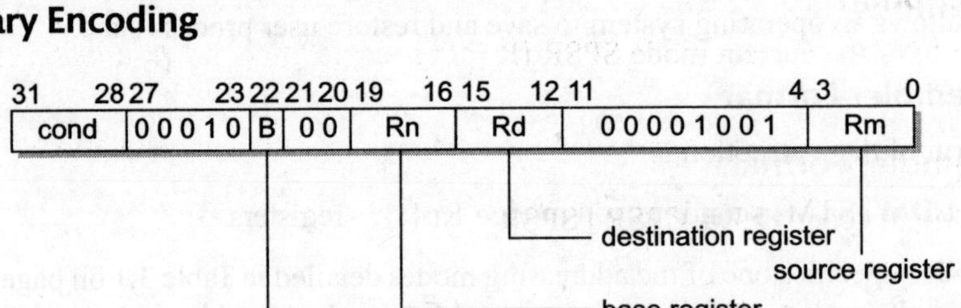

Figure 5.12 Swap memory and register instruction binary encoding

5.13.2 | Description

The instruction loads the word (B = 0) or unsigned byte (B = 1) at the memory location addressed by Rn into Rd, and stores the same data type from Rm into the same memory location. Rd and Rm may be the same register (but should both be distinct from Rn), in which case the register and memory values are exchanged. The ARM executes separate memory read and then memory write cycles, but asserts a 'lock' signal to indicate to the memory system that the two cycles should not be separated.

5.13.3 | Assembler Format

SWP{<cond>} {B} Rd, Rm, [Rn]

EXAMPLE

```
ADR     r0, SEMAPHORE
SWPB    r1, r1, [r0]                    ; exchange byte
```

Notes

1. The PC should not be used as any of the registers in this instruction.
2. The base register (Rn) should not be the same as either the source (Rm) or the destination (Rd) register.

5.14 | Status Register to General Register Transfer Instructions

When it is necessary to save or modify the contents of the CPSR or the SPSR of the current mode, those contents must first be transferred into a general register, the selected bits modified and then the value returned to the status register. These instructions perform the first step in this sequence.

5.14.1 | Binary Encoding

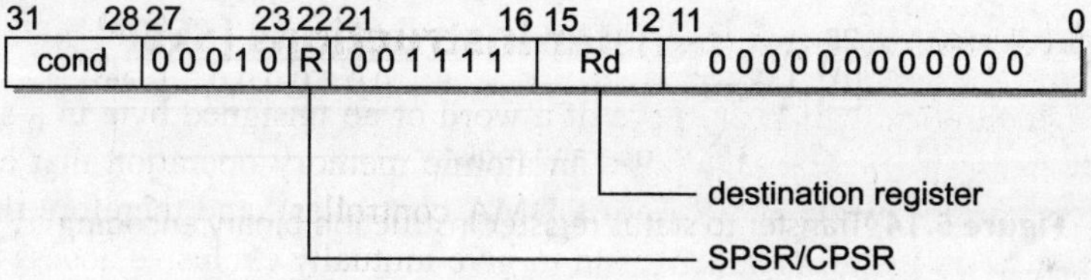

Figure 5.13 Status register to general register transfer instruction binary encoding

5.14.2 | Description

The CPSR (R = 0) or the current mode SPSR (R = 1) is copied into the destination register (Rd). All 32 bits are copied.

5.14.3 | Assembler Format

MRS{<cond>} Rd, CPSR | SPSR

EXAMPLES

```
MRS     r0, CPSR        ; move the CPSR to r0
MRS     r3, SPSR        ; move the SPSR to r3
```

Notes

1. The SPSR form should not be used in user or system mode since there is no accessible SPSR in those modes.
2. When modifying the CPSR or SPSR care should be taken to preserve the values of all the unused bits; this will maximize the probability of compatibility with future uses of those bits. This is best achieved by moving the status register to a general register (using these instructions), modifying only the necessary bits and then moving the result back to the status register.

5.15 | General Register to Status Register Transfer Instructions

When it is necessary to save or modify the contents of the CPSR or the SPSR of the current mode, those contents must first be transferred into a general register, the selected bits modified and then the value returned to the status register. These instructions perform the last step in this sequence.

5.15.1 | Binary Encoding

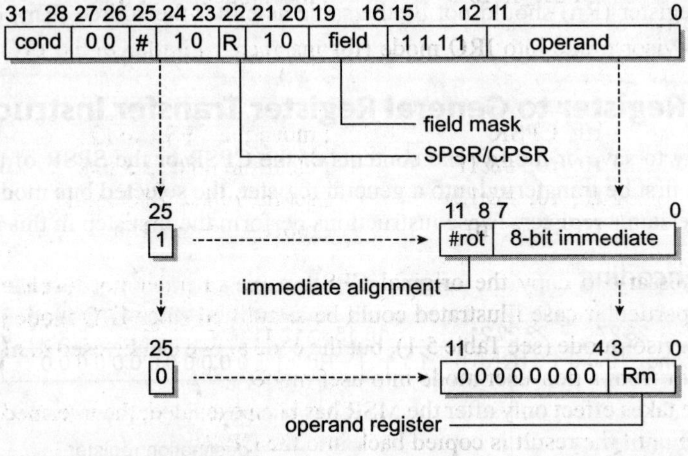

Figure 5.14 Transfer to status register instruction binary encoding

5.15.2 | Description

The operand, which may be a register (Rm) or a rotated 8-bit immediate (specified in the same way as the immediate form of operand2 in the data processing instructions), is moved under a field mask to the CPSR (R = 0) or current mode SPSR (R = 1).

The field mask controls the update of the four byte fields within the PSR register. Instruction bit 16 determines whether PSR[7:0] is updated, bit 17 controls PSR[15:8], bit 18 controls PSR[23:16] and bit 19 controls PSR[31:24].

When an immediate operand is used only the flags (PSR[31:24]) may be selected for update. (These are the only bits that may be updated by user-mode code.)

5.15.3 | Assembler Format

MSR{<cond>} CPSR_f | SPSR_f, #<32-bit immediate>
MSR{<cond>} CPSR_<field> | SPSR_<field>, Rm

where <field> is one of:

- c – the control field – PSR[7:0].
- x – the extension field – PSR[15:8] (unused on current ARMs).
- s – the status field – PSR[23:16] (unused on current ARMs).
- f – the flags field – PSR[31:24].

EXAMPLES

To set the N, Z, C and V flags:

```
MSR  CPSR_f,  #&f0000000; set all the flags
```

To set just the C flag, preserving N, Z and V:

```
MRS     r0, CPSR              ; move the CPSR to r0
ORR     r0, r0, #&20000000    ; set bit 29 of r0
MSR     CPSR_f, r0            ; move back to CPSR
```

To switch from supervisor mode into IRQ mode (for instance, to initialize the IRQ stack pointer at start up):

```
MRS     r0,  CPSR             ; move the CPSR to r0
BIC     r0,  r0,  #&1f        ; clear the bottom 5 bits
ORR     r0,  r0,  #&12        ; set the bits to IRQ mode
MSR     CPSR_c,  r0           ; move back to CPSR
```

In this case it is necessary to copy the original CPSR value in order not to change the interrupt enable settings. The particular case illustrated could be simplified since IRQ mode just requires one bit cleared from supervisor mode (see Table 5.1), but the code above can be used to move between any two non-user modes or from a non-user mode into user mode.

The mode change takes effect only after the MSR has been executed; the intermediate working has no effect on the mode until the result is copied back into the CPSR.

Notes

1. Attempts to modify any of CPSR[23:0] whilst in user mode have no effect.
2. Attempts to access the SPSR whilst in user or system mode should be avoided, since they have unpredictable results as there is no SPSR in these modes.

5.16 | Coprocessor Instructions

The ARM architecture supports a general mechanism for extending the instruction set through the addition of coprocessors. The most common use of a coprocessor is the system coprocessor used to control on-chip functions such as the cache and memory management unit on the ARM720. A floating-point ARM coprocessor has also been developed, and application-specific coprocessors are a possibility.

5.16.1 | Coprocessor Registers

ARM coprocessors have their own private register sets and their state is controlled by instructions that mirror the instructions that control ARM registers.

The ARM has sole responsibility for control flow, so the coprocessor instructions are concerned with data processing and data transfer. Following RISC load-store architectural principles, these categories are cleanly separated. The instruction formats reflect this:

5.16.2 | Coprocessor Data Operations

- Coprocessor data operations are completely internal to the coprocessor and cause a state change in the coprocessor registers. An example would be floating-point addition, where two registers in the floating-point coprocessor are added together and the result placed into a third register.

5.16.3 | Coprocessor Data Transfers

- Coprocessor data transfer instructions load or store the values in coprocessor registers from or to memory. Since coprocessors may support their own data types, the number of words transferred for each register is coprocessor dependent. The ARM generates the memory address, but the coprocessor controls the number of words transferred. A coprocessor may perform some type conversion as part of the transfer (for instance the floating-point coprocessor converts all loaded values into its 80-bit internal representation).

5.16.4 | Coprocessor Register Transfers

- In addition to the above, it is sometimes useful to move values between ARM and coprocessor registers. Again taking the floating-point coprocessor as an illustration, a 'FIX' instruction takes a floating-point value from a coprocessor register, converts it to an integer, and moves the integer into an ARM register. A floating-point comparison produces a result which is often needed to affect control flow, so the result of the compare must be moved to the ARM CPSR. Taken together these instructions support a generalized extension of the ARM instruction set to support application-specific datatypes and functions.

5.17 | Coprocessor Data Operations

These instructions are used to control internal operations on data in coprocessor registers. The standard format follows the 3-address form of ARM's integer data processing instructions, but other interpretations of all the coprocessor fields are possible.

5.17.1 | Binary Encoding

31 28	27 24	23 20	19 16	15 12	11 8	7 5	4	3 0
cond	1 1 1 0	Cop1	CRn	CRd	CP#	Cop2	0	CRm

Figure 5.15 Coprocessor data processing instruction binary encoding

5.17.2 | Description

The ARM offers this instruction to any coprocessors that may be present. If it is accepted by one of them the ARM proceeds to the next instruction; if it is not accepted the ARM takes the undefined instruction trap (which may be used to implement a software emulation of the missing coprocessor).

Normally the coprocessor identified with the coprocessor number CP# will accept the instruction and perform the operation defined by the Cop1 and Cop2 fields, using CRn and CRm as the source operands and placing the result in CRd.

5.17.3 | Assembler Format

```
CDP{<cond>} <CP#>, <Cop1>, CRd, CRn, CRm{, <Cop2>}
```

EXAMPLES

```
CDP      p2, 3, C0, C1, C2
CDPEQ    p3, 6, C1, C5, C7, 4
```

Note

1. The interpretation of the Cop1, CRn, CRd, Cop2 and CRm fields is coprocessor-dependent. The above interpretation is recommended and will maximize compatibility with ARM development tools.

5.18 | Coprocessor Data Transfers

The coprocessor data transfer instructions are similar to the immediate offset forms of the word and unsigned byte data transfer instructions described earlier, but with the offset limited to eight bits rather than 12.

Auto-indexed forms are available, with pre- and post-indexed addressing.

5.18.1 | Binary encoding

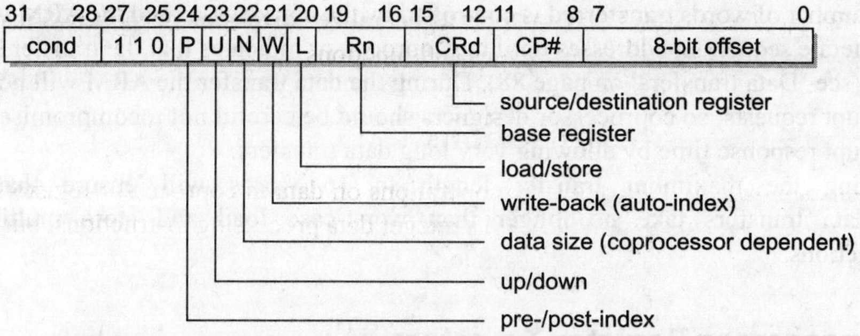

Figure 5.16 Coprocessor data transfer instruction binary encoding

5.18.2 | Description

The instruction is offered to any coprocessors which may be present; if none accepts it ARM takes the undefined instruction trap and may use software to emulate the coprocessor. Normally the coprocessor with coprocessor number CP#, if present, will accept the instruction.

The address calculation takes place within the ARM, using an ARM base register (Rn) and an 8-bit immediate offset which is scaled to a word offset by shifting it left two bit positions. The addressing mode and auto-indexing are controlled in the same way as the ARM word and unsigned byte transfer instructions. This defines the first transfer address; subsequent words are transferred to or from incrementing word addresses.

The data is supplied by or received into a coprocessor register (CRd), with the number of words transferred being controlled by the coprocessor and the N bit selecting one of two possible lengths.

5.18.3 | Assembler Format

The pre-indexed form:

```
LDC | STC{<cond>} {L} <CP#>,   CRd,   [Rn,  <offset>]{!}
```

The post-indexed form:

```
LDC | STC{<cond>} {L} <CP#>,   CRd,   [Rn], <offset>
```

In both cases LDC selects a load from memory into the coprocessor register, STC selects a store from the coprocessor register into memory. The L flag, if present, selects the long data type (N = 1). <offset> is # + /–<8-bit immediate>.

EXAMPLES

```
LDC       p6,  CO, [rl]
STCEQL    p5,  C1, [r0], #4
```

Notes

1. The interpretation of the N and CRd fields is coprocessor-dependent. The use shown above is recommended and will maximize compatibility with ARM development tools.
2. If the address is not word-aligned the two least significant bits will be ignored, though some ARM systems may raise an exception.
3. The number of words transferred is controlled by the coprocessor and the ARM will continue to generate sequential addresses until the coprocessor indicates that the transfer should complete (see 'Data transfers' on page 88). During the data transfer the ARM will not respond to interrupt requests, so coprocessor designers should be careful not tocompromise the system interrupt response time by allowing very long data transfers.
   Limiting the maximum transfer length to 16 words will ensure that coprocessor data transfers take no longer than worst-case load and store multiple register instructions.

5.19 | Coprocessor Register Transfers

These instructions allow an integer generated in a coprocessor to be transferred directly into a ARM register or the ARM condition code flags.

Typical uses are:

- A floating-point FIX operation which returns the integer to an ARM register;
- A floating-point comparison which returns the result of the comparison directly to the ARM condition code flags where it can determine the control flow;
- A FLOAT operation which takes an integer value from an ARM register and sends it to the coprocessor where it is converted to floating-point representation and placed in a coprocessor register.

The system control coprocessors used to control the cache and memory management functions on the more complex ARM CPUs (Central Processing Units) generally use these instructions to access and modify the on-chip control registers.

5.19.1 | Binary Encoding

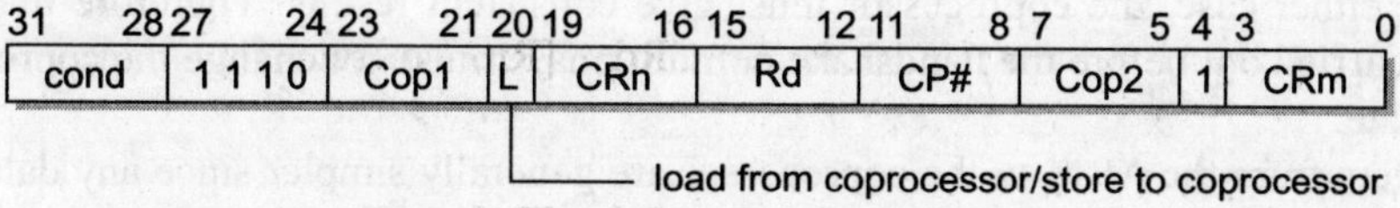

Figure 5.17 Coprocessor register transfer instruction binary encoding

5.19.2 | Description

The instruction is offered to any coprocessors present; normally the coprocessor with coprocessor number CP# will accept the instruction. If no coprocessor accepts the instruction ARM raises an undefined instruction trap.

If a coprocessor accepts a load from coprocessor instruction, it will normally perform an operation defined by Cop1 and Cop2 on source operands CRn and CRm and return a 32-bit integer result to the ARM which will place it in Rd.

If a coprocessor accepts a store to coprocessor instruction, it will accept a 32-bit integer from the ARM register Rd and do something with it.

If the PC is specified as the destination register Rd in a load from coprocessor instruction, the top four bits of the 32-bit integer generated by the coprocessor are placed into the N, Z, C and V flags in the CPSR.

5.19.3 | Assembler Format

Move to ARM register from coprocessor:

MRC{<cond>} <CP#>, <Cop1>, Rd, CRn, CRm{,<Cop2>}

Move to coprocessor from ARM register:

MCR{<cond>} <CP#>, <Cop1>, Rd, CRn, CRm{, <Cop2>}

EXAMPLES

```
MCR      p14, 3,  r0, C1, C2
MRCCS    p2, 4,   r3, C3, C4, 6
```

Notes

1. The Cop1, CRn, Cop2 and CRm fields are interpreted by the coprocessor. The above interpretations are recommended to maximize compatibility with ARM development tools.
2. Where the coprocessor must perform some internal work to prepare a 32-bit value for transfer to the ARM (for example, a floating-point FIX operation has to convert the floating-point value into its equivalent fixed-point value), this must take place before the coprocessor commits to the transfer. Therefore it will often be necessary for the coprocessor hand-shake to 'busy-wait' while the data is prepared.

   The ARM can take interrupts during the busy-wait period and if it does get interrupted it will break off from the handshake to service the interrupt. It will probably retry the coprocessor instruction when it returns from the interrupt service routine, but it may not; the interrupt may cause a task switch, for example.

In either case, the coprocessor must give consistent results. Therefore the preparation work carried out before the handshake commit phase must not change the coprocessor's visible state.

3. Transfers from the ARM to the coprocessor are generally simpler since any data conversion work can take place in the coprocessor after the transfer has completed.

5.20 | Breakpoint Instruction (BKPT – Architecture v5T Only)

Breakpoint instructions are used for software debugging purposes; they cause the processor to break from normal instruction execution and enter appropriate debugging procedures.

5.20.1 | Binary Encoding

31 28	27 20	19 16	15 12	11 8	7 4	3 0
1110	00010010	xxxx	xxxx	xxxx	0111	xxxx

Figure 5.18 Breakpoint instruction binary encoding

5.20.2 | Description

This instruction causes the processor to take a prefetch abort when the debug hardware unit is configured appropriately.

5.20.3 | Assembler Format

BRK

EXAMPLE

BRK ; !

Notes

1. Only processors that implement ARM architecture v5T support the BKPT instruction (see Section 5.23).
2. BKPT instructions are unconditional – the condition field must contain the 'ALWAYS' code.

5.21 | Unused Instruction Space

Not all of the 2^{32} instruction bit encodings have been assigned meanings; the encodings that have not been used so far are available for future instruction set extensions.

The unused instruction encodings each fall into particular gaps left in the used encodings, and their likely future use can be inferred from where they lie.

5.21.1 | Unused Arithmetic Instructions

These instructions look very like the multiply instructions described in Section 5.8. This would be a likely encoding, for example, for an integer divide instruction.

31 28	27 22	21 20	19 16	15 12	11 8	7 4	3 0
cond	0 0 0 0 0 1	op	Rn	Rd	Rs	1 0 0 1	Rm

Figure 5.19 Arithmetic instruction extension space

5.21.2 | Unused Control Instructions

These instructions include the branch and exchange instructions described in Section 5.5 and the status register transfer instructions described in Sections 5.14 and 5.15. The gaps here could be used to encode other instructions that affect the processor operating mode.

31 28	27 23	22 21	20	19 16	15 12	11 8	7	6 5	4	3 0
cond	0 0 0 1 0	op1	0	Rn	Rd	Rs	op2		0	Rm
cond	0 0 0 1 0	op1	0	Rn	Rd	Rs	0	op2	1	Rm
cond	0 0 1 1 0	op1	0	Rn	Rd	#rot	8-bit immediate			

Figure 5.20 Control instruction extension space

5.21.3 | Unused Load/store Instructions

There are unused encodings in the areas occupied by the swap instructions described in Section 5.13 and the load and store half-word and signed byte instructions described in Section 5.11. These are likely to be used to support additional data transfer instructions, should these be required in the future.

31 28	27 25	24	23	22	21	20	19 16	15 12	11 8	7	6 5	4	3 0
cond	0 0 0	P	U	B	W	L	Rn	Rd	Rs	1	op1	1	Rm

Figure 5.21 Data transfer instruction extension space

5.21.4 | Unused Coprocessor Instructions

The following instruction format is similar to the coprocessor data transfer instruction described in Section 5.18, and is likely to be used to support any additional coprocessor instructions that may be required:

31 28	27 24	23 22	21	20	19 16	15 12	11 8	7 0
cond	1 1 0 0	op	0	X	Rn	CRd	CP#	offset

Figure 5.22 Coprocessor instruction extension space

5.21.5 | Undefined Instruction Space

The largest area of undefined instructions looks like the word and unsigned byte data transfer instruction described in Section 5.10. However the future options on this space are being kept completely open.

5.21.6 | Behaviour of Unused Instructions

All current ARM processors will take the undefined instruction trap if an attempt is made to execute an instruction that matches the encoding shown in Figure 5.23, in the undefined instruction space.

31 28	27 25	24 5	4	3 0
cond	0 1 1	XXXXXXXXXXXXXXXXXXXX	1	XXXX

Figure 5.23 Undefined instruction space

The latest ARM processors should take the undefined instruction trap if any unused opcode is executed, but previous versions (including ARM6 and ARM7) will behave unpredictably. Therefore these instructions should be avoided!

5.22 | Memory Faults

ARM processors allow the memory system (or, more usually, the memory management unit) to fault on any memory access. What this means is that instead of returning the requested value from memory, the memory system returns a signal that indicates that the memory access has failed to complete correctly. The processor will then enter an exception handler and the system software will attempt to recover from the problem. The most common sources of a memory fault in a general-purpose machine are:

5.22.1 | Page Absent

- The addressed memory location has been paged out to disk.

In a virtual memory system infrequently used pages are held on disk. An attempt to access instructions or data on such a page will fail, causing the MMU to abort the access. The system software must identify the cause of the abort, fetch the required page into memory from disk, change the translation tables in the MMU accordingly and retry the aborted access.

Since fetching a page from disk is a slow process, the operating system will often switch out the faulted process and schedule another task while the transfer takes place.

5.22.2 | Page Protected

- The addressed memory location is temporarily inaccessible.

When a page is loaded into memory, the operating system may initially make it read only. An attempt to write the page will fault, alerting the operating system to the fact that the page has been modified and must be saved when it is swapped out to disk again. (An unmodified page need not be written to disk again if the old copy is still there.)

Some operating systems will periodically make pages inaccessible in order to generate statistics about their use for the paging algorithm.

5.22.3 | Soft Memory Errors

- A soft error has been detected in the memory.

A large memory system has a not-insignificant error rate due to alpha particle radiation changing the state of a dynamic RAM storage cell. Where the memory system has simple error detection (such as a parity check) the fault is not recoverable so the faulting process must be terminated. Where the memory system has full error check and correct (ECC) hardware the processor will usually be unaware of the error, though a fault could still be generated in order that the operating system can accumulate statistics on the memory error rate. In the intermediate case, where the memory has a hardware error detector but relies on software error correction, the fault, correct and retry sequence is followed.

5.22.4 | Embedded Systems

In a typical small embedded ARM application, a hard disk is usually unavailable, and in any case paging to disk is usually incompatible with the real-time constraints that the system must meet. Furthermore the memory system is usually small (a few megabytes at most, comprising a handful of memory chips) so the soft error rate is negligible and error detection is rarely incorporated. Therefore many embedded systems will not use memory faults at all.

A typical use in an embedded system might be to store a library of routines in compressed form in ROM and to use the virtual memory technique to trap calls to individual routines, expanding them as required into RAM for execution. The benefit of storing them in compressed form is the reduction in the size and cost of the ROM; the penalty is the time taken for decompression.

An additional use in an embedded system might be to offer some protection for processes running under a real-time operating system.

5.22.5 | Memory Faults

The ARM handles memory faults detected during instruction fetches (*prefetch aborts*) and those detected during data transfers (*data aborts*) separately.

5.22.6 | Prefetch Aborts

If an instruction fetch faults, the memory system raises the abort signal (a dedicated input to the processor) and returns a meaningless instruction word. Internally ARM puts the meaningless instruction into the instruction pipeline along with the abort flag, and then continues with business as usual until the instruction enters the decode stage, whereupon the abort flag overrides the instruction and causes the decoder to generate an exception entry sequence using the prefetch abort vector.

If the aborted instruction does not get executed, for instance because it was fetched immediately after a branch instruction that was ultimately taken, then no exception is raised and the fault is ignored.

5.22.7 | Data Aborts

Memory faults which arise during an access to memory for a data value are far more complex to handle. The memory system need not differentiate the instruction and data cases; it simply raises the abort input when it sees an address that it can't handle. The processor has to work much harder in response to a data abort, however, since this is a problem with the instruction that is currently executing whereas a prefetch abort is a problem with an instruction that has not yet entered decode.

Since the objective, in some cases, is to retry the instruction when the cause of the fault has been resolved, the instruction should do its best to ensure that its state (that is, its register values) after an abort is unchanged from its state before it started executing. Failing that, it should at least ensure that enough state can be recovered so that after the instruction has been executed a second time its state is the same as it would have been had the instruction completed the first time.

5.22.8 | LDM Data Abort

To see just how hard this can get, consider a load multiple instruction with 16 registers in the register list using r0 as the base register. Initially the addresses are fine, so the loading begins. The first data value to arrive overwrites r0, then successive registers get written until the final address (destined for the PC) crosses a page boundary and faults. Most of the processor state has been lost. How can the processor recover?

The abort signal is just in time to prevent the PC from being overwritten, so at least we have an address for the instruction that caused the fault. But we appear to have lost the base register a long time back, so how can the instruction be retried? Fortunately the processor has kept a copy of the base register value (possibly after auto-indexing) in a dark corner while the instruction was proceeding, so the last act of the instruction, when it should have been changing the PC to the new value had the PC access not faulted, is instead to copy this preserved value back into the base register.

So we have preserved the PC and the (modified) base register, but we have overwritten several other registers in the meantime. The base register modification can be reversed by software, since we can inspect the instruction and determine the number of registers in the list and the addressing mode. The overwritten registers are exactly those that we will load again with the correct values when we retry the instruction, so all is well (just!).

5.22.9 | An Historical Note

The requirement to recover from data aborts was added fairly late in the development of the first ARM processor chip. Up to that point, the various load and store multiple addressing modes had been implemented starting from the base address and incrementing up or decrementing down memory according to the mode. The chip was therefore designed with an address incrementer/decrementer unit.

When it became clear that support for virtual memory was needed it was rapidly seen that the decrementing mode made abort recovery much harder, since the PC could be overwritten before the abort was signalled. Therefore the implementation was changed always to increment the address. The memory addresses used were the same, and the mapping of register to memory was unchanged (see Figure 3.2 on page 54); just the order of the transfer was changed to lowest address first, PC last.

This change was implemented too late to affect the layout of the address generating logic, so the first ARM silicon has an address incrementer/decrementer hard-wired always to increment. Needless to say, this redundancy was not carried forward to subsequent implementations.

5.22.10 | Abort Timing

The earlier a processor gets an indication of a fault from the memory system, the better placed it is to preserve state. The earlier a processor requires the fault signal, the harder the memory system is to design. There is therefore a tension between the architectural simplicity of the processor's fault handling and the engineering efficiency of the memory system.

This tension doesn't affect just the memory management unit. Where the processor has a cache memory, the cache design can also be affected by the abort timing.

Early ARM processors required the abort signal by the end of phase 1 of the clock cycle (see Figure 4.8 on page 75), before half-way through the memory access. A fully associative cache with a CAM-RAM (CAM is Content Addressable Memory) organization can be designed to generate its hit/miss signal from the CAM access only, in time either to confirm a satisfactory access or to halt the processor in phase 1. Once the processor is halted the MMU has time to control the generation of the abort signal. A set-associative cache, on the other hand will usually produce its hit/miss signal at the end of the cycle, too late to defer a miss to the MMU (which may generate an abort) without a significant performance loss. (The ARM710, which has a set-associative RAM-RAM cache, does not follow this rule, and the cache still generates its hit/miss signal and the MMU its protection information before the end of phase 1.)

In order to ease the constraints on the cache and MMU designs, later ARMs were redesigned to allow aborts to be flagged at the end of the cycle, with a similar timing to the read data. The compromise that had to be accepted was that now the processor state has changed further so there is more work for the abort recovery software to do.

Some ARM processors may be configured (by external hard-wiring or using the L bit, bit 6 of CP15 register 1, see Section 11.2 on page 252) to work with either early or late abort timing.

5.22.11 | ARM Data Aborts

The state of the ARM after a data abort depends on the particular processor and, with some processors, on the early/late abort configuration:

- In all cases the PC is preserved (so on data abort exception entry r14_abt contains the address of the faulting instruction plus eight bytes).
- The base register will either be unmodified, or will contain a value modified by auto-indexing (it will not be overwritten by a loaded value).
- Other load destination registers may have been overwritten, but the correct value will be loaded when the instruction is retried.

Because the base register may be modified by auto-indexing, certain (not very useful) auto-indexing modes should be avoided. For example:

```
LDR    r0, [r1], r1
```

This instruction uses r1 as the address for the load, then uses post-indexing to add r1 to itself, losing the top bit in the process. If, following a data abort, only the modified value of r1 is available, it is not possible to recover the original transfer address. In general, using the same register for the base and the index in an addressing mode should be avoided.

5.23 | ARM Architecture Variants

The ARM architecture has undergone a number of revisions in the course of its development. The various architecture versions are described below.

5.23.1 | Version 1

ARM architecture version 1 describes the first ARM processor, developed at Acorn Computers Limited between 1983 and 1985. These first ARM chips supported only 26-bit addressing and had no multiply or coprocessor support. Their only use in a product was in the ARM second processor attachments to the BBC microcomputer; these were made in very small numbers, but established the ARM as the first commercially exploited single-chip RISC microprocessor. They were also used internally within Acorn in prototypes of the Archimedes personal workstation.

5.23.2 | Version 2

The ARM2 chip was sold in volume in the Acorn Archimedes and A3000 products. It was still a 26-bit address machine, but included the 32-bit result multiply instructions and coprocessor support. ARM2 employs the architecture that ARM Limited now calls ARM architecture version 2.

5.23.3 | Version 2a

The ARM3 chip was the first ARM with an on-chip cache. The architecture was very similar to version 2, but added the atomic load and store (SWP) instruction and introduced the use of coprocessor 15 as the system control coprocessor to manage the cache.

5.23.4 | Version 3

The first ARM processor designed by ARM Limited following their establishment as a separate company in 1990 was the ARM6, sold as a macrocell, a stand-alone processor (the ARM60) and as an integrated CPU with an on-chip cache, MMU and write buffer (the ARM600, and the ARM610 used in the Apple Newton). The ARM6 introduced ARM architecture version 3, which had 32-bit addressing, separate CPSR and SPSRs, and added the undefined and abort modes to allow coprocessor emulation and virtual memory support in supervisor mode.

ARM architecture version 3 is backwards compatible with version 2a, allowing either hard-wired 26-bit operation or process-by-process mixed 26- and 32-bit operation.

5.23.5 | Version 3G

ARM architecture version 3G is version 3 without backwards compatibility to version 2a.

5.23.6 | Version 3M

ARM architecture version 3M introduces the signed and unsigned multiply and multiply-accumulate instructions that generate the full 64-bit result.

5.23.7 | Version 4

Version 4 of the architecture adds the signed and unsigned half-word and signed byte load and store instructions and reserves some of the SWI space for architecturally defined operations. The system mode (a privileged mode that uses the user registers) is introduced and several unused corners of the instruction space are trapped as undefined instructions.

At this stage those uses of r15 which yielded 'pc + 12' in earlier ARMs are declared to give unpredictable results (so architecture version 4 compliant implementations need not reproduce the 'pc + 12' behaviour). This is the first architecture version to have a full formal definition.

5.23.8 | Version 4T

The 16-bit Thumb compressed form of the instruction set is introduced in version 4T of the architecture.

5.23.9 | Version 5T

Version 5T of the ARM architecture has been introduced recently, and at the time of writing is supported only by ARM10 processors (and these will soon support v5TE). It is a superset of architecture version 4T, adding the BLX, CLZ and BRK instructions.

5.23.10 | Version 5TE

Version 5TE adds the signal processing instruction set extensions described in Section 8.9 to architecture version 5T.

5.23.11 | Summary

Table 5.7 summarizes the use of the ARM architecture versions by each core.

Table 5.7 Summary of ARM architectures

Core	Architecture
ARM1	v1
ARM2	v2
ARM2aS, ARM3	v2a
ARM6, ARM600, ARM610	v3
ARM7, ARM700, ARM710	v3
ARM7TDMI, ARM710T, ARM720T, ARM740T	v4T
StrongARM, ARM8, ARM810	v4
ARM9TDMI, ARM920T, ARM940T	v4T
ARM9E-S	v5TE
ARM10TDMI, ARM1020E	v5TE

5.24 | Example and Exercises

(See also Sections 3.4 and 3.5.)

EXAMPLE 5.1

Write a scalar product program which is significantly faster than that given in Section 5.8.

The original program takes ten cycles plus the (data dependent) multiply time for each pair of data values. Each data value costs three cycles to load and the branch costs three cycles per loop.

The load costs may be reduced by using multiple register loads and the branch cost by 'loop unrolling'. Combining these two techniques gives a program such as:

```
        MOV     r11, #20          ; initialize loop counter
        MOV     r10, #0           ; initialize total
LOOP    LDMIA   r8!, {r0–r3}      ; load 4 1st vector values..
        LDMIA   r9!, {r4–r7}      ; .. and 4 2nd vector values
        MLA     r10, r0, r4, r10  ; accumulate 1st product
        MLA     r10, r1, r5, r10  ; accumulate 2nd product
        MLA     r10, r2, r6, r10  ; accumulate 3rd product
        MLA     r10, r3, r7, r10  ; accumulate 4th product
        SUBS    r11, r11, #4      ; decrement loop count by 4
        BNE     LOOP              ; loop if not finished
```

Now the loop overhead is 16 cycles plus the multiply time for four pairs of data values, or four cycles for each pair.

Exercise 5.1.1

Write a program which arranges 10 numbers (which are in memory) in descending order.

The sorted array must not overwrite the unsorted one.

Exercise 5.1.2

Repeat the previous exercise using the technique demonstrated in the above example to improve the performance. Assume that both source and destination strings are word-aligned and the string is a multiple of 16 bytes long.

Exercise 5.1.3

Now assume that the source string is word-aligned but the destination string may have any byte alignment. The string is still a multiple of 16 bytes long. Write a program which handles 16 byte blocks at a time, using multiple register transfers for the bulk of the storing but byte stores for the end conditions.

6

Architectural Support for High-level Languages

SUMMARY OF CHAPTER CONTENTS

High-level languages allow a program to be expressed in terms of abstractions such as data types, structures, procedures, functions, and so on. Since the RISC approach represents a movement away from instruction sets that attempt to support these high-level concepts directly, we need to be satisfied that the more primitive RISC instruction set still offers building blocks that can be assembled to give the necessary support.

In this chapter we will look at the requirements that a high-level language imposes on an architecture and see how those requirements may be met. We will use C as the example high-level language (though some might debate its qualification for this role!) and the ARM instruction set as the architecture that the language is compiled onto.

In the course of this analysis, it will become apparent that a RISC architecture such as that of the ARM has a vanilla flavour and leaves a number of important decisions open for the compiler writer to take according to taste. Some of these decisions will affect the ease with which a program can be built up from routines generated from different source languages. Since this is an important issue, there is a defined *ARM Procedure Call Standard* that compiler writers should use to ensure the consistency of entry and exit conditions.

Another area that benefits from agreement across compilers is the support for floating-point operations, which use data types that are not defined in the ARM hardware instruction set.

6.1 | Abstraction in Software Design

We have already met a level of abstraction that is important to software design. The essence of an ARM processor is captured in the ARM instruction set which was described in Chapter 5. We shall see in Chapter 9 that there are many ways to implement the ARM architecture, but the whole point of an architecture is to ensure that the programmer need not be concerned with particular implementation details. If a program works correctly on one implementation it should work correctly on them all (with certain provisos).

6.1.1 | Assembly-level Abstraction

A programmer who writes at the assembly programming level works (almost) directly with the raw machine instruction set, expressing the program in terms of instructions, addresses, registers, bytes and words.

A good programmer, faced with a non-trivial task, will begin by determining higher levels of abstraction that simplify the program design; for instance a graphics program may do a lot of line drawing, so a subroutine that will draw a line given the end coordinates will be useful. The rest of the program can then work just in terms of these end coordinates.

Abstraction is important, then, at the assembly programming level, but all the responsibility for supporting the abstraction and expressing it in terms of the machine primitives rests with the programmer, who must therefore have a good understanding of those primitives and be prepared to return frequently to think at the level of the machine.

6.1.2 | High-level Languages

A high-level language allows the programmer to think in terms of abstractions that are above the machine level; indeed, the programmer may not even know on which machine the program will ultimately run. Parameters such as the number of registers vary from architecture to architecture, so clearly these must not be reflected in the design of the language.

The job of supporting the abstractions used in the high-level language on the target architecture falls upon the *compiler*. Compilers are themselves extremely complex pieces of software, and the efficiency of the code they produce depends to a considerable extent on the support that the target architecture offers them to do their job.

At one time, the conventional wisdom was that the best way to support a compiler was to raise the complexity of the instruction set to implement the high-level operations of the language directly. The introduction of the RISC philosophy reversed that approach, focusing instruction set design on flexible primitive operations from which the compiler can build its high-level operations.

This chapter describes the requirements of high-level languages and shows how they are met by the ARM architecture, which is based on this RISC philosophy.

6.2 | Data Types

It is possible, though not very convenient, to express any computer program in terms of the basic Boolean logic variables 'true' (1) and 'false' (0). We can see that this is possible, since at the gate level that is all that the hardware can handle.

The definition of the ARM instruction set already introduces an abstraction away from logic variables when it expresses the functions of the processor in terms of instructions, bytes, words, addresses, and so on. Each of these terms describes a collection of logic variables viewed in a particular way. Note, for example, that an instruction, a data word and an address are all 32 bits long and a 32-bit memory location which contains one of these is indistinguishable from one that contains another of a different type. The difference is not in the way the information is stored but in the way it is used. A computer data type can therefore be characterized by:

- the number of bits it requires;
- the ordering of those bits;
- the uses to which the group of bits is put.

Some data types, such as addresses and instructions, exist principally to serve the purposes of the computer, whereas others exist to represent information in a way that is accessible to human users. The most basic of the latter category, in the context of computation, is the number.

6.2.1 | Numbers

What started as a simple concept, presumably as a means of checking that no sheep had been stolen overnight, has evolved over the ages into a very complex mechanism capable of computing the behaviour of transistors a thousandth of a millimetre wide switching a hundred million times a second.

6.2.2 | Roman Numerals

Here is a number written by a human:

MCMXCV

6.2.3 | Decimal Numbers

The interpretation of this **Roman** numeral is complex; the value of a symbol depends on the symbol and its positional relationship to its neighbours. This way of writing a number has largely (but not entirely; see the page numbers in the front matter of this book) been replaced by the **decimal** scheme where the same number appears as:

1995

Here we understand that the right-hand digit represents the number of units, the digit to its left the number of tens, then hundreds, thousands, and so on. Each time we move left one place the value of the digit is increased by a factor of 10.

6.2.4 | Binary Coded Decimal

To represent such a number as a group of Boolean variables, the simplest thing appears to be to find a representation for each digit and then use four of these to represent the whole number. We need four Boolean variables to be able to represent each digit from 0 to 9 differently, so the first form of this number that could easily be handled by logic gates is:

0001 1001 1001 0101

This is the binary coded decimal scheme which is supported by some computers and is commonly used in pocket calculators.

6.2.5 | Binary Notation

Most computers, most of the time, abandon the human-oriented decimal scheme altogether in favour of a pure binary notation where the same number becomes:

11111001011

Here the right-hand digit represents units, the next one 2, then 4, and so on. Each time we move left one place the value of the digit doubles. Since a value of 2 in one column can be represented by a value of 1 in the next column left, we never need a digit to have any value other than 0 or 1, and hence each binary digit (**bit**) can be represented by a single Boolean variable.

6.2.6 | Hexadecimal Notation

Although machines use binary numbers extensively internally, a typical 32-bit binary number is fairly unmemorable, but rather than convert it to the familiar decimal form (which is quite hard work and error-prone), computer users often describe the number in **hexadecimal** (base 16) notation. This is easy because the binary number can be split into groups of four binary digits and each group replaced by a hexadecimal number. Because, in base 16, we need symbols for numbers from 0 to 15, the early letters of the alphabet have been pressed into service where the decimal symbols run out: we use 0 to 9 as themselves and A to F to represent 10 to 15. Our number becomes:

7CB

(At one time it was common to use octal, base 8, notation in a similar role. This avoids the need to use alphabetic characters, but groups of three bits are less convenient to work with than groups of four, so the use of octal has largely been abandoned.)

6.2.7 | Number Ranges

When writing on paper, we use the number of decimal digits that are required to represent the number we want to write. A computer usually reserves a fixed number of bits for a number, so if the number gets too big it cannot be represented. The ARM deals efficiently with 32-bit quantities, so the first data type that the architecture supports is the 32-bit (unsigned) integer, which has a value in the range:

$$0 \text{ to } 4\,294\,967\,295_{10} = 0 \text{ to } \mathrm{FFFFFFFF}_{16}$$

(The subscript indicates the number base, so the range above is expressed in decimal first and in hexadecimal second. Note how the hexadecimal value 'F' represents a binary number of all '1's.)

This looks like a large range, and indeed is adequate for most purposes, though the programmer must be aware of its limitations. Adding two unsigned numbers near the maximum value within the range will give the wrong answer, since the correct answer cannot be represented within 32 bits. The C flag in the program status register gives the only indication that something has gone wrong and the answer is not to be trusted.

If a large number is subtracted from a small number, the result will be negative and cannot be represented by an unsigned integer of any size.

6.2.8 | Signed Integers

In many cases it is useful to be able to represent negative numbers as well as positive ones. Here the ARM supports a 2's complement binary notation where the value of the top bit is made negative; in a 32-bit signed integer all the bits have the same value as they have in the unsigned case apart from bit 31, which has the value -2^{31} instead of $+2^{31}$. Now the range of numbers is:

$$-2\,147\,483\,648_{10} \text{ to } +2\,147\,483\,647_{10} = 80000000_{16} \text{ to } \mathrm{7FFFFFFF}_{16}$$

Note that the sign of the number is determined by bit 31 alone, and the positive integer values have exactly the same representation as their unsigned equivalents.

The ARM, in common with most processors, uses the 2's complement notation for signed integers because adding or subtracting them requires exactly the same Boolean logic functions as are needed for unsigned integers, so there is no need to have separate instructions (the exception being multiplication with a full 64-bit result; here ARM *does* have separate signed and unsigned instructions).

The 'architectural support' for signed integers is the V flag in the program status registers which has no use when the operands are unsigned but indicates an overflow (out of range) error when signed operands are combined. The source operands cannot be out of range since they are represented as 32-bit values, but when two numbers near the extremes of the range are added or subtracted, the result could fall outside the range; its 32-bit representation will be an in-range number of the wrong value and sign.

6.2.9 | Other Number Sizes

The natural representation of a number in the ARM is as a signed or unsigned 32-bit integer; indeed, internally to the processor that is all that there is. However, all ARM processors will perform unsigned 8-bit (byte) loads and stores, allowing small positive numbers to occupy a smaller space in memory than a 32-bit word, and all but the earliest versions of the processor also support signed byte and signed and unsigned 16-bit transfers, also principally to reduce the memory required to store small values.

Where a 32-bit integer is too small, larger numbers can be handled using multiple words and multiple registers. A 64-bit addition can be performed with two 32-bit additions, using the C flag in the status register to propagate the carry from the lower word to the higher word:

```
        ; 64-bit addition of [r1, r0] to [r3, r2]
        ADDS   r2, r2, r0        ; add low, save carry
        ADC    r3, r3, r1        ; add high with carry
```

6.2.10 | Real Numbers

So far we have just considered integers, or whole numbers. 'Real' numbers are used to represent fractions and transcendental values that are useful when dealing with physical quantities.

The representation of real numbers in computers is a big issue that is deferred to the next section. An ARM core has no support for real data types, though ARM Limited has defined a set of types and instructions that operate on them. These instructions are either executed on a floating-point coprocessor or emulated in software.

6.2.11 | Printable Characters

After the number, the next most basic data type is the printable character. To control a standard printer we need a way to represent all the normal characters such as the upper and lower case alphabet, decimal digits from 0 to 9, punctuation marks and a number of special characters such as £, $, %, and so on.

6.2.12 | ASCII

Counting all these different characters, the total rapidly approaches a hundred or so. Some time ago the binary representation of these characters was standardized in the 7-bit ASCII (American Standard for Computer Information Interchange) code, which includes these printable characters and a number of control codes whose names reflect the teletype origins of the code, such as 'carriage return', 'line feed', and 'bell'.

The normal way to store an ASCII character in a computer is to put the 7-bit binary code into an 8-bit byte. Many systems extend the code using, for example, the 8-bit ISO character set where the other 128 binary codes within the byte represent special characters (for instance, characters with

accents). The most flexible way to represent characters is the 16-bit 'Unicode' which incorporates many such 8-bit character sets within a single encoding.
'1995' encoded as 8-bit printable characters is:

$$00110001\ 00111001\ 00111001\ 00110101 = 31\ 39\ 39\ 35_{16}$$

6.2.13 | ARM Support for Characters

The support in the ARM architecture for handling characters is the unsigned byte load and store instructions; these have already been mentioned as being available to support small unsigned integers, but that role is rare compared with their frequency of use for transferring ASCII characters.

There is nothing in the ARM architecture that reflects the particular codes defined by ASCII; any other encoding is equally well supported provided it uses no more than eight bits. However, it would be perverse these days to choose a different code for characters without having a very good reason.

6.2.14 | Byte Ordering

The above ASCII example highlights an area of some potential difficulty. It is written to be read from left to right, but if it is read as a 32-bit word, the least significant byte is at the right. A character output routine might print characters at successive increasing byte addresses, in which case, with 'little-endian' addressing, it will print '5991'. We clearly need to be careful about the order of bytes within words in memory.

(ARMs can operate with either little- or big-endian addressing. See 'Memory organization' on page 92.)

6.2.15 | High-level Languages

A high-level language defines the data types that it needs in its specification, usually without reference to any particular architecture that it may run on. Sometimes the number of bits used to represent a particular data type is architecture-dependent in order to allow a machine to use its most efficient size.

6.2.16 | ANSI C Basic Data Types

The dialect of the 'C' language defined by the American National Standards Institute (ANSI), and therefore known as 'ANSI standard C' or simply 'ANSI C', defines the following basic data types:

- Signed and unsigned **characters** of at least eight bits.
- Signed and unsigned **short integers** of at least 16 bits.
- Signed and unsigned **integers** of at least 16 bits.
- Signed and unsigned **long integers** of at least 32 bits.
- **Floating-point, double** and **long double** floating-point numbers.
- **Enumerated** types.
- **Bitfields.**

The ARM C compiler adopts the minimum sizes for each of these types except the standard integer, where it uses 32-bit values since this is the most frequently used data type and the ARM supports 32-bit operations more efficiently than 16-bit operations.

Enumerated types (where variables have one value out of a specified set of possible values) are implemented as the smallest integer type with the necessary range of values. Bitfield types (sets of

Boolean variables) are implemented within integers; several may share one integer, with the first declared holding the lowest bit position, but may not straddle word boundaries.

6.2.17 | ANSI C Derived Data Types

In addition, the ANSI C standard defines derived data types:

- **Arrays** of several objects of the same type.
- **Functions** which return an object of a given type.
- **Structures** containing a sequence of objects of various types.
- **Pointers** (which are usually machine addresses) to objects of a given type.
- **Unions** which allow objects of different types to occupy the same space at different times.

ARM pointers are 32 bits long (the size of ARM native addresses) and resemble unsigned integers, though note that they obey different arithmetic rules.

The ARM C compiler aligns characters on byte boundaries (that is, at the next available address), short integers at even addresses and all other types on word boundaries. A structure always starts on a word boundary with the first-named component, then subsequent components are packed as closely as possible consistent with these alignment rules. (**Packed** structures violate the alignment rules; use of memory is discussed more extensively in Section 6.9.)

6.2.18 | ARM Architectural Support for C Data Types

We have seen above that the ARM integer core provides native support for signed and unsigned 32-bit integers and for unsigned bytes, covering the C integer (given the decision to implement these as 32-bit values), long integer and unsigned character types. Pointers are implemented as native ARM addresses and are therefore supported directly.

The ARM addressing modes provide reasonable support for arrays and structures: base plus scaled index addressing allows an array of objects of a size which is 2^n bytes to be scanned using a pointer to the start of the array and a loop variable as the index; base plus immediate offset addressing gives access to an object within a structure. However, additional address calculation instructions will be necessary for more complex accesses.

Current versions of the ARM include signed byte and signed and unsigned 16-bit loads and stores, providing some native support for short integer and signed character types.

Floating-point types are discussed in the next section, however here we can note that the basic ARM core offers little direct support for them. These types (and the instructions that manipulate them) are, in the absence of specific floating-point support hardware, handled by complex software emulation routines.

6.3 | Floating-point Data Types

Floating-point numbers attempt to represent real numbers with uniform accuracy. A generic way to represent a real number is in the form:

$$R = a \times b^n \qquad \text{Equation 13}$$

where n is chosen so that a falls within a defined range of values; b is usually implicit in the data type and is often equal to 2.

6.3.1 | IEEE 754

There are many complex issues to resolve with the handling of floating-point numbers in computers to ensure that the results are consistent when the same program is run on different machines. The consistency problem was greatly aided by the introduction in 1985 of the IEEE Standard for Binary Floating-Point Arithmetic (ANSI/IEEE Standard 754-1985, sometimes referred to simply as IEEE 754) which defines in considerable detail how floating-point numbers should be represented, the accuracy with which calculations should be performed, how errors should be detected and returned, and so on.

The most compact representation of a floating-point number defined by IEEE 754 is the 32-bit 'single precision' format:

6.3.2 | Single Precision

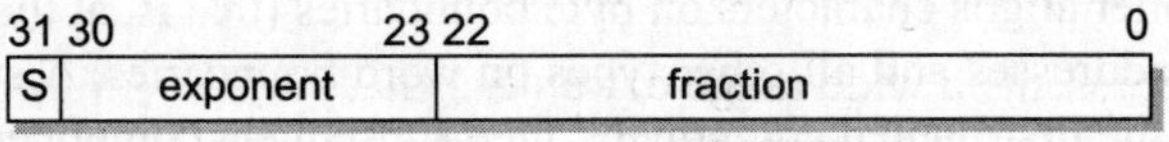

Figure 6.1 IEEE 754 single precision floating-point number format

The number is made up from a **sign bit** ('S'), an **exponent** which is an unsigned integer value with a 'bias' of +127 (for normalized numbers) and a **fractional** component. See Figure 6.1. A number of terms in the previous sentence may be unfamiliar. To explain them, let us look at how a number we recognize, '1995', is converted into this format.

We start from the binary representation of 1995, which has already been presented:

$$11111001011$$

This is a positive number, so the S bit will be zero.

6.3.3 | Normalized Numbers

The first step is to normalize the number, which means convert it into the form shown in Equation 13 where $1 \le a < 2$ and $b = 2$. Looking at the binary form of the number, a can be constrained within this range by inserting a 'binary point' (similar in interpretation to the more familiar decimal point) after the first '1'. The implicit position of the binary point in the binary integer representation is to the right of the right-most digit, so here we have to move it left ten places. Hence the normalized representation of 1995 is:

$$1995 = 1.1111001011 \times 2^{1010} \qquad \text{Equation 14}$$

where a and n are both in binary notation.

When any number is normalized, the bit in front of the binary point in a will be a '1' (otherwise the number is not normalized). Therefore there is no need to store this bit.

6.3.4 | Exponent Bias

Finally, since the format is required to represent very small numbers as well as very large ones, some numbers may require negative exponents in their normalized form. Rather than use a signed exponent, the standard specifies a 'bias'. This bias (+127 for single precision normalized numbers) is added to the exponent value. Hence 1995 is represented as shown in Figure 6.2.

Figure 6.2 IEEE 754 single precision representation of '1995'

The exponent is 127 + 10 = 137; the fraction is zero-extended to the right to fill the 23-bit field.

6.3.5 | Normalized Value

In general, the value of a 32-bit normalized number is given by:

$$\text{value (norm)} = (-1)^S \times 1.\ \text{fraction} \times 2^{(\text{exponent} - 127)} \qquad \text{Equation 15}$$

Although this format represents a wide range of values efficiently, it has one rather glaring problem: there is no way to represent zero. Therefore the IEEE 754 standard reserves numbers where the exponent is either zero or 255 to represent special values:

- Zero is represented by a zero exponent and fraction (but either sign value, so positive and negative zeros can be represented).
- Plus or minus infinity are represented by the maximum exponent value with a zero fraction and the appropriate sign bit.
- NaN (**Not a Number**) is indicated by the maximum exponent and a non-zero fraction; 'quiet' NaNs have a '1' in the most significant fraction bit position and 'signalling' NaNs have a '0' in that bit (but a '1' somewhere else, otherwise they look like infinity).
- **Denormalized** numbers, which are numbers that are just too small to normalize within this format, have a zero exponent, a non-zero fraction and a value given by:

$$\text{value (denorm)} = (-1)^S \times 0.\ \text{fraction} \times 2^{(-126)} \qquad \text{Equation 16}$$

The 'NaN' format is used to represent the results of invalid floating-point operations, such as taking the logarithm of a negative number, and prevents a series of operations from producing an apparently valid result when an intermediate error condition was not checked.

6.3.6 | Double Precision

For many purposes the accuracy offered by the single precision format is inadequate. Greater accuracy may be achieved by using the double precision format which uses 64 bits to store each floating-point value.

The interpretation is similar to that for single precision values, but now the exponent bias for normalized numbers is +1023 as shown in Figure 6.3.

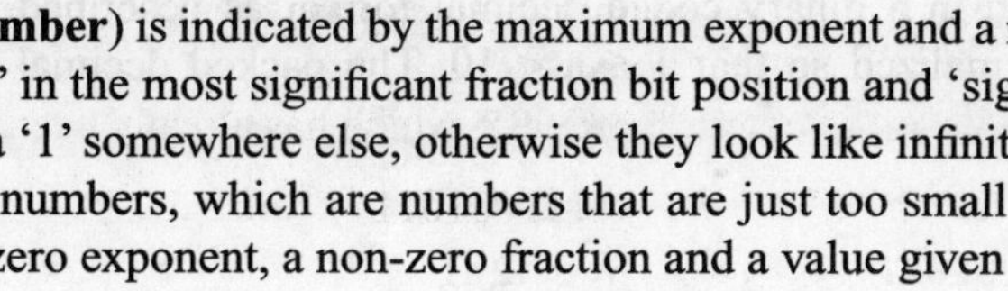

Figure 6.3 IEEE 754 double precision floating-point number format

6.3.7 | Double Extended Precision

Even greater accuracy is available from the double extended precision format, which uses 80 bits of information spread across three words. The exponent bias is 16383, and the J bit is the bit to the left of the binary point (and is a '1' for all normalized numbers). See Figure 6.4.

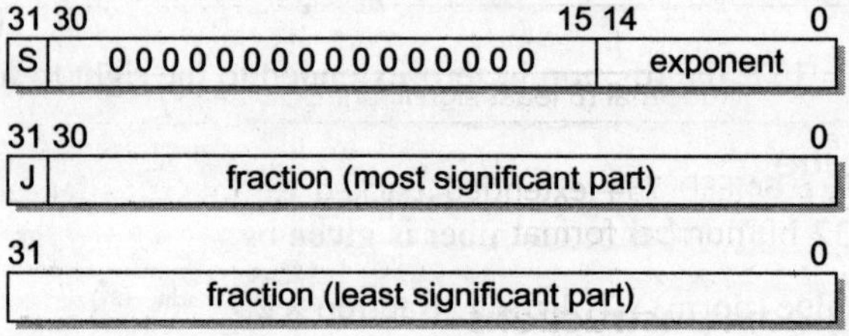

Figure 6.4 IEEE 754 double extended precision floating-point number format

6.3.8 | Packed Decimal

In addition to the binary floating-point representations detailed above, the IEEE 754 standard also specifies packed decimal formats. Referring back to Equation 13, in these packed formats *b* is 10 and *a* and *n* are stored in a binary coded decimal format as described in 'Binary coded decimal'. The number is normalized so that $1 \le a < 10$. The packed decimal format is shown as in Figure 6.5.

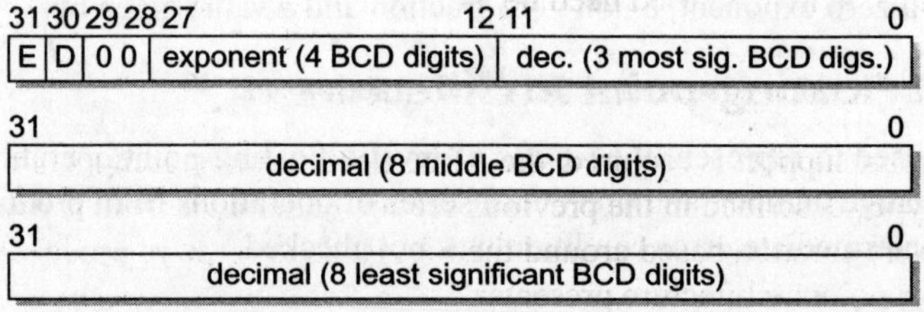

Figure 6.5 IEEE 754 packed decimal floating-point number format

The sign of the exponent is held in bit 31 of the first word ('E') and the sign of the decimal in bit 30 ('D'). The value of the number is:

$$\text{Value (packed)} = (-1)^{D} \times \text{decimal} \times 10^{((-1))^{E} \times \text{exponent})} \qquad \text{Equation 17}$$

6.3.9 | Extended Packed Decimal

The extended packed decimal format occupies four words to give higher precision. The value is still as given by Equation 17 above and the format is as shown in Figure 6.6.

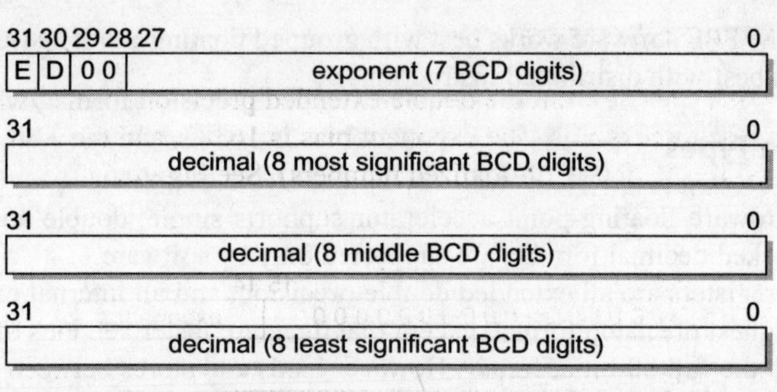

Figure 6.6 IEEE 754 extended packed decimal floating-point number format

6.3.10 | ARM Floating-point Instructions

Although there is no direct support for any of these floating-point data types in a standard ARM integer core, ARM Limited has defined a set of floating point instructions within the coprocessor instruction space. These instructions are normally implemented entirely in software through the undefined instruction trap (which collects any coprocessor instructions that are not accepted by a hardware coprocessor), but a subset may be handled in hardware by the FPA10 floating-point coprocessor.

6.3.11 | ARM Floating-point Library

As an alternative to the ARM floating-point instruction set (and the only option for Thumb code), ARM Limited also supplies a C floating-point library which supports IEEE single and double precision formats. The C compiler has a flag to select this route which produces code that is both faster (by avoiding the need to intercept, decode and emulate the floating-point instructions) and more compact (since only the functions which are used need be included in the image) than software emulation.

6.4 | The ARM Floating-point Architecture

Where full floating-point support is required, the ARM floating-point architecture provides extensive support for the data types described in the previous section either entirely in software or using a combined software/hardware solution based around the FPA10 floating-point accelerator.

The ARM floating-point architecture presents:

- An interpretation of the coprocessor instruction set when the coprocessor number is 1 or 2. (The floating-point system uses two logical coprocessor numbers.)
- Eight 80-bit floating-point registers in coprocessors 1 and 2 (the same physical registers appear in both logical coprocessors).
- A user-visible floating-point status register (FPSR) which controls various operating options and indicates error conditions.
- Optionally, a floating-point control register (FPCR) which is user-invisible and should be used only by the support software specific to the hardware accelerator.

Note that the ARM coprocessor architecture allows the floating-point emulator (FPE) software to be used interchangeably with the combination of the FPA10 and the floating-point accelerator support code (FPASC), or any other hardware-software combination that supports the same set of instructions. Application binaries will work with either support environment, though the compiler optimization strategy is different (the FPE software works best with grouped floating-point instructions whereas the FPA10/FPASC works best with distributed instructions).

6.4.1 | FPA10 Data Types

The ARM FPA10 hardware floating-point accelerator supports single, double and extended double precision formats. Packed decimal formats are supported only by software.

The coprocessor registers are all extended double precision, and all internal calculations are carried out in this, the highest precision format, except that there are faster versions of some instructions which do not produce the full 80-bit accuracy. However loads and stores between memory and these registers can convert the precision as required. This is shown in Figure 6.7.

This is similar to the treatment of integers in the ARM integer architecture, where all internal operations are on 32-bit quantities, but memory transfers can specify bytes and half-words.

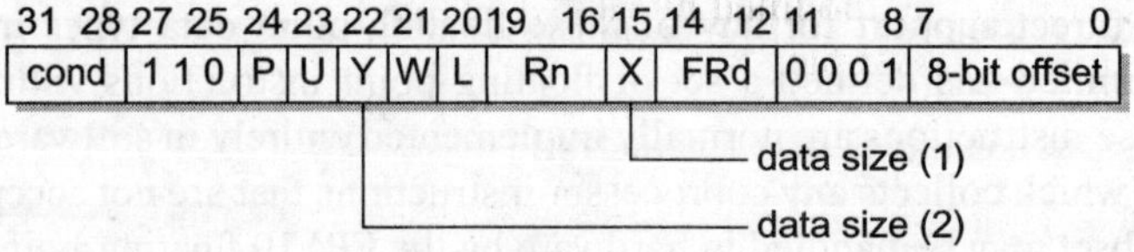

Figure 6.7 Load and store floating binary encoding

6.4.2 | Load and Store Floating Instructions

Since there are only eight floating-point registers, the register specifier field in the coprocessor data transfer instruction (shown in Figure 5.16 on page 119) has a spare bit which is used here as an additional data size specifier:

The other fields in this format are described in Section 5.18 on page 119. The X and Y bits allow one of four precisions to be specified choosing between single, double, double extended and packed decimal. (The choice between packed decimal and extended packed decimal is controlled by a bit in the FPSR.)

6.4.3 | Load and Store Multiple Floating

The load and store multiple floating-point registers instructions are used to save and restore the floating-point register state. Each register is saved using three memory words, and the precise format is not defined; it is intended that the only use for the saved values will be to reload them using the equivalent load multiple floating instruction to restore the context. 'FRd' specifies the first register to be transferred and 'X' and 'Y' encode the number of registers transferred which can be from one to four. Note that these instructions use coprocessor number 2, whereas the other floating-point instructions use coprocessor number 1. Figure 6.8 shows the binary encoding for this.

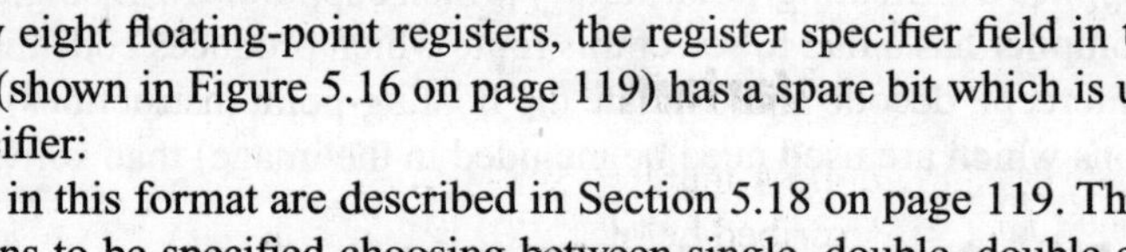

Figure 6.8 Load and store multiple floating binary encoding

6.4.4 | Floating-point Data Operations

The floating-point data operations perform arithmetic functions on values in the floating-point registers; their only interaction with the outside world is to confirm that they should complete through the ARM coprocessor handshake. (Indeed, a floating-point coprocessor may begin executing one of these instructions before the handshake begins so long as it waits for confirmation from the ARM before committing a state change.)

31 28	27 24	23 20	19	18 16	15	14 12	11 8	7 5	4	3	2 0
cond	1 1 1 0	Cop1	e	FRn	j	FRd	0 0 0 1	Cop2	0	i	FRm

Figure 6.9 Floating-point data processing binary encoding

The instruction format has a number of opcode bits, augmented by extra bits from each of the three register specifier fields since only three bits are required to specify one of the eight floating-point registers:

- 'i' selects between a register ('FRm') or one of eight constants for the second operand.
- 'e' and 'Cop2' control the destination size and the rounding mode.
- 'j' selects between monadic (single operand) and dyadic (two operand) operations (Figure 6.9).

The instructions include simple arithmetic operations (add, subtract, multiply, divide, remainder, power), transcendental functions (log, exponential, sin, cos, tan, arcsin, arccos, arctan) and assorted others (square root, move, absolute value, round).

6.4.5 | Floating-point Register Transfers

The register transfer instructions accept a value from or return a value to an ARM register. This is generally combined with a floating-point processing function (Figure 6.10).

31 28	27 24	23 21	20	19	18 16	15 12	11 8	7 5	4	3	2 0
cond	1 1 1 0	Cop1	L	e	FRn	Rd	0 0 0 1	Cop2	1	i	FRm

Figure 6.10 Floating-point register transfer binary encoding

Transfers from ARM to the floating-point unit include 'float' (convert an integer in an ARM register to a real in a floating-point register) and writes to the floating-point status and control registers; going the other way there is 'fix' (convert a real in a floating-point register to an integer in an ARM register) and reads of the status and control registers.

The floating-point compare instructions are special cases of this instruction type, where Rd is r15. Two floating-registers are compared and the result of the comparison is returned to the N, Z, C and V flags in the ARM CPSR where they can directly control the execution of conditional instructions:

- N indicates 'less than'.
- Z indicates equality.
- C and V indicate more complex conditions, including 'unordered' comparison results which can arise when an operand is a 'NaN' (not a number).

6.4.6 | Floating-point Instruction Frequencies

The design of the FPA10 is guided by the typical frequencies of the various floating-point instructions. These were measured running compiled programs using the floating-point emulator software and are summarized in Table 6.1.

Table 6.1 Floating-point instruction frequencies

Instruction	Frequency
Load/store	67%
Add	13%
Multiply	10.5%
Compare	3%
Fix and float	2%
Divide	1.5%
Others	3%

The statistics are dominated by the number of load and store operations that take place. As a result, the FPA10 has been designed to allow these to operate concurrently with internal arithmetic operations.

6.4.7 | FPA10 Organization

The internal organization of the FPA10 is illustrated in Figure 6.11. Its external interface is to the ARM data bus and the coprocessor handshake signals, so it has a modest pin-count requirement. The major components are:

- The coprocessor pipeline follower (see Section 4.5 on page 87).
- The load/store unit that carries out format conversion on floating-point data types as they are loaded from and stored to memory.
- The register bank which stores eight 80-bit extended precision floating-point operands.
- The arithmetic unit which incorporates an adder, a multiplier and a divider, together with rounding and normalizing hardware.

The load/store unit operates concurrently with the arithmetic unit, enabling new operands to be loaded from memory while previously loaded operands are being processed. Hardware interlocks protect against data hazards.

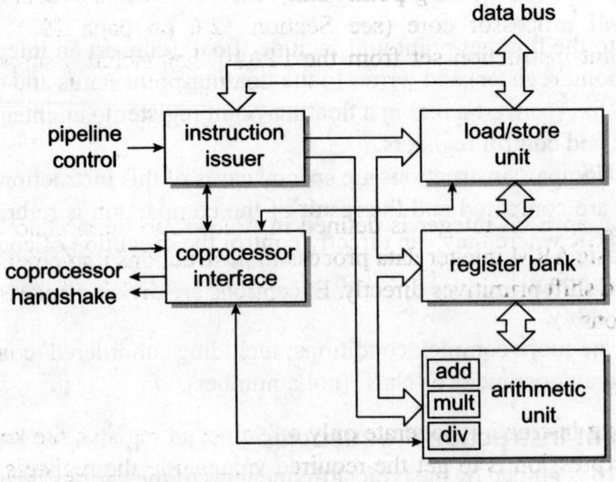

Figure 6.11 FPA10 internal organization

6.4.8 | FPA10 Pipeline

The FPA10 arithmetic unit operates in four pipeline stages:

1. Prepare: align operands.
2. Calculate: add, multiply or divide.
3. Align: normalize the result.
4. Round: apply appropriate rounding to the result.

A floating-point operation can begin as soon as it is detected in the instruction pipeline (that is, before the ARM handshake has occurred), but the result write-back must await the handshake.

6.4.9 | Floating-point Context Switches

The FPA registers represent additional process state which must be saved and restored across context switches. However, typically only a small number of active processes use floating-point instructions. Therefore saving and restoring the FPA registers on every switch is an unnecessary overhead. Instead, the software minimizes the number of saves and restores by the following algorithm:

- When a process using the FPA is switched out, the FPA registers are not saved but the FPA is turned off.
- If a subsequent process executes a floating-point instruction this will trap; the trap code will save the FPA state and enable the FPA.

Thus the FPA state saving and restoring overhead is only incurred for processes which use the FPA; in a typical system with only one process using the FPA, the overhead is avoided altogether.

6.4.10 | FPA10 Applications

The FPA10 is used as a macrocell on the ARM7500FE chip (see Section 13.5 on page 308).

6.4.11 | The VFP10

A much higher performance floating-point unit, the VFP10, has been designed to operate with the ARM10TDMI processor core (see Section 12.6 on page 291). The VFP10 supports a different floating-point instruction set from the FPA10 that includes support for vector floating -point operations.

6.5 | Expressions

Unsigned arithmetic on an n-bit integer is defined in ANSI C to be modulo 2^n, so overflow cannot occur. Therefore the basic ARM integer data processing instructions implement most of the C integer arithmetic, bit-wise and shift primitives directly. Exceptions are division and remainder which require several ARM instructions.

6.5.1 | Register Use

Since all data processing instructions operate only on values in register, the key to the efficient evaluation of a complex expression is to get the required values into the registers in the right order and to ensure that frequently used values are normally resident in registers. There is clearly a trade-off between the number of values that can be held in registers and the number of registers remaining for intermediate results during expression evaluation (remembering that registers are also needed to hold the addresses of operands that must be fetched from memory). Optimizing this trade-off is a major task for the compiler, as is sorting out the right order to load and combine operands to achieve the result prescribed by the operator precedence defined in the language.

6.5.2 | ARM Support

The 3-address instruction format used by the ARM gives the compiler the maximum flexibility in how it preserves or re-uses registers during expression evaluation.

Thumb instructions are generally 2-address, which restricts the compiler's freedom to some extent, and the smaller number of general registers also makes its job harder (and will result in less efficient code).

6.5.3 | Accessing Operands

A procedure will normally work with operands that are presented in one of the following ways, and can be accessed as indicated:

1. As an argument passed through a register.
   The value is already in a register, so no further work is necessary.
2. As an argument passed on the stack.
   Stack pointer (r13) relative addressing with an immediate offset known at compile-time allows the operand to be collected with a single LDR.
3. As a constant in the procedure's literal pool.
   PC-relative addressing, again with an immediate offset known at compile-time, gives access with a single LDR.
4. As a local variable.
   Local variables are allocated space on the stack and are accessed by a stack pointer relative LDR.
5. As a global variable.
   Global (and static) variables are allocated space in the static area and are accessed by static base relative addressing. The static base is usually in r9 (see the 'ARM Procedure Call Standard').

If the value that is passed is a pointer, an additional LDR (with an immediate offset) may be required to access an operand within the structure that it points to.

6.5.4 | Pointer Arithmetic

Arithmetic on pointers depends on the size of the data type that the pointers are pointing to. If a pointer is incremented it changes in units of the size of the data item in bytes. Thus:

```
int *p;
p = p + 1;
```

will increase the value of p by 4 bytes. Since the size of a data type is known at compile-time, the compiler can scale constants by an appropriate amount. If a variable is used as an offset it must be scaled at run-time:

```
int i = 4;
p = p + i;
```

If p is held in r0 and i in r1, the change to p may be compiled as:

```
ADD        r0, r0, r1, LSL #2    ; scale r1 to int
```

Where the data type is a structure with a size which is not a power of 2 bytes, a multiplication by a small constant is required. The shift and add instructions can usually produce the desired product in a small number of operations, using a temporary register where necessary.

6.5.5 | Arrays

Arrays in C are little more than a shorthand notation for pointer operations, so the above comments apply here too. The declaration:

```
int a[10] ;
```

establishes a name, a, for the array which is just a pointer to the first element, and a reference to a[i] is equivalent to the pointer-plus-offset form *(a + i); the two may be used interchangeably.

6.6 | Conditional Statements

Conditional statements are executed if the Boolean result of a test is true (or false); in C these include if...else statements and switches (C 'case' statements).

6.6.1 | if...else

The ARM architecture offers unusually efficient support for conditional expressions when the conditionally executed statement is small.

For example, here is a C statement to find the maximum of two integers:

```
if (a > b) c = a; else c = b;
```

If the variables a, b and c are in registers r0, r1 and r2, the compiled code could be as simple as:

```
CMP      r0,  r1     ; if (a > b) ...
MOVGT    r2,  r0     ; ..c = a ..
MOVLE    r2,  r1     ; ...else c = b
```

(In this particular case the C compiler can produce a rather more obvious sequence:

```
MOV      r2,  r0     ; c = a
CMP      r0,  r1     ; if (a > b) ...
MOVLE    r2,  r1     ; c = b
```

However, this doesn't scale well to more complex 'if statements so we will ignore it in this general discussion.)

The 'if' and 'else' sequences may be a few instructions long with the same condition on each instruction (provided none of the conditionally executed instructions changes the condition codes), but beyond two or three instructions it is generally better to fall back on the more conventional solution:

```
        CMP     r0,  r1    ; if (a > b) ...
        BLE     ELSE       ; skip clause if false
        MOV     r2,  r0    ; .. c = a ..
        B       ENDIF      ; skip else clause
ELSE    MOV     r2,  r1    ; ... else c = b
ENDIF   ..
```

Here the 'if' and 'else' sequences may be any length and may use the condition codes freely (including, for example, for nested if statements) since they are not required beyond the branch immediately following the compare instruction.

Note, however, that whichever branch is taken, this second code sequence will take approximately twice as long to execute as the first for this simple example. Branches are expensive on the ARM, so the absence of them from the first sequence makes it very efficient.

6.6.2 | Switches

A switch, or case, statement extends the two-way decision of an if...else statement to many ways. The standard C form of a switch statement is:

```
switch (expression) {
        case constant-expression₁: statements₁
        case constant-expression₂: statements₂
        ...
        case constant–expressionN: statementsN
        default: statementsD
}
```

Normally each group of statements ends with a 'break' (or a 'return') to cause the switch statement to terminate, otherwise the C semantics cause execution to fall through to the next group of statements. A switch statement with 'breaks' can always be translated into an equivalent series of if..else statements:

```
temp = expression;
if (temp = = constant – expression₁) {statements₁}
else ...
else if (temp = = constant – expressionN) {statementsN}
else {statementsD}
```

However this can result in slow code if the switch statement has many cases. An alternative is to use a *jump table.* In its simplest form a jump table contains a target address for each possible value of the switch expression:

```
                        ; r0 contains value of expression
        ADR     r1, JUMPTABLE           ; get base of jump table
        CMP     r0, #TABLEMAX           ; check for overrun ..
        LDRLS   pc, [r1, r0, LSL #2]    ; ..if OK get pc
                ; statementsD           ; ..otherwise default
        B       EXIT                    ; break
L1      ..      ; statements1
        B       EXIT                    ; break
        ..
LN      ..      ; statementsN
EXIT    ..
```

Clearly it is not possible for the jump table to contain an address for every possible value of a 32-bit integer, and equally clearly it is vital that the jump table look-up does not fall past the end of the table, so some checking is necessary.

Another way of compiling a switch statement is illustrated by a procedure in the 'Dhrystone' benchmark program which ends (effectively) as follows:

```
    switch (a) {
      case 0:   *b = 0; break;
      case 1:   if (C > 100) *b = 0; else *b = 3; break;
      case 2:   *b = 1; break
      case 3:   break;
      case 4:   *b = 2; break;
    } /* end of switch */
  } /* end of procedure */
```

The code which is generated highlights a number of aspects of the ARM instruction set. The switch statement is implemented by adding the value of the expression (in v2; the register naming convention follows the ARM Procedure Call Standard which will be described in Section 6.8) to the PC after scaling it to a word offset. The overrun case falls through the add instruction into the slot left free by the PC offset. Any cases which require a single instruction (such as case 3), and the last case whatever its length, can be completed in line; others require a branch. This example also illustrates an if..then...else implemented using conditional instructions.

```
          ; on entry a1 = 0,  a2 = 3, v2 = switch expression
          CMP      v2, #4                       ; check value for overrun ..
          ADDLS    pc, pc, v2, LSL #2           ; if OK,  add to pc (+8)
          LDMDB    fp, {v1, v2, fp, sp, pc}     ; .. if not OK, return
          B        L0                           ; case 0
          B        L1                           ; case 1
          B        L2                           ; case 2
          LDMDB    fp, {v1, v2, fp, sp, pc}     ; case 3 (return)
          MOV      a1,#2                        ; case 4
          STR      a1, [v1]
          LDMDB    fp, {v1, v2, fp, sp, pc}     ; return
L0        STR      a1, [v1]
          LDMDB    fp, {v1, v2, fp, sp, pc}     ; return
L1        LDR      a3, c_ADDR                   ; get address of c
          LDR      a3, [a3]                     ; get c
          CMP      a3,#&64                      ; C > 100?..
          STRLE    a2, [v1]                     ; .. No:   *b = 3
          STRGT    a1, [v1]                     ; .. Yes:  *b = 0
          LDMDB    fp, {v1, v2, fp, sp, pc}     ; return
c_ADDR    DCD      <address of c>
L2        MOV      a1, #1
          STR      a1, [v1]                     ; *b = 1
          LDMDB    fp, {v1, v2, fp, sp, pc}     ; return
```

6.7 | Loops

The C language supports three forms of loop control structure:

- for (e1; e2; e3) {..}
- while (el) {..}
- do {..} while (el)

Here el, e2 and e3 are expressions which evaluate to 'true' or 'false' and {..} is the body of the loop which is executed a number of times determined by the control structure. Often the body of a loop is very simple, which puts the onus on the compiler to minimize the overhead of the control structure. Each loop must have at least one branch instruction, but any more would be wasteful.

6.7.1 | for Loops

A typical 'for' loop uses the control expressions to manage an index:

```
for (i = 0;  i < 10;  i++)   {a[i] = 0}
```

The first control expression is executed once before the loop begins, the second is tested each time the loop is entered and controls whether the loop is executed, and the third is executed at the end of each pass through the loop to prepare for the next pass. This loop could be compiled as:

```
        MOV     r1, #0                  ; value to store in a[i]
        ADR     r2, a[0]                ; r2 points to a[0]
        MOV     r0, #0                  ; i = 0
LOOP    CMP     r0, #10                 ; i < 10 ?
        BGE     EXIT                    ; if i >= 10 finish
        STR     r1, [r2, r0, LSL #2]    ; a[i] = 0
        ADD     r0, r0,  #1             ; i++
        B       LOOP
EXIT    ..
```

(This example illustrates the optimization technique of *strength reduction*, which means moving fixed operations outside the loop. The first two instructions are logically inside the loop in the C program, but have been moved outside since they are initializing registers to the same constants each time round the loop.)

This code may be improved by omitting the conditional branch to EXIT and applying the opposite condition to the following instructions, causing the program to fall through rather than branch round them when the terminating condition is met. However, it can be further improved by moving the test to the bottom of the loop (which is possible here since the initialization and test are with constants, so the compiler can be sure that the loop will be executed at least once).

6.7.2 | while Loops

A 'while' loop has a simpler structure and generally controls loops where the number of iterations is not a constant or clearly defined by a variable at run-time. The standard conceptual arrangement of a 'while' loop is as follows:

```
LOOP    ..                              ; evaluate expression
        BEQ     EXIT
```

```
                ..                          ; loop body
            B           LOOP
EXIT        ..
```

The two branches appear to be necessary since the code must allow for the case where the body is not executed at all. A little reordering produces more efficient code:

```
            B       TEST
LOOP        ..                      ; loop body
TEST        ..                      ; evaluate expression
            BNE     LOOP
EXIT        ..
```

This second code sequence executes the loop body and evaluates the control expression exactly the same way as the original version and has the same code size, but it executes one fewer (untaken) branch per iteration, so the second branch has been removed from the loop overhead. An even more efficient code sequence can be produced by the compiler:

```
            ..                      ; evaluate expression
            BEQ     EXIT            ; skip loop if necessary
LOOP        ..                      ; loop body
TEST        ..                      ; evaluate expression
            BNE     LOOP
EXIT        ..
```

The saving here is that one fewer branch is executed each time the complete 'while' structure is encountered (assuming that the body is executed at least once). This is a modest gain and costs extra instructions, so it is worthwhile only if performance matters much more than code size.

6.7.3 | do..while Loops

The conceptual arrangement of a 'do..while' loop is similar to the improved 'while' loop above, but without the initial branch since the loop body is executed before the test (and is therefore always executed at least once):

```
LOOP        ..                      ; loop body
            ..                      ; evaluate expression
            BNE     LOOP
EXIT        ..
```

6.8 | Functions and Procedures

6.8.1 | Program Design

Good programming practice requires that large programs are broken down into components that are small enough to be thoroughly tested; a large, monolithic program is too complex to test fully and is likely to have 'bugs' in hidden corners that do not emerge early enough in the program's life to be fixed before the program is shipped to users.

Each small software component should perform a specified operation using a well-defined interface. How it performs this operation should be of no significance to the rest of the program (this is the principle of **abstraction;** see Section 6.1).

6.8.2 | Program Hierarchy

Furthermore, the full program should be designed as a **hierarchy** of components, not simply a flat list.

A typical hierarchy is illustrated in Figure 6.12. The top of the hierarchy is the program called *main*. The remaining hierarchy is fairly informal; lower-level routines may be shared by higher-level routines, calls may skip levels, and the depth may vary across the hierarchy.

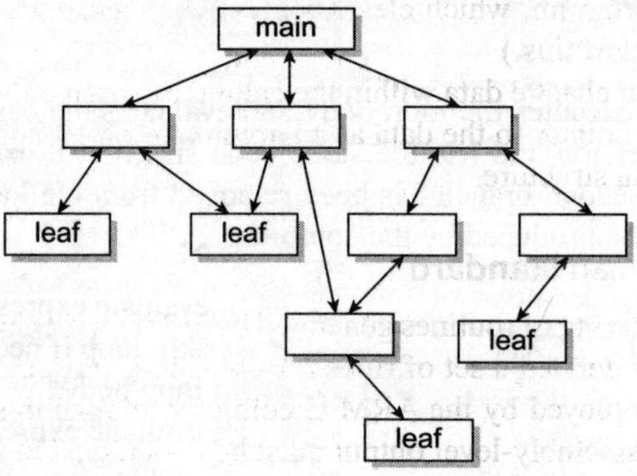

Figure 6.12 Typical hierarchical program structure

6.8.3 | Leaf Routines

At the lowest level of the hierarchy there are **leaf** routines; these are routines which do not themselves call any lower-level routines. In a typical program some of the bottom-level routines will be **library** or **system** functions; these are predefined operations which may or may not be leaf routines (that is, they may or may not have internal structure).

6.8.4 | Terminology

There are several terms that are used to describe components of this program structure, often imprecisely. We shall attempt to apply terms as follows:

- **Subroutine:** a generic term for a routine that is called by a higher-level routine, particularly when viewing a program at the assembly language level.
- **Function:** a subroutine which returns a value through its name. A typical invocation looks like:
  c = max (a, b) ;
- **Procedure:** a subroutine which is called to carry out some operation on specified data item(s). A typical invocation looks like:
  printf ("Hello World\n");

6.8.5 | C Functions

Some programming languages make a clear distinction between functions and procedures, but C does not. In C all subroutines are functions, but they can have side-effects in addition to returning a value, and when the returned value is of type 'void' it is effectively suppressed and only the side-effects remain, giving a behaviour which looks just like a procedure.

6.8.6 | Arguments and Parameters

An **argument** is an expression passed to a function call; a value received by the function is a **parameter**. C uses a strict 'call by value' semantics, so a copy is made of each argument when a function is called and, though the function may change the values of its parameters, since these are only copies of the arguments the arguments themselves are not affected.

(A **call by reference** semantics would cause any change to a parameter within a function to be passed back to the calling program, which clearly only makes sense when the argument is a simple variable, but C does not support this.)

The way a C function can change data within the calling program, other than by returning a single value, is when it is passed a pointer to the data as an argument. The function can then use the pointer to access and modify the data structure.

6.8.7 | ARM Procedure Call Standard

In order to support flexible mixing of routines generated by different compilers and written in assembly language, ARM Limited has defined a set of rules for procedure entry and exit. The ARM Procedure Call Standard **(APCS)** is employed by the ARM C compiler, though this is of significance to the C programmer only when the assembly-level output must be understood in detail.

The APCS imposes a number of conventions on the otherwise 'vanilla' flavour of the ARM architecture:

- It defines particular uses for the 'general-purpose' registers.
- It defines which form of stack is used from the full/empty, ascending/descending choices supported by the ARM instruction set.
- It defines the format of a stack-based data structure used for back-tracing when debugging programs.
- It defines the function argument and result passing mechanism to be used by all externally visible functions and procedures. ('Externally visible' means that the procedure interface is offered outside the current programming module. A function which is used only within the current module may be optimized by deviating from this convention.)
- It supports the ARM shared library mechanism, which means it supports a standard way for shared (re-entrant) code to access static data.

6.8.8 | APCS Register Usage

The convention for the use of the 16 currently visible ARM registers is summarized in Table 6.2. The registers are divided into three sets:

Table 6.2 APCS register use convention

Register	APCS name	APCS role
0	a1	Argument 1/integer result/scratch register
1	a2	Argument 2/scratch register

(Continued)

Table 6.2 APCS register use convention (*Continued*)

Register	APCS name	APCS role
2	a3	Argument 3/scratch register
3	a4	Argument 4/scratch register
4	v1	Register variable 1
5	v2	Register variable 2
6	v3	Register variable 3
7	v4	Register variable 4
8	v5	Register variable 5
9	sb/v6	Static base/register variable 6
10	sl/v7	Stack limit/register variable 7
11	fp	Frame pointer
12	iP	Scratch reg./new sb in inter-link-unit calls
13	sp	Lower end of current stack frame
14	lr	Link address/scratch register
15	pc	Program counter

1. Four argument registers which pass values into the function.
   The function need not preserve these so it can use them as scratch registers once it has used or saved its parameter values. Since they will not be preserved across any calls this function makes to other functions, they must be saved across such calls if they contain values that are needed again. Hence, they are **caller-saved** register variables when so used.
2. Five (to seven) register variables which the function must return with unchanged values.
   These are **callee-saved** register variables. This function must save them if it wishes to use the registers, but it can rely on functions it calls not changing them.
3. Seven (to five) registers which have a dedicated role, at least some of the time.
   The link register (lr), for example, carries the return address on function entry, but if it is saved (as it must be if the function calls subfunctions) it may then be used as a scratch register.

6.8.9 | APCS Variants

There are several (16) different variants of the APCS which are used to generate code for a range of different systems. They support:

- 32-or 26-bit PCs.
  Older ARM processors operated in a 26-bit address space and some later versions continue to support this for backwards compatibility reasons.
- Implicit or explicit stack-limit checking.
  Stack overflow must be detected if code is to operate reliably. The compiler can insert instructions to perform explicit checks for overflow.
  Where memory management hardware is available, an ARM system can allocate memory to the stack in units of a page. If the next logical page is mapped out, a stack overflow will cause a data abort and be detected. Therefore the memory management unit can perform stack-limit checking and there is no need for the compiler to insert instructions to perform explicit checks.

- Two ways to pass floating-point arguments.
  The ARM floating-point architecture (see Section 6.4) specifies a set of eight floating-point registers. The APCS can use these to pass floating-point arguments into functions, and this is the most efficient solution when the system makes extensive use of floating-point variables. If, however, the system makes little or no use of floating-point types (and many ARM systems do not) this approach incurs a small overhead which is avoided by passing floating-point arguments in the integer registers and/or on the stack.
- Re-entrant or non-re-entrant code.
  Code specified as re-entrant is position-independent and addresses all data indirectly through the static base register (sb). This code can be placed in a ROM and can be shared by several client processes. Generally, code to be placed in a ROM or a shared library should be re-entrant whereas application code will not be.

6.8.10 | Argument Passing

A C function may have many (or even a variable number of) arguments. The APCS organizes the arguments as follows:

1. If floating-point values are passed through floating-point registers, the first four floating-point arguments are loaded into the first four floating-point registers.
2. All remaining arguments are organized into a list of words; the first four words are loaded into a1 to a4, then the remaining words are pushed onto the stack in reverse order.

Note that multi-word arguments, including double precision floating-point values, may be passed in integer registers, on the stack, or even split across the registers and the stack.

6.8.11 | Result Return

A simple result (such as an integer) is returned through a1. A more complex result is returned in memory to a location specified by an address which is effectively passed as an additional first argument to the function through a1.

6.8.12 | Function Entry and Exit

A simple leaf function which can perform all its functions using only a1 to a4 can be compiled into code with a minimal calling overhead:

```
        BL      leaf1
        ..
leaf1   ..
        MOV     pc, lr          ; return
```

In typical programs somewhere around 50% of all function calls are to leaf functions, and these are often quite simple.

Where registers must be saved, the function must create a stack frame. This can be compiled efficiently using ARM's load and store multiple instructions:

```
        BL      leaf2
        ..
leaf2   STMFD   p!, {regs, lr}     ; save registers
        ..
        LDMFD   sp!, {regs, pc}    ; restore and return
```

Here the number of registers which are saved and restored will be the minimum required to implement the function. Note the value saved from the link register (lr) is returned directly to the program counter (pc), and therefore lr is available as a scratch register in the body of the function (which it was not in the simple case above).

More complex function entry sequences are used where needed to create stack backtrace data structures, handle floating-point arguments passed in floating-point registers, check for stack overflow, and so on.

6.8.13 | Tail Continued Functions

Simple functions that call another function immediately before returning often do not incur any significant call overhead; the compiler will cause the code to return directly from the continuing function. This makes veneer functions (functions that simply reorder arguments, change their type or add an extra argument) particularly efficient.

6.8.14 | ARM Efficiency

Overall the ARM supports functions and procedures efficiently and flexibly. The various flavours of the procedure call standard match different application requirements well, and all result in efficient code. The load and store multiple register instructions are exploited to good effect by the compiler in this context; without them calls to non-leaf functions would be much more costly.

The compiler is also able to make effective optimizations for leaf and tail continued functions, thereby encouraging good programming styles. Programmers can use better structured design when leaf function calls are efficient and can exploit abstraction better when veneer functions are efficient.

6.9 | Use of Memory

An ARM system, like most computer systems, has its memory arranged as a linear set of logical addresses. A C program expects to have access to a fixed area of program memory (where the application image resides) and to memory to support two data areas that grow dynamically and where the compiler often cannot work out a maximum size. These dynamic data areas are:

- The stack.
  Whenever a (non-trivial) function is called, a new activation frame is created on the stack containing a backtrace record local (non-static) variables, and so on. When a function returns its stack space is automatically recovered and will be reused for the next function call.
- The heap.
  The heap is an area of memory used to satisfy program requests (malloc ()) for more memory for new data structures. A program which continues to request memory over a long period of time should be careful to free up *all* sections that are no longer needed otherwise the heap will grow until memory runs out.

6.9.1 | Address Space Model

The normal use of memory is illustrated in Figure 6.13. Where an application can use the entire memory space (or where a memory management unit can allow an application to think it has the entire memory space), the application image is loaded into the lowest address, the heap grows upwards from the top of the application and the stack grows downwards from the top of memory.

The unused memory between the top of the heap and the bottom of the stack is allocated on demand to the heap or the stack, and if it runs out the program stops due to lack of memory.

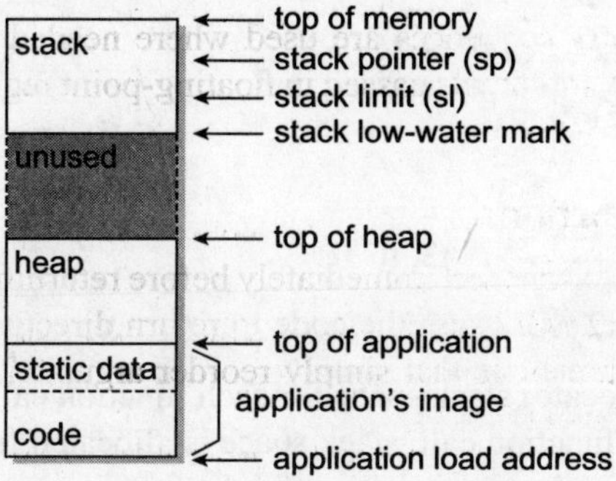

Figure 6.13 The standard ARM C program address space model

In a typical memory managed ARM system the logical space allocated to a single application will be very large, in the range of 1 to 4 Gbytes. The memory management unit will allocate additional pages, on demand, to the heap or the stack, until it runs out of pages to allocate (either due to having allocated all the physical memory pages, or, in a system with virtual memory, due to running out of swap space on the hard disk). This will usually be a long time before the top of the heap meets the bottom of the stack.

In a system with no memory management support the application will be allocated all (if it is the only application to run at the time) or part (if more than one application is to run) of the physical memory address space remaining once the operating system has had its requirements met, and then the application runs out of memory precisely when the top of the heap meets the bottom of the stack.

6.9.2 | Chunked Stack Model

Other address space models are possible, including implementing a 'chunked' stack where the stack is a series of chained chunks within the heap. This causes the application to occupy a single contiguous area of memory, which grows in one direction as required, and may be more convenient where memory is very tight.

6.9.3 | Stack Behaviour

It is important to understand the dynamic behaviour of the stack while a program is running, since it sheds some light on the scoping rules for local variables (which are allocated space on the stack). Consider this simple program structure:

```
Main () {
    ..                  /* t1 */
    func1 ();
    ..                  /* t5 */
    func2 ();
    ..                  /* t7 */
```

```
} /* end of main */
func1 () {
    ..                  /* t2 */
    func2  ();
    ..                  /* t4 */
} /* end of func1 */
func2 () {
                        /* t3, t6 */
    ..
} /* end of func2 */
```

Assuming that the compiler allocates stack space for each function call, the stack behaviour will be as shown in Figure 6.14. At each function call, stack space is allocated for arguments (if they cannot all be passed in registers), to save registers for use within the function, to save the return address and the old stack pointer, and to allocate memory on the stack for local variables.

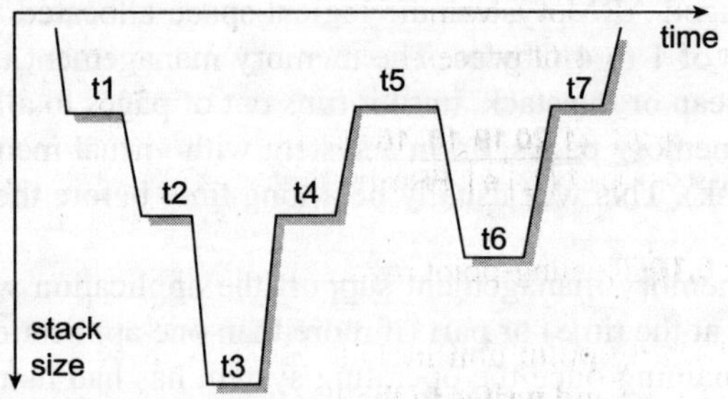

Figure 6.14 Example stack behaviour

Note how all the stack space is recovered on function exit and reused for subsequent calls, and how the two calls to func2() are allocated different memory areas (at times t3 and t6 in Figure 6.14), so even if the memory used for a local variable in the first call had not been overwritten in an intervening call to another function, the old value cannot be accessed in the second call since its address is not known. Once a procedure has exited, local variable values are lost forever.

6.9.4 | Data Storage

The various data types supported in C require differing amounts of memory to store their binary representations. The basic data types occupy a byte (chars), a half-word (short ints), a word (ints, single precision float) or multiple words (double precision floats). Derived data types (structs, arrays, unions, and so on) are defined in terms of multiple basic data types.

The ARM instruction set, in common with many other RISC processors, is most efficient at loading and storing data items when they are appropriately aligned in memory. A byte access can be made to any byte address with equal efficiency, but storing a word to a non-word-aligned address is very inefficient, taking up to seven ARM instructions and requiring temporary work registers.

6.9.5 | Data Alignment

Therefore the ARM C compiler generally aligns data items on appropriate boundaries:

- Bytes are stored at any byte address.
- Half-words are stored at even byte addresses.
- Words are stored on four-byte boundaries.

Where several data items of different types are declared at the same time, the compiler will introduce padding where necessary to achieve this alignment:

```
struct S1 {char c;  int x;  short s;} example1;
```

This structure will occupy three words of memory as shown in Figure 6.15. (Note that structures are also padded to end on a word boundary.)

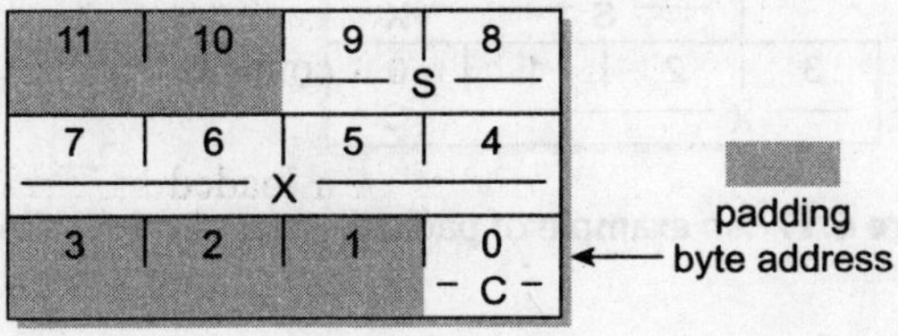

Figure 6.15 An example of normal struct memory allocation

Arrays are laid out in memory by repeating the appropriate basic data item, obeying the alignment rules for each item.

6.9.6 | Memory Efficiency

Given the data alignment rules outlined above, the programmer can help the compiler to minimize memory wastage by organizing structures appropriately. A structure with the same contents as above, but reordered as below, occupies only two memory words instead of the original three:

```
struct S2 {char c;  short s;  int x;} example2;
```

This will result in the memory occupancy illustrated in Figure 6.16. In general, ordering structure elements so that types smaller than a word can be grouped within a word will minimize the amount of padding that the compiler has to insert to maintain efficient alignment.

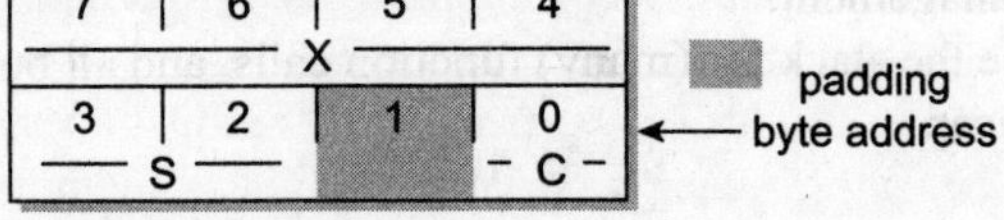

Figure 6.16 An example of more efficient struct memory allocation

6.9.7 | Packed Structs

Sometimes it is necessary to exchange data with other computers that follow different alignment conventions, or to pack data tightly to minimize memory use even though this will reduce performance. For such purposes the ARM C compiler can produce code that works with packed data structures where all the padding is removed:

```
__packed struct S3 {char c; int x; short s;} example3;
```

A packed struct gives precise control of the alignment of all the fields but incurs the overhead of the ARM's relatively inefficient access to non-aligned operands, and therefore should only be used when strictly necessary. The memory occupancy of the packed structure declared above is illustrated in Figure 6.17.

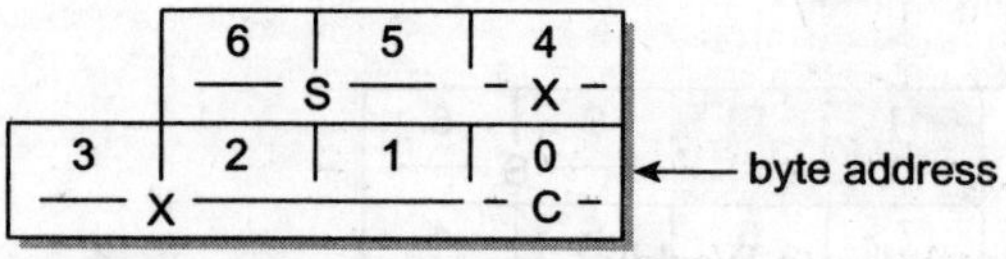

Figure 6.17 An example of packed struct memory allocation

6.10 | Run-time Environment

A C program requires an environment in which to operate; this is usually provided through a library of functions that the C program can call. In a PC or workstation a C programmer can expect to find the full ANSI C library, giving access to a broad range of functions such as file management, input and output (printf()), the realtime clock, and so on.

6.10.1 | Minimal Run-time Library

In a small embedded system such as a mobile telephone, most of these functions are irrelevant. ARM Limited supplies a minimal stand-alone run-time library which, once ported to the target environment, allows basic C programs to run. This library therefore reflects the minimal requirements of a C program. It comprises:

- Division and remainder functions.
  Since the ARM instruction set does not include divide instructions, these are implemented as library functions.
- Stack-limit checking functions.
  A minimal embedded system is unlikely to have memory management hardware available for stack overflow detection; therefore these library functions are needed to ensure programs operate safely.
- Stack and heap management.
  All C programs use the stack for (many) function calls, and all but the most trivial create data structures on the heap.
- Program start up.
  Once the stack and heap are initialized, the program starts with a call to main().

- Program termination.
  Most programs terminate by calling _exit(); even a program which runs forever should terminate if an error is detected.

The total size of the code generated for this minimal library is 736 bytes, and it is implemented in a way that allows the linker to omit any unreferenced sections to reduce the library image to around half a kilobyte in many cases. This is a great deal smaller than the full ANSI C library.

6.11 | Examples and Exercises

EXAMPLE 6.1

Write, compile and run a 'Hello World' program written in C.

The following program has the required function:

```
/* Hello World in C */
#include <stdio.h>
int main()
{
        printf("Hello World\n" );
        return( 0 );
}
```

The principal things to note from this example are:

- The '#include' directive which allows this program to use all the standard input and output functions available in C.
- The declaration of the 'main' procedure. Every C program must have exactly one of these as the program is run by calling it.
- The 'printf(..)' statement calls a function provided in stdio which sends output to the standard output device. By default this is the display terminal.

As with the assembly programming exercises, the major challenge is to establish the flow through the tools from editing the text to compiling, linking and running the program. Once this program is working, generating more complex programs is fairly straightforward (at least until the complexity reaches the point where the design of the program becomes a challenge in itself).

Using the ARM software development tools, the above program should be saved as 'HelloW.c'. Then a new project should be created using the Project Manager and this file added (as the only file in the project). A click on the 'Build' button will cause the program to be compiled and linked then the 'Go' button will run it on the ARMulator, hopefully giving the expected output in the terminal window.

Exercise 6.1.1

The early versions of the ARM processor had no 'divide' instructions. Write an assembly version of division being accomplished by repeated subtraction.

Exercise 6.1.2

The stacks used in ARM may be descending or ascending types. Discuss how a descending stack is created using multiple load/store instructions.

EXAMPLE 6.2

Write the number 2001 in 32-bit binary, binary-coded decimal, ASCII and single-precision floating-point notation.

Binary: 2001 = 1024 + 512 + 256 + 128 + 64 + 16 + 1
= $00000000000000000000011111010001_2$

BCD: 2001 = 0010 0000 0000 0001

ASCII: 2001 = 00110010 00110000 00110000 00110001

F–P: 2001 = $1.1111010001 \times 2^{1010}$
= 01001001 11110100 01000000 00000000

Exercise 6.2.1

Write a C program to convert a date presented in Roman numerals into decimal form.

EXAMPLE 6.3

Show how the following data is organized in memory:

```
struct S1 {char c;  int x;};
struct S2 {
char c2 [5];
S1  s1 [2];
} example;
```

The first structure statement only declares a type, so no memory is allocated. The second establishes a structure called 'example' comprising an array of five characters followed by an array of two structures of type S1. The structures must start on a word boundary, so the character array will be padded out to fill two words and each structure will also occupy two words. The memory organization is therefore as shown below:

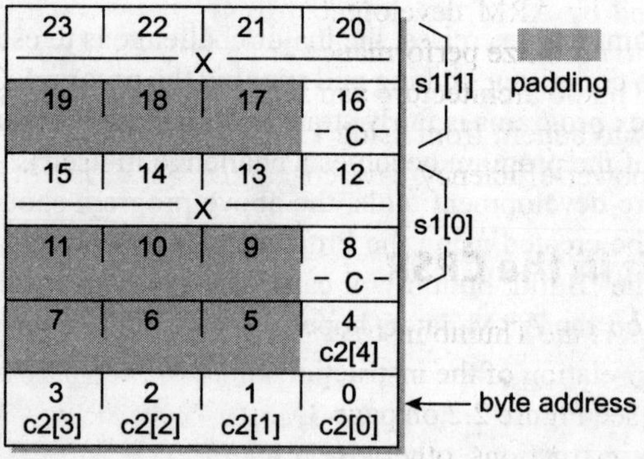

Exercise 6.3.1

Show how the same structure would be organized in memory if it were packed.

7

The Thumb Instruction Set

SUMMARY OF CHAPTER CONTENTS

The Thumb instruction set addresses the issue of code density. It may be viewed as a compressed form of a subset of the ARM instruction set. Thumb instructions map onto ARM instructions, and the Thumb programmer's model maps onto the ARM programmer's model. Implementations of Thumb use dynamic decompression in an ARM instruction pipeline and then instructions execute as standard ARM instructions within the processor.

Thumb is not a complete architecture; it is not anticipated that a processor would execute Thumb instructions without also supporting the ARM instruction set. Therefore the Thumb instruction set need only support common application functions, allowing recourse to the full ARM instruction set where necessary (for instance, all exceptions automatically enter ARM mode).

Thumb is fully supported by ARM development tools, and an application can mix ARM and Thumb subroutines flexibly to optimize performance or code density on a routine-by-routine basis.

This chapter covers the Thumb architecture and implementation, and suggests the characteristics of applications that are likely to benefit from using Thumb. In the right application, use of the Thumb instruction set can improve power-efficiency, save cost and enhance performance all at once.

7.1 | The Thumb Bit in the CPSR

ARM processors which support the Thumb instruction set can also execute the standard 32-bit ARM instruction set, and the interpretation of the instruction stream at any particular time is determined by bit 5 of the CPSR, the T bit (see Figure 2.2 on page 35). If T is set the processor interprets the instruction stream as 16-bit Thumb instructions, otherwise it interprets it as standard ARM instructions.

Not all ARM processors are capable of executing Thumb instructions; those that are have a T in their name, such as the ARM7TDMI described in Section 9.1 on page 213.

7.1.1 | Thumb Entry

ARM cores start up, after reset, executing ARM instructions. The normal way they switch to execute Thumb instructions is by executing a Branch and Exchange instruction (BX, see Section 5.5 on page 100). This instruction sets the T bit if the bottom bit of the specified register was set, and switches the program counter to the address given in the remainder of the register. Note that since the instruction causes a branch it flushes the instruction pipeline, removing any ambiguity over the interpretation of any instructions already in the pipeline (they are simply not executed).

Other instructions which change from ARM to Thumb code include exception returns, either using a special form of data processing instruction or a special form of load multiple register instruction (see 'Exception return' on page 95). Both of these instructions are generally used to return to whatever instruction stream was being executed before the exception was entered and are not intended for a deliberate switch to Thumb mode. Like BX, they also change the program counter and therefore flush the instruction pipeline.

7.1.2 | Thumb Exit

An explicit switch back to an ARM instruction stream can be caused by executing a Thumb BX instruction as described in Section 7.3.

An implicit return to an ARM instruction stream takes place whenever an exception is taken, since exception entry is always handled in ARM code.

7.1.3 | Thumb Systems

It should be clear from the above that all Thumb systems include some ARM code, if only to handle initialization and exception entry.

It is likely, however, that most Thumb applications will make more than this minimal use of ARM code. A typical embedded system will include a small amount of fast 32-bit memory on the same chip as the ARM core and will execute speed-critical routines (such as digital signal processing algorithms) in ARM code from this memory. The bulk of the code will not be speed critical and may execute from a 16-bit off-chip ROM. This is discussed further at the end of the chapter.

7.2 | The Thumb Programmer's Model

The Thumb instruction set is a subset of the ARM instruction set and the instructions operate on a restricted view of the ARM registers. The programmer's model is illustrated in Figure 7.1. The instruction set gives full access to the eight 'Lo' general purpose registers r0 to r7, and makes extensive use of r13 to r15 for special purposes:

- r13 is used as a stack pointer.
- r14 is used as the link register.
- r15 is the program counter (PC).

These uses follow very closely the way these registers are used by the ARM instruction set, though the use of r13 as a stack pointer in ARM code is purely a software convention, whereas in Thumb code it is somewhat hard-wired. The remaining registers (r8 to r12 and the CPSR) have only restricted access:

- A few instructions allow the 'Hi' registers (r8 to r15) to be specified.
- The CPSR condition code flags are set by arithmetic and logical operations and control conditional branching.

7.2.1 | Thumb-ARM Similarities

All Thumb instructions are 16 bits long. They map onto ARM instructions so they inherit many properties of the ARM instruction set:

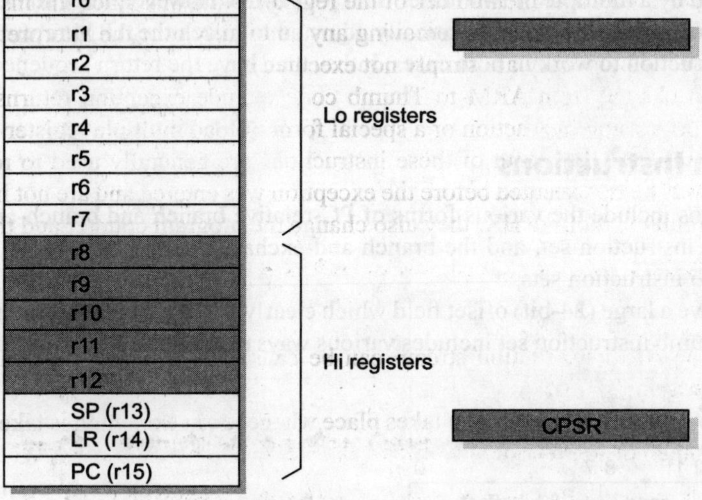

Figure 7.1 Thumb accessible registers

- The load-store architecture with data processing, data transfer and control flow instructions.
- Support for 8-bit byte, 16-bit half-word and 32-bit word data types where half-words are aligned on 2-byte boundaries and words are aligned on 4-byte boundaries.
- A 32-bit unsegmented memory.

7.2.2 | Thumb-ARM Differences

However, in order to achieve a 16-bit instruction length a number of characteristic features of the ARM instruction set have been abandoned:

- Most Thumb instructions are executed unconditionally.
  (*All* ARM instructions are executed conditionally.)
- Many Thumb data processing instructions use a 2-address format (the destination register is the same as one of the source registers).
  (ARM data processing instructions, with the exception of the 64-bit multiplies, use a 3-address format.)
- Thumb instruction formats are less regular than ARM instruction formats, as a result of the dense encoding.

7.2.3 | Thumb Exceptions

All exceptions return the processor to ARM execution and are handled within the ARM programmer's model. Since the T bit resides in the CPSR, it is saved on exception entry in the appropriate SPSR, and the same return from exception instruction will restore the state of the processor and leave it executing ARM or Thumb instructions according to the state when the exception arose.

Note that the ARM exception return instructions, described in 'Exception return' on page 95, involve return address adjustments to compensate for the ARM pipeline behaviour. Since Thumb instructions are two bytes rather than four bytes long, the natural offset should be different when an exception is entered from Thumb execution, since the PC value copied into the exception-mode link register will have incremented by a multiple of two rather than four bytes. However, the Thumb architecture requires that the link register value be automatically adjusted to match the ARM return offset, allowing the same return instruction to work in both cases, rather than have the return sequence made more complex.

7.3 | Thumb Branch Instructions

These control flow instructions include the various forms of PC-relative branch and branch-and-link instruction seen in the ARM instruction set, and the branch-and-exchange instruction for switching between the ARM and Thumb instruction sets.

The ARM instructions have a large (24-bit) offset field which clearly will not fit in a 16-bit instruction format. Therefore the Thumb instruction set includes various ways of subsetting the functionality.

7.3.1 | Binary Encodings

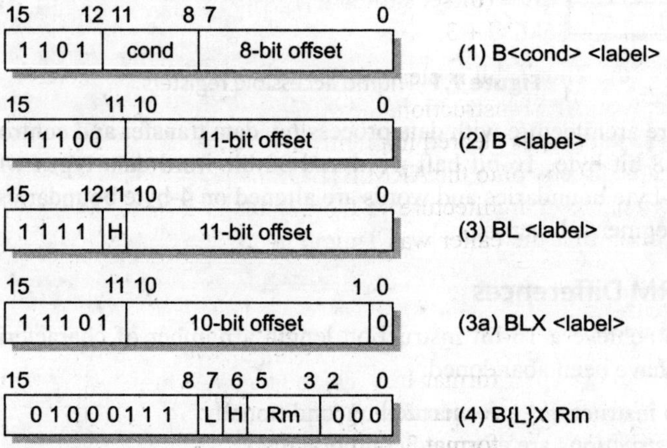

Figure 7.2 Thumb branch instruction binary encodings

7.3.2 | Description

Typical uses of branch instructions include:

1. short conditional branches to control (for example) loop exit;
2. medium-range unconditional branches to 'goto' sections of code;
3. long-range subroutine calls.

ARM handles all these with the same instruction, typically wasting many bits of the 24-bit offset in the first two cases. Thumb has to be more efficient, using different formats for each of these cases, numbered respectively in Figure 7.2.

The first two formats show how the condition field is traded off against the offset length. The condition field in the first format is the same as that in all ARM instructions (see Section 5.3 on page 96); in both cases the offset is shifted left one bit (to give half-word alignment) and sign-extended to 32 bits.

The third format is more subtle. The branch and link subroutine mechanism often needs to have a long range, which is difficult within a 16-bit instruction format. Therefore Thumb uses two instructions, both with this format, to give a combined 22-bit half-word offset (which is sign-extended to 32 bits). The range of the instruction is therefore +/− 4 Mbytes. In order to make the two instructions independent, so that, for example, an interrupt can be taken between them, the link register is used as temporary storage. It will be overwritten at the end of the instruction pair anyway, so it can't contain anything useful. The operation of the instruction pair is:

1. (H=0) LR := PC + (sign-extended offset shifted left 12 places);
2. (H=l) PC := LR + (offset shifted left 1 place);
   LR := oldPC + 3.

Here 'oldPC' is the address of the second instruction; the return address has two bytes added to point to the next instruction and the bottom bit set to indicate that the caller is a Thumb routine.

Format 3a is an alternative second step which gives the BLX variant; it is only available in architecture v5T. It uses the same first step as BL above:

1. (BL, H=0) LR := PC + (sign-extended offset shifted left 12 places);
2. (BLX) PC := LR + (offset shifted left 1 place) & 0xfffffffc;
   LR := oldPC + 3;
   the Thumb bit is cleared.

Note that as the target is an ARM instruction, the offset only requires 10 bits and the computed PC value may still have bit [1] set, so it is cleared implicitly.

The fourth format maps directly onto the ARM B{L}X instructions (see Section 5.5 on page 105, except that with BLX (available in architecture v5T only) r14 is set to the address of the following instruction plus 1, indicating that the caller was Thumb code). Here 'H' can be set to select a 'Hi' register (r8 to rl5).

7.3.3 | Assembler Format

```
B<cond> <label>     ; format 1  - Thumb target
B       <label>     ; format 2  - Thumb target
BL      <label>     ; format 3  - Thumb target
BLX     <label>     ; format 3a - ARM target
B{L}X   Rm          ; format 4  - ARM or Thumb target
```

A branch and link generates both format 3 instructions. It is not intended that format 3 instructions are used individually; they should always appear in pairs. Likewise, BLX generates a format 3 instruction and a format 3a instruction.

The assembler will compute the relevant offset to insert into the instruction from the current instruction address, the address of the target label, and a small correction for the pipeline behaviour. If the target is out of range an error message will be output.

7.3.4 | Equivalent ARM Instruction

Although formats 1 to 3 are very similar to the ARM branch and branch-with-link instructions, the ARM instructions support only word (4-byte) offsets whereas the Thumb instructions require half-word (2-byte) offsets. Therefore there is no direct mapping from these Thumb instructions into the ARM instruction set. The ARM cores that support Thumb are slightly modified to support half-word branch offsets, with ARM branch instructions being mapped to even half-word offsets.

Format 4 is equivalent to the ARM instruction with the same assembler syntax. The BLX variant is supported only by ARM processors that implement architecture v5T.

7.3.5 | Subroutine Call and Return

The above instructions, and the equivalent ARM instructions, allow for subroutine calls to functions written in an instruction set the same as, or opposite to, the caller.

Functions that are called only from the same instruction set can use the conventional BL call and MOV pc, r14 or LDMFD sp!, {..,pc} (in Thumb code, POP {..., pc}) return sequences.

Functions that can be called from the opposite instruction set or from either instruction set can return with BX lr or LDMFD sp!,{..., rN}BX rN (in Thumb code, POP {...,rN} ; BX rN).

ARM processors that support architecture v5T can also return with LDMFD sp!, {..., pc} (in Thumb code, POP {..., pc}) as these instructions use the bottom bit of the loaded PC value to update the Thumb bit, but this is not supported in architectures earlier than v5T.

7.4 | Thumb Software Interrupt Instruction

The Thumb software interrupt instruction behaves exactly like the ARM equivalent and the exception entry sequence causes the processor to switch to ARM execution.

7.4.1 | Binary Encoding

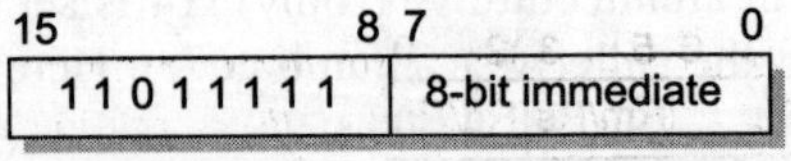

Figure 7.3 Thumb software interrupt binary encoding

7.4.2 | Description

This instruction causes the following actions:

- The address of the next Thumb instruction is saved in r14_svc.
- The CPSR is saved in SPSR_svc.
- The processor disables IRQ, clears the Thumb bit and enters supervisor mode by modifying the relevant bits in the CPSR.
- The PC is forced to address 0x08.

The ARM instruction SWI handler is then entered. The normal return instruction restores the Thumb execution state.

7.4.3 | Assembler Format

SWI <8-bit immediate>

7.4.4 | Equivalent ARM Instruction

The equivalent ARM instruction has an identical assembler syntax; the 8-bit immediate is zero-extended to fill the 24-bit field in the ARM instruction.

Clearly, this limits the SWIs available to Thumb code to the first 256 of the 16 million potential ARM SWIs.

7.5 | Thumb Data Processing Instructions

Thumb data processing instructions comprise a highly optimized set of fairly complex formats covering the operations most commonly required by a compiler.

The functions of these instructions are clear enough. The selection of those to include and those to leave out is far less obvious, but is based on a detailed understanding of the needs of typical application programs.

Figures 7.3 to 7.7 illustrate the binary encoding used for each of the instructions shown alongside the encoded format.

7.5.1 | Binary encodings

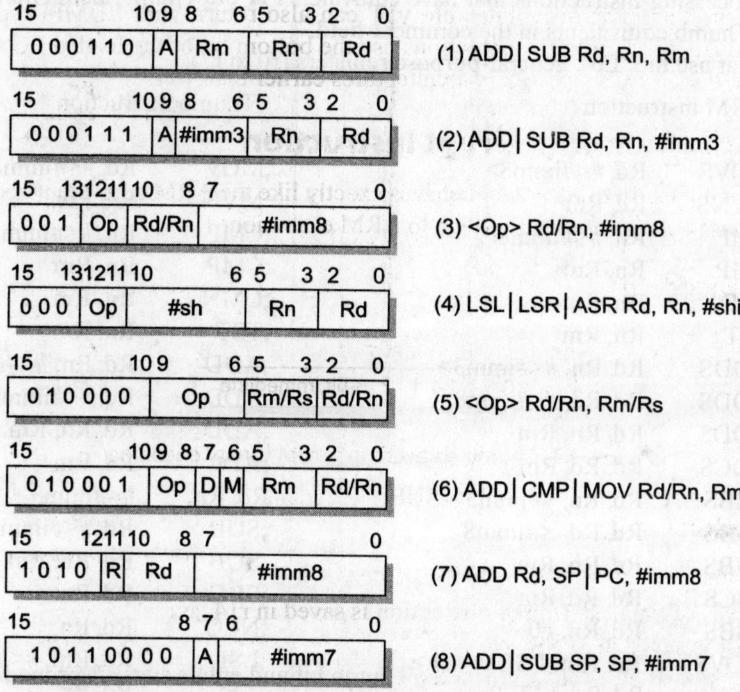

Figure 7.4 Thumb data processing instruction binary encodings

7.5.2 | Description

These instructions all map onto ARM data processing (including multiply) instructions. Although ARM supports a generalized shift on one operand together with an ALU operation in a single instruction, the Thumb instruction set separates shift and ALU operations into separate instructions, so here the shift operation is presented as an opcode rather than as an operand modifier.

7.5.3 | Assembler Format

The various instruction formats are:

```
1:   <op>   Rd, Rn,   Rm           ; <op> = ADD|SUB
2:   <op>   Rd, Rn,   #<#imm3>     ; <op> = ADD|SUB
3:   <op>   Rd|Rn,    #<#imm8>     ; <op> = ADD|SUB|MOV|CMP
```

```
4:    <op>      Rd, Rn, #<#sh>           ; <op> = LSL|LSR|ASR
5:    <op>      Rd|Rn, Rm|Rs             ; <op> = MVN|CMP|CMN|..
     ;..TST|ADC|SBC|NEG|MUL|LSL|LSR|ASR|ROR| AND|EOR|ORR|BIC
6:    <op>      Rd|Rn, Rm                ; <op> = ADD|CMP| MOV
     ;                                     (Hi regs)
7:    ADD       Rd, SP|PC, #<#imm8>
8:    <op>      SP, SP, #<#imm7>         ;<op> = ADD|SUB
```

7.5.4 | Equivalent ARM Instructions

The ARM data processing instructions that have equivalents in the Thumb instruction set are listed below, with their Thumb equivalents in the comment field.

Instructions that use the 'Lo', general-purpose registers (r0 to r7):

```
;ARM instruction                      Thumb instruction

MOVS   Rd, #<#imm8>                   ;MOV   Rd, #<#imm8>
MVNS   Rd, Rm                         ;MVN   Rd, Rm
CMP    Rn, #<#imm8>                   ;CMP   Rn, #<#imm8>
CMP    Rn, Rm                         ;CMP   Rn, Rm
CMN    Rn, Rm                         ;CMN   Rn, Rm
TST    Rn, Rm                         ;TST   Rn, Rm
ADDS   Rd, Rn, #<#imm3>               ;ADD   Rd, Rn, #<#imm3>
ADDS   Rd, Rd, #<#imm8>               ;ADD   Rd, #<#imm8>
ADDS   Rd, Rn, Rm                     ;ADD   Rd, Rn, Rm
ADCS   Rd, Rd, Rm                     ;ADC   Rd, Rm
SUBS   Rd, Rn, <#imm3>;SUB            Rd, Rn, #<#imm3>
SUBS   Rd, Rd, <#imm8>                ;SUB   Rd, #<#imm8>
SUBS   Rd, Rn, Rm                     ;SUB   Rd, Rn, Rm
SBCS   Rd, Rd, Rm                     ;SBC   Rd, Rm
RSBS   Rd, Rn, #0                     ;NEG   Rd, Rn
MOVS   Rd, Rm, LSL #<#sh>             ;LSL   Rd, Rm, #<#sh>
MOVS   Rd, Rd, LSL Rs                 ;LSL   Rd, Rs
MOVS   Rd, Rm, LSR #<#sh>             ;LSR   Rd, Rm, #<#sh>
MOVS   Rd, Rd, LSR Rs                 ;LSR   Rd, Rs
MOVS   Rd, Rm, ASR #<#sh>             ;ASR   Rd, Rm, #<#sh>
MOVS   Rd, Rd, ASR Rs                 ;ASR   Rd, Rs
MOVS   Rd, Rd, ROR Rs                 ;ROR   Rd, Rs
ANDS   Rd, Rd, Rm                     ;AND   Rd, Rm
EORS   Rd, Rd, Rm                     ;EOR   Rd, Rm
ORRS   Rd, Rd, Rm                     ;ORR   Rd, Rm
BICS   Rd, Rd, Rm                     ;BIC   Rd, Rm
MULS   Rd, Rm, Rd                     ;MUL   Rd, Rm
```

Instructions that operate with or on the 'Hi' registers (r8 to r15), in some cases in combination with a 'Lo' register:

```
;ARM instruction                          Thumb instruction
ADD     Rd, Rd, Rm                        ;ADD    Rd, Rm (1/2 Hi regs)
CMP     Rn, Rm                            ;CMP    Rn, Rm (1/2 Hi regs)
MOV     Rd, Rm                            ;MOV    Rd, Rm (1/2 Hi regs)
ADD     Rd, PC, #<#imm8>                  ;ADD    Rd, PC, #<#imm8>
ADD     Rd, SP,  #<#imm8>                 ;ADD    Rd, SP,  #<#imm8>
ADD     SP, SP,  #<#imm7>                 ;ADD    SP,  SP,  #<#imm7>
SUB     SP, SP,  #<#imm7>                 ;SUB    SP,  SP,  #<#imm7>
```

Notes

1. *All* the data processing instructions that operate with and on the 'Lo' registers update the condition code bits (the S bit is set in the equivalent ARM instruction).
2. The instructions that operate with and on the 'Hi' registers do *not* change the condition code bits, with the exception of CMP which only changes the condition codes.
3. The instructions that are indicated above as requiring '1 or 2 Hi regs' must have one or both register operands specified in the 'Hi' register area.
4. #imm3, #imm7 and #imm8 denote 3-, 7- and 8-bit immediate fields respectively. #sh denotes a 5-bit shift amount field.

7.6 | Thumb Single Register Data Transfer Instructions

Again the choice of ARM instructions which are represented in the Thumb instruction set appears complex, but is based on the sort of things that compilers like to do frequently.

Note the larger offsets for accesses to the literal pool (PC-relative) and to the stack (SP-relative), and the restricted support given to signed operands (base plus register addressing only) compared with unsigned operands (base plus offset or register).

7.6.1 | Binary Encodings

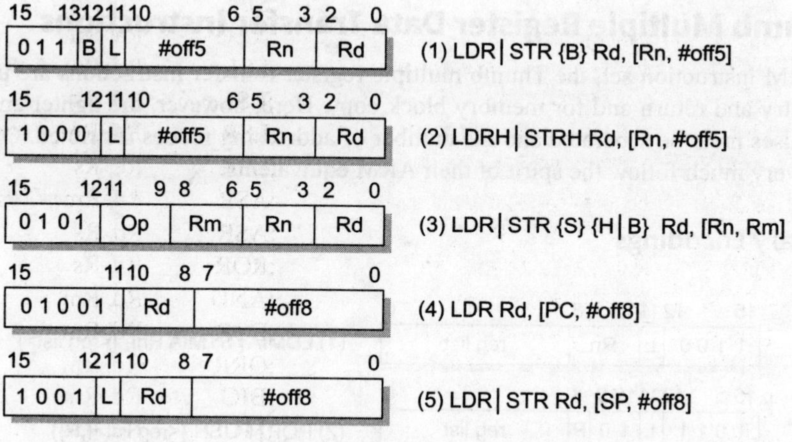

Figure 7.5 Thumb single register data transfer binary encodings

7.6.2 | Description

These instructions are a carefully derived subset of the ARM single register transfer instructions, and have exactly the same semantics as the ARM equivalent.

In all cases the offset is scaled to the size of the data type, so, for instance, the range of the 5-bit offset is 32 bytes in a load or store byte instruction, 64 bytes in a load or store half-word instruction and 128 bytes in a load or store word instruction.

7.6.3 | Assembler Format

The various assembler formats are:

```
1:  <op>   Rd, [Rn,  #<#off5>]    ; <op> = LDR|LDRB|STR|STRB
2:  <op>   Rd, [Rn,  #<#off5>]    ; <op> = LDRH|STRH
3:  <op>   Rd, [Rn,  Rm]          ; <op> = ..
                                  ; .. LDR| LDRH|LDRSH|LDRB|LDRSB| STR|STRH| STRB
4:  LDR    Rd, [PC,  #<#off8>]
5:  <op>   Rd, [SP,  #<#off8>]    ; <op> = LDR| STR
```

7.6.4 | Equivalent ARM Instruction

The ARM equivalents to these Thumb instructions have identical assembler formats.

Notes

1. #off 5 and #off 8 denote 5- and 8-bit immediate offsets respectively. The assembler format specifies the offset in bytes in all cases. The 5- or 8-bit offset in the instruction binary is scaled by the size of the data type.
2. As with the ARM instructions, the signed variants are only supported by the load instructions since store signed and store unsigned have exactly the same effect.

7.7 | Thumb Multiple Register Data Transfer Instructions

As in the ARM instruction set, the Thumb multiple register transfer instructions are useful both for procedure entry and return and for memory block copy. Here, however, the tighter encoding means that the two uses must be separated and the number of addressing modes restricted. Otherwise these instructions very much follow the spirit of their ARM equivalents.

7.7.1 | Binary Encodings

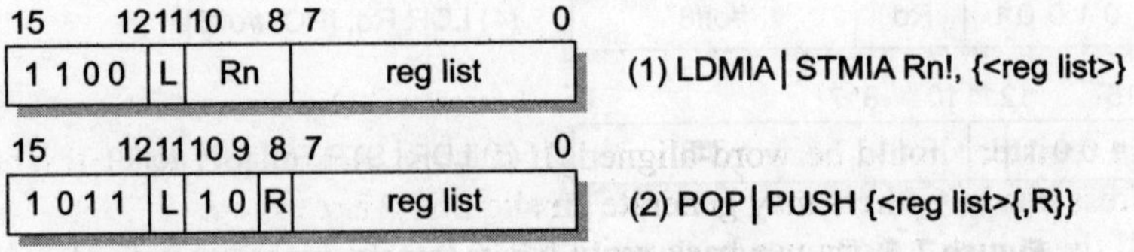

Figure 7.6 Thumb multiple register data transfer binary encodings

7.7.2 | Description

The block copy forms of the instruction use the LDMIA and STMIA addressing modes (see Figure 3.2 on page 48). The base register may be any of the 'Lo' registers (r0 to r7), and the register list may include any subset of these registers but should not include the base register itself since write-back is always selected (and the result of a load or store multiple register with the base register in the list and write-back selected is unpredictable).

The stack forms use SP (r13) as the base register and again always use write-back. The stack model is fixed as full-descending. In addition to the eight registers which may be specified in the register list, the link register (LR, or rl4) may be included in the 'PUSH' instruction and the PC (rl5) may be included in the 'POP form, optimizing procedure entry and exit sequences as is often done in ARM code.

7.7.3 | Assembler Format

<reg list> is a list of registers and register ranges from r0 to r7.

```
LDMIA  Rn!,  {<reg list>}
STMIA  Rn!,  {<reg list>)
POP          {<reg list>{, pc}}
PUSH         {<reg list>{, lr}}
```

7.7.4 | Equivalent ARM Instruction

The equivalent ARM instructions have the same assembler format in the first two cases, and replace POP and PUSH with the appropriate addressing mode in the second two cases.

Block copy:

```
LDMIA     Rn!, {<reg list>}
          STMIA  Rn!, {<reg list>}
```

Pop:

```
LDMFD     SP!, {<reg list>{, pc}}
```

Push:

```
          STMFD SP!, {<reg list>{, lr}}
```

Notes

1. The base register should be word-aligned. If it is not, some systems will ignore the bottom two address bits but others may generate an alignment exception.
2. Since all these instructions use base write-back, the base register should not be included in the register list.

3. The register list is encoded with one bit for each register; bit 0 indicates whether r0 will be transferred, bit 1 controls r1, etc. The R bit controls the PC and LR options in the POP and PUSH instructions.
4. In architecture v5T only, the bottom bit of a loaded PC updates the Thumb bit, enabling a direct return to a Thumb or ARM caller.

7.8 | Thumb Breakpoint Instruction

The Thumb breakpoint instruction behaves exactly like the ARM equivalent. Breakpoint instructions are used for software debugging purposes; they cause the processor to break from normal instruction execution and enter appropriate debugging procedures.

7.8.1 | Binary Encoding

15 ... 8	7 ... 0
1 0 1 1 1 1 1 0	x x x x x x x x

Figure 7.7 Thumb breakpoint binary encoding

7.8.2 | Description

This instruction causes the processor to take a prefetch abort when the debug hardware unit is configured appropriately.

7.8.3 | Assembler Format

BKPT

7.8.4 | Equivalent ARM Instruction

The equivalent ARM instruction has an identical assembler syntax. The BKPT instruction is supported only by ARM processors that implement ARM architecture v5T.

7.9 | Thumb Implementation

The Thumb instruction set can be incorporated into a 3-stage pipeline ARM processor macrocell with relatively minor changes to most of the processor logic (the 5-stage pipeline implementations are trickier). The biggest addition is the Thumb instruction decompressor in the instruction pipeline; this logic translates a Thumb instruction into its equivalent ARM instruction. The organization of this logic is shown in Figure 7.8.

The addition of the decompressor logic in series with the instruction decoder might be expected to increase the decode latency, but in fact the ARM7 pipeline does relatively little work in phase 1 of the decode cycle. Therefore the decompression logic can be accommodated here without compromising the cycle time or increasing the pipeline latency, and the ARM7TDMI Thumb pipeline operates in exactly the way described in 'The 3-stage pipeline' on page 65.

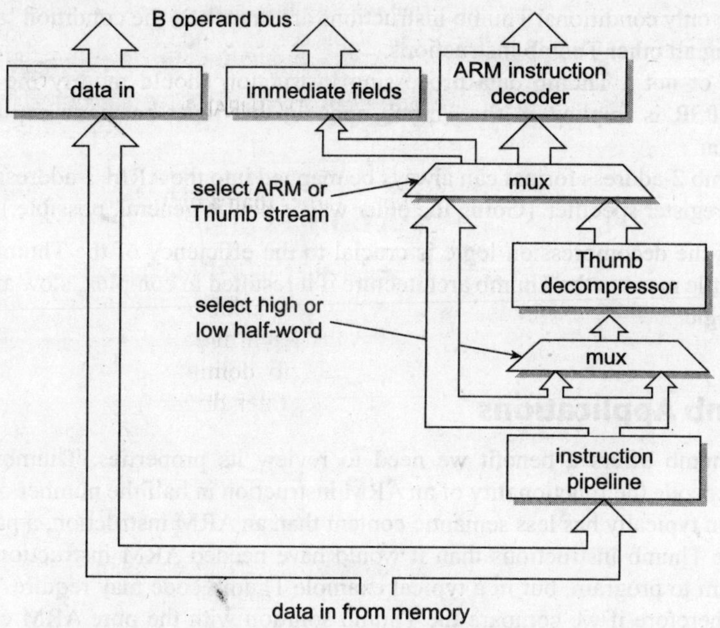

Figure 7.8 The Thumb instruction decompressor organization

7.9.1 | Instruction Mapping

The Thumb decompressor performs a static translation from the 16-bit Thumb instruction into the equivalent 32-bit ARM instruction. This involves performing a look-up to translate the major and minor opcodes, zero-extending the 3-bit register specifiers to give 4-bit specifiers and mapping other fields across as required.

As an example, the mapping of a Thumb 'ADD Rd, #imm8' instruction (see Section 7.5) to the corresponding ARM 'ADDS Rd, Rd, #imm8' instruction (described in Section 5.7 on page 103) is shown in Figure 7.9. Note that:

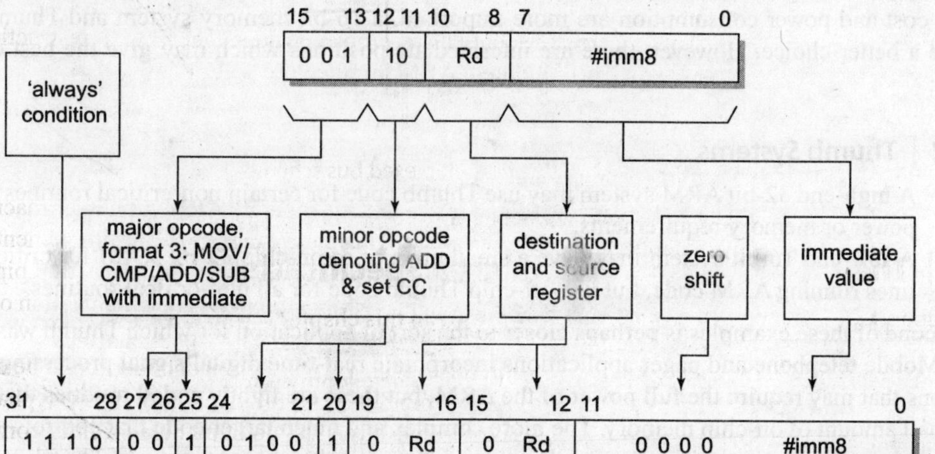

Figure 7.9 Thumb to ARM instruction mapping

- Since the only conditional Thumb instructions are branches, the condition 'always' is used in translating all other Thumb instructions.
- Whether or not a Thumb data processing instruction should modify the condition codes in the CPSR is implicit in the Thumb opcode; this must be made explicit in the ARM instruction.
- The Thumb 2-address format can always be mapped into the ARM 3-address format by replicating a register specifier. (Going the other way is not, in general, possible.)

The simplicity of the decompression logic is crucial to the efficiency of the Thumb instruction set. There would be little merit in the Thumb architecture if it resulted in complex, slow and power-hungry decompression logic.

7.10 | Thumb Applications

To see where Thumb offers a benefit we need to review its properties. Thumb instructions are 16 bits long and encode the functionality of an ARM instruction in half the number of bits, but since a Thumb instruction typically has less semantic content than an ARM instruction, a particular program will require more Thumb instructions than it would have needed ARM instructions. The ratio will vary from program to program, but in a typical example Thumb code may require 70% of the space of ARM code. Therefore if we compare the Thumb solution with the pure ARM code solution, the following characteristics emerge:

7.10.1 | Thumb Properties

- The Thumb code requires 70% of the space of the ARM code.
- The Thumb code uses 40% more instructions than the ARM code.
- With 32-bit memory, the ARM code is 40% faster than the Thumb code.
- With 16-bit memory, the Thumb code is 45% faster than the ARM code.
- Thumb code uses 30% less external memory power than ARM code.

So where performance is all-important, a system should use 32-bit memory and run ARM code. Where cost and power consumption are more important, a 16-bit memory system and Thumb code may be a better choice. However, there are intermediate positions which may give the best of both worlds:

7.10.2 | Thumb Systems

- A high-end 32-bit ARM system may use Thumb code for certain non-critical routines to save power or memory requirements.
- A low-end 16-bit system may have a small amount of on-chip 32-bit RAM for critical routines running ARM code, but use off-chip Thumb code for all non-critical routines.

The second of these examples is perhaps closer to the sort of application for which Thumb was developed. Mobile telephone and pager applications incorporate real-time digital signal processing (DSP) functions that may require the full power of the ARM, but these are tightly coded routines that can fit in a small amount of on-chip memory. The more complex and much larger code that controls the user interface, battery management system, and so on, is less time-critical, and the use of Thumb code will enable off-chip ROMs to give good performance on an 8- or 16-bit bus, saving cost and improving battery life.

7.11 | Example and Exercises

EXAMPLE 7.1

Rewrite the 'Hello World' program in Section 3.4 on page 60 to use Thumb instructions. How do the ARM and Thumb code sizes compare?

Here is the original ARM program:

```
            AREA        HellOW, CODE, READONLY
SWI_WriteC              EQU     &0              ; output character in r0
SWI_Exit                EQU     &11             ; finish program
            ENTRY                               ; code entry point
START       ADR         r1, TEXT                ; r1 -> "Hello World"
LOOP        LDRB        r0, [r1], #1            ; get the next byte
            CMP         r0, #0                  ; check for text end
            SWINE       SWI_WriteC              ; if not end print ..
            BNE         LOOP                    ; .. and loop back
            SWI         SWI_Exit                ; end of execution
TEXT        =           "Hello World", &0a, &0d, 0
            END                                 ; end of program source
```

Most of these instructions have direct Thumb equivalents; however, some do not. The load byte instruction does not support auto-indexing and the supervisor call cannot be conditionally executed. Hence the Thumb code needs to be slightly modified:

```
            AREA        HelloW_Thumb, CODE, READONLY
SWI_WriteC              EQU     &0                      ;output character in r0
SWI_Exit                EQU     &11                     ;finish program
            ENTRY                                       ;code entry point
            CODE32                                      ;enter in ARM state
            ADR         rO,     START+1                 ;get Thumb entry address
            BX          r0                              ;enter Thumb area
            CODE16                                      ;Thumb code follows..
START       ADR         r1,     TEXT                    ;r1 -> "Hello World"
LOOP        LDRB        r0,     [r1]                    ;get the next byte
            ADD         r1,     r1,     #1              ;increment pointer **T
            CMP         r0,     #0                      ;check for text end
            BEQ         DONE                            ;finished?      **T
            SWI         SWI_WriteC                      ;if not end print  ..
            B           LOOP                            ;..and loop back
DONE        SWI         SWI_Exit                        ;end of execution
            ALIGN                                       ;to ensure ADR works
TEXT        DATA
            =           "Hello World", &0a, &0d, &00
`           end
```

The two additional instructions required to compensate for the features absent from the Thumb instruction set are marked with '**T' in the above listing. The ARM code size is six instructions plus 14 bytes of data, 38 bytes in all. The Thumb code size is eight instructions plus 14 bytes of data (ignoring the preamble required to switch the processor to executing Thumb instructions), making 30 bytes in all.

This example illustrates a number of important points to bear in mind when writing Thumb code:

- The assembler needs to know when to produce ARM code and when to produce Thumb code. The 'CODE32' and 'CODE16' directives provide this information. (These are instructions to the assembler and do not themselves cause any code to be generated.)
- Since the processor is executing ARM instructions when it calls the code, explicit provision must be made to instruct it to execute the Thumb instructions. The 'BX r0' instruction achieves this, provided that r0 has been initialized appropriately. Note particularly that the bottom bit of r0 is set to cause the processor to execute Thumb instructions at the branch target.
- In Thumb code 'ADR' can only generate word-aligned addresses. As Thumb instructions are half-words, there is no guarantee that a location following an arbitrary number of Thumb instructions will be word-aligned. Therefore the example program has an explicit 'ALIGN' before the text string.

In order to assemble and run this program on the ARM software development toolkit, an assembler that can generate Thumb code must be invoked and the ARMulator must emulate a 'Thumb-aware' processor core. The default setting of the Project Manager targets an ARM6 core and generates only 32-bit ARM code. This may be changed by choosing 'Project' from the 'Options' menu within the Project Manager and selecting 'TCC/TASM' in the 'Tools' dialogue box before generating the code. The 'Target Processor' will automatically switch to the Thumb-aware ARM7T when this is done.

Otherwise, assembling and running Thumb code is just like using ARM code.

Exercise 7.1.1

Convert the other programs in Sections 3.4 and 3.5 on pages 60 and 62 into Thumb code and compare their sizes with the original ARM code.

Exercise 7.1.2

All ARM instructions are executed 'conditionally' while THUMB instructions are executed 'unconditionally'. To compare the code length for ARM and THUMB, write a program for calculating the factorial of a number in both ARM and THUMB assembly language. Now compare them in terms of the number of instructions, execution times and memory utilised.

8

Architectural Support for System Development

SUMMARY OF CHAPTER CONTENTS

Designing any computer system is a complex task; designing an embedded 'system-on-chip' is a daunting one. The development often takes place entirely within a CAD environment, and the first silicon must not only function but it must deliver the necessary performance and be manufacturable. The only scope for fixing design flaws is in the software; to modify the chip in order to correct errors takes too long and usually incurs considerable cost.

For the past two decades the principal approach to microprocessor system development has been based upon the *In-Circuit Emulator* (ICE). The system itself was a printed circuit board incorporating a microprocessor chip and various memory and peripheral devices. To use the ICE, the microprocessor was removed from its socket and replaced by a header plug with an umbilical connection to the ICE equipment. The ICE emulated the function of the microprocessor and gave the user an inside view on the internal state of the system, giving access to read and modify processor registers and memory values, to set breakpoints, and so on.

Now that the microprocessor itself has become just a cell on a larger chip, this whole approach has collapsed. It is not possible to unplug part of a chip! There is, as yet, no approach that has replaced the ICE in all its roles, but there are several techniques that contribute, some of which require explicit support in the processor's architecture. This chapter covers the techniques available to support the development of system chips based on ARM cores and the architectural features built into the cores to assist in this process.

8.1 | The ARM Memory Interface

In this section we look at the general principles involved in connecting an ARM processor to a memory system built from standard memory parts. The efficiency of the memory interface is an important determinant of the system performance, so these principles must be well understood by the designer who wishes to develop a high-performance system.

More recent ARM cores have direct AMBA interfaces (see Section 8.2), but many of the basic issues discussed here still apply.

8.1.1 | Arm Bus Signals

ARM processor chips vary in the details of their bus interfaces, but they are generally similar in nature. The memory bus interface signals include the following:

- A 32-bit address bus, *A*[31:0], which gives the byte address of the data to be accessed.
- A 32-bit bidirectional data bus, *D*[31:0], along which the data is transferred.
- Signals that specify whether the memory is needed (*mreq*) and whether the address is sequential (*seq*); these are issued in the previous cycle so that the memory control logic can prepare appropriately.
- Signals that specify the direction ($\overline{r}/w$) and size ($\overline{b}/w$) on earlier processors; *mas*[1:0] on later processors) of the transfer.
- Bus timing and control signals (*abe, ale, ape, dbe, lock, bl*[3:0]).

8.1.2 | Simple Memory Interface

The simplest form of memory interface is suitable for operation with ROM and static RAM **(SRAM)**. These devices require the address to be stable until the end of the cycle, which may be achieved by disabling the address pipeline (tying *ape* low) on later processors or retiming the address bus (connecting *ale* to $\overline{mclk}$) on earlier processors. The address and data buses may then be connected directly to the memory parts as shown in Figure 8.1 which also shows the output enable signals ($\overline{RAMoe}$ and $\overline{ROMoe}$) and the write enables ($\overline{RAMwe}$).

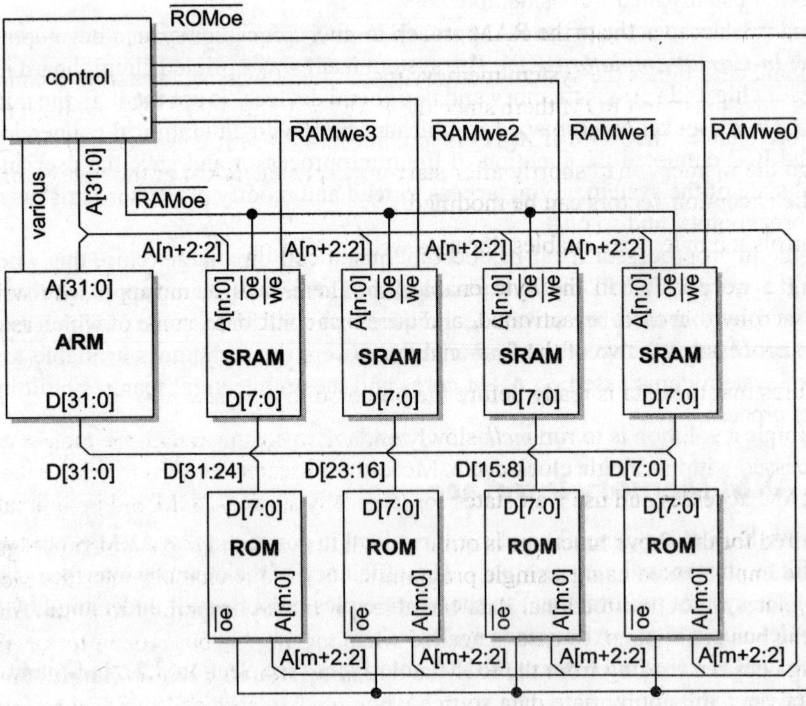

Figure 8.1 A basic ARM memory system

This figure illustrates the connection of 8-bit memory parts, which are a standard configuration for SRAMs and ROMs. Four parts of each type are required to form a 32-bit memory and an individual device is connected to a single byte section of the bus. The notation on the figure shows the device's bus numbering inside the device and the bus wires to which it is connected outside the device, so, for example, the SRAM shown nearest the ARM has its pins *D*[7:0] connected to bus pins *D*[31:24] which are connected to the ARM's pins *D*[31:24].

Since the bottom two address lines, *A*[1:0], are used for byte selection, they are used by the control logic and not connected to the memory. Therefore the address lines on the memory devices are connected to *A*[2] and upwards, the precise number used depending on the size of the memory part (for example, a 128 Kbyte ROM part will use *A*[18:2]).

Although the ARM performs reads of both bytes and words, the memory system can ignore the difference (at the cost of some power wastage) and always simply supply a word quantity. The ARM will extract the addressed byte and ignore the remainder of the word. Therefore the ROMs do not need individual enables and using 16-bit devices causes no problems. Byte *writes*, however, do require individual byte enables, so the control logic must generate four byte write enable controls. This makes the use of wider RAMs difficult (and inefficient) unless they incorporate separate byte enables, since writing an individual byte would require a read-modify-write memory operation. Since many processors require support for writing bytes, it is likely that if RAMs do become available with a data width greater than a byte, they will incorporate individual byte enables.

8.1.3 | Control Logic

The control logic performs the following functions:

- It decides when to activate the RAM and when to activate the ROM.

  This logic determines the system memory map. The processor starts from location zero after a reset, so it must find ROM there since the RAM is uninitialized. The simplest memory map therefore enables the ROM if *A*[31] is low and the RAM if it is high. (Most ARM systems change the memory map shortly after start-up to put the RAM at the bottom of memory so that the exception vectors can be modified.)

- It controls the byte write enables during a write operation.

  During a word write all the byte enables should be active, during a byte write only the addressed byte should be activated, and where the ARM supports half-words a half-word write should activate two of the four enables.

- It ensures that the data is ready before the processor continues.

  The simplest solution is to run *mclk* slowly enough to ensure that all the memory devices can be accessed within a single clock cycle. More sophisticated systems may have the clock set to suit RAM accesses and use wait states for (typically slower) ROM and peripheral accesses.

The logic required for the above functions is quite straightforward and is illustrated in Figure 8.2. (All this logic can be implemented using a single programmable logic device.) Perhaps the trickiest aspect of the design relates to the bidirectional data bus. Here it is very important to ensure that only one device drives the bus at any time, so care is needed when turning the bus around for a write cycle, or when switching between reading from the ROM and reading from the RAM. The solution illustrated in the figure activates the appropriate data source when *mclk* is high and turns all sources off when *mclk* is low, so *dbe*, the processor's data bus enable, should also be connected to *mclk*. This is a very conservative solution which will often compromise the performance of the system by limiting the maximum clock frequency that can be used.

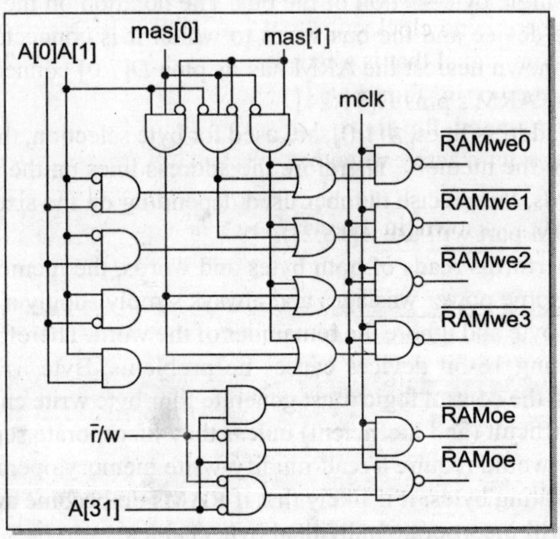

Figure 8.2 Simple ARM memory system control logic

Note that this design assumes that the ARM outputs are stable to the end of the clock cycle, which will be the case on newer processors with the address pipeline enable (*ape*) control input tied low. Older processors should use $ale = mclk$ to retime the address outputs, but will need an external transparent latch which is open when *mclk* is low to retime $(\overline{r}/w)$ and $(\overline{b}/w)$ (which replaces *mas* [1], and *mas*[0] is tied low).

This simple memory system makes no use of $\overline{mreq}$ (or *seq*); it simply activates the memory on every cycle. This is safe since the ARM will only request a write cycle on a genuine memory access. The $(\overline{r}/w)$ control remains low during all internal and coprocessor register transfer cycles.

8.1.4 | Wait States

If we try to speed up the clock in this system it will stop working when the slowest path fails. This will normally be the ROM access. We can get a lot more performance from the system if the clock is tuned to the RAM access time and wait states are introduced to allow the ROM more access time. Usually the ROM will be allowed a fixed number of clock cycles per access, the exact number being determined by the clock rate and the ROM data sheet. We will assume an access time of four clock cycles.

The memory control logic must now incorporate a simple finite state machine to control the ROM access. A suitable state transition diagram is shown in Figure 8.3.

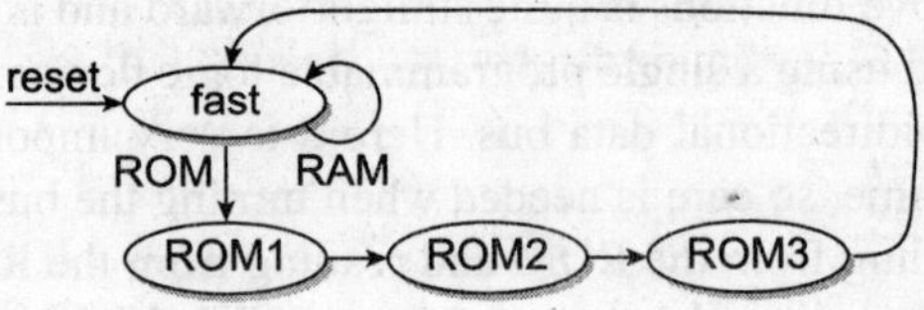

Figure 8.3 ROM wait control state transition diagram

The three ROM states are used to stretch the ROM access time to four cycles by asserting the ARM's *wait* input. A design problem here is that since the addresses have been retimed to become valid early in the current cycle and *wait* must be asserted before *mclk* rises, *wait* cannot be generated as a simple state machine output since there is no clock edge that can be used to generate it. Another problem is to generate a stretched *ROMoe* signal that is glitch-free.

A possible circuit is shown in Figure 8.4. The state machine is a synchronous counter which uses the two edge-triggered flip-flops. Only the state ROM3 is of significance, since it de-activates *wait* which is otherwise active whenever a ROM access is detected. The two level-sensitive latches are used to generate a clean, stretched *ROMoe* using *wait* as the starting point. A timing diagram for this circuit is shown in Figure 8.5, which should clarify the operation of the logic.

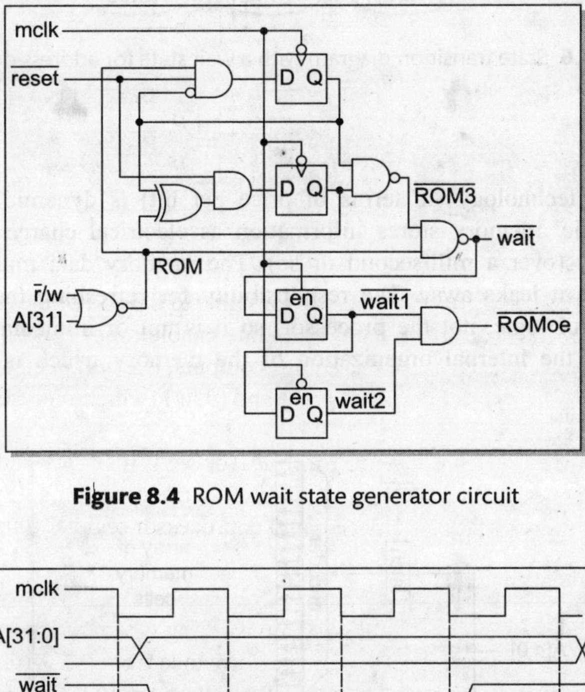

Figure 8.4 ROM wait state generator circuit

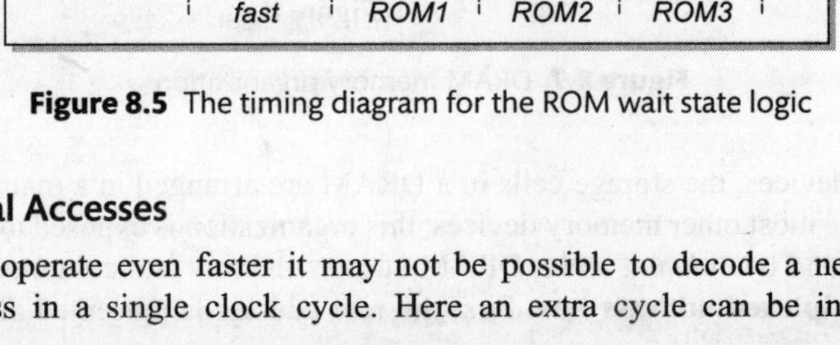

Figure 8.5 The timing diagram for the ROM wait state logic

8.1.5 | Sequential Accesses

If the system is to operate even faster it may not be possible to decode a new address and perform a RAM access in a single clock cycle. Here an extra cycle can be inserted whenever an unknown address is issued to allow time for address decoding. The only addresses that are not unknown are sequential ones, but these represent around 75% of all addresses in a typical program.

We should also now begin to recognize cycles that do not use the memory, since there is no reason why they should not operate at the full clock rate. A suitable state transition diagram is shown in Figure 8.6.

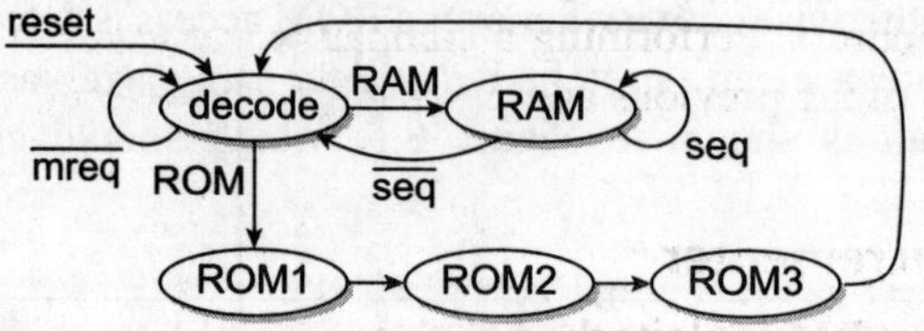

Figure 8.6 State transition diagram with a wait state for address decoding

8.1.6 | DRAM

The cheapest memory technology (in terms of price per bit) is dynamic random access memory **(DRAM)**. 'Dynamic' memory stores information as electrical charge on a capacitor where it gradually leaks away (over a millisecond or so). The memory data must be read and rewritten ('refreshed') before it leaks away. The responsibility for refreshing the memory usually lies with the memory control logic, not the processor, so it is not of immediate concern to us here. What is of concern is the internal organization of the memory which is shown in Figure 8.7.

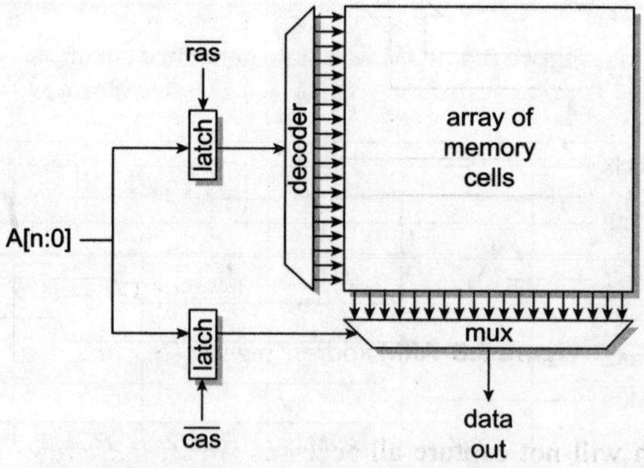

Figure 8.7 DRAM memory organization

Like most memory devices, the storage cells in a DRAM are arranged in a matrix which is approximately square. Unlike most other memory devices, this organization is exposed to the user. The matrix is addressed by *row* and by *column*, and a DRAM accepts the row and column addresses separately down the same **multiplexed address bus**. First the row address is presented and latched using the active-low **row address strobe** signal ($\overline{ras}$), then the column address is presented and latched using the active-low **column address strobe** ($\overline{cas}$). If the next access is within the same row, a new column address may be presented without first supplying a new row address. Since a $\overline{cas}$-only access does not activate the cell matrix it can deliver its data two to three times faster than a full $\overline{ras}$-$\overline{cas}$ access and consumes considerably less power. It is therefore very advantageous to use $\overline{cas}$-only accesses whenever possible.

The difficulty is in detecting early enough in the memory access that the new address is in the same row as the previous address. Performing a comparison of the relevant bits of the new address with the corresponding bits of the previous address is almost always too slow.

8.1.7 | ARM Address Incrementer

The solution adopted on the ARM exploits the fact that most addresses (typically 75%) are generated in the address incrementer. The ARM address selection logic (shown in Figure 8.8) picks the address for the next cycle from one of four sources. One of these sources is the incrementer. The ARM indicates to the outside world whenever the next address is coming from the incrementer by asserting the *seq* output. External logic can then look at the previous address to check for row boundaries; if the previous address is *not* at the end of a row and the *seq* signal is asserted then a $\overline{cas}$-only memory access can be performed.

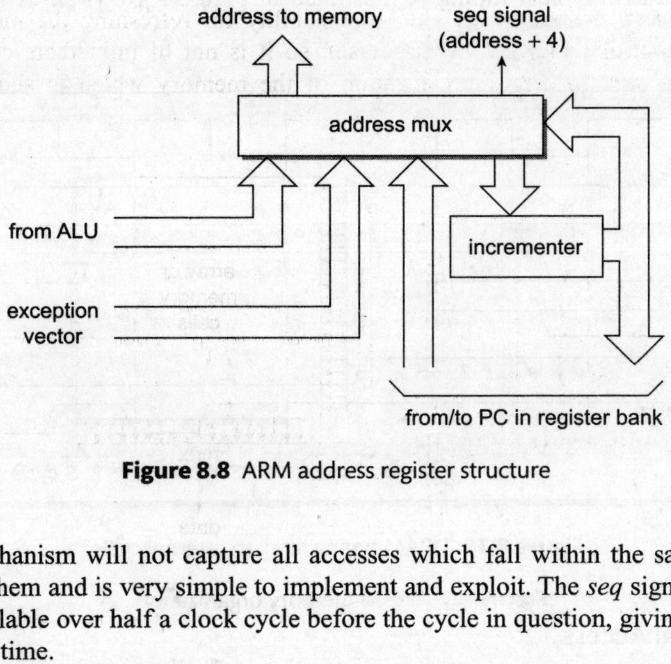

Figure 8.8 ARM address register structure

Although this mechanism will not capture all accesses which fall within the same DRAM row, it does find most of them and is very simple to implement and exploit. The *seq* signal and the previous address are all available over half a clock cycle before the cycle in question, giving the memory control logic plenty of time.

A typical DRAM timing diagram is shown in Figure 8.9. The first, non-sequential access takes two clock cycles as the row address is strobed in, but subsequent sequential addresses use a $\overline{cas}$-only access and operate in a single clock cycle. (Note that early address timing is now used with *ape* or *ale* high.)

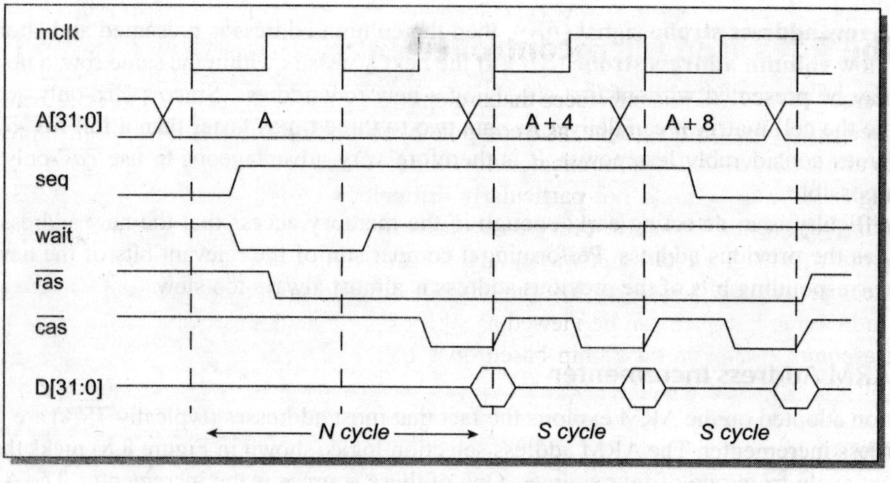

Figure 8.9 DRAM timing illustration

The other use of the *seq* signal, to indicate a cycle which will use the same address as the preceding internal or coprocessor register transfer cycle, can also be exploited to improve DRAM access times. The DRAM access is started in the preceding cycle, which is only possible because *seq* is available so early. Typical timing is illustrated in Figure 8.10. (*wait* is inactive during this sequence.)

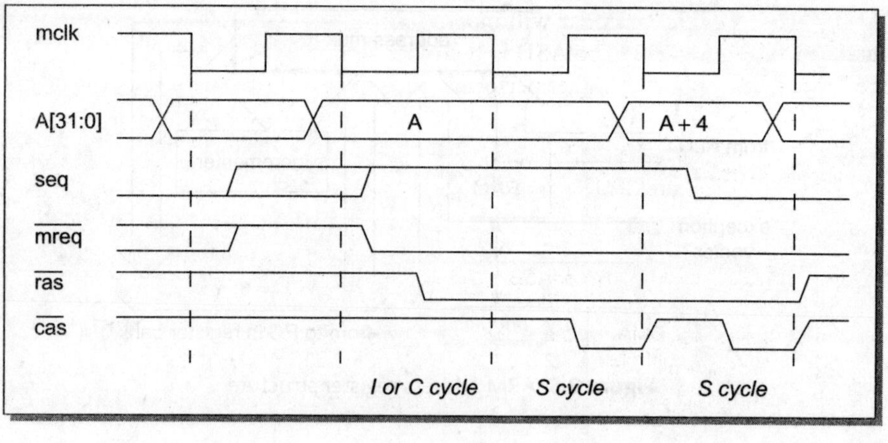

Figure 8.10 DRAM timing after an internal cycle

8.1.8 | Peripheral Access

Most systems incorporate peripheral devices in addition to the memory components described so far. These often have slow access speeds, but can be interfaced using techniques similar to those described above for ROM access.

8.2 | The Advanced Microcontroller Bus Architecture (AMBA)

ARM processor cores have bus interfaces that are optimized for high-speed cache interfacing. Where a core is used, with or without a cache, as a component on a complex system chip, some interfacing is required to allow the ARM to communicate with other on-chip macrocells.

Although this interfacing is not particularly difficult to design, there are many potential solutions. Making an *ad hoc* choice in every case consumes design resource and inhibits the reuse of peripheral macrocells. To avoid this waste, ARM Limited specified the Advanced Microcontroller Bus Architecture, **AMBA**, to standardize the on-chip connection of different macrocells. Macrocells designed to this bus interface can be viewed as a kit of parts for future system chips, and ultimately designing a complex system on a chip based on a new combination of existing macrocells could become a straightforward task.

8.2.1 | AMBA Buses

Three buses are defined within the AMBA specification:

- The *Advanced High-performance Bus* (**AHB**) is used to connect high-performance system modules. It supports burst mode data transfers and split transactions, and all timing is referenced to a single clock edge.
- The *Advanced System Bus* (**ASB**) is used to connect high-performance system modules. It supports burst mode data transfers.
- The *Advanced Peripheral Bus* (**APB**) offers a simpler interface for low-performance peripherals.

A typical AMBA-based microcontroller will incorporate either an AHB or an ASB together with an APB as illustrated in Figure 8.11. The ASB is the older form of system bus, with AHB being introduced later to improve support for higher performance, synthesis and timing verification.

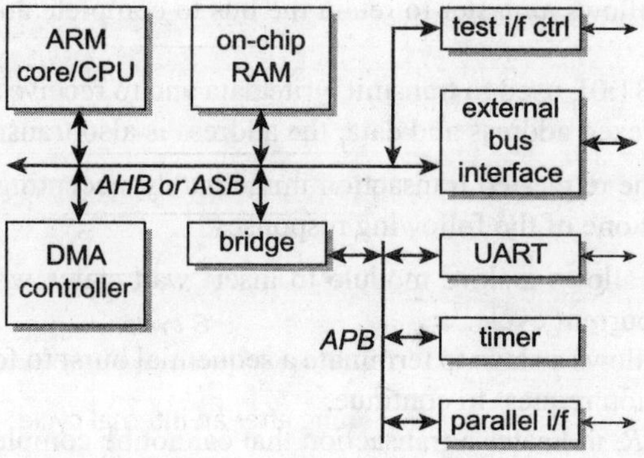

Figure 8.11 A typical AMBA-based system

The APB is generally used as a local secondary bus which appears as a single slave module on the AHB or ASB.

In the following sections we assume the system bus is an ASB. More details on the AHB are provided at the end of the section.

8.2.2 | Arbitration

A bus transaction is initiated by a bus master which requests access from a central arbiter. The arbiter decides priorities when there are conflicting requests, and its design is a system-specific issue. The ASB only specifies the protocol which must be followed:

- The master, *x*, issues a request (*AREQx*) to the central arbiter.
- When the bus is available, the arbiter issues a grant (*AGNTx*) to the master. (The arbitration must take account of the bus lock signal (*BLOK*) when deciding which grant to issue to ensure that atomic bus transactions are not violated.)

8.2.3 | Bus Transfers

When a master has been granted access to the bus, it issues address and control information to indicate the type of the transfer and the slave device which should respond. The following signal is used to define the transaction timing:

- The bus clock, *BCLK*. This will usually be the same as *mclk*, the ARM processor clock.

The bus master which holds the grant then proceeds with the bus transaction using the following signals:

- Bus transaction, *BTRAN*[1:0], indicates whether the next bus cycle will be address-only, sequential or non-sequential. It is enabled by the grant signal and is ahead of the bus cycle to which it refers.
- The address bus, *BA*[31:0]. (Not all address lines need be implemented in systems with modest address-space requirements, and in a multiplexed implementation the address is sent down the data bus.)
- Bus transfer direction, *BWRITE*.
- Bus protection signals, *BPROT*[1:0], which indicate instruction or data fetches and supervisor or user access.
- The transfer size, *BSIZE*[1:0], specifies a byte, half-word or word transfer.
- Bus lock, *BLOK*, allows a master to retain the bus to complete an atomic read-modify-write transaction.
- The data bus, *BD*[31:0], used to transmit write data and to receive read data. In an implementation with multiplexed address and data, the address is also transmitted down this bus.

A slave unit may process the requested transaction immediately, accepting write data or issuing read data on *BD*[31:0], or signal one of the following responses:

- Bus wait, *BWAIT*, allows a slave module to insert wait states when it cannot complete the transaction in the current cycle.
- Bus last, *BLAST*, allows a slave to terminate a sequential burst to force the bus master to issue a new bus transaction request to continue.
- Bus error, *BERROR*, indicates a transaction that cannot be completed. If the master is a processor it should abort the transfer.

8.2.4 | Bus Reset

The ASB supports a number of independent on-chip modules, many of which may be able to drive the data bus (and some control lines). Provided all the modules obey the bus protocols, there will only be one module driving any bus line at any time. Immediately after power-on, however, all the modules come up in unknown states. It takes some time for a clock oscillator to stabilize after power-up, so there may be no reliable clock available to sequence all the modules into a known state. In any case, if two or more modules power-up trying to drive bus lines in opposite directions, the output drive clashes may cause power supply crow-bar problems which may prevent the chip from powering up properly at all.

Correct ASB power-up is ensured by imposing an asynchronous reset mode that forces all drivers off the bus independently of the clock.

8.2.5 | Test Interface

A possible use of the AMBA is to provide support for a modular testing methodology through the *Test Interface Controller*. This approach allows each module on the AMBA to be tested independently by allowing an external tester to appear as a bus master on the ASB.

The only requirement for test mode to be supported is that the tester has access to the ASB through a 32-bit bidirectional port. Where a 32-bit bidirectional data bus interface to external memory or peripheral devices exists, this suffices. Where the off-chip data interface interface is only 16 or 8 bits wide other signals such as address lines are required to give 32 lines for test access.

The test interface allows control of the ASB address and data buses using protocols defined on the two test request inputs (*TREQA* and *TREQB*) and an address latch and incrementer in the controller. A suitably designed macrocell module can then allow access to all of its interface signals in groups of up to 32 bits. For example, the ARM7 macrocell has a 13-bit control and configuration input, a 32-bit data input, a 15-bit status output and 32-bìt address and data outputs. The test vectors are applied and the responses sensed following a sequence defined by a finite state automaton whose state transitions are controlled by *TREQA* and *TREQB*.

The AMBA macrocell test methodology may be compared with the JTAG-based methodology proposed in 'Macrocell testing'. Although perhaps less general, the AMBA approach will reduce test cost due its parallel tester interface.

8.2.6 | Advanced Peripheral Bus

The ASB offers a relatively high-performance on-chip interconnect which suits processor, memory and peripheral macrocells with some built-in interface sophistication. For very simple, low-performance peripherals, the overhead of the interface is too high. The **Advanced Peripheral Bus** is a simple, static bus which operates as a stub on an ASB to offer a minimalist interface to very simple peripheral macrocells.

The bus includes address (*PADDR*[*n*:0]; the full 32 bits are not usually required) and read and write data (*PRDATA*[*m*:0] and *PWDATA*[*m*:0], where *m* is 7, 15 or 31) buses which are no wider than necessary for the connected peripherals, a read/write direction indicator (*PWRITE*), individual peripheral select strobes (*PSELx*) and a peripheral timing strobe (*PENABLE*). APB transfers are timed to *PCLK*, and all APB devices are reset with *PRESETn*.

The address and control signals are all set up and held with respect to the timing strobe to allow time for local decoding with the select acting as the local enable. Peripherals which are slave devices based around simple register mapping may be interfaced directly with minimal logic overhead.

8.2.7 | Advanced High-performance Bus

The AHB is intended to replace the ASB in very high performance systems, for example those based on the ARM1020E (described in Section 12.6 on page 291).

The following features differentiate the AHB from the ASB:

- It supports split transactions, where a slave with a long response latency can free up the bus for other transfers while it prepares its data for transmission.
- It uses a single clock edge to control all of its operations, aiding synthesis and design verification (through the use of static timing analysis and similar tools).

- It uses a centrally multiplexed bus scheme rather than a bidirectional bus with tristate drivers (see Figure 8.12).
- It supports wider data bus configurations of 64 or 128 bits.

The multiplexed bus scheme may appear to introduce a lot of excess wiring, but bidirectional buses create a number of problems for designers and even more for synthesis systems. For example, as chip feature sizes shrink wire delays begin to dominate performance issues, and unidirectional buses can benefit from the insertion of repeater drivers that are very hard to add to a bidirectional bus.

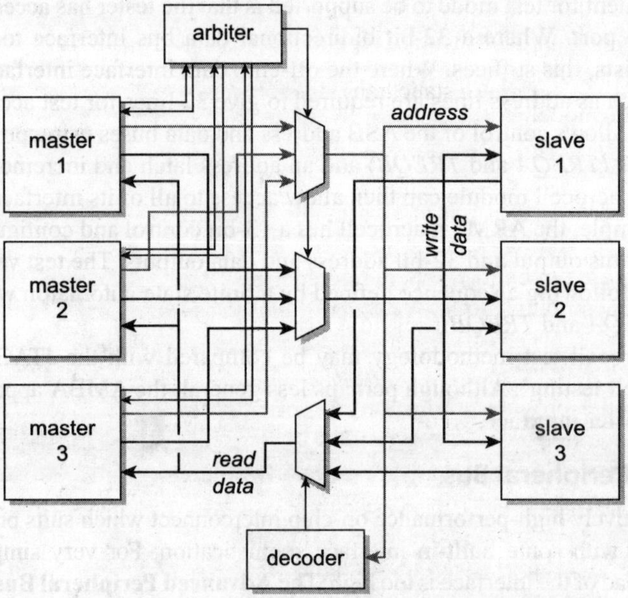

Figure 8.12 AHB multiplexed bus scheme

8.3 | The ARM Reference Peripheral Specification

The support for system development described so far in this chapter is principally aimed at testing and providing low-level access to processor and system state. AMBA offers a systematic way to connect hardware components together on a chip, but software development must still start from first principles on each new chip.

If a system developer wishes to start from a higher baseline, for example to base the software on a particular real-time operating system, then a number of components must be available to support the basic operating system functions. The **ARM reference peripheral specification** defines such a basic set of components, providing a framework within which an operating system can run but leaving full scope for application-specific system extensions.

The objective of the reference peripheral specification is to ease the porting of software between compliant implementations and thereby raise the level from which software development begins on a new system.

8.3.1 | Base Components

The reference peripheral specification defines the following components:

- A memory map which allows the base address of the interrupt controller, the counter timers and the reset controller to vary but defines the offsets of the various registers from these base addresses.
- An interrupt controller with a defined set of functions, including a defined interrupt mechanism for a transmit and receive communications channel (though the mechanism of the channel itself is not defined).
- A counter timer with various defined functions.
- A reset controller with defined boot behaviour, power-on reset detection, a 'wait for interrupt' pause mode and an identification register.

The particular ARM core used with these components is not specified since this does not affect the system programmer's model.

8.3.2 | Memory Map

The system must define the base addresses of the interrupt controller (**ICBase**), the counter-timer (**CTBase**) and the reset and pause controller (**RPCBase**).

These addresses are not defined by the reference peripheral specification, but all the addresses of the registers are defined relative to one or other of these base addresses.

8.3.3 | Interrupt Controller

The interrupt controller provides a uniform way of enabling, disabling and examining the status of up to 32 level-sensitive IRQ sources and one FIQ source. Each interrupt source has a mask bit which enables that source. Memory locations are defined with fixed offsets from *ICBase* to examine the unmasked, mask and masked interrupt status and to set or clear interrupt sources.

Five IRQ sources are defined by the reference peripheral specification, corresponding to the communication receive and transmit functions, one for each counter-timer and one which can be generated directly by software (principally to enable an FIQ handler to generate an IRQ).

8.3.4 | Counter-timers

Two 16-bit counter-timers are required, though more may be added. These are controlled by registers with fixed offsets relative to *CTBase*. The counters operate from the system clock with selectable pre-scaling of 0, 4 or 8 bits (so the input frequency is the system clock frequency divided by 1, 16 or 256).

Each counter-timer has a control register which selects the pre-scaling, enables or disables the counter and specifies the mode of operation as free-running or periodic, and a load register which specifies the value that the count starts from. A write to the 'load' register initializes the count value, which is then decremented to zero when an interrupt is generated. A write to the 'clear' register clears the interrupt. In free-running mode the counter continues to decrement past zero, whereas in periodic mode it is reloaded with the value in the 'load' register and decrements from there.

The current count value may be read from the 'value' register at any time.

8.3.5 | Reset and Pause Controller

The reset and pause controller includes registers which are addressed at fixed offsets from *RPCBase*. The readable registers give identification and reset status information, including whether or not a power-on reset has occurred. The writeable registers can set or clear the reset status (though not the power-on reset status bit; this can only be set by a hardware power-on reset), clear the reset map (for instance to switch the ROM from location zero, where it is needed after power-on for the ARM reset vector, to the normal memory map), and put the system into pause mode where it uses minimal power until an interrupt wakes it up again.

8.3.6 | System Design

Any ARM system which incorporates this basic set of components can support a suitably configured operating system kernel. System design then consists of adding further application-specific peripherals and software, building upwards from a functional base.

Since most applications require these components there is little overhead incurred in using the reference peripheral specification as the starting point for system development, and there is considerable benefit in starting from a functional system.

8.4 | Hardware System Prototyping Tools

The task facing today's system-on-chip designer is daunting. The number of gates on a chip continues to grow at an exponential rate, and is already in the millions. With the best software design tools available on the market, designers cannot produce fully tested systems of this complexity within the time-to-market constraints.

The first step towards addressing this problem, as has already been indicated, is to base a significant proportion of the design on pre-existing design components. Design reuse can reduce the amount of new design work to a small fraction of the total number of gates on the chip. A systematic approach to on-chip interconnect through the use of a bus such as AMBA further reduces the design task. However, there are still difficult problems to be solved, such as:

- How can the designer be sure that all of the selected re-usable blocks, which may come from various sources, will really work together correctly?
- How can the designer be sure that the specified system meets the performance requirements, which often include complex real-time issues?
- How can the software designers progress their work before the chip is available?

Simulating the system using software tools usually results in a performance that is several orders of magnitude lower than that of the final system, rendering software development and full system verification impractical.

A solution that goes a considerable way towards addressing all these issues is the use of hardware prototyping: building a hardware system that combines all of the required components in a form that makes no attempt to meet the power and size constraints of the final system, but does provide a platform for system verification and software development. The ARM 'Integrator' is one such system; another is the 'Rapid Silicon Prototyping' system from VLSI Technology, Inc.

8.4.1 | Rapid Silicon Prototyping

VLSI Technology, Inc., have introduced a development system called 'Rapid Silicon Prototyping'. The basis of this system is to use specially developed reference chips, each offering a particular plentiful set of on-chip components and support for off-chip extensions, which can be used to prototype a system-on-chip design. The target system is modelled in two steps:

1. The selected reference chip is 'deconfigured' to render those on-chip blocks that are not required in the target system inactive.
2. The blocks required in the target system that are not available on the reference chip are implemented as off-chip extensions. These may be either existing integrated circuits with the necessary functionality or FPGAs configured to the required function (usually by synthesis from a high-level language such as VHDL).

The use of pre-existing blocks, interconnected using standard buses such as AMBA, minimizes the technical risk in producing the final chip. All of the blocks in the reference chip exist as synthesizable components. The high-level language descriptions of the required functions are taken together with the high-level language source used to configure the FPGAs, the deconfigured functions are discarded and the result resynthesized to give the target chip. This process is illustrated in Figure 8.13.

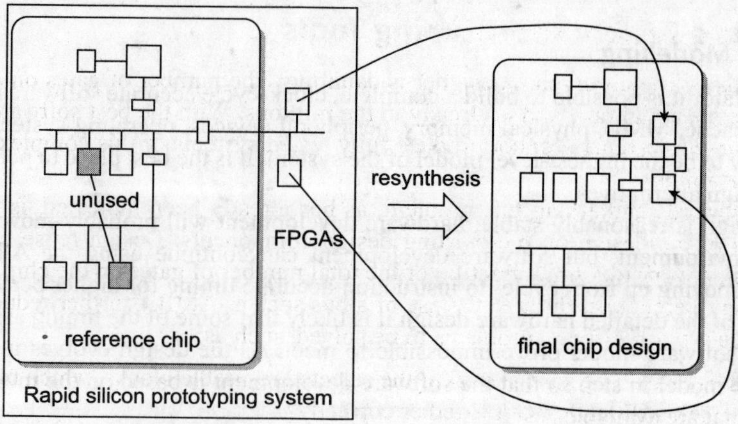

Figure 8.13 Rapid silicon prototyping principle

It is clear that this approach depends on the reference chip containing appropriate key components, such as the CPU core and possibly a signal processing system (where this is demanded by the target application). Although in principle it might be possible to build a single reference chip that contains every different ARM processor core (including all the different cache and MMU configurations), in practice such a chip would not be economic even for prototyping purposes. The success of the approach therefore depends on a careful choice of the components on the reference chip to ensure that it can cover a wide spread of systems, and different reference chips with different CPU and other key cores being built for different application domains.

8.5 | The ARMulator

The ARMulator is part of the cross-development toolkit described in Section 2.4 on page 38. It is a software emulator of the ARM processor which supports the debugging and evaluation of ARM code without requiring an ARM processor chip.

The ARMulator has a role in embedded system design. It supports the high-level prototyping of various parts of the system to support the development of software and the evaluation of architectural alternatives. It is made up of four components:

- The processor core model, which can emulate any current ARM core, including the Thumb instruction set.
- A memory interface which allows the characteristics of the target memory system to be modelled. Various models are supplied to support rapid prototyping, but the interface is fully customizable to incorporate the level of detail required.
- A coprocessor interface that supports custom coprocessor models.
- An operating system interface that allows individual system calls to be handled by the host or emulated on the ARM model.

The processor core model incorporates the remote debug interface, so the processor and system state are visible from ARMsd, the ARM symbolic debugger. Programs can be loaded, run and debugged through this interface.

8.5.1 | System Modelling

Using the ARMulator it is possible to build a complete, clock-cycle accurate software model of a system including a cache, MMU, physical memory, peripheral devices, operating system and software. Since this is likely to be the highest-level model of the system, it is the best place to perform the initial evaluation of design alternatives.

Once the design is reasonably stable, hardware development will probably move into a timing-accurate CAD environment, but software development can continue using the ARMulator-based model (probably moving up from cycle- to instruction-accurate timing for higher performance).

In the course of the detailed hardware design it is likely that some of the timing assumptions built into the original software model prove impossible to meet. As the design evolves it is important to keep the software model in step so that the software development is based on the most accurate estimates of timing that are available.

It is now common for complex systems development to be supported by multiple computer models of the target system built upon different levels of abstraction. Unless the lower-level models are synthesized automatically from the more abstract models, maintaining consistency between the models always takes considerable care and effort.

8.6 | The JTAG Boundary Scan Test Architecture

Two difficult areas in the development of a product based around an application-specific embedded system chip are the production testing of the VLSI component and the production testing of the assembled printed circuit board.

The second of these is addressed by the IEEE standard number 1149, 'Standard Test Access Port and Boundary-Scan Architecture'. This standard describes a 5-pin serial protocol for accessing and controlling the signal levels on the pins of a digital circuit, and has extensions for testing the circuitry on the chip itself. The standard was developed by the *Joint Test Action Group* (hence JTAG), and the architecture described by the standard is known either as 'JTAG boundary scan' or as 'IEEE 1149'.

The general structure of the JTAG boundary scan test interface is shown in Figure 8.14. All the signals between the core logic and the pins are intercepted by the serial scan path which can connect the core logic to the pins in normal operating mode, or can read out the original value and replace it with a new value in test mode.

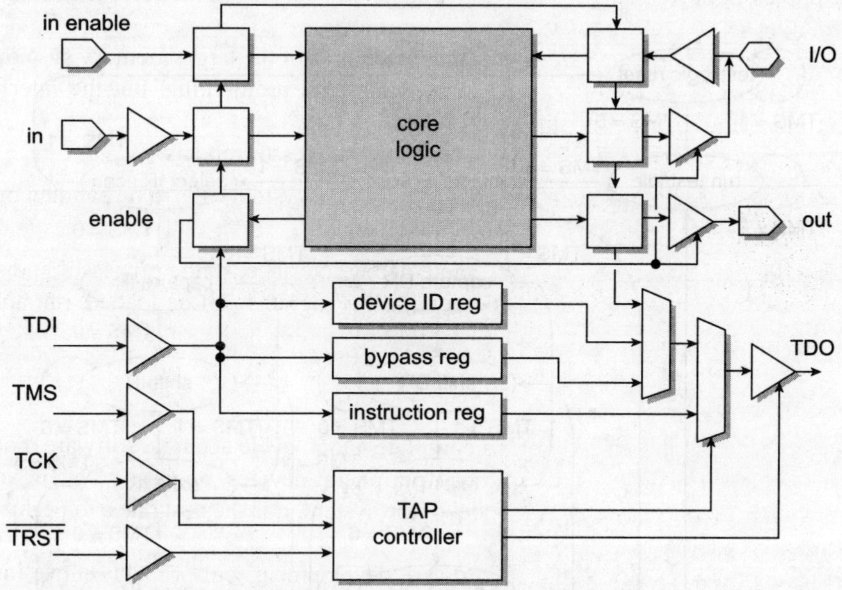

Figure 8.14 JTAG boundary scan organization

8.6.1 | Test Signals

The interface works with five dedicated signals which must be provided on each chip that supports the test standard:

- $\overline{TRST}$ is a test reset input which initializes the test interface.
- *TCK* is the test clock which controls the timing of the test interface independently from any system clocks.
- *TMS* is the test mode select which controls the operation of the test interface state machine.
- *TDI* is the test data input line which supplies the data to the boundary scan or instruction registers.
- *TDO* is the test data output line which carries the sampled values from the boundary scan chain and propagates data to the next chip in the serial test circuit.

The normal organization of the test circuit on a board that incorporates several chips with JTAG support is to connect $\overline{TRST}$, *TCK* and *TMS* to every chip in parallel and to connect *TDO* from one chip to *TDI* of the next in a single loop, so the board test interface has the same five signals listed above.

8.6.2 | TAP Controller

The operation of the test interface is controlled by the Test Access Port (**TAP**) controller. This is a state machine whose state transitions are controlled by *TMS*; the state transition diagram is shown in

Figure 8.15. All the states have two exits so the transitions can be controlled by one signal, *TMS*. The two main paths in the state transition diagram control the operation of a data register (**DR**) and the instruction register (**IR**).

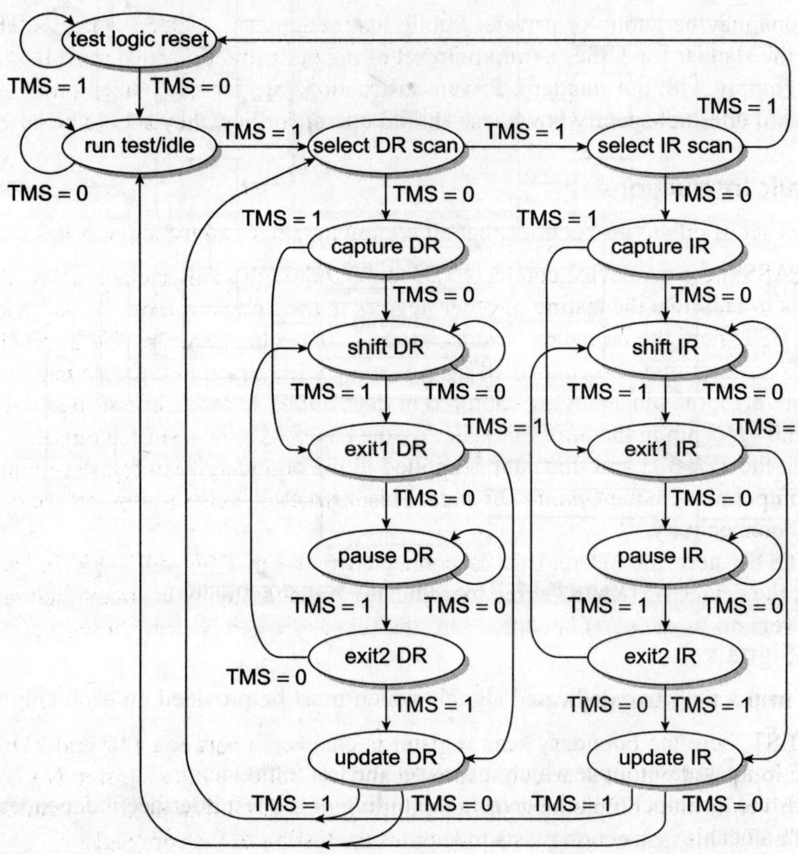

Figure 8.15 Test Access Port (TAP) controller state transition diagram

8.6.3 | Data Registers

The behaviour of a particular chip is determined by the contents of the test instruction register, which can select between various different data registers:

- The **device ID** register reads out an identification number which is hard-wired into the chip.
- The **bypass** register connects *TDI* to *TDO* with a 1-clock delay to give the tester rapid access to another device in the test loop on the same board.
- The **boundary scan** register intercepts all the signals between the core logic and the pins and comprises the individual register bits which are shown as the squares connected to the core logic in Figure 8.14.
- Other registers may be employed on the chip to test other functions as required.

8.6.4 | Instructions

The normal operation of a JTAG test system is to enter an instruction which specifies the sort of test to be carried out next and the data register to be used for that test into the *instruction* register, and then to use the data register to carry out the test.

Instructions may be public or private. Public instructions are declared and available for general test use, and the standard specifies a minimum set of public instructions that must be supported by all devices that comply with the standard. Private instructions are for specialized on-chip test purposes and the standard does not specify how these should operate or how they should be used.

8.6.5 | Public Instructions

The minimum set of public instructions that all compliant devices must support is:

- BYPASS: here the device connects *TDI* to *TDO* though a single clock delay. This instruction exists to facilitate the testing of other devices in the same test loop.
- EXTEST: here the boundary scan register is connected between *TDI* and *TDO* and the pin states are captured and controlled by the register. Referring to the state transition diagram in Figure 8.15, the pin states are captured in the *Capture DR* state and shifted out of the register via the *TDO* pin in the *Shift DR* state. As the captured data is shifted out, new data is shifted in via the *TDI* pin, and this data is applied to the boundary scan register outputs (and hence the output pins) in the *Update DR* state. This instruction exists to support the testing of board-level connectivity.
- IDCODE: here the ID register is connected between *TDI* and *TDO*. In the *Capture DR* state the device ID (a hard-wired identification number giving the manufacturer, part number and version of the part) is copied into the register which is then shifted out in the *Shift DR* state.

Other public instructions may include:

- INTEST: here the boundary scan register is connected between *TDI* and *TDO* and the core logic input and output states are captured and controlled by the register. Note that the inputs are driven to the complement of the values supplied. Otherwise the operation is similar to EXTEST. This instruction exists to support the testing of the core logic.

8.6.6 | PCB Testing

The principal goal of the JTAG test circuit is to enable the continuity of tracks and the connectivity of solder connections on printed circuit boards (*PCBs*) to be tested. This has become difficult since the introduction of surface mount packages which do not require through-holes in the circuit board. Previously 'bed of nails' testers could contact all the pins on each IC package from the back of the PCB to check continuity; surface mount packages typically have the pins closer together and the tracks accessible only on the component side of the board, making the 'bed of nails' approach inapplicable.

When the surface mount components have a JTAG test interface, this can be used (using the EXTEST instruction) to control outputs and observe inputs independently of the normal function of the chip, so board-level connectivity can readily be checked from chip to chip. If the board also contains components which do not have a JTAG interface these will require 'bed of nails' contacts, but these can be used together with the JTAG interfaces where available to minimize the cost and difficulty of building the production test equipment.

8.6.7 | VLSI Testing

High-complexity integrated circuits require extensive production testing to identify faulty devices before they get built into product. A production IC tester is a very expensive piece of equipment, and the time each device spends on the tester is an important factor in its manufacturing cost. Since the JTAG test circuitry operates through serial access, it is not a high-speed way to apply test vectors to the core logic. Furthermore, it is not possible to apply test vectors through the JTAG port at the normal operating speed of the device to check its performance.

Therefore the JTAG architecture is not a generic solution to all the problems of VLSI production testing. However, it can solve a number of problems:

- The JTAG port can be used for in-circuit functional testing of an IC (provided that the INTEST instruction is supported).
- It gives good control of the IC pins for parametric testing (checking the drive of the output buffers, leakage, input thresholds, and so on). This uses only the EXTEST instruction which is required on all JTAG compliant devices.
- It can be used to access internal scan paths to improve the controllability and observability of internal nodes that are hard to access from the pins.
- It can be used to give access to on-chip debug functions with no additional pins and without interfering with the system functions. This is exploited by the ARM EmbeddedICE debug architecture described briefly below and in detail in Section 8.7.
- It offers an approach to the functional testing of macrocell-based designs as described below.

These uses are all in addition to its principal purpose, which is in the production testing of printed circuit boards.

8.6.8 | Embedded-ICE

The ARM debug architecture, described in Section 8.7, is based on an extension of the JTAG test port. The EmbeddedICE module introduces breakpoint and watchpoint registers which are accessed as additional data registers using special JTAG instructions, and a trace buffer which is similarly accessed. The scan path around the ARM core macrocell is used to introduce instructions into the ARM pipeline without interfering with other parts of the system and these instructions can be used to access and modify the ARM and system state.

The debug architecture gives most of the functionality of a conventional In-Circuit Emulation system to debug an ARM macrocell on a complex system chip, and since the JTAG test access port is used to control the debug hardware, no additional pins are required on the chip.

8.6.9 | Macrocell Testing

A growing trend in the design of complex system chips is to incorporate a number of complex, pre-designed macrocells, together with some application-specific custom logic. The ARM processor core is itself one such macrocell; the others may come from ARM Limited, a semiconductor partner or some third party supplier. In such cases the designer of the system chip will have limited knowledge of the macrocells and will depend on the macrocell suppliers for the production test patterns for each macrocell.

Since the macrocells are buried within the system chip, the designer is faced with the problem of devising a way to apply the supplied test vectors to each of the macro-cells in turn. Test patterns must also be generated for the custom logic part of the design, but the designer is assumed to understand that part of the logic.

There are various approaches to getting the test patterns onto the edges of the macrocells:

- Test modes may be provided which multiplex the signals from each macrocell in turn onto the pins of the system chip.
- An on-chip bus may support direct test access to each macrocell which is attached to it (see Section 8.2).
- Each macrocell may have a boundary scan path through which the test patterns may be applied using an extension of the JTAG architecture.

This last approach is illustrated in Figure 8.16. The chip has a peripheral boundary scan path to support the public EXTEST operation and additional paths around each macrocell, designed into the macrocell, for applying functional tests as supplied. The custom logic designed specifically for this chip may have its own scan path or, as shown in the figure, rely on the fact that all its interface signals must intercept one of the existing scan paths.

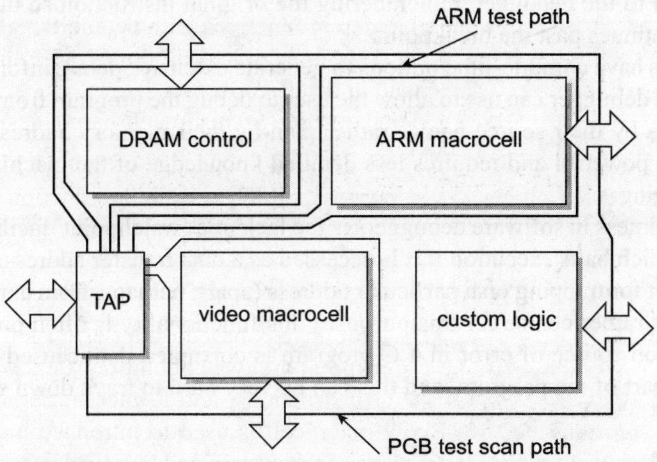

Figure 8.16 A possible JTAG extension for macrocell testing

It should be recognized that although perfectly feasible for functional testing, the scan path approach to macrocell testing has the same drawbacks as using the JTAG boundary scan path to test the core logic on a chip. The serial access is much slower than parallel access through the pins and performance testing at speed is not possible.

The most promising production test methodology for macrocell-based system chips appears to be to exploit the on-chip bus to give parallel access to the macrocell's periphery (especially where the macrocell has been designed specifically to give good access through this route). Multiplexing is used to give external access to peripheral macrocell signals that are important for performance testing and cannot conveniently be accessed via the on-chip bus, and the JTAG port is used to access other signals and internal state where necessary via scan chains. We have seen this approach as it is supported by ARM's Advanced Microcontroller Bus Architecture' (AMBA) which is described in Section 8.2.

The JTAG system continues to be very important for board-level testing, and can also be used for in-circuit testing of the core logic and to access on-chip debug facilities. It is incorporated into most ARM designs and is an important component of their test and debug methodologies.

8.7 | The ARM Debug Architecture

Debugging any computer system can be a complex task. There are two basic approaches to debugging, the simplest being based on watching a system from the outside using test equipment such as a logic analyser, and the more powerful being based on viewing a system from the inside with tools that support single stepping, the setting of breakpoints, and so on.

8.7.1 | Desktop Debugging

When the system to be debugged is a piece of software running on a desktop machine, all the user interface components are readily available and the debugger may itself simply be another piece of software running on the same machine. Breakpoints are set by replacing an instruction in the object program with a call to the debugger, remembering the original instruction so that it can be replaced when execution continues past the breakpoint.

Often compilers have compile-time options to generate extensive debug information such as symbol tables which the debugger can use to allow the user to debug the program from a source-level view, addressing variables by their source names rather than by their memory address. This 'source-level debugging' is more powerful and requires less detailed knowledge of the machine environment than object-level debugging.

A common weakness in software debuggers is the lack of a 'watchpoint' facility. A watchpoint is a memory address which halts execution if it is accessed as a data transfer address. Since many processors have no support for trapping on a particular address (apart, perhaps, from a memory management page fault, which is rather coarse for this purpose) this functionality is often omitted. This is a pity, since a very common source of error in a C program is corrupted data caused by an errant pointer in some unrelated part of the program, and this can be very hard to track down without a watchpoint facility.

8.7.2 | Embedded Debugging

Debugging becomes significantly more difficult when the target system is embedded. Now there is probably no user interface in the system, so the debugger must run on a remote host through some sort of communication link to the target. If the code is in ROM, instructions cannot simply be replaced by calls to the debugger since the locations are not writeable.

The standard solution here is the *In-Circuit Emulator* **(ICE)**. The processor in the target system is removed and replaced by a connection to an emulator. The emulator may be based around the same processor chip, or a variant with more pins (and more visibility of its internal state), but it will also incorporate buffers to copy the bus activity off to a 'trace buffer' (which stores the signals on all the pins in each clock cycle for some number of cycles) and various hardware resources which can watch for particular events, such as execution passing through a breakpoint. The trace buffer and hardware resources are managed by software running on a host desktop system.

When a 'trigger' event occurs, the trace buffer is frozen so the user can observe activity around the point of interest. The host software will present the trace buffer data, give a view on the processor and system state and allow it to be modified and generally attempt to appear as similar to a debugger in a desktop system as possible.

8.7.3 | Debugging Processor Cores

The ICE approach depends on the system having an identifiable processor chip which can be removed and replaced by the ICE. Clearly, once the processor has become just one macrocell of many on a complex system chip, this is no longer possible.

Although simulation using software models such as the ARMulator should remove many of the design bugs before the physical system is built, it is often impossible to run the full software system under emulation, and it can be difficult to model all the real-time constraints accurately. Therefore it is likely that some debugging of the complete hardware and software system will be necessary. How can this be achieved? This is still an area of active research to identify the best overall strategy with acceptable hardware overhead costs, but considerable progress has been made over the last few years in developing practical approaches, and the rest of this section presents the approach developed by ARM Limited.

8.7.4 | ARM Debug Hardware

To provide debug facilities comparable with those offered by a typical ICE, the user must be able to set breakpoints and watchpoints (for code running in ROM as well as RAM), to inspect and modify the processor and system state, to see a trace of processor activity around the point of interest, and to do all this from the comfort of a desk-top system with a good user interface. The trace mechanism used in ARM systems is separate from the other debug facilities, and is discussed in Section 8.8. In this section we restrict our attention to the breakpoint, watchpoint and state inspection resources.

The communication between the target system and the host is achieved by extending the functionality of the JTAG test port. Since the JTAG test pins are included in most designs for board testing, accessing the debug hardware through this port requires no additional dedicated pins, sparing the most precious resource on the chip from further pressure. JTAG scan chains are used to access the breakpoint and watchpoint registers and also to force instructions into the processor to access processor and system state.

The breakpoint and watchpoint registers represent a fairly small hardware overhead that can often be accepted on production parts. The host system runs the standard ARM development tools, communicating with the target through a serial port and/or a parallel port. Special protocol conversion hardware sits between the host serial line and the target JTAG port.

In addition to the breakpoint and watchpoint events, it may also be desirable to halt the processor when a system-level event occurs. The debug architecture includes external inputs for this purpose.

The on-chip cell containing these facilities is called the *EmbeddedICE* module.

8.7.5 | Embedded-ICE

The EmbeddedICE module consists of two watchpoint registers and control and status registers. The watchpoint registers can halt the ARM core when the address, data and control signals match the value programmed into the watchpoint register. Since the comparison is performed under a mask, either watchpoint register can be configured to operate as a breakpoint register capable of halting the processor when an instruction in either ROM or RAM is executed.

The comparison and mask logic is illustrated in Figure 8.17.

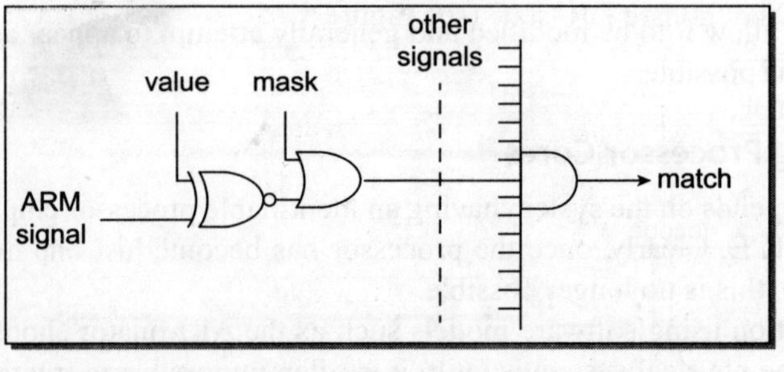

Figure 8.17 EmbeddedICE signal comparison logic

8.7.6 | Chaining

Each watchpoint can look for a particular combination of values on the ARM address bus, data bus, $\overline{trans}$, $\overline{opc}$, $\overline{mas}$ [1:0] and $\overline{r}/w$ control signals, and if either combination is matched the processor is stopped. Alternatively, the two watchpoints may be chained to halt the processor when the second watchpoint is matched only after the first has previously been matched.

8.7.7 | Registers

EmbeddedICE registers are programmed via the JTAG test port, using a dedicated scan chain. The scan chain is 38 bits long, with 32 data bits, 5 address bits and a $\overline{r}/w$ bit which controls whether the register is read or written. The address bits specify the particular register following the mapping detailed in Table 8.1.

Table 8.1 EmbeddedICE register mapping

Address	Width	Function
00000	3	Debug control
00001	5	Debug status
00100	6	Debug comms control register
00101	32	Debug comms data register
01000	32	Watchpoint 0 address value
01001	32	Watchpoint 0 address mask
01010	32	Watchpoint 0 data value
01011	32	Watchpoint 0 data mask
01100	9	Watchpoint 0 control value
01101	8	Watchpoint 0 control mask
10000	32	Watchpoint 1 address value
10001	32	Watchpoint 1 address mask
10010	32	Watchpoint 1 data value
10011	32	Watchpoint 1 data mask
10100	9	Watchpoint 1 control value
10101	8	Watchpoint 1 control mask

The use of the JTAG scan chain is illustrated in Figure 8.18. The read or write takes place when the TAP controller enters the 'update DR' state (see Figure 8.15).

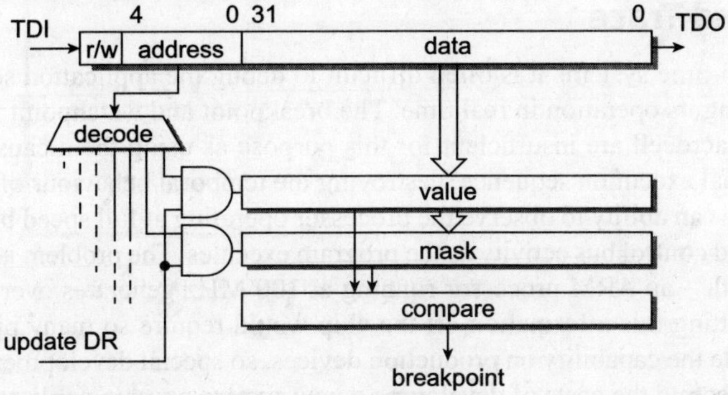

Figure 8.18 EmbeddedICE register read and write structure

8.7.8 | Accessing State

The EmbeddedICE module allows a program to be halted at specific points, but it does not directly allow the processor or system state to be inspected or modified. This is achieved via further scan paths which are also accessed through the JTAG port.

The mechanism employed to access the processor state is to halt the processor, then to force an instruction such as a store multiple of all the registers into the processor's instruction queue. Then clocks are applied to the processor, again via the scan chain, causing it to write the registers out through its data port. Each register is collected by the scan chain and shifted out.

System state is harder to glean, since there may be system locations that cannot be read at the very low speeds that the scan path can generate. Here the processor is preloaded with a suitable instruction, then allowed to access the system location at system speed. This transfers the required system state into a processor register, whereupon it may be passed to the external debugger through the JTAG port as described above.

8.7.9 | Debug Comms

In additions to the breakpoint and watchpoint registers, the EmbeddedICE module also includes a **debug comms** port whereby the software running on the target system can communicate with the host. The software in the target system sees the comms port as a 6-bit control register and 32-bit data read and write registers which are accessed using MRC and MCR instructions to coprocessor 14. The host sees these registers in the EmbeddedICE register map as shown in Table 8.1.

8.7.10 | Debugging

An ARM-based system chip which includes the EmbeddedICE module connects to a host computer through the JTAG port and a protocol converter. This configuration supports the normal breakpoint, watchpoint and processor and system state access that the programmer is accustomed to using for native or ICE-based debugging (in addition to the comms port described above), and with suitable host software gives a full source-level debugging capability with low hardware overhead.

The only facility that is missing is the ability to trace code in real time. This is the function of the *Embedded Trace Macrocell* described in the next section.

8.8 | Embedded Trace

When debugging real-time systems it is often difficult to debug the application software without the capability of observing its operation in real time. The breakpoint and watchpoint facilities offered by the EmbeddedICE macrocell are insufficient for this purpose as using them causes the processor to deviate from its normal execution sequence, destroying the temporal behaviour of the software.

What is required is an ability to observe the processor operating at full speed by generating a trace of its address, data and control bus activity as the program executes. The problem is that this represents a huge data bandwidth – an ARM processor running at 100 MHz generates over 1 Gbyte/s of interface information. Getting this information off the chip would require so many pins that it would be uneconomic to include the capability on production devices, so special development devices would be needed, adversely affecting the costs of developing a new system-on-chip application.

8.8.1 | Trace Compression

The solution adopted by ARM Limited is to reduce the interface bandwidth using intelligent trace compression techniques. For example:

- Most ARM addresses are sequential, so it is not necessary to send every address off chip. Instead, the sequential information can be sent on most cycles and the full address only when a branch is taken.
- If there is off-chip logic which has access to the code which is running on the processor, it will know when the processor is executing a branch instruction and where the target of the branch is. The only information which must be sent off chip is whether or not the branch is taken.
- Fuller address information is now required only when the branch target is not known, such as in a subroutine return or jump table instruction. Even here, only those low-order address bits that change need be issued.
- The address information is now very bursty. A first-in-first-out (FIFO) buffer can be used to smooth the data rate so that the necessary address information can be transmitted in 4-, 8- or 16-bit packets at a steadier rate.

Using a number of techniques similar along these lines, the ARM Embedded Trace Macrocell can compress the trace information to the extent necessary to allow it to be communicated off chip through 9, 13 or 21 pins depending on the configuration. These pins could be used for other purposes when trace output is not required.

8.8.2 | Real-time Debug

A complete real-time debug solution is as shown in Figure 8.19. The EmbeddedICE unit supports breakpoint and watchpoint functionality, and communication channels between the host and target software. The Embedded Trace Macrocell compresses the processor's interface information and sends it off chip through the Trace port. The JTAG port is used to control both units. The external EmbeddedICE controller is used to connect the host system to the JTAG port, and the external Trace Port Analyser interfaces the host system to the Trace port. The host may connect to both the trace port analyser and the EmbeddedICE controller via a network.

The user has control of the breakpoint and watchpoint settings and various trace functions. All the application software may be traced, or just particular routines. Trigger conditions can be specified, and the trace can be collected before or after the trigger or with the trigger in the centre of the trace. Data accesses can be selected to be included in the trace or not, and the trace may collect just the address of the data access, or just the data itself, or both.

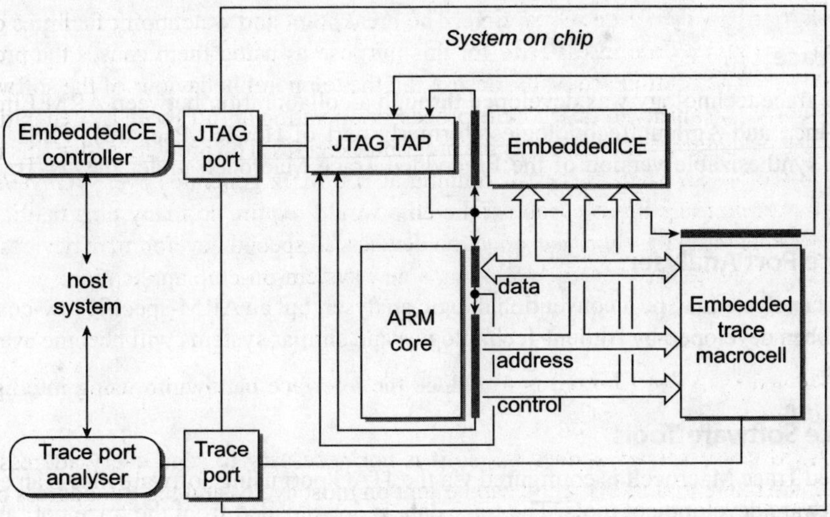

Figure 8.19 Real-time debug system organization

8.8.3 | Embedded Trace Options

As noted above, the Embedded Trace Macrocell may be synthesized in several different configurations allowing the functionality of the unit to be traded off against cost (measured in terms of the numbers of gates and pins used).

- The minimal system requires 5 pins to issue pipeline information and 4 pins to issue data (in addition to the 5-pin JTAG interface). This is sufficient for execution tracing, but will only support very limited data tracing and has restricted triggering and filtering capabilities. A 9-byte FIFO is used to smooth the data transfer rate, and the hardware cost of this implementation is approximately 15 Kgates.
- A maximal system uses 5 pins to issue pipeline information and 16 pins to issue data (again, in addition to the 5-pin JTAG interface). It is capable of tracing the flow of execution and all but the very-worst-case data activity. A 40-byte FIFO is used to smooth the data flow, and the hardware cost is approximately 50 Kgates.

Between these two extremes several intermediate configurations are possible. All allow for external inputs (that is, inputs from other logic on the chip) to control the trace triggering, and for triggering from the EmbeddedICE breakpoint logic.

8.8.4 | Trace Overflow

With all of the implementations of the Embedded Trace Macrocell there are some circumstances where the trace FIFO buffer can overflow. The unit can be configured either to stall the processor or to discontinue tracing when this happens. In either case, real-time tracing is lost, although only temporarily while the FIFO drains.

Fundamentally what has happened is the information bandwidth has exceeded the capability of the compression algorithm to reduce it to match the bandwidth capacity of the trace port. If this happens, the filtering setup must be modified to reduce the amount of data that is being traced.

8.8.5 | N-Trace

The real-time trace technology was developed through a collaboration between ARM Limited, VLSI Technology, Inc., and Agilent Technologies (formerly part of Hewlett-Packard). VLSI Technology, Inc., offers a synthesizable version of the Embedded Trace Macrocell under the 'N-Trace' product name.

8.8.6 | Trace Port Analyser

The trace port analyser may be a conventional logic analyser, but an ARM-specific low-cost trace port analyser has been developed by Agilent Technologies and similar systems will become available from other vendors.

8.8.7 | Trace Software Tools

The Embedded Trace Macrocell is configured via the JTAG port using software that is an extension to the ARM software development tools. The trace data is downloaded from the trace port analyser and decompressed using source code information. It is then presented as an assembly listing with interspersed data accesses, and has links back to the source code.

With EmbeddedICE and the Embedded Trace facility the ARM system-on-chip designer has all the facilities offered by traditional in-circuit emulation (ICE) tools. These technologies give full visibility of the real-time behaviour of the application code with the ability to set breakpoints and inspect and change processor registers and memory locations, always with firm links back to the high-level language source code.

8.9 | Signal Processing Support

Many applications that use an ARM processor as a controller also require significant digital signal processing performance. A typical GSM mobile telephone handset is a case in point; first-generation ARM-based designs typically incorporate a DSP core on the same chip as the ARM core, and the system designer has to make careful choices regarding which system functions are best implemented on the DSP core and which on the ARM core.

DSP cores have programmers' models that are very different from the ARM's model. They employ several separate data memories, and often require the programmer to schedule their internal pipeline very carefully if maximum throughput is to be obtained. Synchronizing the DSP code with the ARM code that is running concurrently is a complex task.

ARM Limited has introduced two different extensions to the ARM architecture in attempting to simplify the system design task in applications which require both controller and signal processing functions: the Piccolo coprocessor, and the signal processing instruction set extensions in ARM architecture v5TE.

8.9.1 | Piccolo

The Piccolo coprocessor is a sophisticated 16-bit signal processing engine that uses the ARM coprocessor interface to cooperate with the ARM core in the transfer of operands and results from and to memory, but also executes its own instruction set.

The organization of Piccolo is illustrated in Figure 8.20. Operands are loaded and results stored via the ARM coprocessor interface, so suitable addresses must be generated by the ARM core. The input and output buffers allow these transfers to move many 16-bit values in a single instruction, and values are transferred in pairs, making full use of the ARM's 32-bit bus width. The input buffer stores values until they are called upon by the signal processing code, and they may be accessed out of order from the buffer.

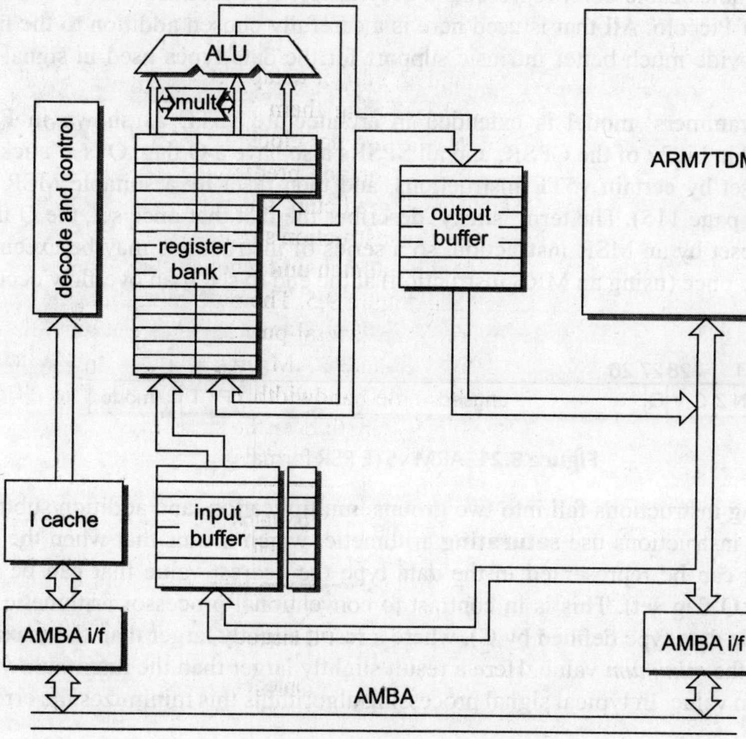

Figure 8.20 Piccolo organization

The Piccolo register set holds operands that may be 16 bits, 32 bits or 48 bits wide. The four 48-bit registers are used to accumulate results such as inner products without risk of overflow. The processing logic can compute a 16×16 product and add the result to one of these 48-bit accumulator registers in a single cycle. It also offers good support for fixed point operations and supports saturating arithmetic.

The signal processing operations that use values held in the register file are specified in a separate instruction set which Piccolo loads from memory via the AMBA bus into a local instruction cache.

An objective of the Piccolo architecture is to provide sufficient local storage, in the form of registers, the instruction cache and the input and output buffers, that a single AMBA bus can support good throughput. This contrasts with conventional signal processor designs that use two independent data memories and a separate instruction memory. As a result, Piccolo offers a much more straightforward programming model than does a system that combines an ARM core with a conventional signal processing core. However, some care is still required to synchronize the ARM code with the Piccolo code, and in an intensive signal processing application the ARM core is kept quite busy with the operand and result transfers, and is therefore unable to carry out extensive control functions at the same time. An even more straightforward programming model is offered by the ARM architecture v5TE instruction set extensions.

8.9.2 | v5TE Signal Processing Instructions

The signal processing instruction set extension defined by ARM architecture v5TE, first implemented on the ARM9E-S synthesizable core, represents a very different approach to the problem from that used in the design of Piccolo. All that is used here is a carefully chosen addition to the native ARM instruction set to provide much better intrinsic support for the data types used in signal processing applications.

The ARM programmers' model is extended in architecture v5TE as shown in Figure 8.21. The 'Q' flag is added in bit 27 of the CPSR, and all SPSRs also have a Q flag. Q is a 'sticky' overflow flag which may be set by certain v5TE instructions, and then reset by a suitable MSR instruction (see Section 5.14 on page 115). The term 'sticky' describes the fact that once set, the Q flag remains set until explicitly reset by an MSR instruction, so a series of instructions may be executed and the Q flag inspected only once (using an MRS instruction) at the end to see if an overflow occurred at any point in the sequence.

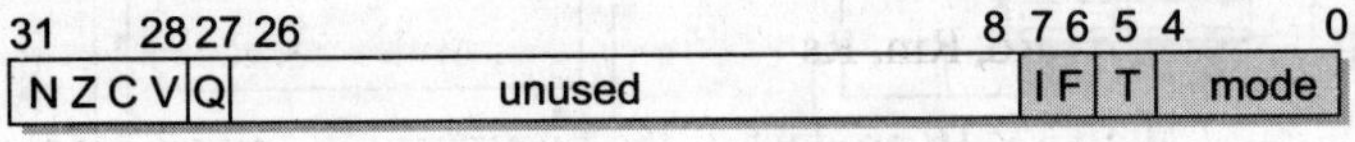

Figure 8.21 ARM v5TE PSR format

The signal processing instructions fall into two groups: multiplication, and addition/subtraction. The addition/subtraction instructions use **saturating** arithmetic, which means that when the result overflows the range that can be represented in the data type the nearest value that can be represented is returned (and the Q flag set). This is in contrast to conventional processor arithmetic (and to the modulo 2^{32} arithmetic data type defined by C), where a result slightly larger than the maximum value has a value close to the *minimum* value. Here a result slightly larger than the maximum value simply returns the maximum value. In typical signal processing algorithms this minimizes the error and gives optimum results.

8.9.3 | v5TE Multiply Instructions

The multiply instructions all improve the ability of the processor to handle 16-bit data types, and assume that a 32-bit ARM register may hold two 16-bit values. They therefore give efficient access to values held in the upper or lower half of a register. The binary encoding of these instructions is shown in Figure 8.22.

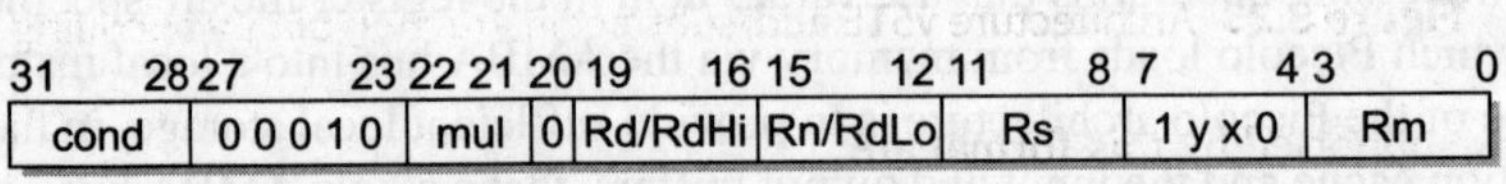

Figure 8.22 Architecture v5TE multiply instruction binary encoding

The instructions supported by this format are:

SMLAxy{cond} Rd, Rm, Rs, Rn ; mul = 00

This instruction computes the 16 × 16 product of the two signed 16-bit values from the lower (x = 0) or upper (x = 1) half of Rm and the lower (y = 0) or upper (y = 1) half of Rs. The 32-bit product is added to the 32-bit value in Rn, and the result placed in Rd. The assembly format replaces x and y with 'B' for the lower (bottom) halfword or 'T' for the upper (top) halfword.

SMLAWy{cond} Rd, Rm, Rs, Rn ; mul = 01, x = 0

This instruction computes the 32 × 16 product of the 32-bit value in Rm and the 16-bit value in the lower (y = 0) or upper (y = 1) half of Rs. The most significant 32 bits of the 48-bit product are added to the 32-bit value in Rn, and the result placed in Rd.

SMULWy{cond} Rd, Rm, Rs ; mul = 01, x = 1, Rn = 0

This instruction computes the 32 × 16 product of the 32-bit value in Rm and the 16-bit value in the lower (y = 0) or upper (y = 1) half of Rs. The most significant 32 bits of the 48-bit product are placed in Rd.

SMLALxy{cond} RdLo, RdHi, Rm, Rs ; mul = 10

This instruction computes the 16 × 16 product of the two signed 16-bit values from the lower (x = 0) or upper (x = 1) half of Rm and the lower (y = 0) or upper (y = 1) half of Rs. The 32-bit product is added to the 64-bit value in RdHi:RdLo, and the result placed in RdHi:RdLo.

SMULxy{cond} Rd, Rm, Rs ; mul = 11, Rn = 0

This instruction computes the 16 × 16 product of the two signed 16-bit values from the lower (x = 0) or upper (x = 1) half of Rm and the lower (y = 0) or upper (y = 1) half of Rs. The 32-bit product is placed in Rd.

In all the above instructions the CPSR flags N, Z, C and V are *not* affected by the instruction, and the PC (r15) should not be used for any of the operand or result registers. If the addition in the accumulation (in SMLA and SMLAW) overflows the Q bit in the CPSR is set, but the addition uses conventional modulo 2^{32} rather than saturating arithmetic.

8.9.4 | v5TE Add/Subtract Instructions

The other group of instructions in the architecture v5TE extensions are 32-bit addition and subtraction instructions that use saturating arithmetic. In each case there is an additional instruction which also doubles one of the operands before performing the addition and subtraction, which improves the efficiency of certain signal processing algorithms. The binary encoding of these instructions is shown in Figure 8.23.

31–28	27–23	22–21	20	19–16	15–12	11–8	7–4	3–0
cond	0 0 0 1 0	op	0	Rn	Rd	0 0 0 0	0 1 0 1	Rm

Figure 8.23 Architecture v5TE add/subtract instruction binary encoding

The instructions supported by this format are:

QADD{cond} Rd, Rm, Rn ; op = 00

This instruction performs a 32-bit saturating addition of Rm and Rn, placing the result in Rd.

```
QSUB {cond}    Rd, Rm, Rn          ; op = 01
```

This instruction performs a 32-bit saturating subtraction of Rn from Rm, placing the result in Rd.

```
QDADD {cond}    Rd, Rm, Rn         ; op = 10
```

This instruction doubles Rn (with saturation) and then performs a 32-bit saturating addition of the result and Rm, placing the result in Rd.

```
QDSUB {cond}    Rd, Rm, Rn         ; op = 11
```

This instruction doubles Rn (with saturation) and then performs a 32-bit saturating subtraction of the result from Rm, placing the result in Rd.

Again, in all the above instructions the CPSR flags N, Z, C and V are *not* affected by the instruction, and the PC (r15) should not be used for any of the operand or result registers. If the saturating addition or subtraction overflows, or doubling Rn (where specified) causes overflow, the Q bit in the CPSR is set.

8.9.5 | v5TE Code Example

To illustrate the use of these instructions, consider the problem of generating the inner ('dot') product of two vectors of 16-bit signed numbers held memory on an ARM9E-S core, which supports the architecture v5TE extensions, and an ARM9TDMI core, which does not. Computing an inner product is a very common procedure in signal processing applications. To minimize errors, saturating arithmetic should be used. The v5TE code for the central loop is as follows:

```
Loop    SMULBB    r3, r1, r2       ; 16x16 multiply
        SUBS      r4, r4, #2       ; decrement loop counter
        QDADD     r5, r5, r3       ; saturating x2 & accumulate
        SMULTT    r3, r1, r2       ; 16x16 multiply
        LDR       r1, [r6], #4     ; get next two multipliers
        QDADD     r5, r5, r3       ; saturating x2 & accumulate
        LDR       r2, [r7], #4     ; get next two multiplicands
        BNE       loop
```

This code example illustrates several important points:

- The instructions are 'scheduled' to avoid pipeline stalls. On an ARM9E-S this means that the result of a load or 16-bit multiply should not be used in the following cycle.
- Although the operands are 16-bit halfwords, they are loaded in pairs as 32-bit words. This is a more efficient way to use ARM"s 32-bit memory interface than using halfword loads, and the v5TE multiply instructions can access the individual 16-bit operands directly from the registers.
- The saturating 'double and accumulate' instructions are used to scale the product before accumulation. This is useful because the fixed point arithmetic used in signal processing generally assumes operands in the range −1 to +1 but certain algorithms need coefficients greater than 1. The doubling operation gives an effective range from −2 to +2, which is sufficient for most algorithms.

8.9.6 | Performance Comparison

The single-cycle 32 × 16 multiplier on the ARM9E-S enables it to complete the above loop in 10 clock cycles, of which 4 are loop overhead (decrementing the loop counter and branching back at the end of the loop). Each loop computes two products, so each product requires 5 cycles. With loop unrolling (replicating the code to compute many more products in a single loop iteration) the cost for each product reduces towards 3 cycles. The best an ARM9TDMI can achieve is one product in 10 cycles, over three times slower. The difference is accounted for partly by the slower multiplier on the ARM9TDMI, partly by its less efficient handling of 16-bit operands, and the remainder by the extra instructions required to test and correct for saturation.

8.10 | Example and Exercises

EXAMPLE 8.1

Estimate the proportion of the number of test vectors required to test an ARM core via the JTAG and AMBA interfaces.

An ARM core has in the region of 100 interface connections (32 data, 32 address, control, clock, bus, mode, and so on). The JTAG interface is serial. If the tester allows one vector to specify a pulse on *TCK* it will take 100 vectors to apply a parallel pattern to the ARM core. The AMBA test interface accesses the ARM periphery in five sections (see 'Test interface'), requiring five vectors on a standard tester.

The JTAG interface therefore appears to require 20 times the number of vectors. (Remember that JTAG is intended for PCB testing, not production VLSI testing.) In fact both the JTAG-based EmbeddedICE and AMBA interfaces include optimizations to improve the efficiency of getting instructions into the ARM core, which is the dominant requirement in testing it, but a very detailed analysis would be required to take these into account in the estimate.

Exercise 8.1.1

Summarize the problem areas in the production VLSI testing of complex macrocell-based system chips and discuss the relative merits of the various solutions.

Exercise 8.1.2

Make a study of digital signal processing requirements, and make a model of a DSP core that can be added to the ARM core ,as a coprocessor. To answer this question, it is necessary to make a study of general filtering operations done as part of DSP.

Exercise 8.1.3

What problem does the Advanced Microprocessor Bus Architecture address and what problem does the ARM reference peripheral specification address? How might they be related?

Exercise 8.1.4

Sketch a system development plan for an embedded system chip showing at which stage the ARMulator, AMBA, the reference peripheral specification, EmbeddedICE and JTAG are (i) designed into the chip, and/or (ii) used to assist in the development process.

9

ARM Processor Cores

SUMMARY OF CHAPTER CONTENTS

An ARM processor core is the engine within a system that fetches ARM (and possibly Thumb) instructions from memory and executes them. ARM cores are very small, typically occupying just a few square millimetres of chip area. Modern VLSI technology allows a large number of additional system components to be incorporated on the same chip. These may be closely related to the processor core, such as cache memory and memory management hardware, or they may be unrelated system components such as signal processing hardware. They may even include further ARM processor cores. Among all of these components the processor cores stand out as being the most densely complex components which place the greatest demand on software development and debugging tools. The correct choice of processor core is one of the most critical decisions in the specification of a new system.

In this chapter the principal current ARM processor core products are described. They offer a choice of cost, complexity and performance points from which the most effective solution can be selected.

Many applications require the processor core to be supported by closely coupled cache and memory management subsystems. A number of standard configurations combining these components are described in Chapter 12, 'ARM CPU Cores', on page 271.

Further ARM-compatible processor cores are described in Chapter 14, 'The AMULET Asynchronous ARM Processors', on page 321. These processor cores are research prototypes and not yet commercial products.

9.1 | ARM7TDMI

The ARM7TDMI is the current low-end ARM core and is widely used across a range of applications, most notably in many digital mobile telephones.

It evolved from the first ARM core to implement the 32-bit address space programming model, the ARM6, which it now supersedes. The ARM6 used circuit techniques that prevented it from operating reliably with a power supply of less than 5 volts. The ARM7 corrected this deficiency, and then 64-bit multiply instructions, on-chip debug support, the Thumb instruction set and the EmbeddedICE watchpoint hardware were all added over a fairly short period of time to give the ARM7TDMI.

The origins of the name are as follows:

- The **ARM7**, a 3 volt compatible rework of the ARM6 32-bit integer core, with:
- the Thumb 16-bit compressed instruction set;
- on-chip **D**ebug support, enabling the processor to halt in response to a debug request;
- an enhanced **M**ultiplier, with higher performance than its predecessors and yielding a full 64-bit result; and
- Embedded**I**CE hardware to give on-chip breakpoint and watchpoint support.

The ARM7TDMI has been fabricated on a large number of different CMOS process technologies, some supporting clock rates over 100 MHz and others enabling operation at 0.9 V (thereby allowing a single-cell battery to be used as the source of power). Typical applications in production at the time of writing use a 3.3 V supply on a 0.35 μm process yielding a clock rate of up to 66 MHz, but the trend is, of course, towards smaller transistors, lower supply voltages and higher clock frequencies.

9.1.1 | ARM7TDMI Organization

The organization of the ARM7TDMI is illustrated in Figure 9.1. The ARM7TDMI core is a basic ARM integer core using a 3-stage pipeline (see Section 4.1 on page 65) with a number of important features and extensions:

- It implements ARM architecture version 4T, with support for 64-bit result multiplies, half-word and signed byte loads and stores and the Thumb instruction set.
- It includes the EmbeddedICE module to support embedded system debugging. (This was described in Section 8.7 on page 200.)

As the debug hardware is accessed via the JTAG test access port, the JTAG control logic (described in Section 8.6 on page 194) is considered part of the processor macrocell.

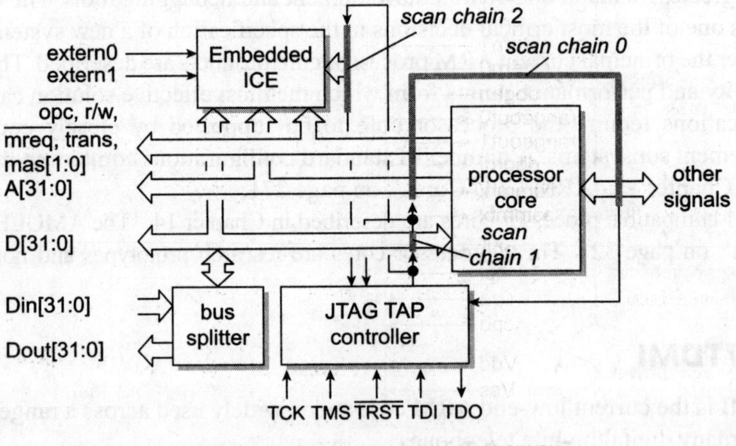

Figure 9.1 ARM7TDMI organization

9.1.2 | Hardware Interface

The ARM7TDMI hardware interface signals are shown in Figure 9.2. The apparently bewildering number of signals is rather misleading as it suggests a complexity of behaviour that belies the intrinsic simplicity of the basic ARM interface. Numerically the interface signals are dominated by the principal 32-bit address and data buses, and a simple memory interface will use these and a few control signals as described below. The other signals are dedicated to more esoteric functions such as on-chip debug, JTAG boundary scan extensions, and so on.

In Figure 9.2 the interface signals are shown grouped by function, and the role of each group is described below with, where appropriate, information on the individual signals and the interface timing.

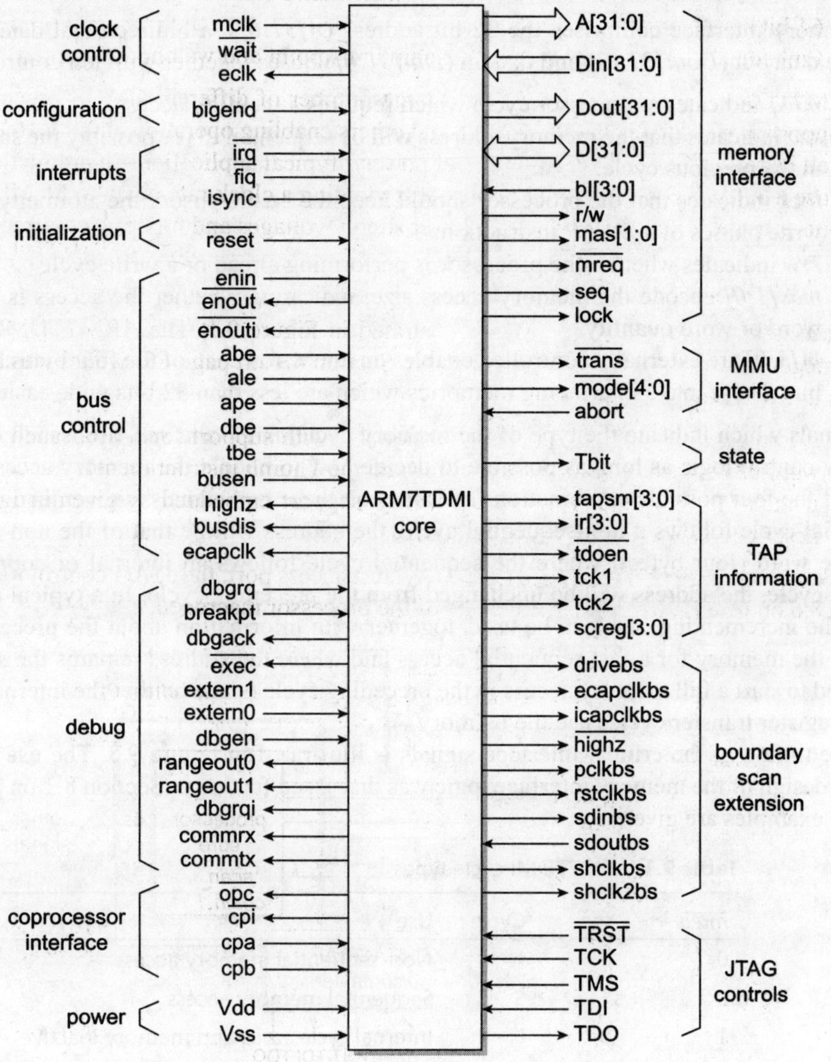

Figure 9.2 The ARM7TDMI core interface signals

9.1.3 | Clock Control

All state changes within the processor are controlled by *mclk*, the memory clock. Although this clock may be manipulated externally to cause the processor to wait for a slow access, it is often simpler to supply a free-running clock and to use $\overline{wait}$ to skip clock cycles. The internal clock is effectively just a logical AND of *mclk* and $\overline{wait}$, so $\overline{wait}$ must only change when *mclk* is low.

The *eclk* clock output reflects the clock used by the core, so it normally reflects the behaviour of *mclk* after $\overline{wait}$ has been gated in, but it also reflects the behaviour of the debug clock when in debugging mode.

9.1.4 | Memory Interface

The memory interface comprises the 32-bit address (*A[31:0]*), a bidirectional data bus (*D[31:0]*), separate data out (*Dout[31:0]*) and data in (*Din[31:0]*) buses together with ten control signals.

- $\overline{mreq}$ indicates a processor cycle which requires a memory access.
- *seq* indicates that the memory address will be sequential to (or possibly the same as) that used in the previous cycle.
- *lock* indicates that the processor should keep the bus to ensure the atomicity of the read and write phases of a SWAP instruction.
- $\overline{r}/w$ indicates whether the processor is performing a read or a write cycle.
- *mas[1:0]* encode the memory access size, indicating whether the access is for a byte, half-word or word quantity.
- b*l[3:0]* are externally controlled enables on latches on each of the four bytes on the data input bus. These make interfacing memories which are less than 32 bits wide easier.

The signals which indicate the type of the memory cycle, $\overline{mreq}$ and *seq*, are issued early to give the memory control logic as long as possible to decide how to handle the memory access. The interpretation of the four possible combinations of values on these two signals is given in Table 9.1. When a sequential cycle follows a non-sequential cycle, the address will be that of the non-sequential cycle plus one word (four bytes); where the sequential cycle follows an internal or coprocessor register transfer cycle, the address will be unchanged from the preceding cycle. In a typical memory organization the incrementing case can be used, together with information about the preceding address, to prepare the memory for a fast sequential access and where the address remains the same this can be exploited to start a full memory access in the preceding cycle (since neither the internal nor the coprocessor register transfer cycles use the memory).

The timing of the critical interface signals is illustrated in Figure 9.3. The use of these signals and the design of the memory interface logic was discussed further in Section 8.1 on page 179, where specific examples are given.

Table 9.1 ARM7TDMI cycle types

$\overline{mreq}$	*seq*	Cycle	Use
0	0	N	Non-sequential memory access
0	1	S	Sequential memory access
1	0	I	Internal cycle – bus and memory inactive
1	1	C	Coprocessor register transfer – memory inactive

9.1.5 | MMU Interface

The interface signals to the MMU provide information which is used to control access to areas of memory. The $\overline{trans}$ (translation control) signal indicates whether the processor is in a user

(*$\overline{trans}$* = 0) or privileged (*$\overline{trans}$* = 1) mode so that some areas of memory can be restricted to supervisor-only access and, where appropriate, different translation tables can be used for user and supervisor code (though this is rarely done). Where more detailed information about the operating mode is required, *$\overline{mode}$ [4:0]* reflects the bottom five bits of the CPSR (inverted), though memory management at this level is rarely used; the detailed mode information is probably of most use when debugging.

Where an access is disallowed, this is signalled on the *abort* input. The timing of *abort* is such that it must be valid at the end of the cycle, with the data. This is illustrated in Figure 9.3.

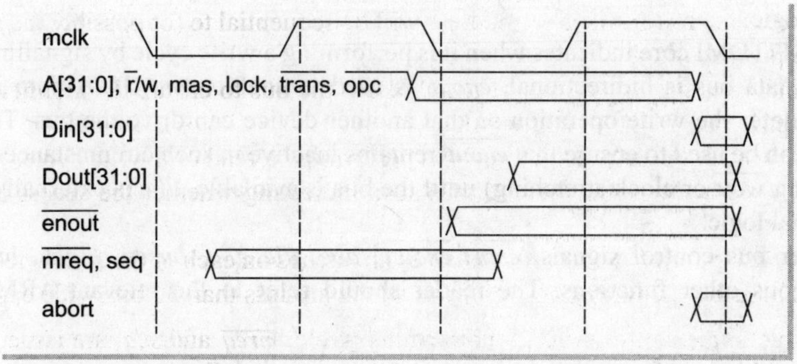

Figure 9.3 ARM7TDMI core memory and MMU interface timing

An aborted memory access causes the processor to take a prefetch or data abort, depending on the value of $\overline{opc}$ during the access.

The MMU may also use the $\overline{opc}$ signal where it is desired to support execute-only areas of memory, but it should be noted that this precludes the use of literal pools held in the code area for PC-relative access. For this reason execute-only protection is not widely used in ARM systems (and, in particular, is not supported in the ARM MMU architecture described in Section 11.6 on page 258).

9.1.6 | State

The *Tbit* output tells the environment whether the processor is currently executing ARM or Thumb instructions.

9.1.7 | Configuration

bigend switches the byte ordering between little- and big-endian (see 'Memory organization' on page 92 for an explanation of endianness). This input configures the way the processor operates and is not expected to change dynamically, although it can be changed during phase 2 of the clock if necessary.

9.1.8 | Interrupts

The two interrupt inputs may be asynchronous to the processor clock since they pass through synchronizing latches before entering the processor's control logic. The fast interrupt request, $\overline{fig}$, has higher priority than the normal interrupt request, $\overline{irq}$.

The *isync* input allows the interrupt synchronizers to be bypassed when the environment supplies inputs that are already synchronous to *mclk*; this removes the synchronizing delay from the interrupt latency.

9.1.9 | Initialization

$\overline{reset}$ starts the processor from a known state, executing from address 00000000_{16}.

9.1.10 | Bus Control

Normally, the ARM7TDMI core issues a new address as soon as it is available to maximize the time the MMU or memory controller has to process it. However, in simple systems where the address bus is connected directly to ROM or SRAM it is necessary to hold the old address to the end of the cycle. The core incorporates a transparent latch controlled by *ape*, which can retime the address as required by external logic.

The ARM7TDMI core indicates when it is performing a write cycle by signalling on $\overline{enout}$. Where the external data bus is bidirectional, $\overline{enout}$ is used to enable *dout[31:0]* onto it. Sometimes it is desirable to defer the write operation so that another device can drive the bus. The data bus enable signal, *dbe*, can be used to ensure that $\overline{enout}$ remains inactive in such circumstances. The core must be stopped (using $\overline{wait}$ or clock stretching) until the bus is available. *dbe* is externally timed as required by the external logic.

The other bus control signals, $\overline{enin}$, $\overline{enouti}$, *abe*, *ale*, *tbe*, *busen*, *highz*, *busdis* and *ecapclk*, perform various other functions. The reader should refer to the relevant ARM7TDMI datasheet for details.

9.1.11 | Debug Support

The ARM7TDMI implements the ARM debug architecture described in Section 8.7 on page 200. The EmbeddedICE module contains the breakpoint and watchpoint registers which allow code to be halted for debugging purposes. These registers are controlled through the JTAG test port using scan chain 2 (see Figure 9.1). When a breakpoint or watchpoint is encountered, the processor halts and enters debug state. Once in debug state, the processor registers may be inspected by forcing instructions into the instruction pipeline using scan chain 1. A store multiple of all the registers will present the register values on the data bus, where they can be sampled and shifted out again using scan chain 1. Accessing the banked registers requires instructions to be forced in to cause a mode change (note that in debug state the usual bar against switching into a privileged mode from user mode is removed).

Inspecting system state is achieved by causing the ARM to access memory locations at system speed and then switch immediately back into debug state.

9.1.12 | Debug Interface

The debug interface extends the functionality provided by the integrated EmbeddedICE macrocell by allowing external hardware to enable debug support (via *dbgen*) and make an asynchronous debug request (on *dbgrq*) or an instruction-synchronous request (on *breakpt*). External hardware is informed of when the core is in debug mode via *dbgack*. The internal debug request signal is exported on *dbgrqi*.

External events may contribute to the triggering of watchpoints via *extern0* and *extern1*, and EmbeddedICE watchpoint matches are signalled on *rangeout0* and *rangeout1*.

An empty communication transmission buffer is signalled on *commtx*, and an empty reception buffer on *commrx*.

The processor indicates whether or not the current instruction in the execution stage is being executed on $\overline{exec}$. An instruction is not executed if, for example, it fails its condition code test.

9.1.13 | Coprocessor Interface

The *cpi*, *cpa* and *cpb* coprocessor interface signals were described in Section 4.5 on page 87. The additional signal provided to the coprocessors is $\overline{opc}$, which indicates whether a memory access is to fetch an instruction or a data item. This is used by the coprocessor pipeline follower to track the ARM instruction execution. Where there is no requirement to connect a coprocessor, *cpa* and *cpb* should be tied high. This will cause all coprocessor instructions to take the undefined instruction trap.

9.1.14 | Power

The ARM7TDMI core is designed to operate with a nominal 5 volt or 3 volt supply, though this is dependent on the capabilities of the process technology as well as the circuit design style employed in the core.

9.1.15 | JTAG Interface

The JTAG control signals are as prescribed by the standard described in Section 8.6 on page 194 and are connected to an off-chip test controller via dedicated pins.

9.1.16 | TAP Information

These signals are used to support the addition of further scan chains to the JTAG system, along with the boundary scan extension signals detailed below.

tapsm[3:0] indicates the state the TAP controller is in; *ir[3:0]* gives the contents of the TAP instruction register; *screg[3:0]* is the address of the scan register currently selected by the TAP controller; *tck1* and *tck2* form a non-overlapping pair of clocks to control extension scan chains, and *tdoen* indicates when serial data is being driven out on *tdo*.

9.1.17 | Boundary Scan Extension

The ARM7TDMI cell contains a full JTAG TAP controller to support the EmbeddedICE functionality, and this TAP controller is capable of supporting any other on-chip scan facilities that are accessed through the JTAG port. The *drivebs*, *ecapclkbs*, *icapclkbs*, $\overline{highz}$, *pclkbs*, *rstclkbs*, *sdinbs*, *sdoutbs*, *shclkbs* and *shclk2bs* interface signals are therefore made available to allow arbitrary additional scan paths to be added to the system. The reader should refer to the relevant ARM7TDMI datasheet for details of the individual functions of these signals.

9.1.18 | ARM7TDMI Core

A plot of the ARM7TDMI processor core is shown in Figure 9.4. The characteristics of the 0.35 μm core when executing 32-bit ARM code are summarized in Table 9.2.

On a suitable process technology exceedingly high power-efficiencies have been obtained with ARM7TDMI cores. One example used a 0.25 μm process technology with a 0.9 V power supply to deliver 12,000 MIPS/W.

© ARM Limited

Figure 9.4 The ARM7TDMI processor core

Table 9.2 ARM7TDMI characteristics

Process	0.35 μm	**Transistors**	74,209	**MIPS**	60
Metal layers	3	**Core area**	2.1 mm^2	**Power**	87 mW
Vdd	3.3 V	**Clock**	0–66 MHz	**MIPS/W**	690

9.1.19 | ARM7TDMI for Synthesis

The standard ARM7TDMI processor core is a 'hard' macrocell, which is to say that it is delivered as a piece of physical layout, customized to the appropriate process technology. The ARM7TDMI-S is a synthesizable version of the ARM7TDMI, delivered as a high-level language module which can be synthesized using any suitable cell library in the target technology. It is therefore easier to port to a new process technology than is the hard macrocell.

The synthesis process supports a number of optional variations on the processor core functionality. These include:

- omitting the EmbeddedICE cell;
- replacing the full 64-bit result multiplier with a smaller and simpler multiplier that supports only the ARM multiply instructions that produce a 32-bit result.

Either of these options will result in a smaller synthesized macrocell with reduced functionality. The full version is 50% larger and 50% less power-efficient than the hard macrocell.

9.1.20 | ARM7TDMI Applications

The ARM7TDMI processor core has found many applications in systems with simple memory configurations, usually including a few kilobytes of simple on-chip RAM. A typical example is a mobile telephone handset (where the same chip usually incorporates sophisticated digital signal processing hardware and associated memories), where the ARM7TDMI has become the de-facto standard processor for the control and user interface functions.

Where significantly higher performance is required than can be delivered by a straightforward ARM7TDMI with a simple memory system, the system complexity will inevitably increase. The first step is to add a cache memory to the ARM7TDMI, probably in the form of an ARM CPU macrocell. This will enhance the performance of the software running from off-chip memory. If this still does not yield sufficient performance for the application, a more complex ARM core must be used that is capable of operating at yet higher performance levels. The ARM9TDMI and ARM10TDMI are such cores and are described later in this chapter.

9.2 | ARM8

The ARM8 core was developed at ARM Limited from 1993 to 1996 to supply the demand for an ARM core with a higher performance than was achievable with the ARM7 3-stage pipeline. It has now been superseded by the ARM9TDMI and ARM10TDMI, but its design raises some points of interest.

As was discussed in Section 4.2 on page 68, the performance of a processor core can be improved by:

- Increasing the clock rate.

  This requires the logic in each pipeline stage to be simplified and, therefore, the number of pipeline stages to be increased.

- Reducing the CPI (clock cycles per instruction).

  This requires either that instructions which occupy more than one pipeline slot in an ARM7 are re-implemented to occupy fewer slots, or that pipeline stalls caused by dependencies between instructions are reduced, or a combination of both.

9.2.1 | Reducing the CPI

Again repeating the argument presented earlier, the fundamental problem with reducing the CPI relative to an ARM7 core is related to the von Neumann bottleneck – any stored-program computer with a single instruction and data memory will have its performance limited by the available memory bandwidth. An ARM7 core accesses memory on (almost) every clock cycle either to fetch an instruction or to transfer data. To get a significantly better CPI than ARM7 the memory system must deliver more than one value in each clock cycle either by delivering more than 32 bits per cycle from a single memory or by having separate memories for instruction and data accesses.

9.2.2 | Double-bandwidth Memory

ARM8 retains a unified memory (either in the form of cache or on-chip RAM) but exploits the sequential nature of most memory accesses to achieve *double-bandwidth* from a single memory. It assumes that the memory it is connected to can deliver one word in a clock cycle and deliver the next sequential word half a cycle later concurrently with starting the next access. Typical memory organizations are quite capable of supplying the extra data with only a little extra hardware cost. Restricting the extra bandwidth to sequential accesses may seem to limit its usefulness, but instruction fetches are highly sequential and ARM's load multiple instructions generate sequential addresses (as do the store multiple instructions, though these do not exploit the double-bandwidth memory on ARM8), so the occurrence of sequential accesses is quite high in typical ARM code.

A 64-bit wide memory has the required characteristics, but delaying the arrival of the second word by half a clock cycle allows a 32-bit bus to be used and can save area since routing a 32-bit bus requires less area than routing a 64-bit bus.

9.2.3 | Core Organization

The ARM8 processor consists of a prefetch unit and an integer datapath. The prefetch unit is responsible for fetching instructions from memory and buffering them (in order to exploit the double-bandwidth memory). It then supplies up to one instruction per clock cycle to the integer unit, along with its PC value. The prefetch unit is responsible for branch prediction and uses static prediction based on the branch direction (backwards branches are predicted 'taken', whereas forwards branches are predicted 'not taken') to attempt to guess where the instruction stream will go; the integer unit will compute the exact stream and issue corrections to the prefetch unit where necessary.

The overall organization of the core is shown in Figure 9.5. The double-bandwidth memory will normally be on-chip, in the form of a cache memory on a general-purpose device such as the ARM810 (described in Section 12.2 on page 277) or as addressable RAM in an embedded application. The remaining memory may comprise conventional, single-bandwidth devices, but without some fast memory in the system the ARM8 core will show little benefit over the simpler ARM cores.

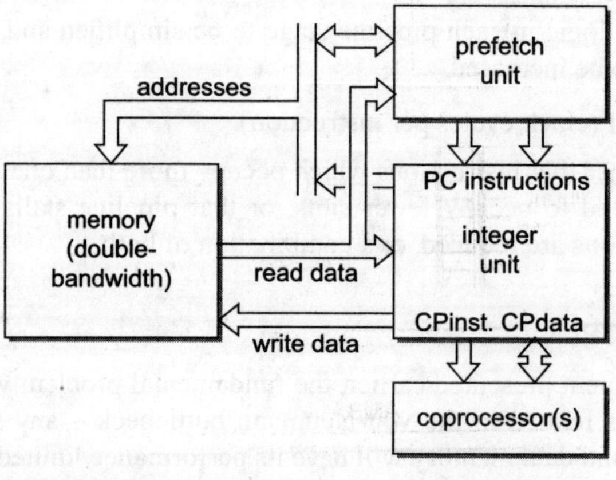

Figure 9.5 ARM8 processor core organization

9.2.4 | Pipeline Organization

The processor uses a 5-stage pipeline with the prefetch unit occupying the first stage and the integer unit using the remaining four stages:

1. Instruction prefetch.
2. Instruction decode and register read.
3. Execute (shift and ALU).
4. Data memory access.
5. Write-back results.

9.2.5 | Integer Unit Organization

The organization of the ARM8 integer unit is illustrated in Figure 9.6. The instruction stream and associated PC values are supplied by the prefetch unit through the interface shown at the top of the figure; the system control coprocessor connects through the dedicated coprocessor instruction and data buses to the left of the figure; the interface to the data memory is to the right of the figure and comprises an address bus, a write data bus and a read data bus.

Note that the read memory data bus supports double-bandwidth transfers on load multiple instructions, and both register write ports are used in load multiple instructions to store the double-bandwidth data stream. Since load multiple instructions transfer word quantities only, it does not matter that half of the data stream bypasses the byte alignment and sign extension logic.

9.2.6 | ARM8 Applications

ARM8 was designed as a general-purpose processor core that can readily be manufactured by ARM Limited's many licensees, so it is not highly optimized for a particular process technology. It offers significantly (two to three times) higher performance than the simpler ARM7 cores for a similar increase in silicon area, and requires the support of double-bandwidth on-chip memory if it is to realize its full potential.

One application of the ARM8 core is to build a high-performance CPU such as the ARM810, described in Section 12.2 on page 277. There the double-bandwidth memory is in the form of a cache, and the chip also incorporates a memory management unit and system control coprocessor CP15.

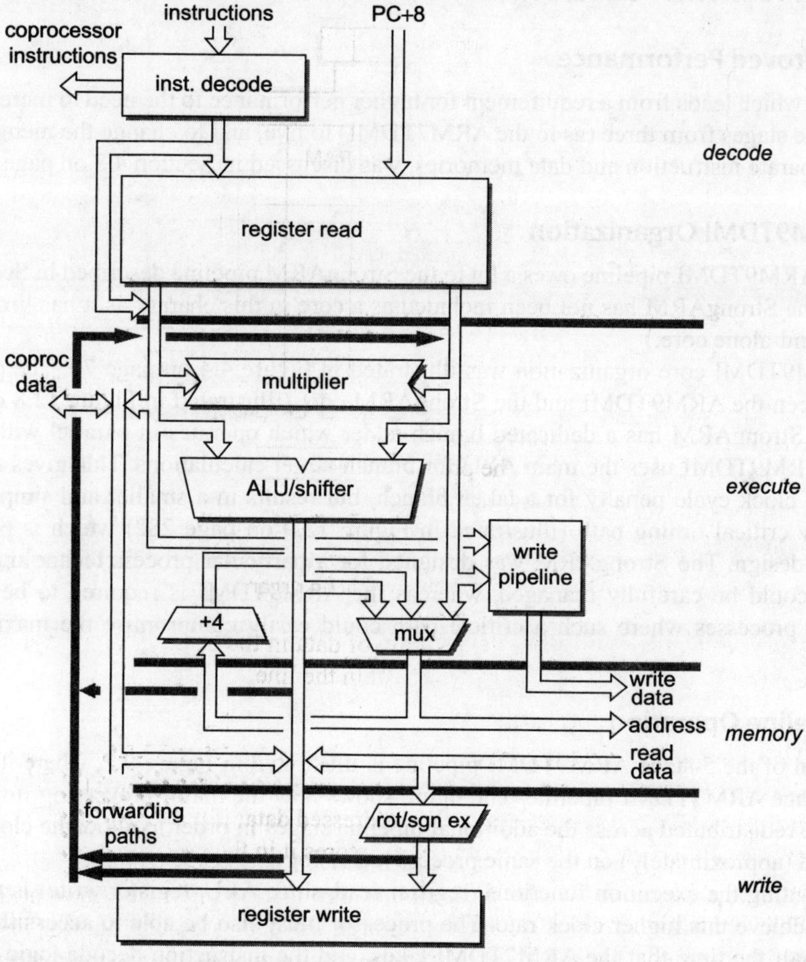

Figure 9.6 ARM8 integer unit organization

9.2.7 | ARM8 Silicon

The ARM8 core uses 124,554 transistors and operates at speeds up to 72 MHz on a 0.5 µm CMOS process with three metal layers.

The core layout can be seen in the ARMS10 die photograph in Figure 12.6 on page 278 in the upper left-hand area of the die.

9.3 | ARM9TDMI

The ARM9TDMI core takes the functionality of the ARM7TDMI up to a significantly higher performance level. Like the ARM7TDMI (and unlike the ARM8) it includes support for the Thumb instruction set and an EmbeddedICE module for on-chip debug support. The performance improvement is achieved by adopting a 5-stage pipeline to increase the maximum clock rate and by using separate instruction and data memory ports to allow an improved CPI (Clocks Per Instruction – a measure of how much work a processor does in a clock cycle).

9.3.1 | Improved Performance

The rationale which leads from a requirement for higher performance to the need to increase the number of pipeline stages from three (as in the ARM7TDMI) to five, and to change the memory interface to employ separate instruction and data memories, was discussed in Section 4.2 on page 68.

9.3.2 | ARM9TDMI Organization

The 5-stage ARM9TDMI pipeline owes a lot to the StrongARM pipeline described in Section 12.3 on page 279. (The StrongARM has not been included as a core in this chapter as it has limited applicability as a stand-alone core.)

The ARM9TDMI core organization was illustrated in Figure 4.4 on page 70. The principal difference between the ARM9TDMI and the StrongARM core (illustrated in Figure 12.8 on page 281) is that while StrongARM has a dedicated branch adder which operates in parallel with the register read stage, ARM9TDMI uses the main ALU for branch target calculations. This gives ARM9TDMI an additional clock cycle penalty for a taken branch, but results in a smaller and simpler core, and avoids a very critical timing path (illustrated in Figure 12.9 on page 282) which is present in the StrongARM design. The StrongARM was designed for a particular process technology where this timing path could be carefully managed, whereas the ARM9TDMI is required to be readily portable to new processes where such a critical path could easily compromise the maximum usable clock rate.

9.3.3 | Pipeline Operation

The operation of the 5-stage ARM9TDMI pipeline is illustrated in Figure 9.7, where it is compared with the 3-stage ARM7TDMI pipeline. The figure shows how the major processing functions of the processor are redistributed across the additional pipeline stages in order to allow the clock frequency to be doubled (approximately) on the same process technology.

Redistributing the execution functions (register read, shift, ALU, register write) is not all that is required to achieve this higher clock rate. The processor must also be able to access the instruction memory in half the time that the ARM7TDMI takes, and the instruction decode logic must also be restructured to allow the register read to take place concurrently with a substantial part of the decoding.

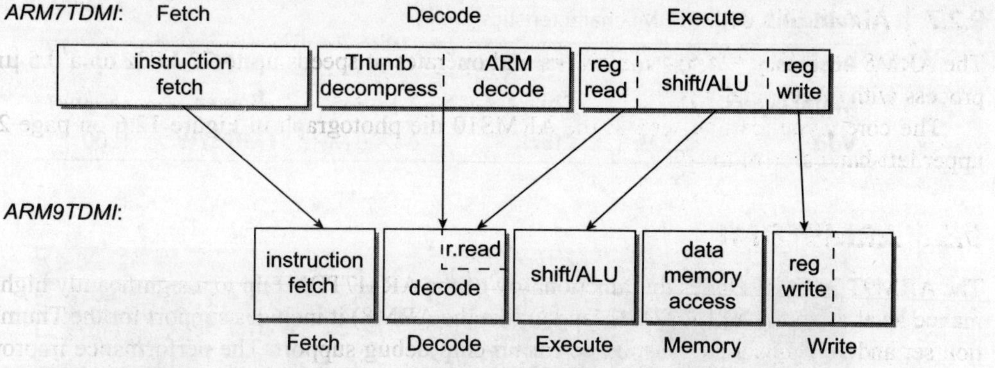

Figure 9.7 ARM7TDMI and ARM9TDMI pipeline comparison

9.3.4 | Thumb Decoding

The ARM7TDMI implements the Thumb instruction set by 'decompressing' Thumb instructions into ARM instructions using slack time in the ARM7 pipeline. The ARM9TDMI pipeline is much tighter and does not have sufficient slack time to allow Thumb instructions to be first translated into ARM instructions and then decoded; instead it has hardware to decode both ARM and Thumb instructions directly.

The extra 'Memory' stage in the ARM9TDMI pipeline does not have any direct equivalent in the ARM7TDMI. Its function is performed by additional 'Execute' cycles that interrupt the pipeline flow. This interruption is an inevitable consequence of the single memory port used by the ARM7TDMI for both instruction and data accesses. During a data access an instruction fetch cannot take place. The ARM9TDMI avoids this pipeline interruption through the provision of separate instruction and data memories.

9.3.5 | Coprocessor Support

The ARM9TDMI has a coprocessor interface which allows on-chip coprocessors for floating-point, digital signal processing or other special-purpose hardware acceleration requirements to be supported. (At the clock speeds it supports there is little possibility of off-chip coprocessors being useful.)

9.3.6 | On-chip Debug

The EmbeddedICE functionality in the ARM9TDMI core gives the same system-level debug features as that on the ARM7TDMI core (see Section 8.7 on page 200), with the following additional features:

- Hardware single-stepping is supported.
- Breakpoints can be set on exceptions in addition to the address/data/control conditions supported by ARM7TDMI.

9.3.7 | Low Voltage Operation

Although the first ARM9TDMI core was implemented on a 0.35 μm 3.3 V technology, the design has been ported onto 0.25 μm and 0.18 μm processes using power supplies down to 1.2 V

9.3.8 | ARM9TDMI Core

The characteristics of the 0.25 μm ARM9TDMI core when executing 32-bit ARM code are summarized in Table 9.3. A plot of the core is shown in Figure 9.8.

Table 9.3 ARM9TDMI characteristics

Process	0.25 μm	**Transistors**	111,000	**MIPS**	220
Metal layers	3	**Core area**	2.1 mm^2	**Power**	150 mW
Vdd	2.5 V	**Clock**	0–200 MHz	**MIPS/W**	1500

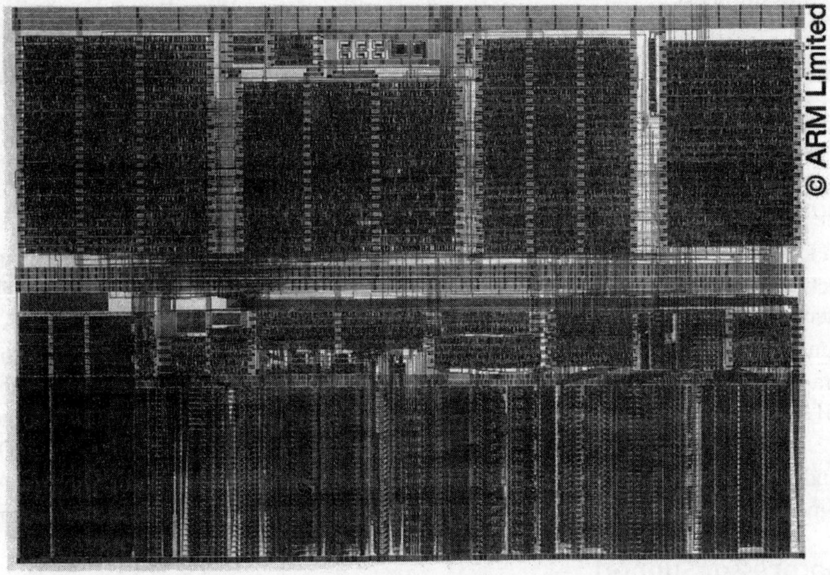

Figure 9.8 The ARM9TDMI processor core

9.3.9 | ARM9TDMI Applications

An ARM9TDMI core has separate instruction and data memory ports. While in principle it may be possible to connect these ports to a single unified memory, in practice doing so would negate many of the reasons for choosing the ARM9TDMI core over the smaller and cheaper ARM7TDMI core in the first place. Similarly, although it is not necessary to exploit the higher clock rate supported by the ARM9TDMI's 5-stage pipeline in comparison to the ARM7TDMI's 3-stage pipeline, not to do so would negate the rationale for using the ARM9TDMI. Therefore, any application that justifies the use of an ARM9TDMI core is going to have to cope with a complex high-speed memory subsystem.

The most common way of handling this memory requirement will be to incorporate separate instruction and data cache memories as exemplified by the various standard ARM CPU cores based around the ARM9TDMI. The ARM920T and ARM940T CPU cores are described in Section 12.4 on page 286. The caches in these CPU cores satisfy most of the memory bandwidth requirements of the ARM9TDMI and reduce the external bandwidth requirement to something that can be satisfied by conventional unified memories connected via a single AMBA bus.

An alternative solution, particularly applicable in embedded systems where the performance-critical code is relatively well contained, is to use an appropriate amount of separate directly addressed local instruction and data memory instead of caches.

9.3.10 | ARM9E-S

The ARM9E-S is a synthesizable version of the ARM9TDMI core. It implements an extended version of the ARM instruction set compared with the 'hard' core. In addition to the ARM architecture v4T instructions supported by the ARM9TDMI, the ARM9E-S supports the full ARM architecture version v5TE (see Section 5.23 on page 127), including the signal processing instruction set extensions described in Section 8.9 on page 206.

The ARM9E-S is 30% larger than the ARM9TDMI on the same process. It occupies 2.7 mm^2 on a 0.25 μm CMOS process.

9.4 | ARM10TDMI

The ARM10TDMI is the current high-end ARM processor core and is still under development at the time of writing. Just as the ARM9TDMI delivers approximately twice the performance of the ARM7TDMI on the same process, the ARM10TDMI is positioned to operate at twice the performance of the ARM9TDMI. It is intended to deliver 400 dhrystone 2.1 MIPS at 300 MHz on 0.25 μm CMOS technology.

In order to achieve this level of performance, starting from the ARM9TDMI, two approaches have been combined (again, see the discussion in Section 4.2 on page 68):

1. The maximum clock rate has been increased.
2. The CPI (average number of Clocks Per Instruction) has been reduced.

Since the ARM9TDMI pipeline is already fairly optimal, how can these improvements be achieved without resorting to a very complex organization, such as superscalar execution, which would compromise the low power and small core size that are the hallmarks of an ARM core?

9.4.1 | Increased Clock Rate

The maximum clock rate that an ARM core can support is determined by the slowest logic path in any of the pipeline stages.

The 5-stage ARM9TDMI is already well balanced (see Figure 9.7); four of the five stages are heavily loaded. The pipeline could be extended to spread the logic over many more stages, but the benefits of such a 'super-pipelined' organization tend to be offset by the worsened CPI that results from the increased pipeline dependencies unless very complex mechanisms are employed to minimize these effects.

Instead, the ARM10TDMI approach is to retain a very similar pipeline to the ARM9TDMI but to support a higher clock rate by optimizing each stage in a particular way (see Figure 9.9):

- The fetch and memory stages are effectively increased from one to one-and-a-half clock cycles by providing the address for the next cycle early. To achieve this in the memory stage, memory addresses are computed in a separate adder that can produce its result faster than the main ALU (because it implements only a subset of the ALU's functionality).
- The execute stage uses a combination of improved circuit techniques and restructuring to reduce its critical path. For example, the multiplier does not feed into the main ALU to resolve its partial sum and product terms; instead it has its own adder in the memory stage (multiplications never access memory, so this stage is free.)
- The instruction decode stage is the only part of the processor logic that could not be streamlined sufficiently to support the higher clock rate, so here an additional 'Issue' pipeline stage was inserted.

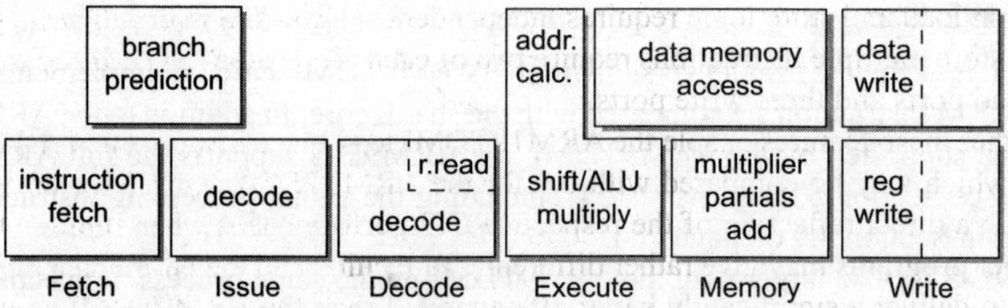

Figure 9.9 The ARM1OTDMI pipeline

The result is a 6-stage pipeline that can operate faster than the 5-stage ARM9TDMI pipeline, but requires its supporting memories- to be little faster than the ARM9TDMF's memories. This is of significance since very fast memories tend to be power-hungry. The extra pipeline stage, inserted to allow more time for instruction decode, only incurs pipeline dependency costs when an unpredicted branch is executed. Since the extra stage comes before the register read takes place it introduces no new operand dependencies and requires no new forwarding paths. With the inclusion of a branch prediction mechanism this pipeline will give a very similar CPI to the ARM9TDMI pipeline while supporting the higher clock rate.

9.4.2 | Reduced CPI

The pipeline enhancements described above support a 50% higher clock rate without compromising the CPI. This is a good start, but will not yield the required 100% performance improvement. For this an improved CPI is needed on top of the increased clock rate.

Any plan to improve the CPI must start from a consideration of memory bandwidth. The ARM7TDMI uses its single 32-bit memory on (almost) every clock cycle, so the ARM9TDMI moved to a Harvard memory organization to release more bandwidth. The ARM9TDMI uses its instruction memory on (almost) every clock cycle. Although its data memory is only around 50% loaded, it is hard to exploit this to improve its CPI. The instruction bandwidth must be increased somehow.

The approach adopted in the ARM10TDMI is to employ 64-bit memories. This effectively removes the instruction bandwidth bottleneck and enables a number of CPI-improving features to be added to the processor organization:

- Branch prediction: the ARM10TDMI branch prediction logic goes beyond what is required simply to maintain the pipeline efficiency as discussed above. Because instructions are fetched at a rate of two per clock cycle, the branch prediction unit (which is in the fetch pipeline stage) can often recognize branches before they are issued and effectively remove them from the instruction stream, reducing the cycle cost of the branch to zero.

  The ARM10TDMI employs a *static* branch prediction mechanism: conditional branches that branch backwards are predicted to be taken; those that branch forwards are predicted not to be taken.
- Non-blocking load and store execution: a load or store instruction that cannot complete in a single memory cycle, either because it is referencing slow memory or because it is transferring multiple registers, does not stall the execution pipeline until an operand dependency arises.
- The 64-bit data memory enables load and store multiple instructions to transfer two registers in each clock cycle.

The non-blocking load and store logic requires independent register file read and write ports, and the 64-bit load and store multiple instructions require two of each. The ARM10TDMI register bank therefore has four read ports and three write ports.

Taken together these features enable the ARM10TDMI to achieve a dhrystone 2.1 MIPS per MHz figure of 1.25, which may be compared with 0.9 for the ARM7TDMI and 1.1 for the ARM9TDMI. These figures are a direct reflection of the respective CPI performances when running the dhrystone benchmark; other programs may give rather different CPI results, and the 64-bit data buses enable the ARM10TDMI to deliver a significantly better effective CPI than the ARM9TDMI on complex tasks such as booting an operation system.

9.4.3 | ARM10TDMI Applications

It was noted in the discussion of 'ARM9TDMI applications' that at least some local high-speed memory was required to release the performance potential of the core. The same is true of the ARM10TDMI: without separate local 64-bit instruction and data memories the core will not be able to deliver its full performance, and it will go no faster than a smaller and cheaper ARM core.

Again, the usual (though not the only) way to resolve this problem is through the provision of local cache memories as exemplified by the ARM1020E described in Section 12.6 on page 291. Since the performance of the ARM10TDMI core is critically dependent on the availability of fast 64-bit local memory, discussion of its performance characteristics will be presented later in the context of the ARM1020E.

9.5 | Discussion

All early ARM processor cores, up to and including the ARM7TDMI, were based on a simple 3-stage fetch-decode-execute pipeline. From the first ARM1, developed at Acorn Computers in the early 1980s, through to the ARM7TDMI cores in most of today's mobile telephone handsets, the basic principles of operation have barely changed. The development work carried out in the ARM's first decade focused on the following aspects of the design:

- performance improvement through critical path optimization and process shrinkage;
- low-power applications through static CMOS logic, power supply voltage reduction and code compression (the Thumb instruction set);
- support for system development through the addition of on-chip debug facilities, on-chip buses and software tools.

The ARM7TDMI represents the pinnacle of this development process, and its commercial success demonstrates the viability of the original very simple 3-stage pipeline in a world dominated by PCs with ever-increasingly complex superscalar, superpipelined, high-performance (and very power-hungry) microprocessors.

The second decade of ARM development has seen a careful diversification of the ARM organization in the quest for higher performance levels:

- The first step to a 5-stage pipeline yields a doubling of performance (all other factors being equal) at the cost of some forwarding logic in the core and either a double-bandwidth memory (as in the ARM8) or separate instruction and data memories (as in the ARM9TDMI and StrongARM).

- The next doubling of performance, achieved in the ARM10TDMI, is rather harder-won. The 6-stage pipeline is quite similar to the 5-stage pipeline used before, but the time slots allocated to memory access have been extended to enable the memories to support higher clock rates without burning excessive power. The processor core also incorporates more decoupling: in the prefetch unit to allow branches to be predicted and removed from the instruction stream, and in the data memory interface to allow the processor to continue executing when a data access takes some time to resolve (for example, due to a cache miss).

Performance improvement is achieved through a combination of increased clock rate and reduced CPI – the average number of clocks per instruction. The increased clock rate will usually require a deeper pipeline that will tend to worsen the CPI, so remedial measures are required to recover the CPI loss and then improve it further.

To date, all ARM processors have been based on organizations that issue at most one instruction per clock cycle, and always in program order. The ARM10TDMI and the AMULET3 processor (described in Section 14.5 on page 332) handle out-of-order completion in order to be able to keep instructions flowing during a slow data access, and both of these processors also include branch prediction logic to reduce the cost of refilling their pipelines on branch instructions. AMULET3 suppresses the fetching of predicted branch instructions but still executes them; ARM10TDMI fetches branch instructions but suppresses their execution. But by the standards of today's high-end PC and workstation processors, these are still very simple machines. This simplicity has direct benefits in system-on-chip applications in that simple processors require fewer transistors than complex processors and therefore occupy less die area and consume less power.

9.6 | Example and Exercises

EXAMPLE 9.1

How should the ARM7TDMI address bus be retimed to interface to static RAM or ROM devices?

Normally the ARM7TDMI outputs new addresses as soon as they are available, which is towards the end of the preceding clock cycle. To interface to static memory devices the address must be held stable until after the end of the cycle, so this pipelining must be removed. This is most simply achieved by using *ape*, the address pipeline enable signal. In systems where some memory devices benefit from early addresses and some are static, either an external latch should be used to retime the addresses to the static devices or *ape* should be controlled to suit the currently addressed device.

Exercise 9.1.1

Review the processor cores described in this chapter and discuss the basic techniques used to increase the core performance by a factor of eight in going from the ARM7TDMI to the ARM10TDMI.

Exercise 9.1.2

In a system where the designer is free to vary the supply voltage to the processor it is possible to trade off performance (which scales in proportion to *Vdd*) against power-efficiency (which scales as $1/Vdd^2$). A measure of architectural power-efficiency that factors out the effect of power supply variations is therefore $MIPS^3/W$.

Compare each of the processor cores presented here on the basis of this measure.

Exercise 9.1.3

Increasing the clock speed of a processor to get improved performance is not a sustainable technique because it increases power dissipation. What are the new techniques incorporated in ARM10 to enhance performance by reducing the CPI (Cycles per instruction)?

10

Memory Hierarchy

SUMMARY OF CHAPTER CONTENTS

A modern microprocessor can execute instructions at a very high rate. To exploit this potential performance fully the processor must be connected to a memory system which is both very large and very fast. If the memory is too small, it will not be able to hold enough programs to keep the processor busy. If it is too slow, the memory will not be able to supply instructions as fast as the processor can execute them.

Unfortunately, the larger a memory is the slower it is. It is therefore not possible to design a single memory which is both large enough and fast enough to keep a high-performance processor busy.

It is, however, possible to build a composite memory system which combines a small, fast memory and a large, slow *main* memory to present an external behaviour which, with typical program statistics, appears to behave like a large, fast memory much of the time. The small, fast memory component is the *cache*, which automatically retains copies of instructions and data that the processor is using most frequently. The effectiveness of the cache depends on the *spatial locality* and *temporal locality* properties of the program.

This two-level memory principle can be extended into a memory hierarchy of many levels, and the computer backup (disk) store can be viewed as part of this hierarchy. With suitable *memory management* support, the size of a program is limited not by the computer's main memory but by the size of the hard disk, which may be very much larger than the main memory.

10.1 | Memory Size and Speed

A typical computer memory hierarchy comprises several levels, each level having a characteristic size and speed.

- The processor registers can be viewed as the top of the memory hierarchy. A RISC processor will typically have around thirty-two 32-bit registers making a total of 128 bytes, with an access time of a few nanoseconds.
- On-chip cache memory will have a capacity of eight to 32 Kbytes with an access time around ten nanoseconds.
- High-performance desktop systems may have a second-level off-chip cache with a capacity of a few hundred Kbytes and an access time of a few tens of nanoseconds.

- Main memory will be megabytes to tens of megabytes of dynamic RAM with an access time around 100 nanoseconds.
- Backup store, usually on a hard disk, will be hundreds of Mbytes up to a few Gbytes with an access time of a few tens of milliseconds.

Note that the performance difference between the main memory and the backup store is very much greater than the difference between any other adjacent levels, even when there is no secondary cache in the system.

The data which is held in the registers is under the direct control of the compiler or assembler programmer, but the contents of the remaining levels of the hierarchy are usually managed automatically. The caches are effectively invisible to the application program, with blocks or 'pages' of instructions and data migrating up and down the hierarchy under hardware control. Paging between the main memory and the backup store is controlled by the operating system, and remains transparent to the application program. Since the performance difference between the main memory and the backup store is so great, much more sophisticated algorithms are required here to determine when to migrate data between the levels.

An embedded system will not usually have a backing store and will therefore not exploit paging. However, many embedded systems incorporate caches, and ARM CPU chips employ a range of cache organizations. We will therefore look at cache organizational issues in some detail.

10.1.1 | Memory Cost

Fast memory is more expensive per bit than slow memory, so a memory hierarchy also aims to give a performance close to the fastest memory with an average cost per bit approaching that of the slowest memory.

10.2 | On-chip Memory

Some form of on-chip memory is essential if a microprocessor is to deliver its best performance. With today's clock rates, only on-chip memory can support zero wait state access speeds, and it will also give better power-efficiency and reduced electromagnetic interference than off-chip memory.

10.2.1 | On-chip RAM Benefits

In many embedded systems simple on-chip RAM is preferred to cache for a number of reasons:

- It is simpler, cheaper, and uses less power.

  We will see in the following sections that cache memory carries a significant overhead in terms of the logic that is required to enable it to operate effectively. It also incurs a significant design cost if a suitable off-the-shelf cache is unavailable.
- It has more deterministic behaviour.

  Cache memories have complex behaviours which can make difficult to predict how well they will operate under particular circumstances. In particular, it can be hard to guarantee interrupt response time.

The drawback with on-chip RAM *vis-à-vis* cache is that it requires explicit management by the programmer, whereas a cache is usually transparent to the programmer.

Where the program mix is well-defined and under the control of the programmer, on-chip RAM can effectively be used as a software-controlled cache. Where the application mix cannot be predicted this control task becomes very difficult. Hence a cache is usually preferred in any general-purpose system where the application mix is unknown.

One important advantage of on-chip RAM is that it enables the programmer to allocate space in it using knowledge of the *future* processing load. A cache left to its own devices has knowledge only of *past* program behaviour, and it can therefore never prepare in advance for critical future tasks. Again, this is a difference which is most likely to be significant when critical tasks must meet strict realtime constraints.

The system designer must decide which is the right approach for a particular system, taking all these factors into account. Whatever form of on-chip memory is chosen, it must be specified with great care. It must be fast enough to keep the processor busy and large enough to contain critical routines, but neither too fast (or it will consume too much power) nor too large (or it will occupy too much chip area).

10.3 | Caches

The first RISC processors were introduced at a time when standard memory parts were faster than their contemporary microprocessors, but this situation did not persist for long. Subsequent advances in semiconductor process technology which have been exploited to make microprocessors faster have been applied differently to improve memory chips. Standard DRAM parts have got a little faster, but mostly they have been developed to have a much higher capacity.

10.3.1 | Processor and Memory Speeds

In 1980 a typical DRAM part could hold 4 Kbits of data, with 16 Kbit chips arriving in 1981 and 1982. These parts would cycle at 3 or 4 MHz for random accesses, and at about twice this rate for local accesses (in page mode). Microprocessors at that time could request around two million memory accesses per second.

In 2000 DRAM parts have a capacity of 256 Mbits per chip, with random accesses operating at around 30 MHz. Microprocessors can request several hundred million memory accesses per second. If the processor is so much faster than the memory, it can only deliver its full performance potential with the help of a **cache** memory.

A cache memory is a small, very fast memory that retains copies of recently used memory values. It operates transparently to the programmer, automatically deciding which values to keep and which to overwrite. These days it is usually implemented on the same chip as the processor. Caches work because programs normally display the property of **locality**, which means that at any particular time they tend to execute the same instructions many times (for instance in a loop) on the same areas of data (for instance a stack).

10.3.2 | Unified and Harvard Caches

Caches can be built in many ways. At the highest level a processor can have one of the following two organizations:

- A unified cache.

  This is a single cache for both instructions and data, as illustrated in Figure 10.1.

- Separate instruction and data caches.

  This organization is sometimes called a **modified Harvard** architecture as shown in Figure 10.2.

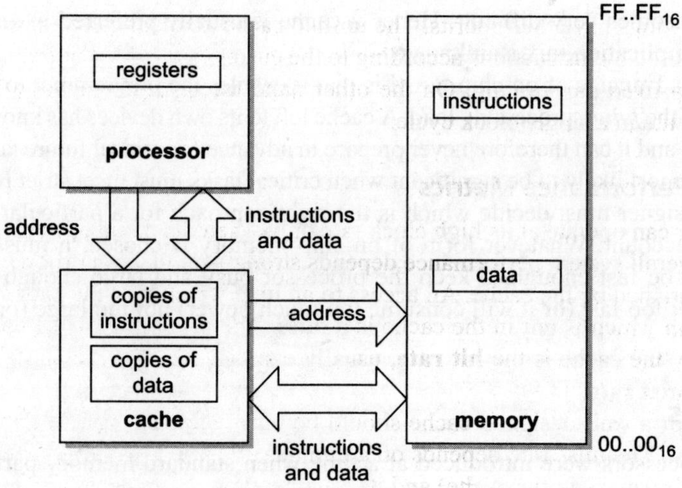

Figure 10.1 A unified instruction and data cache

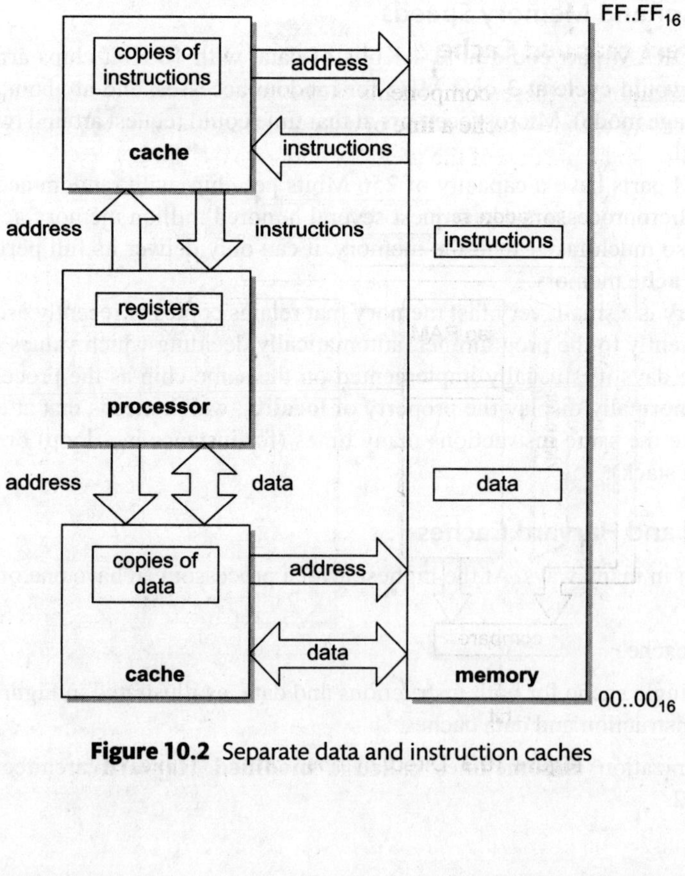

Figure 10.2 Separate data and instruction caches

Both these organizations have their merits. The unified cache automatically adjusts the proportion of the cache memory used by instructions according to the current program requirements, giving a better performance than a fixed partitioning. On the other hand the separate caches allow load and store instructions to execute in a single clock cycle.

10.3.3 | Cache Performance Metrics

Since the processor can operate at its high clock rate only when the memory items it requires are held in the cache, the overall system performance depends strongly on the proportion of memory accesses which cannot be satisfied by the cache. An access to an item which is in the cache is called a **hit**, and an access to an item which is not in the cache is a **miss**. The proportion of all the memory accesses that are satisfied by the cache is the **hit rate**, usually expressed as a percentage, and the proportion that are not is the **miss rate**.

The miss rate of a well-designed cache should be only a few per cent if a modern processor is to fulfil its potential. The miss rate depends on a number of cache parameters, including its size (the number of bytes of memory in the cache) and its organization.

10.3.4 | Cache Organization

Since a cache holds a dynamically varying selection of items from main memory, it must have storage for both the data and the address at which the data is stored in main memory.

10.3.5 | The Direct-mapped Cache

The simplest organization of these components is the direct-mapped cache which is illustrated in Figure 10.3. In the direct-mapped cache a **line** of data is stored along with an address **tag** in a memory which is addressed by some portion of the memory address (the **index**).

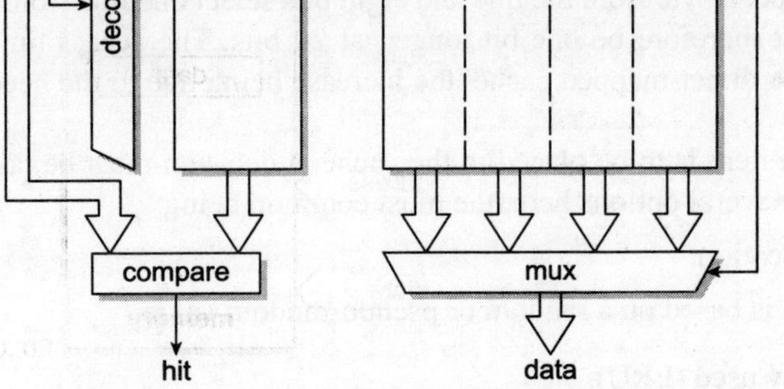

Figure 10.3 Direct-mapped cache organization

To check whether or not a particular memory item is stored in the cache, the index address bits are used to access the cache entry. The top address bits are then compared with the stored tag; if they are equal, the item is in the cache. The lowest address bits can be used to access the desired item within the line.

This, simplest, cache organization has a number of properties that can be contrasted with those of more complex organizations:

- A particular memory item is stored in a unique location in the cache; two items with the same cache address field will contend for use of that location.
- Only those bits of the address that are not used to select within the line or to address the cache RAM need be stored in the tag field.
- The tag and data access can be performed at the same time, giving the fastest cache access time of any organization.
- Since the tag RAM is typically a lot smaller than the data RAM, its access time is shorter, allowing the tag comparison to be completed within the data access time.

A typical direct-mapped cache might store 8 Kbytes of data in 16-byte lines. There would therefore be 512 lines. A 32-bit address would have four bits to address bytes within the line and nine bits to select the line, leaving a 19-bit tag which requires just over one Kbyte of tag store.

When data is loaded into the cache, a **block** of data is fetched from memory. There is little point in having the line size smaller than the block size. If the block size is smaller than the line size, the tag store must be extended to include a valid bit for each block within the line. Choosing the line and block sizes to be equal results in the simplest organization.

10.3.6 | The Set-associative Cache

Moving up in complexity, the set-associative cache aims to reduce the problems due to contention by enabling a particular memory item to be stored in more than one cache location. A 2-way set-associative cache is illustrated in Figure 10.4. As the figure suggests, this form of cache is effectively two direct-mapped caches operating in parallel. An address presented to the cache may find its data in either half, so each memory address may be stored in either of two places. Each of two items which were in contention for a single location in the direct-mapped cache may now occupy one of these places, allowing the cache to hit on both.

The 8 Kbyte cache with 16 byte lines will have 256 lines in each half of the cache, so four bits of the 32-bit address select a byte from the line and eight bits select one line from each half of the cache. The address tag must therefore be one bit longer, at 20 bits. The access time is only very slightly longer than that of the direct-mapped cache, the increase being due to the need to multiplex the data from the two halves.

When a new data item is to be placed in the cache, a decision must be taken as to which half to place it in. There are several options here, the most common being:

- Random allocation.

  The decision is based on a random or pseudo-random value.

- Least recently used (LRU).

  The cache keeps a record of which location of a pair was last accessed and allocates the new data to the other one.

- Round-robin (also known as 'cyclic').

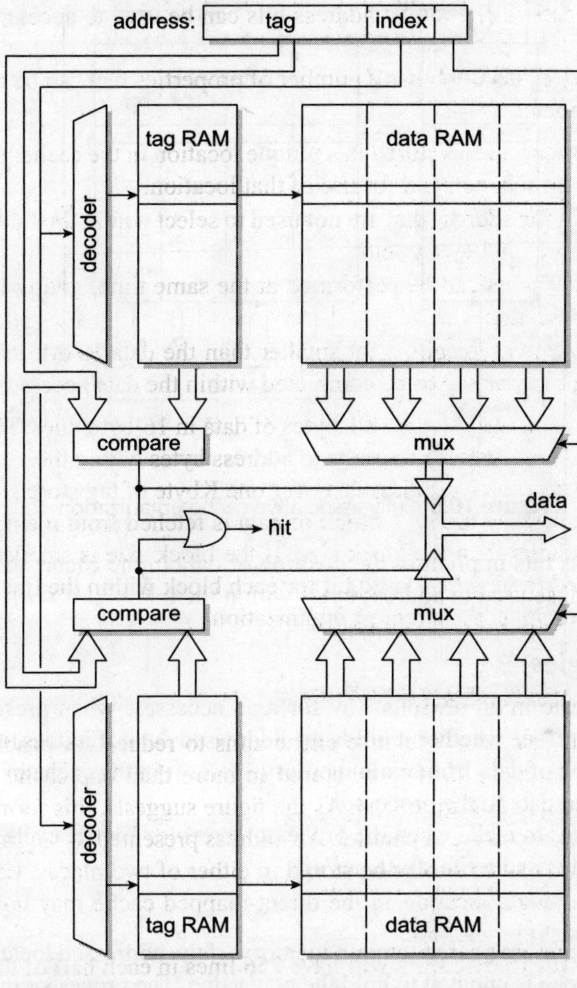

Figure 10.4 Two-way set-associative cache organization

The cache keeps a record of which location of a pair was last allocated and allocates the new data to the other one.

The set-associative approach extends beyond 2-way up to any degree of associativity, but in practice the benefits of going beyond 4-way associativity are small and do not warrant the extra complexity incurred.

10.3.7 | The Fully Associative Cache

At the other extreme of associativity, it is possible to design a fully associative cache in VLSI technology. Rather than continuing to divide the direct-mapped cache into ever smaller components, the tag store is designed differently using content addressed memory **(CAM)**. A CAM cell is a RAM cell with an inbuilt comparator, so a CAM based tag store can perform a parallel search to locate an address in any location. The organization of a fully associative cache is illustrated in Figure 10.5.

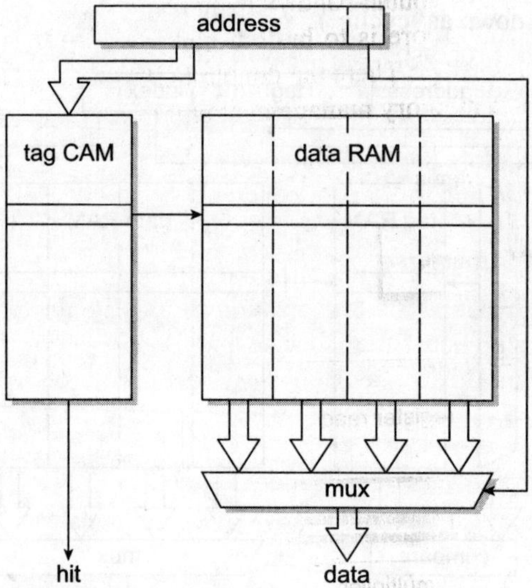

Figure 10.5 Fully associative cache organization

Since there are no address bits implicit in the position of data in the cache, the tag must store all the address bits apart from those used to address bytes within the line.

10.3.8 | Write Strategies

The above schemes operate in an obvious way for read accesses: when presented with a new read address the cache checks to see whether it holds the addressed data; if it does, it supplies the data; if it does not, it fetches a block of data from main memory, stores it in the cache in some suitable location and supplies the requested data to the processor.

There are more choices to make when the processor executes a write cycle. In increasing order of complexity, the commonly used write strategies are:

- **Write-through**.

  All write operations are passed to main memory; if the addressed location is currently held in the cache, the cache is updated to hold the new value. The processor must slow down to main memory speed while the write takes place.
- **Write-through with buffered write**.

  Here all write operations are still passed to main memory and the cache updated as appropriate, but instead of slowing the processor down to main memory speed the write address and data are stored in a **write buffer** which can accept the write information at high speed. The write buffer then transfers the data to main memory, at main memory speed, while the processor continues with its next task.
- **Copy-back** (also known as **write-back**).

  A copy-back cache is not kept coherent with main memory. Write operations update only the cache, so cache lines must remember when they have been modified (usually using a **dirty** bit on each line or block). If a dirty cache line is allocated to new data it must be copied back to memory before the line is reused.

The write-through cache is the simplest to implement and has the merit that the memory is kept up to date; the drawback is that the processor must slow to memory speeds on every write transfer. The addition of a write buffer allows the processor to continue until the write traffic exceeds the external write bandwidth. The copy-back cache reduces the external write bandwidth requirement since a location may be written many times before the final value gets written back to memory, but the implementation is considerably more complex and the loss of coherency is hard to manage.

10.3.9 | Cache Feature Summary

The various parameters that define the organization of a cache are summarized in Table 10.1. The first of these is the relationship between the cache and the memory management unit **(MMU)** which will be discussed further in 'Virtual and physical caches'; the others have been covered in this section.

Table 10.1 Summary of cache organizational options

Organizational feature	Options		
Cache-MMU relationship	Physical cache	Virtual cache	
Cache contents	Unified instruction and data cache	Separate instruction and data caches	
Associativity	Direct-mapped RAM-RAM	Set-associative RAM-RAM	Fully associative CAM-RAM
Replacement strategy	Round-robin	Random	LRU
Write strategy	Write-through	Write-through with write buffer	Copy-back

10.4 | Cache Design - An Example

The choice of organization for a cache requires the consideration of several factors as discussed in Section 10.3, including the size of the cache, the degree of associativity, the line and block sizes, the replacement algorithm, and the write strategy. Detailed architectural simulations are required to analyse the effects of these choices on the performance of the cache.

10.4.1 | The ARM3 Cache

The ARM3, designed in 1989, was the first ARM chip to incorporate an on-chip cache, and detailed studies were carried out into the effects of these parameters on performance and bus use. These studies used specially designed hardware to capture address traces while running several benchmark programs on an ARM2; software was then used to analyse these traces to model the behaviour of the various organizations. (Today special hardware is generally unnecessary since desktop machines have sufficient performance to simulate large enough programs without hardware support.)

The study started by setting an upper bound on the performance benefit that could be expected from a cache. A 'perfect' cache, which always contains the requested data, was modelled to set this bound. Any real cache is bound to miss some of the time, so it cannot perform any better than one which always hits.

Three forms of perfect cache were modelled using realistic assumptions about the cache and external memory speeds (which were 20 MHz and 8 MHz respectively): caches which hold either just instructions, mixed instructions and data, or just data. The results are shown in Table 10.2, normalized to the performance of a system with no cache. They show that instructions are the most important values to hold in the cache, but including data values as well can give a further 25% performance increase.

Table 10.2 'Perfect' cache performance

Cache form	Performance
No cache	1
Instruction-only cache	1.95
Instruction and data cache	2.5
Data-only cache	1.13

Although a decision was taken early on that the cache write strategy would be write-through (principally on the grounds of simplicity), it is still possible for the cache to detect a write miss and load a line of data from the write address. This 'allocate on write miss' strategy was investigated briefly, but proved to offer a negligible benefit in exchange for a significant increase in complexity, so it was rapidly abandoned. The problem was reduced to finding the best organization, consistent with chip area and power constraints, for a unified instruction and data cache with allocation on a read miss.

Various different cache organizations and sizes were investigated, with the results show in Figure 10.6. The simplest cache organization is the direct-mapped cache, but even with a size of 16 Kbytes, the cache is significantly worse than the 'perfect' case. The next step up in complexity is the dual set associative cache; now the performance of the 16 Kbyte cache is within a per cent or so of the perfect cache. But at the time of the design of the ARM3 (1989) a 16 Kbyte cache required a large chip area,

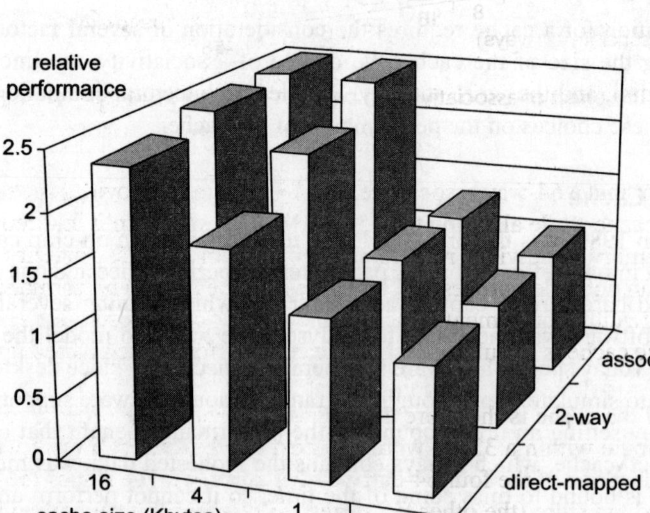

Figure 10.6 Unified cache performance as a function of size and organization

and the 4 Kbyte cache does not perform so well. (The results depend strongly on the program used to generate the address traces used, but these are typical.)

Going to the other extreme, a fully associative cache performs significantly better at the smaller size, delivering the 'perfect' performance on the benchmark program used for the tests. Here the replacement algorithm is random; LRU (least recently used) gives very similar results.

The cache model was then modified to use a quad-word line which is necessary to reduce the area cost of the tag store. This change had minimal effect on the performance.

The fully associative cache requires a large CAM (Content Addressable Memory) tag store which is likely to consume significant power, even with a quad-word line. The power can be reduced a lot by segmenting the CAM into smaller components, but this reduces the associativity. An analysis of the sensitivity of the system performance on the degree of associativity, using a 4 Kbyte cache, is shown in Figure 10.7. This shows the performance of the system for all associativities from fully (256-way) associative down to direct-mapped (1-way). Although the biggest performance increase is in going from direct-mapped to dual-set associative, there are noticeable improvements all the way up to 64-way associativity.

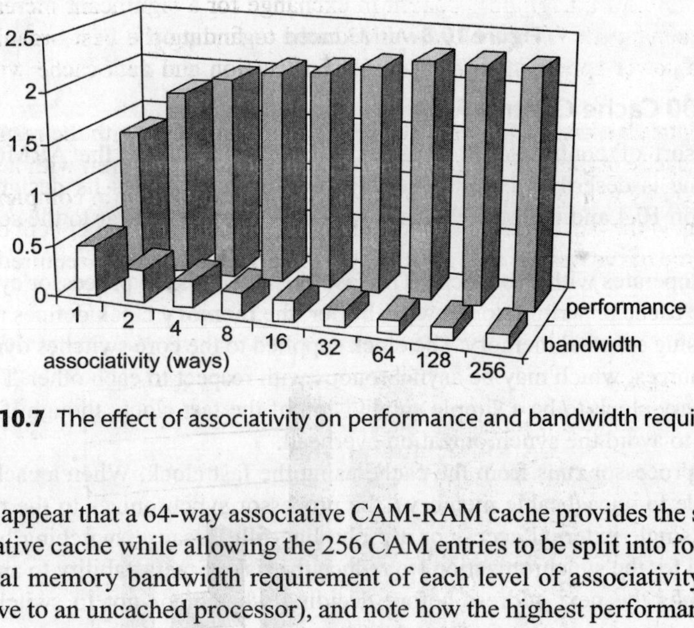

Figure 10.7 The effect of associativity on performance and bandwidth requirement

It would therefore appear that a 64-way associative CAM-RAM cache provides the same performance as the fully associative cache while allowing the 256 CAM entries to be split into four sections to save power. The external memory bandwidth requirement of each level of associativity is also shown in Figure 10.7 (relative to an uncached processor), and note how the highest performance corresponds to the lowest external bandwidth requirement. Since each external access costs a lot of energy compared with internal activity, the cache is simultaneously increasing performance and reducing system power requirements.

The organization of the cache is therefore that shown in Figure 10.8. The bottom two bits of the virtual address select a byte within a 32-bit word, the next two bits select a word within a cache line and the next two bits select one of the four 64-entry CAM tag stores. The rest of the virtual address is presented to the selected tag store (the other tag stores are disabled to save power) to check whether the data is in the cache, and the result is either a miss, or a hit together with the address of the data in the cache data RAM.

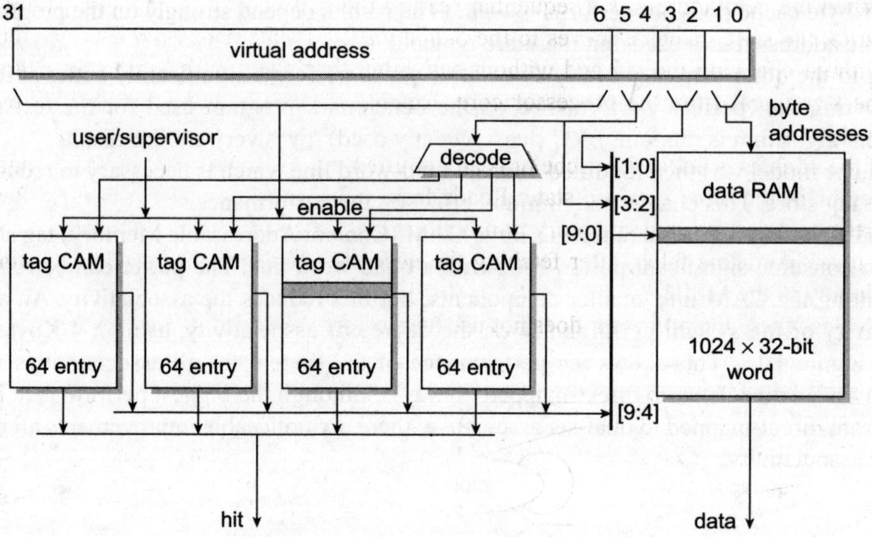

Figure 10.8 ARM3 cache organization

10.4.2 | ARM600 Cache Control FSM

To illustrate the sort of control logic required to manage a cache, the ARM600 cache control finite state machine is described below. The ARM600 cache borrows its design from the ARM3 described in Section 10.4 and it also includes a translation system similar to the scheme described in Section 10.5.

The ARM600 operates with two clocks. The **fast** clock defines the processor cycle time when it is operating from the cache or writing to the write buffer; the **memory** clock defines the speed when the processor is accessing external memory. The clock supplied to the core switches dynamically between these two clock sources, which may be asynchronous with respect to each other. There is no requirement for the memory clock to be a simple subdivision of the fast clock, though if it is the processor can be configured to avoid the synchronization overhead.

Normally the processor runs from the cache using the fast clock. When a cache miss occurs (or a reference is made to uncacheable memory), the processor synchronizes to the memory clock and either performs a single external access or a cache line-fill. Because switching between the clocks incurs an overhead for the synchronization (to reduce the risk of metastability to an acceptable level), the processor checks the next address before deciding whether or not to switch back to the fast clock.

The finite state machine that controls this activity is shown in Figure 10.9. Following initialization, the processor enters the *Check tag* state running from the fast clock. Depending on whether or not the addressed data is found in the cache, the processor can proceed in one of the following ways:

- So long as the address is non-sequential, does not fault in the MMU and is either a read found in the cache or a buffered write, the state machine remains in the *Check tag* state and a data value is returned or written every clock cycle.

- When the next address is a sequential read in the same cache line or a sequential buffered write, the state machine moves to the *Sequential fast* state where the data may be accessed without checking the tag and without activating the MMU. This saves power, and exploits the *seq* signal from the processor core. Again a data value is read or written every clock cycle.
- If the address is not in the cache or is an unbuffered write an external access is required. This begins in the *Start external* state. Reads from uncacheable memory and unbuffered writes are completed as single memory transactions in the *External* state. Cacheable reads perform a quad-word line fetch, after fetching the necessary translation information if this was not already in the MMU.
- Cycles where the processor does not use memory are executed in the *Idle* state.

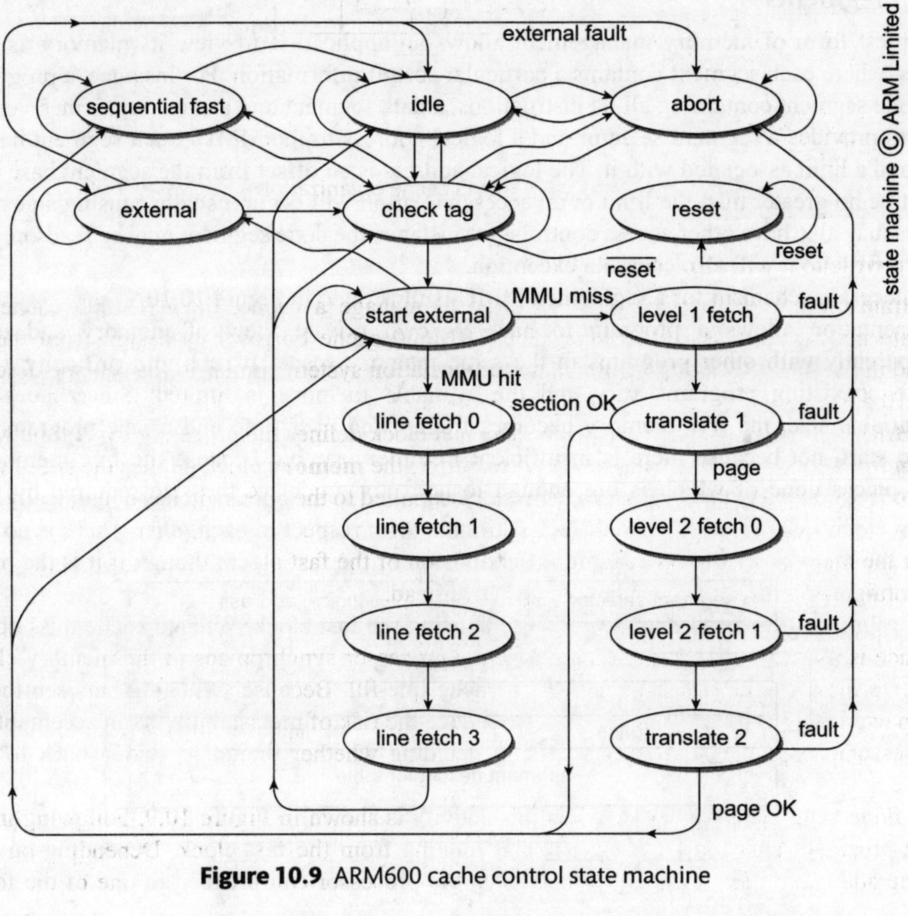

Figure 10.9 ARM600 cache control state machine

At several points in the translation process it may become clear that the access cannot be completed and the *Abort* state is entered. Uncacheable reads and unbuffered writes may also be aborted by external hardware.

10.5 | Memory Management

Modern computer systems typically have many programs active at the same time. A single processor can, of course, only execute instructions from one program at any instant, but by switching rapidly between the active programs they all appear to be executing at once, at least when viewed on a human timescale.

The rapid switching is managed by the operating system, so the application programmer can write his or her program as though it owns the whole machine. The mechanism used to support this illusion is described by the term **memory management unit** (MMU). There are two principal approaches to memory management, called **segmentation** and **paging**.

10.5.1 | Segments

The simplest form of memory management allows an application to view its memory as a set of segments, where each segment contains a particular sort of information. For instance, a program may have a code segment containing all its instructions, a data segment and a stack segment. Every memory access provides a segment selector and a logical address to the MMU. Each segment has a base address and a limit associated with it. The logical address is an offset from the segment base address, and must be no greater than the limit or an access violation will occur, usually causing an exception. Segments may also have other access controls, for instance the code segment may be read-only and an attempt to write to it will also cause an exception.

The access mechanism for a segmented MMU is illustrated in Figure 10.10.

Segmentation allows a program to have its own private view of memory and to coexist transparently with other programs in the same memory space. It runs into difficulty, however, when the coexisting programs vary and the available memory is limited. Since the segments are of variable size, the free memory becomes fragmented over time and a new program may be unable to start, not because there is insufficient free memory, but because the free memory is all in small pieces none of which is big enough to hold a segment of the size required by the new program.

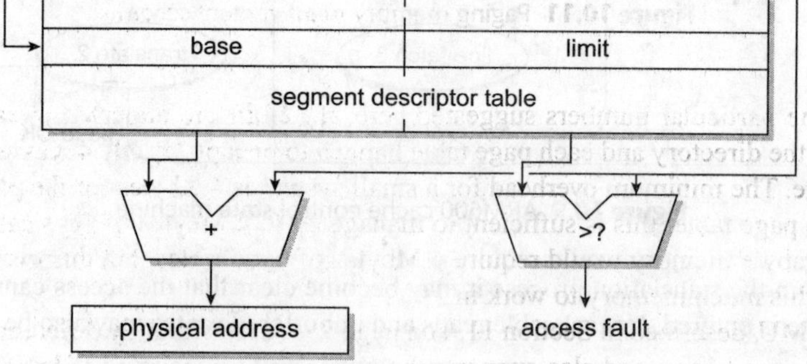

Figure 10.10 Segmented memory management scheme

The crisis can be alleviated by the operating system moving segments around in memory to coalesce the free memory into one large piece, but this is inefficient, and most processors now incorporate a memory mapping scheme based on fixed-size chunks of memory called **pages**. Some architectures include segmentation and paging, but many, including the ARM, just support paging without segmentation.

10.5.2 | Paging

In a paging memory management scheme both the logical and the physical address spaces are divided into fixed-size components called pages. A page is usually a few kilobytes in size, but different architectures use different page sizes. The relationship between the logical and physical pages is stored in **page tables**, which are held in main memory.

A simple sum shows that storing the translation in a single table requires a very large table: if a page is 4 Kbytes, 20 bits of a 32-bit address must be translated, which requires $2^{20} \times 20$ bits of data in the table, or a table of at least 2.5 Mbytes. This is an unreasonable overhead to impose on a small system.

Instead, most paging systems use two or more levels of page table. For example, the top ten bits of the address can be used to identify the appropriate second-level page table in the first-level page table directory, and the second ten bits of the address then identify the page table entry which contains the physical page number. This translation scheme is illustrated in Figure 10.11.

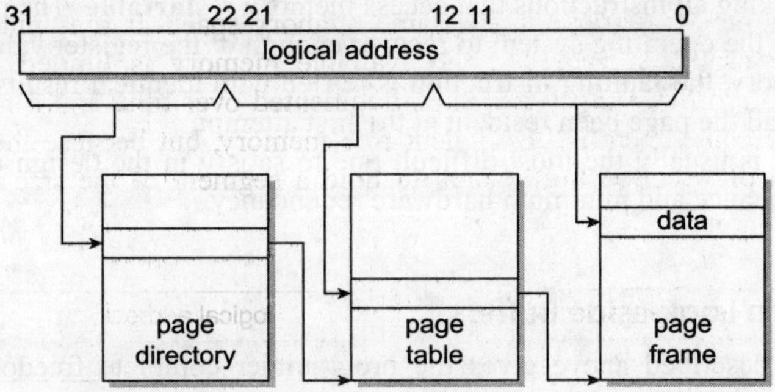

Figure 10.11 Paging memory management scheme

Note that with the particular numbers suggested here, if 32 bits are allocated to each directory and page table entry, the directory and each page table happen to occupy exactly 4 Kbytes each, or exactly one memory page. The minimum overhead for a small system is 4 Kbytes for the page directory plus 4 Kbytes for one page table; this is sufficient to manage up to 4 Mbytes of physical memory. A fully populated 32 gigabyte memory would require 4 Mbytes of page tables, but this overhead is probably acceptable with this much memory to work in.

The ARM MMU, described in Section 11.6 on page 258, uses a slightly different allocation of bits from the one described here (and also supports the single-level translation of larger blocks of memory), but the principle is the same.

10.5.3 | Virtual Memory

One possibility with either memory management scheme is to allow a segment or page to be marked as absent and an exception to be generated whenever it is accessed. Then an operating system which has run out of memory to allocate can transparently move a page or a segment out of main memory into backup store, which for this purpose is usually a hard disk, and mark it as absent. The physical memory can then be allocated to a different use. If the program attempts to access an absent page or segment the exception is raised and the operating system can bring the page or segment back into main memory, then allow the program to retry the access.

When implemented with the paged memory management scheme, this process is known as **demand-paged virtual memory**. A program can be written to occupy a virtual memory space that is larger than the available physical memory space in the computer where it is run, since the operating system can wheel bits of program and data in as they are needed. Typical programs work some parts of their code very hard and rarely touch others; leaving the infrequently used routines out on disk will not noticeably affect performance. However, over-exploiting this facility causes the operating system to switch pages in and out of memory at a high rate. This is described as **thrashing**, and *will* adversely affect performance.

10.5.4 | Restartable Instructions

An important requirement in a virtual memory system is that any instruction that can cause a memory access fault must leave the processor in a state that allows the operating system to page-in the requested memory and resume the original program as though the fault had not happened. This is often achieved by making all instructions that access memory **restartable**. The processor must retain enough state to allow the operating system to recover enough of the register values so that, when the page is in main memory, the faulting instruction is retried with identical results to those that would have been obtained had the page been resident at the first attempt.

This requirement is usually the most difficult one to satisfy in the design of a processor while retaining high-performance and minimum hardware redundancy.

10.5.5 | Translation Look-aside Buffers

The paging scheme described above gives the programmer complete freedom and transparency in the use of memory, but it would seem that this has been achieved at considerable cost in performance since each memory access appears to have incurred an overhead of two additional memory accesses, one to the page directory and one to the page table, before the data itself is accessed.

This overhead is usually avoided by implementing a translation look-aside buffer (**TLB**), which is a cache of recently used page translations. As with instruction and data caches (described in Section 10.3), there are organizational options relating to the degree of associativity and the replacement strategy. The line and block sizes usually equate to a single page table entry, and the size of a typical TLB is much smaller than a data cache at around 64 entries. The locality properties of typical programs enable a TLB of this size to achieve a miss rate of a per cent or so. The misses incur the table-walking overhead of two additional memory accesses.

The operation of a TLB is illustrated in Figure 10.12.

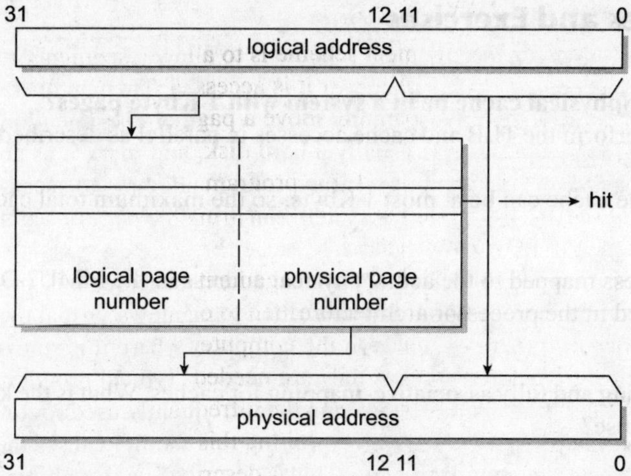

Figure 10.12 The operation of a translation look-aside buffer

10.5.6 | Virtual and Physical Caches

When a system incorporates both an MMU and a cache, the cache may operate either with virtual (pre-MMU) or physical (post-MMU) addresses.

A virtual cache has the advantage that the cache access may start immediately the processor produces an address, and, indeed, there is no need to activate the MMU if the data is found in the cache. The drawback is that the cache may contain **synonyms,** which are duplicate copies of the same main memory data item in the cache. Synonyms arise because address translation mechanisms generally allow overlapping translations. If the processor modifies the data item through one address route it is not possible for the cache to update the second copy, leading to inconsistency in the cache.

A physical cache avoids the synonym problem since physical memory addresses are associated with unique data items. However the MMU must now be activated on every cache access, and with some MMU and cache organizations the address translation must be completed by the MMU before the cache access can begin, leading to much longer cache latencies.

A physical cache arrangement that neatly avoids the sequential access cost exploits the fact that a paging MMU only affects the high-order address bits, while the cache is accessed by the low-order address bits. Provided these sets do not overlap, the cache and MMU accesses can proceed in parallel. The physical address from the MMU arrives at the right time to be compared with the physical address tags from the cache, hiding the address translation time behind the cache tag access. This optimization is not applicable to fully associative caches, and only works if the page size used by the MMU is larger than each directly addressed portion of the cache. A 4 Kbyte page, for example, limits a direct-mapped cache to a maximum size of 4 Kbytes, a 2-way set-associative cache to a maximum size of 8 Kbytes, and so on.

In practice both virtual and physical caches are in commercial use, the former relying on software conventions to contain the synonym problem and the latter either exploiting the above optimization or accepting the performance cost.

10.6 | Examples and Exercises

EXAMPLE 10.1

How big can a 4-way physical cache be in a system with 1 Kbyte pages?

Assume we want to perform the TLB and cache accesses in parallel as described in 'Virtual and physical caches'.

Each section of the cache can be at most 1 Kbyte, so the maximum total cache size is 4 Kbytes.

Exercise 10.1.1

How is a logical address mapped to the actual physical address in the MMU? Discuss with respect to the paging system used in the processor architecture.

Exercise 10.1.2

Compare direct mapping and fully associative mapping for caches. What is the kind of cache mapping that ARM processors use?

EXAMPLE 10.2

How big would a TLB have to be to contain the translations for all of the physical pages?

With 4 Kbyte pages, a 1 Mbyte memory contains 256 pages so the TLB needs 256 entries. The TLB need no longer be an automatic cache. Since a TLB miss means that the page is absent from physical memory a disk transfer is required, and the overhead of maintaining the TLB by software is negligible compared with the cost of the disk transfer.

A TLB which covers all physical memory is a form of **inverted page table**, and just such a translation scheme was used on the early ARM memory controller chips used in the Acorn Archimedes machines. Referring to Figure 10.12, the translation hardware can be a CAM; the physical page number store is a simple hardwired encoder, and the CAM has one entry for each physical page.

The Acorn memory controller chips had CAMs with 128 entries and a page size that varied according to the amount of physical memory in the system. A 1 Mbyte system had 8 Kbyte pages, a 4 Mbyte system had 32 Kbyte pages. To extend beyond 4 Mbytes, the page size stayed at 32 Kbytes and a second memory controller was added. The CAMs were maintained by software, so no complex table-walking hardware was required. The full translation tables were entirely defined by software.

Exercise 10.2.1

Estimate the die area of a 128-entry inverted page table compared with a 64 entry TLB, assuming that one bit of CAM requires twice the area of one bit of RAM.

11

Architectural Support for Operating Systems

SUMMARY OF CHAPTER CONTENTS

The role of an operating system is to provide an environment where several programs may run concurrently with a minimal risk of unwanted interference between them but with support for safe data sharing. The operating system should also provide a clean interface to the hardware facilities of the machine.

Interference between processes is minimized by memory management and protection schemes which enable each process to access only its own area of memory. The process is given its own view of the system memory, and when a process switch takes place the memory view is dynamically transformed to that of the new process, with all the memory used by the previous process being removed from sight. This requires sophisticated hardware support if it is to operate efficiently.

Data sharing implies a loophole in the protection scheme which must be controlled with great care. Haphazard access to shared structures can lead to the most obscure forms of program misbehaviour, so a disciplined approach must be applied.

Access to hardware facilities often involves a lot of low-level bit manipulation, and rather than require each process to do this independently, the details are usually handled centrally by the operating system. Processes can then access input/output functions at a higher level through system calls.

The ARM architecture incorporates features specifically to support all these aspects of the operating system.

11.1 | An Introduction to Operating Systems

The role of an operating system is to present a uniform and clean interface between the underlying hardware resources of the machine and the application programs that run on it. The most sophisticated operating systems are those that provide facilities for multiple general-purpose programs run by several different users at the same time.

11.1.1 | Multi-user Systems

It is very inconvenient if a multi-user system requires each program to make allowances for the presence of other programs in the same machine, since the number and type of concurrent programs is unknown and will vary from one run to the next. Therefore a multi-user operating system presents each program with a complete **virtual machine** in which to operate. Each program can be written as though it is the only program running at the time; the only noticeable effect of the presence of other programs is that the program typically takes longer to run.

Although several programs may be present in the machine at one time, the processor has only one set of registers (we are not concerned with multi-processor systems here), so only one program is executing at any particular time. The apparent concurrency is achieved by **time-slicing**, which means that each program takes a turn in the processor. Since the processor operates at very high speeds by human standards, the effect is that over a period of, say, a second each program will have had several goes in the processor so all programs make some progress. The operating system is responsible for **scheduling** (deciding which program runs when), and it may give each program an equal share of the CPU time or it may use **priority** information to favour some programs over others.

A program is switched out of the processor either because the operating system is invoked by a timer interrupt and decides the program has had enough time for now, or because the program has requested a slow peripheral access (such as a disk access) and cannot do any more useful work until it gets a response. Rather than leave the program idling in the processor, the operating system switches it out and schedules another program that can make useful progress.

11.1.2 | Memory Management

In order to create the virtual machine in which a program runs, the operating system must establish an environment where the program has access to its code and data at the memory locations where it expects to find them. Since one program's expectations of the addresses it will use may conflict with another's, the operating system uses memory translation to present the **physical** memory locations where it has loaded the code and data to the program at appropriate **logical** addresses. The program sees the memory through a logical-to-physical address translation mechanism which is managed by the operating system.

11.1.3 | Protection

Where several users are running programs on the same machine it is highly desirable to ensure that an error in one user's program cannot interfere with the operation of any of the other programs. It is also, unfortunately, necessary to protect against malicious attempts to interfere with other programs.

The memory-mapping hardware which gives each program its own virtual machine can also ensure that a program cannot see any memory belonging to another program, thereby providing a measure of protection. It is not efficient to enforce this too far, however, since sharing areas of memory that contain, for example, libraries of useful functions can save on memory use. A solution here is to make these areas *read-only* or *execute-only* so one program cannot corrupt code that will be used by another.

An obvious route for a malicious user to cause damage to another is to overcome the protection afforded by the memory-management system by assuming operating system status and then changing the translation tables. Most systems address this by providing a privileged system mode which has controlled access and making the translation tables accessible only from this mode.

Designing a computer system to be secure against malicious attacks by clever individuals is a complex issue which requires some architectural support. On the ARM this support is provided by privileged processor modes with controlled access and various forms of memory protection in the memory management units. However, few ARMs are used in systems where protection against malicious users is required, so most of the time these facilities are used to catch inadvertent programming errors and thereby help debug the software.

11.1.4 | Resource Allocation

Two programs which are running concurrently may place conflicting demands on system resources. For example, one program may request data from one part of a disk. It will be switched out while the disk drive seeks the data, and the program that gets switched in may immediately request data from a different part of the disk. If the disk drive responds directly to these requests a situation can easily arise where the programs alternately have control and the disk drive oscillates between the two seeks, never having long enough to find either data area, and the system will live-lock until the disk drive wears out.

In order to avoid this sort of scenario, all requests for input/output activity are channelled through the operating system. It will accept the request from the first program and then queue up the request from the second program to receive attention once the first has been satisfied.

11.1.5 | Single-user Systems

Where a system serves a single user, still possibly running several programs at the same time, much of the above continues to apply. Although the threat of a malicious user sharing the same machine is removed, it is still very useful for each program to run in its own space so that an error in one program does not cause errors in another. The simplification that arises from removing the concern about the malicious user is that it is no longer necessary to make it impossible for a program to assume system privileges, it should merely be extremely unlikely that this will happen inadvertently.

However, desktop machines that appear to belong to one user are increasingly being connected to computer networks that allow other users to run programs on them remotely. Such machines should clearly be viewed as multi-user and incorporate appropriate levels of protection.

11.1.6 | Embedded Systems

An embedded system is quite different from the single- and multi-user general-purpose system discussed above. It typically runs a fixed set of programs and has no mechanism for introducing new programs. Presumably, then, the problem of the malicious user has been removed.

The operating system continues to play a similar role, giving each active program a clean virtual machine in which to run, providing protection for one program from errors in another and scheduling the use of CPU time.

Many embedded systems operate within real-time constraints which must be allowed to determine scheduling priorities. Cost issues also preclude the use of the operating systems that are popular on general-purpose machines, since these tend to demand large memory resources. This has led to the development of the real-time operating system **(RTOS)** which provides the scheduling and hardware interface facilities required by an embedded system using just a few kilobytes of memory.

Smaller embedded systems may not even be able to bear this cost, or they may have such simple scheduling requirements (for example, one fixed program that runs all the time) that they do not need an 'operating system' at all. Here a simple 'monitor' program suffices, providing a few system functions such as sanitized interfaces to input/output functions. Such systems almost certainly dispense with the memory management hardware and use the processor's logical address to access memory directly. If an embedded system includes a cache memory some mechanism is required to define which areas of memory are cacheable (since I/O areas should not be cached), but this can be far simpler than a full memory management system.

11.1.7 | Chapter Structure

The general principles of memory management were described in the previous chapter. Subsequent sections in this chapter introduce the ARM system control coprocessor and the memory management systems it controls, which include a full MMU with address translation and a simpler 'protection unit' for embedded systems that do not require address translation.

Following this there are sections on the important operating system related issues of synchronization, context switching and the handling of input/output devices, including the use of interrupts.

11.2 | The ARM System Control Coprocessor

The ARM system control coprocessor is an on-chip coprocessor, using logical coprocessor number 15, which controls the operation of the on-chip cache or caches, memory management or protection unit, write buffer, prefetch buffer, branch target cache and system configuration signals.

11.2.1 | CP15 Instructions

The control is effected through the reading and writing of the CP15 registers. The registers are all 32 bits long, and access is restricted to MRC and MCR instructions (see Section 5.19 on page 120) which must be executed in supervisor mode. Use of other coprocessor instructions or any attempted access in user mode will cause the undefined instruction trap to be taken. The format of these instructions is shown in Figure 11.1. In most cases the CRm and Cop2 fields are unused and should be zero, though they *are* used in certain operations.

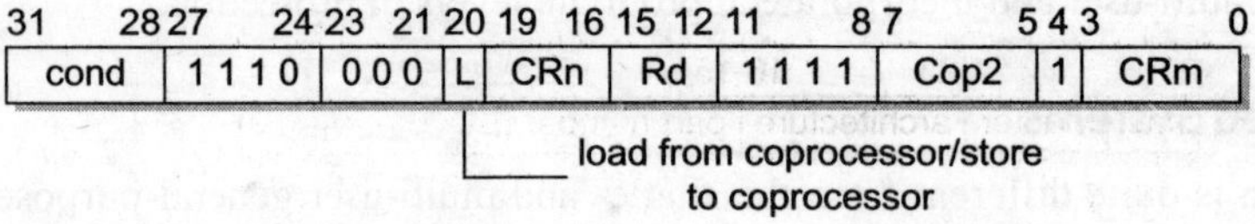

Figure 11.1 CP15 register transfer instructions

11.2.2 | Protection Unit

ARM CPUs which are used in embedded systems with fixed or controlled application programs do not require a full memory management unit with address translation capabilities. For such systems a simpler protection unit is adequate. The CP15 register organization for the ARM protection units is described in Section 11.3, and the operation of the protection unit is described in Section 11.4.

The CPUs which use a protection unit are the ARM740T described in Section 12.1 on page 271 and the ARM940T described in Section 12.4 on page 286.

11.2.3 | MMU

ARM CPUs for use in general-purpose applications where the range and number of application programs is unknown at design time will usually require a full memory management unit with address translation. The CP15 register organization for the ARM MMU is described in Section 11.5 and the operation of the MMU is described in Section 11.6.

CPUs which use the full MMU include all the other CPUs described in Chapter 12.

11.3 | CP15 Protection Unit Registers

The protection unit register structure is illustrated in Table 11.1. The registers are read and written using the CP15 instruction shown in Figure 11.1, with CRn specifying the register to be accessed.

In detail, the register functions are as follows:

Table 11.1 CP15 protection unit register structure

Register	Purpose
0	ID Register
1	Configuration
2	Cache Control
3	Write Buffer Control
5	Access Permissions
6	Region Base and Size
7	Cache Operations
9	Cache Lock Down
15	Test
4, 8, 10–14	UNUSED

- **Register 0** (which is read-only) returns device identification information.

31 24	23 16	15 4	3 0
implementer	architecture	part number (BCD)	revision

Bits [3:0] contain a revision number, bits [15:4] contain a 3-digit part number in binary-coded decimal, bits [23:16] contain the architecture version (0 for version 3, 1 for version 4, 2 for version 4T, 4 for version 5T) and bits [31:24] contain the ASCII code of an implementer's trademark (ASCII 'A' = 41_{16} indicates ARM Limited, 'D' = 44_{16} indicates Digital, and so on).

Some CPUs do not follow the above register 0 format exactly, and recent CPUs have a second register 0 (accessed by changing the Cop2 field in the MRC instruction) which gives details on the cache organization.

- **Register 1** (which is read-write) contains several bits of control information which enable system functions and control system parameters.

31	30	29 28	27	26 25	24	23 14	13	12	11 8	7	6 4	3	2	1	0
iA	nf	Bnk	F	Lck	S	0000000000	V	I	0000	B	000	W	C	0	M

All bits are cleared on reset. If subsequently set, M enables the protection unit, C enables the data or unified cache, W enables the write buffer, B switches from little- to big-endian byte ordering, I enables the instruction cache when this is separate from the data cache, V causes the exception vectors to move to near the top of the address space, S, Lck, F and Bnk are used to control the cache (on the ARM740T), and nf and iA control various clock mechanisms (on the ARM940T).

Note that not all bits are provided in all implementations.

- **Register 2** (which is read-write) controls the cacheability of the eight individual protection regions.

31–8	7	6	5	4	3	2	1	0
000000000000000000000000	7	6	5	4	3	2	1	0

  Bit 0 enables the cache for loads within region 0, bit 1 likewise for region 1, and so on. The ARM940T has separate protection units on its instruction and data ports, and Cop2 (see Figure 11.1) is used to determine which unit is accessed: Cop2 = 0 gives access to the protection unit on the data port; Cop2 = 1 gives access to the protection unit on the instruction port.
- **Register 3** (which is read-write) defines whether or not the write buffer should be used for each of the protection regions. Its format is the same as that for register 2, but note that as the ARM940T instruction port is read-only, the write buffer can only be enabled for the data port and so Cop2 should always be zero.
- **Register 5** (which is read-write) defines the access permissions for each of the protection regions.

31–16	15–14	13–12	11–10	9–8	7–6	5–4	3–2	1–0
0000000000000000	ap7	ap6	ap5	ap4	ap3	ap2	ap1	ap0

- The access permissions cover no access (00), privileged modes only (01), privileged full access and user read only (10) and full access (11). Again the ARM940T uses the Cop2 field to differentiate the instruction (1) and data (0) protection units.
- **Register 6** (which is read-write) defines the start address and size of each of the eight regions.

31–12	11–6	5–1	0
region base address	000000	size	E

  The region base address must be a multiple of the size. The encoding of the size field is shown in Table 11.2. E enables the region.

  The particular region is specified in the CRm field (see Figure 11.1) which should be set from 0 to 7. For a Harvard core such as the ARM940T there are separate region registers for the instruction and data memory ports, and Cop2 specifies which memory port is to be addressed as described above for register 2.

Table 11.2 Protection unit region size encoding

Rd[5:l]	Region size
01011	4 Kbytes
01100	8 Kbytes
01101	16 Kbytes
01110	32 Kbytes
...	...
11100	512 Mbytes
11101	1 Gbyte
11110	2 Gbytes
11111	4 Gbytes

- **Register 7** controls various cache operations and its operation is different for the ARM740T and the ARM940T
- **Register 9** is used in the ARM940T to lock down areas of the cache. (The ARM740T uses certain bits in register 1 for this purpose.)
- **Register 15** is used in the ARM940T to modify the cache allocation algorithm from random to round-robin. This is intended for use only during silicon production testing.

11.4 | ARM Protection Unit

ARM CPUs intended for embedded applications incorporate a memory protection unit which defines various protection and cache functions for different regions of memory so that, for example, I/O regions can be restricted to supervisor access only and made uncacheable. Protection units do not translate addresses. Systems which require address translation should use a full memory management unit, described in Section 11.6. CPUs which incorporate the protection unit include the ARM740T and the ARM940T.

11.4.1 | Protection Unit Structure

The protection unit allows the ARM 4 Gbyte address space to be mapped into eight regions, each with a programmable start address and size and with programmable protection and cache properties. The regions may overlap. A fixed priority scheme defines those characteristics which apply to an address which falls into more than one region.

11.4.2 | Region Definition

Each of the eight regions has a start address and a size defined by writing to CP15 register 6. The format of this register was defined in Section 11.3. The minimum region size is 4 Kbytes, the maximum 4 Gbytes. Rd[5:1], when written to CP15 register 6, defines the size, which can be set to any power of two bytes between the maximum and minimum as shown in Table 11.2. The start address must be a multiple of the selected size and is defined by Rd[31:12]. The region will have no effect unless it is enabled by setting Rd[0].

11.4.3 | Region Priorities

The regions may legitimately be programmed so that they overlap. When an address that falls into more than one region is presented to the protection unit a fixed priority scheme determines which region defines its attributes: region 7 has the highest priority, region 0 the lowest, and the other regions have intermediate priorities in order of their number.

The restriction on the start of a region, which must be a multiple of its size, means that checking whether or not an address falls within a region is simply a matter of comparing some number (up to 20) of the most significant bits of the address against the corresponding bits of the region start address. If they match, the address falls inside that region. If they don't match, the address falls outside the region. No addition or subtraction is required, so the process can be fast. The organization of the protection unit is therefore as shown in Figure 11.2. In this illustration region 0 covers the complete 4 Gbyte address space and therefore all addresses fall into it. Regions 1, 2 and 4 are 4 Kbytes, and regions 3, 6, 7 and 5 have increasing sizes. The example address falls in regions 0, 3 and 6 (as denoted by the black arrows), so the priority encoder selects the attributes for the highest priority region, region 6.

If an address does not fall into any enabled region the protection unit will generate an abort.

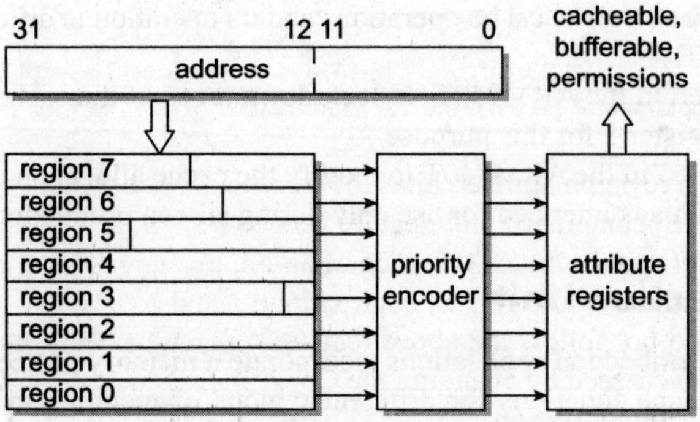

Figure 11.2 Protection unit organization

11.4.4 | Harvard Cores

ARM cores that use a Harvard architecture (such as the ARM940T) have separate protection units on their instruction and data ports, so they have a total of 16 regions.

11.5 | CP15 MMU Registers

The MMU register structure is illustrated in Table 11.3. The registers are read and written using the CP15 instruction shown in Figure 11.1, with CRn specifying the register to be accessed.

Table 11.3 CP15 MMU register structure

Register	Purpose
0	ID Register
1	Control
2	Translation Table Base
3	Domain Access Control
5	Fault Status
6	Fault Address
7	Cache Operations
8	TLB Operations
9	Read Buffer Operations
10	TLB Lockdown
13	Process ID Mapping
14	Debug Support
15	Test and Clock Control
4, 11–12	UNUSED

- **Register 0** (which is read-only) returns identification information.

31 24	23 16	15 4	3 0
implementer	0 0 0 0 0 0 0 A	part number (BCD)	revision

  Bits [3:0] contain a revision number, bits [15:4] contain a 3-digit part number in binary-coded decimal, bits [23:16] contain the architecture version ('A' = 0 for version 3, 'A' = 1 for version 4) and bits [31:24] contain the ASCII code of an implementer's trademark (ASCII 'A' = 41_{16} indicates ARM Limited, 'D' = 44_{16} indicates Digital, and so on).

  Some CPUs do not follow the above register 0 format exactly, and recent CPUs have a second register 0 (accessed by changing the Cop2 field in the MRC instruction) which gives details on the cache organization.

- **Register 1** (which is write-only in architecture version 3 but read-write in version 4) contains several bits of control information which enable system functions and control system parameters.

31 15	14	13	12	11	10	9	8	7	6	5	4	3	2	1	0
00000000000000000	RR	V	I	Z	F	R	S	B	L	D	P	W	C	A	M

  All bits are cleared on reset. If subsequently set, M enables the MMU, A enables address alignment fault checking, C enables the data or unified cache, W enables the write buffer, P switches from 26- to 32-bit exception handling, D switches from 26- to 32-bit address range, L switches to late abort timing, B switches from little- to big-endian byte ordering, S and R modify the MMU system and ROM protection states, F controls the speed of external coprocessor communications, Z enables branch prediction, I enables the instruction cache when this is separate from the data cache, V moves the exception vector base from 0x00000000 to 0xffff0000 and RR controls the cache replacement algorithm (pseudo-random or round-robin). Note that not all bits are provided in all implementations.

  Bits [31:15] are unpredictable on read and should be preserved using read-modify-write accesses. Bits [31:30] are used in the ARM920 and ARM940 for clock control functions, for example.

- **Register 2** (which is write-only in architecture version 3 but read-write in version 4) contains the address of the start of the currently active first-level translation table. This must be aligned on a 16 Kbyte boundary.

31 14	13 0
translation table base address	00000000000000

- **Register 3** (which is write-only in architecture version 3 but read-write in version 4) contains sixteen 2-bit fields, each specifying the access permissions for one of the 16 domains. See 'Domains' for further details.

31 30	29 28	27 26	25 24	23 22	21 20	19 18	17 16	15 14	13 12	11 10	9 8	7 6	5 4	3 2	1 0
D15	D14	D13	D12	D11	D10	D9	D8	D7	D6	D5	D4	D3	D2	D1	D0

- **Register 5** (which is read-write in architecture version 4, but in version 3 it is read-only and writing to it flushes the whole TLB) indicates the type of fault and the domain of the last data access that aborted. D is set on a data breakpoint.

31 10	9	8	7 4	3 0
0000000000000000000000	D	0	domain	status

- **Register 6** (which is read-write in architecture version 4, but in version 3 it is read-only and writing to it flushes a particular TLB entry) contains the address of the last data access that aborted.

31   0
fault address

- **Register 7** (which is read-write in architecture version 4, but in version 3 it is write-only and simply flushes the cache) is used to perform a number of cache, write buffer, prefetch buffer and branch target cache clean and/or flush operations. The data supplied should be either zero or a relevant virtual address.

  Accesses to register 7 use the Cop2 and CRm fields to specify particular operations; the available functions vary from implementation to implementation.
- **Register 8** (which is read-write in architecture version 4 and unavailable in version 3) is used to perform a number of TLB operations, flushing single entries or the whole TLB and supporting unified or separate instruction and data TLBs.
- **Register 9** is used to control the read buffer, if one is present. In some CPUs it is used to control cache lockdown functions.
- **Register 10** is used to control TLB lockdown functions where these are supported.
- **Register 13** is used to remap virtual addresses through a process ID register. This mechanism is used to support Windows CE and is only present on particular CPUs such as the ARM720T, the ARM920T and the SA-1100. If bits [31:25] of the virtual address are zero they are replaced with bits [31:25] of this register.

31 25	24 0
process ID	0000000000000000000000000

- **Register 14** is used for debug support.
- **Register 15** is used for test and in some CPUs for clock control purposes.

11.6 | ARM MMU Architecture

An MMU performs two primary functions:

- It translates virtual addresses into physical addresses.
- It controls memory access permissions, aborting illegal accesses.

The ARM MMU uses a 2-level page table with table-walking hardware and a TLB which stores recently used page translations. Where the processor has separate instruction and data caches it is likely also to have separate instruction and data TLBs.

11.6.1 | Memory Granularity

The memory mapping is performed at several different granularities by the same basic mechanism. The units that can be used are:

- **Sections**. These are 1 Mbyte blocks of memory.
- **Large pages**. These are 64 Kbyte blocks of memory, and within a large page access control is applied to individual 16 Kbyte **subpages**.

- **Small pages**. These are 4 Kbyte blocks of memory, and within a small page access control is applied to individual 1 Kbyte subpages.
- **Tiny pages**. Some of the latest CPUs also support 1 Kbyte 'tiny' pages.

The normal granularity is the 4 Kbyte small page. Large pages and sections exist to allow the mapping of large data areas with a single TLB entry. Forcing a large data area to be mapped in small pages can, under certain circumstances, cause the TLB to perform inefficiently.

11.6.2 | Domains

Domains are an unusual feature of the ARM MMU architecture. A domain is a group of sections and/or pages which have particular access permissions. This allows a number of different processes to run with the same translation tables while retaining some protection from each other. It gives a much more lightweight process switch mechanism than is possible if each process must have its own translation tables.

The access control is based on two sorts of programs:

- **Clients** are users of domains and must observe the access permissions of the individual sections and pages that make up the domain.
- **Managers** are the controllers of the domain and can bypass the access permissions of individual sections or pages.

At any one time a program may be a client of some domains, a manager of some other domains and have no access at all to the remaining domains. This is controlled by CP15 register 3 which contains two bits for each of the 16 domains describing the status of the current program with respect to each domain. The interpretation of the two bits is given in Table 11.4. The relationship of a program to all of the domains can be changed by writing a single new value into CP15 register 3.

Table 11.4 Domain access control bits

Value	Status	Description
00	No access	Any access will generate a domain fault
01	Client	Page and section permission bits are checked
10	Reserved	Do not use
11	Manager	Page and section permission bits are not checked

11.6.3 | Translation Process

The translation of a new virtual address always begins with a first-level fetch. (We ignore for now the TLB, which is only a cache to accelerate the process described below.) This uses the translation base address held in CP15 register 2. Bits [31:14] of the translation base register are concatenated with bits [31:20] of the virtual address to form a memory address which is used to access the first-level descriptor as shown in Figure 11.3.

The first-level descriptor may be either a section descriptor or a pointer to a second-level page table depending on its bottom two bits. '01' indicates a pointer to a second-level coarse page table; '10' indicates a section descriptor; '11' indicates a pointer to a second-level fine page table (only supported by certain CPUs). '00' should be used to indicate a descriptor that causes a translation fault.

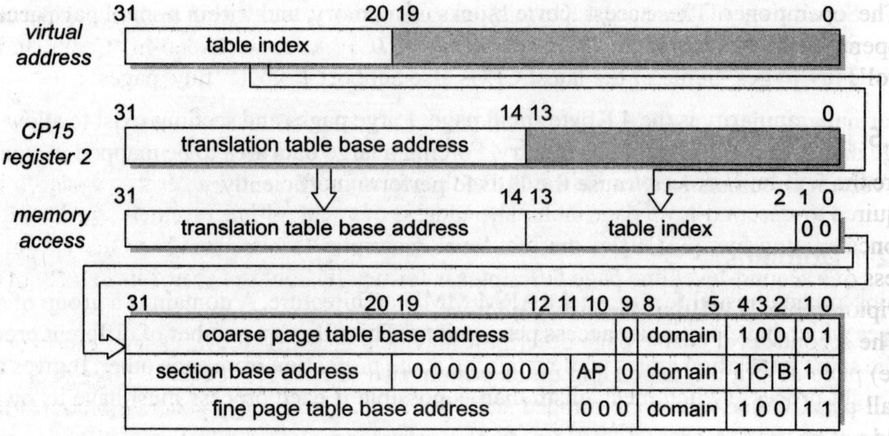

Figure 11.3 First-level translation fetch

11.6.4 | Section Translation

Where the first-level descriptor indicates that the virtual address translates into a section, the domain ('Domain' in the section descriptor) is checked and, if the current process is a client of the domain, the access permissions ('AP' in the section descriptor) are also checked. If the access is permissible, the memory address is formed by concatenating bits [31:20] of the section descriptor with bits [19:0] of the virtual address. This address is used to access the data in memory. The full section translation sequence is shown in Figure 11.4.

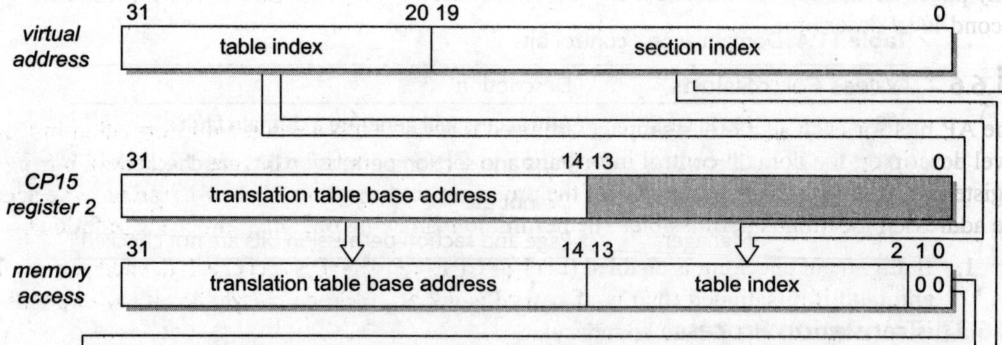

Figure 11.4 Section translation sequence

The operation of the access permission bits (AP) is described in 'Access permissions', and the operation of the bufferable (B) and cacheable (C) bits is described in 'Cache and write buffer control'.

11.6.5 | Page Translation

Where the first-level descriptor indicates that the virtual address translates into a page, a further access is required to a second-level page table. The address of a second-level coarse page descriptor is formed by concatenating bits [31:10] of the first-level descriptor to bits [19:12] of the virtual address. The address of a second-level fine page descriptor is formed by concatenating bits [31:12] of the first-level descriptor to bits [19:10] of the virtual address.

The second-level coarse page descriptor may be a large (64 Kbyte) page descriptor or a small (4 Kbyte) page descriptor, depending on its bottom two bits. '01' indicates a large page; '10' indicates a small page. Other values are trapped, and '00' should be used to generate a translation fault; '11' should not be used. A second-level fine page descriptor may also be a tiny (1 Kbyte) page descriptor, indicated by '11' in its bottom two bits, or it may be a large or small page descriptor as above.

A small page base address is held in bits [31:12] of the page descriptor. Bits [11:4] contain two access permission bits ('AP0-3') for each of the four subpages, where a subpage is a quarter of the size of the page. Bits [3:2] contain the 'bufferable' and 'cacheable' bits. (Bits marked '?' have implementation-specific uses.)

The overall translation sequence for a small page is shown in Figure 11.5. The translation sequence for a large page is similar except bits [15:12] of the virtual address are used both in the page table index and in the page offset. Each page table entry for a large page must therefore be copied 16 times in the page table for every value of these bits in the page table index.

The tiny page translation scheme is also similar, but must start from a fine first-level descriptor. Tiny pages do not support subpages and therefore there is only one set of access permissions in the second-level descriptor.

11.6.6 | Access Permissions

The AP bits for each section or subpage are used together with the domain information in the first-level descriptor, the domain control information in CP15 register 3, the S and R control bits in CP15 register 1 and the user/supervisor state of the processor to determine whether a read or write access to the addressed location is permissible. The permission checking operation proceeds as follows:

1. If alignment checking is enabled (bit 1 of CP15 register 1 is set) check the address alignment and fault if misaligned (that is, if a word is not aligned on a 4-byte boundary or a half-word is not aligned on a 2-byte boundary).
2. Identify the domain of the addressed location from bits [8:5] of the first-level descriptor. (Fetching the first-level descriptor will fault if the descriptor is invalid.)
3. Check in CP 15 register 3, the domain access control register, whether the current process is a client or manager of this domain; if neither, fault here.
4. If a manager of this domain, proceed ignoring access permissions. If a client, check the access permissions against Table 11.5 using the S and R bits from CP15 register 1. Fault if access is not permitted otherwise continue to access data.

The permission checking scheme is illustrated in Figure 11.6 which shows the various faults that can be generated in the course of an address translation. The MMU may generate alignment, translation, domain and permission faults. In addition, the external memory system may fault on cache

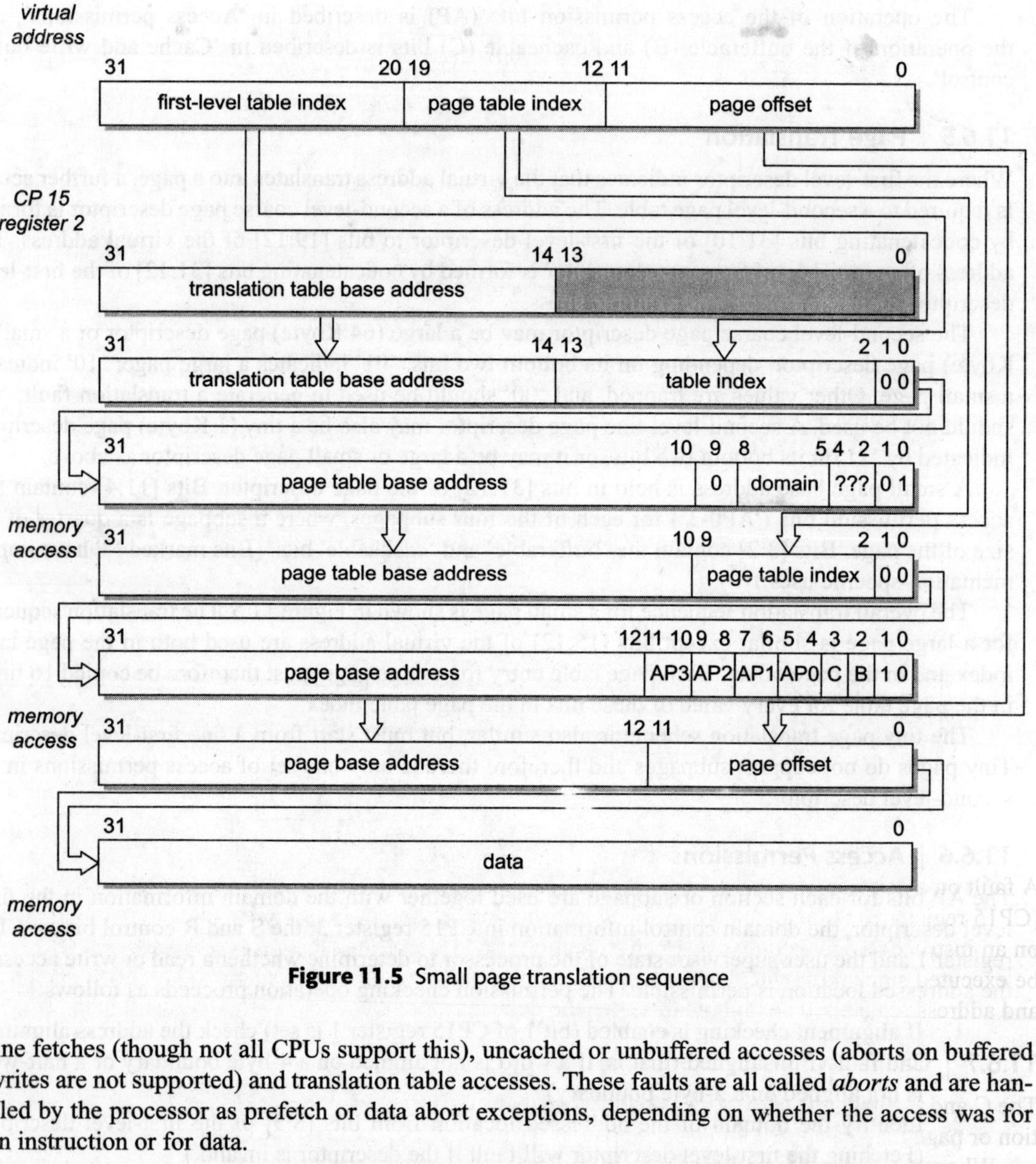

Figure 11.5 Small page translation sequence

line fetches (though not all CPUs support this), uncached or unbuffered accesses (aborts on buffered writes are not supported) and translation table accesses. These faults are all called *aborts* and are handled by the processor as prefetch or data abort exceptions, depending on whether the access was for an instruction or for data.

Table 11.5 Access permissions

AP	S	R	Supervisor	User
00	0	0	No access	No access
00	1	0	Read only	No access
00	0	1	Read only	Read only

(Continued)

Table 11.5 Access permissions (*Continued*)

AP	S	R	Supervisor	User
00	1	1	Do not use	
01	–	–	Read/write	No access
10	–	–	Read/write	Read only
11	–	–	Read/write	Read/write

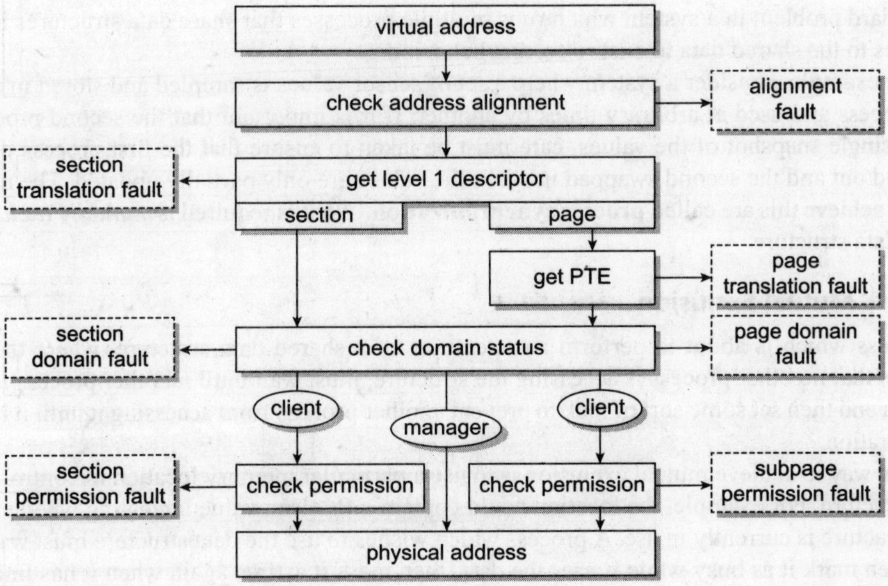

Figure 11.6 Access permission checking scheme

A fault on a data access causes the fault status register (CP15 register 5) and the fault address register (CP15 register 6) to be updated to provide information on the cause and location of the fault. A fault on an instruction access only causes an exception if and when the instruction is executed (it may not be executed since it may be fetched just after a taken branch), and it does not update the fault status and address registers. The fault address may be deduced from the return address in the link register.

11.6.7 | Cache and Write Buffer Control

The C and B bits in the section and second-level page descriptors control whether the data in the section or page may be copied into a cache and/or written back to memory through a write buffer.

Where the cache uses a write-through scheme, C controls whether or not the data is cacheable and B controls whether or not writes may be buffered. Where the cache uses a copy-back scheme the 'cached, unbuffered' combination may alternatively be used to specify a 'write-through, buffered' behaviour. (This cache terminology is described in 'Write strategies' on page 238.)

11.6.8 | External Faults

Note that the processor cannot recover from external faults signalled on buffered writes, because by the time the fault is signalled the processor may have executed several instructions and is therefore unable to recover its state to retry the faulting store instruction. Where recovery is required (for example, to allow the processor to retry a store instruction following a bus fault) unbuffered writes must be used.

In typical ARM applications there are no potentially recoverable sources of external faults, so this is not an issue.

11.7 | Synchronization

A standard problem in a system which runs multiple processes that share data structures is to control accesses to the shared data to ensure correct behaviour.

For example, consider a system where a set of sensor values is sampled and stored in memory by one process and used at arbitrary times by another. If it is important that the second process always sees a single snapshot of the values, care must be taken to ensure that the first process does not get swapped out and the second swapped in when the values are only partially updated. The mechanisms used to achieve this are called **process synchronization**. What is required is *mutually exclusive* access to the data structure.

11.7.1 | Mutual Exclusion

A process which is about to perform an operation on a shared data structure, where the operation requires that no other process is accessing the structure, must wait until no other process *is* accessing the data and then set some sort of lock to prevent another process from accessing it until it has finished the operation.

One way to achieve mutual exclusion is to use a particular memory location to control access to a data structure. For example, the location could contain a Boolean value indicating whether or not the data structure is currently in use. A process which wishes to use the data structure must wait until it is free, then mark it as busy while it uses the data, then mark it as free again when it has finished using it. The problem is that an interrupt can arise between the structure becoming free and it being marked as busy. The interrupt causes a process switch, the new process sees the structure is free, marks it as busy, changes it a bit and then another interrupt returns control to the first process which is in a state where it believes, now incorrectly, that the structure is free.

A standard solution to this problem is to disable interrupts while the Boolean is tested and set. This works, but on a processor with a protected supervisor mode (such as the ARM) user-level code cannot disable interrupts, so a system call is required, which takes several clock cycles to complete and return control to the user process.

11.7.2 | SWAP

A more efficient solution is to use an **atomic** (that is, uninterruptable) 'test and set' instruction. The ARM 'SWAP' instruction (see Section 5.13 on page 114) is just such an instruction which is included in the instruction set for exactly this purpose. A register is set to the 'busy' value, then this register is swapped with the memory location containing the Boolean. If the loaded value is 'free' the process can continue; if it is 'busy' the process must wait, often by **spinning** (repeating the test until it gets the 'free' result) on the lock.

Note that this is the *only* reason for including SWAP in the ARM instruction set. It does not contribute to the processor's performance and its dynamic frequency of use is negligible. It is there just to provide this functionality.

11.8 | Context Switching

A process runs in a **context**, which is all the system state that must be established for the process to run correctly. This state includes:

- the values of all of the processor's registers, including the program counter, stack pointer, and so on;
- the values in the floating-point registers, if the process uses them;
- the translation tables in memory (but not the contents of the TLB since it is just a cache of the values in memory and will automatically reload active values as they are used);
- data values used by the process in memory (but not the values in the cache since they will automatically be reloaded when required).

When a process switch takes place, the context of the old process must be saved and that of the new process restored (if it is resuming rather than starting for the first time).

11.8.1 | When to Switch

Context switching may occur as a result of an external interrupt, for example:

- A timer interrupt causes the operating system to make a new process active according to a time-slicing algorithm.
- A high-priority process which is waiting for a particular event is reactivated in response to that event.

Alternatively, a process may run out of useful work and call the operating system to be made dormant until an external event occurs.

In all cases, the operating system is given or takes control and is responsible for saving the old and restoring the new context. In an ARM-based system, this will normally take place while the processor is in supervisor mode.

11.8.2 | Register State

If all context switches take place in response to IRQs or internal faults or supervisor calls, and the supervisor code does not re-enable interrupts, the process register state may be restricted to the user-mode registers. If context switches may take place in response to FIQs or supervisor code does re-enable interrupts, it may be necessary to save and restore some of the privileged mode registers as well.

The 'architectural support' for register saving and restoring offered on the ARM recognizes the difficulty of saving and restoring user registers from a privileged mode and provides special instructions to assist in this task. These instructions are the special forms of the load and store multiple instructions (see Section 5.12 on page 112) which allow code running in a non-user mode to save and restore the user registers from an area of memory addressed by a non-user mode register.

Without these instructions, an operating system would have to switch into user mode to save or restore the banked user registers and then get back through the protection barrier into supervisor mode. Though possible, this solution is inefficient.

11.8.3 | Floating-point State

The floating-point registers, whether held in a hardware coprocessor or maintained in memory by a software emulator, represent part of the state of any process that uses them. Rather than add to the context switching overhead by saving and restoring them on every process swap, the operating system simply disables user-level use of the floating-point system when a process that uses floating-point is swapped out. If the new process attempts to use the floating-point system, the first use will trap. At that point the operating system will save the old process state and restore the new, then it will re-enable the floating-point system and the new process can use it freely.

Thus the floating-point context switch overhead is incurred only when strictly necessary.

11.8.4 | Translation State

Where the old and new processes have independent translation tables a *heavy-weight* process switch is required. The complete translation table structure can be switched simply by changing the base address of the first-level page table in CP15 register 2, but since this will invalidate existing TLB and (virtually addressed) cache entries, these must be flushed. The TLB and an instruction or write-through data cache can be flushed simply by marking all entries as invalid which on an ARM processor chip requires a single CP15 instruction for each TLB or cache, but a copy-back cache must be purged of all dirty lines which may take many instructions.

(Note that a physically addressed cache avoids this problem, but to date all ARM CPUs have used virtually addressed caches.)

Where the old and new processes share the same translation tables a *light-weight* process switch is required. The 'domain' mechanism in the ARM MMU architecture allows the protection state of 16 different subsets of the virtual address space to be reconfigured with a single update of CP15 register 3.

In order to ensure that the cache does not represent a leak in the protection system, a cache access must be accompanied by a permission check. This could be achieved by storing the domain and access permission information along with the data in each cache line, but current ARM processors check permissions using information in the MMU concurrently with the cache access.

11.9 | Input/Output

The input/output (I/O) functions are implemented in an ARM system using a combination of memory-mapped addressable peripheral registers and the interrupt inputs. Some ARM systems may also include direct memory access **(DMA)** hardware.

11.9.1 | Memory-mapped Peripherals

A peripheral device, such as a serial line controller, contains a number of registers. In a memory-mapped system, each of these registers appears like a memory location at a particular address. (An alternative system organization might have I/O functions in a separate address space from memory devices.) A serial line controller may have a set of registers as follows:

- A transmit data register (write only); data written to this location gets sent down the serial line.
- A receive data register (read only); data arriving along the serial line is presented here.
- A control register (read/write); this register sets the data rate and manages the RTS (request to send) and similar signals.
- An interrupt enable register (read/write); this register controls which hardware events will generate an interrupt.
- A status register (read only); this register indicates whether read data is available, whether the write buffer is full, and so on.

To receive data, the software must set up the device appropriately, usually to generate an interrupt when data is available or an error condition is detected. The interrupt routine must then copy the data into a buffer and check for error conditions.

11.9.2 | Memory-mapped Issues

Note that a memory-mapped peripheral register behaves differently from memory. Two consecutive reads to the read data register will probably deliver different results even though no write to that location has taken place. Whereas reads to true memory are **idempotent** (the read can be repeated many times, with identical results) a read to a peripheral may clear the current value and the next value may be different. Such locations are termed **read-sensitive**.

Programs must be written very carefully where read-sensitive locations are involved, and, in particular, such locations must *not* be copied into a cache memory.

In many ARM systems I/O locations are made inaccessible to user code, so the only way the devices can be accessed is through supervisor calls (SWIs) or through C library functions written to use those calls.

11.9.3 | Direct Memory Access

Where I/O functions have a high data bandwidth, a considerable share of the processor's performance may be consumed handling interrupts from the I/O system. Many systems employ DMA hardware to handle the lowest level I/O data transfers without processor assistance. Typically, the DMA hardware will handle the transfer of blocks of data from the peripheral into a buffer area in memory, interrupting the processor only if an error occurs or when the buffer becomes full. Thus the processor sees an interrupt once per buffer rather than once per byte.

Note, however, that the DMA data traffic will occupy some of the memory bus bandwidth, so the processor performance will still be reduced by the I/O activity (though far less than it would be if it were handling the data traffic on interrupts).

11.9.4 | Fast Interrupt Request

The ARM fast interrupt (FIQ) architecture includes more banked registers than the other exception modes (see Figure 2.1 on page 34) in order to minimize the register save and restore overhead associated with handling one of these interrupts. The number of registers was chosen to be the number required to implement a software emulation of a DMA channel.

If an ARM system with no DMA support has one source of I/O data traffic that has a significantly higher bandwidth requirement than the others, it is worth considering allocating the FIQ interrupt to this source and using IRQ to support all the other sources. It is far less effective to use FIQ for several different data sources at the same time, though switching it on a coarse granularity between sources may be appropriate.

11.9.5 | Interrupt Latency

An important parameter of a processor is its **interrupt latency**. This is a measure of how long it takes to respond to an interrupt in the worst case. For the ARM6 the worst-case FIQ latency is determined by the following components:

1. The time for the request signal to pass through the FIQ synchronizing latches; this is three clock cycles (worst case).
2. The time for the longest instruction (which is a load multiple of 16 registers) to complete; this is 20 clock cycles.

3. The time for the data abort entry sequence; this is three clock cycles. (Remember that data abort has a higher priority than FIQ but does not mask FIQs out; see 'Exception priorities' on page 96.)
4. The time for the FIQ entry sequence; this is two clock cycles.

The total worst-case latency is therefore 28 clock cycles. After this time the ARM6 is executing the instruction at 0x1C, the FIQ entry point. These cycles may be sequential or non-sequential, and memory accesses may be further delayed if they address slow memory devices. The best-case latency is four clock cycles.

The IRQ latency calculation is similar but must include an arbitrary delay for the longest FIQ routine to complete (since FIQ is higher priority than IRQ).

11.9.6 | Cache-I/O Interactions

The usual assumption is that a cache makes a processor go faster. Normally this is true, if the performance is averaged over a reasonable period. But in many cases interrupts are used where worst-case real-time response is critical; in these cases a cache can make the performance significantly worse. An MMU can make things worse still!

Here is the worst-case interrupt latency sum for the ARM710 which we will meet in the next chapter. The latency is the sum of:

1. The time for the request signal to pass through the FIQ synchronizing latches; this is three clock cycles (worst case) as before.
2. The time for the longest instruction (which is a load multiple of 16 registers) to complete; this is 20 clock cycles as before, but …
   …this could cause the write buffer to flush, which can take up to 12 cycles, then incur three MMU TLB misses, adding 18 clock cycles, and six cache misses, adding a further 24 cycles. The original 20 cycles overlap the line fetches, but the total cost for this stage can still reach 66 cycles.
3. The time for data abort entry sequence; this is three clock cycles as before, but …
   … the fetches from the vector space could add an MMU miss and a cache miss, increasing the cost to 12 cycles.
4. The time for the FIQ entry sequence; this is two clock cycles as before, but …
   … it could incur another cache miss, costing six cycles.

The total is now 87 clock cycles, many of which are non-sequential memory accesses. So note that automatic mechanisms which support a memory hierarchy to speed up general-purpose programs *on average* often have the opposite effect on *worst-case* calculations for critical code segments.

11.9.7 | Reducing Latency

How can the latency be reduced when real-time constraints simply must be met?

- A fixed area of fast on-chip RAM (for example, containing the vector space at the bottom of memory) will speed up exception entry.
- Sections of the TLB and cache can be **locked down** to ensure that critical code segments never incur the miss penalty.

Note that even in general-purpose systems where the cache and MMU are generally beneficial there are often critical real-time constraints, for example for servicing disk data traffic or for managing the local area network. This is especially true in low-cost systems with little DMA hardware support.

11.9.8 | Other Cache Issues

There are other things to watch out for when a cache is present, for example:

- Caching assumes that an address will return the same data value each time it is read until a new value is written. I/O devices do not behave like this; each time you read them they give the next piece of data.
- A cache fetches a block (which is typically around four words) of data at a time from sequential addresses. I/O devices often have different register functions at consecutive addresses; reading them all can give unpredictable results.

Therefore the I/O area of memory is normally marked as uncacheable, and accesses bypass the cache. In general, caches interact badly with any *read-sensitive* devices. Display frame buffers also need careful consideration and are often made uncacheable.

11.9.9 | Operating System Issues

Normally, all the low-level detail of the I/O device registers and the handling of interrupts is the responsibility of the operating system. A typical process will send data to the serial port by loading the next byte into r0 and then making the appropriate supervisor call; the operating system will call a subroutine called a **device driver** to check for the transmit buffer being empty, that the line is active, that no transmission errors occur, and so on. There may even be a call which allows the process to pass a pointer to the operating system which will then output a complete buffer of values.

Since it takes some time to send a buffer full of data down a serial line, the operating system may return control to the process until the transmit buffer has space for more data. An interrupt from the serial line hardware device returns control to the operating system, which refills the transmit buffer before returning control to the interrupted process. Further interrupts result in further transfers until the whole buffer has been sent.

It may be the case that the process which requested the serial line activity runs out of useful work, or an interrupt from a timer or another source causes a different process to become active. The operating system must be careful, when modifying the translation tables, to ensure that it does not make the data buffer inaccessible to itself. It must also treat any requests from the second process to output data down the serial line with caution; they must not interfere with the ongoing transfer from the first process. **Resource allocation** is used to ensure that there are no conflicts in the use of shared resources.

A process may request an output function and then go inactive until the output has completed or it may go inactive until a particular input arrives. It can lodge a request with the operating system to be reactivated when the input/output *event* occurs.

11.10 | Example and Exercises

EXAMPLE 11.1

Why, on the ARM, can user-level code not disable interrupts?

To allow a user to disable interrupts would make building a protected operating system impossible. The following code illustrates how a malicious user could destroy all the currently active programs:

```
        MSR   CPSR_f, #&c0      ; disable IRQ and FIQ
HERE    B     HERE              ; loop forever
```

Once interrupts are disabled there is no way for the operating system to regain control, so the program will loop forever. The only way out is a hard reset, which will destroy all currently active programs.

If the user cannot disable interrupts the operating system can establish a regular periodic interrupt from a timer, so the infinite loop will be interrupted and the operating system can schedule other programs. This program will either time-out, if the operating system has an upper limit on the amount of CPU time it is allowed to consume, or it will continue to loop whenever it gets switched in, running up a large bill on a system with accounting.

Exercise 11.1.1

What is meant by protection in the context of a computer system? How are different users protected from intrusion by others? How is it ensured that users don't tromp on the codes of the operating system and corrupt them?

Exercise 11.1.2

If the ARM had no SWAP instruction, devise a hardware peripheral that could be used to support synchronization. (Hint: standard memory will not work; the location must be read-sensitive.)

12

ARM CPU Cores

SUMMARY OF CHAPTER CONTENTS

Although some ARM applications use a simple integer processor core as the basic processing component, others require tightly coupled functions such as cache memory and memory management hardware. ARM Limited offers a range of such 'CPU' configurations based around its integer cores.

The ARM CPU cores described here include the ARM710T, 720T and 740T, the ARM810 (now superseded by the ARM9 series), the StrongARM, the ARM920T and 940T, and the ARM1020E. These CPUs encompass a range of pipeline and cache organizations and form a useful illustration of the issues which arise when designing high-performance processors for low-power applications.

The primary role of a cache memory is to satisfy the processor core's instruction and data bandwidth requirements, so the cache organization is tightly coupled to the particular processor core that it is to serve. In the context of system-on-chip designs the goal is for the cache to reduce the external memory bandwidth requirements of the CPU core to a level that can be handled by an on-chip bus. The higher-performance ARM processor cores would run little faster than the ARM7TDMI if they were connected directly to an AMBA bus, so they will always be used with fast local memory or cache.

Memory management is another complex system function that must be tightly coupled to the processor core, whether it is a full translation-based system or a simpler protection unit. The ARM CPU cores integrate the processor core, cache(s), MMU(s) and (usually) an AMBA interface in a single macrocell.

12.1 | The ARM710T, ARM720T and ARM740T

The ARM710T, ARM720T and ARM740T are based upon the ARM7TDMI processor core (see Section 9.1 on page 213), to which an 8 Kbyte mixed instruction cache and data cache has been added. External memory and peripherals are accessed via an AMBA bus master unit, and a write buffer and memory management (ARM710T and 720T) unit or memory protection (ARM740T) unit are also incorporated.

The organization of the ARM710T and ARM720T CPUs is similar and is illustrated in Figure 12.1.

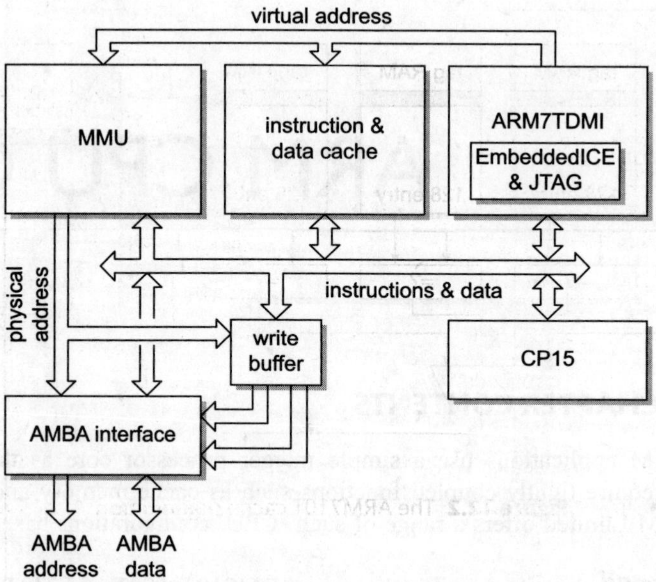

Figure 12.1 ARM710T and ARM720T organization

12.1.1 | ARM710T Cache

Since the ARM7TDMI processor core has a single memory port it is logical for it to be paired with a unified instruction and data cache. The ARM710T incorporates such a cache, with a capacity of 8 Kbytes. The cache is organized with 16-byte lines and is 4-way set associative. A random replacement algorithm selects which of the four possible locations will be overwritten by new data on a cache miss. The cache uses a write-through strategy as the target clock rate is only a few times higher than the rate at which standard off-chip memory devices can cycle.

The organization of the ARM710T cache is illustrated in Figure 12.2. Bits [10:4] of the virtual address are used to index into each of the four tag stores. The tags contain bits [31:11] of the virtual addresses of the corresponding data, so these tags are compared with bits [31:11] of the current virtual address. If one of the tags matches, the cache has hit and the corresponding line can be accessed from the data RAM using the same index (bits [10:4] of the virtual address) together with two bits which encode the number of the tag store which produced the matching tag. Virtual address bits [3:2] select the word from the line and, if a byte or half-word access is requested, bits [1:0] select the byte or half-word from the word.

It is interesting to compare the ARM710T cache organization with that of the ARM3 and ARM610 (described in detail in Section 10.4 on page 239) since they illustrate the sorts of issues that arise in designing a cache for both good performance and low-power operation. Although there is, as yet, no final word on the correct way to design a cache for this sort of application, the designer can be guided by the following observations on the examples presented in these ARM chips.

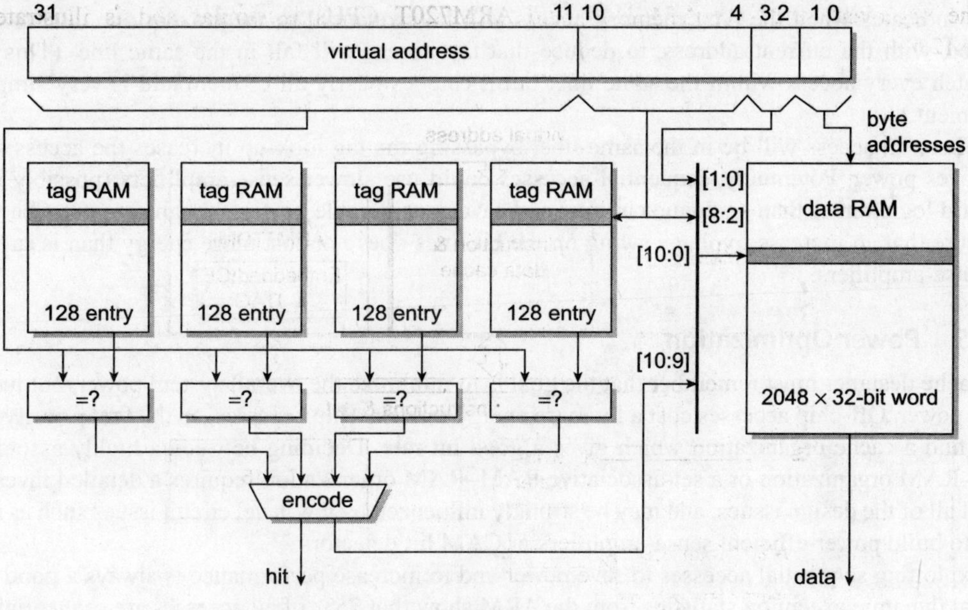

Figure 12.2 The ARM710T cache organization

12.1.2 | Cache Speed

High-associativity caches give the best hit rate, but require sequential CAM then RAM accesses which limits how fast the cycle time can become. Caches with a lower associativity can perform parallel tag and data accesses to give faster cycle times, and although a direct mapped cache has a significantly lower hit rate than a fully associative one, most of the associativity benefits accrue going from direct-mapped to 2- or 4-way associative; beyond 4-way the benefits of increased associativity are small. However, a fully associative CAM-RAM cache is much simpler than a 4-way associative RAM–RAM cache.

12.1.3 | Cache Power

CAM is somewhat power-hungry, requiring a parallel comparison with every entry on each cycle. Segmenting the cache by reducing the associativity a little and activating only a subsection of the CAM reduces the power cost significantly for a small increase in complexity.

In a static RAM the main users of power are the analogue sense-amplifiers. A 4-way cache must activate four times as many sense-amplifiers in the tag store as a direct-mapped cache; if it exploits the speed advantage offered by parallel tag and data accesses, it will also uses four times as many sense-amplifiers in the data store. (RAM–RAM caches can, alternatively, perform serial tag and data accesses to save power, only activating a particular data RAM when a hit is detected in the corresponding tag store.) Waste power can be minimized by using self-timed power-down circuits to turn off the sense-amplifiers as soon as the data is valid, but the power used in the sense-amplifiers is still significant.

12.1.4 | Sequential Accesses

Where the processor is accessing memory locations which fall within the same cache line it should be possible to bypass the tag look-up for all but the first access. The ARM generates a signal which indicates when the next memory access will be sequential to the current one, and this can be used, with the current address, to deduce that the access will fall in the same line. (This does not catch every access within the same line, but it catches nearly all of them and is very simple to implement.)

Where an access will be in the same line, bypassing the tag look-up increases the access speed and saves power. Potentially, sequential accesses could use slower sense-amplifiers (possibly using standard logic rather than analogue circuits) and save considerable power, though care must be taken to ensure that an increased voltage swing on the bit lines does not cost more energy than is saved in the sense-amplifiers.

12.1.5 | Power Optimization

The cache designer must remember that the goal is to minimize the overall system power, not just the cache power. Off-chip accesses cost a lot more energy than on-chip accesses, so the first priority must be to find a cache organization which gives a good hit rate. Deciding between a highly associative CAM-RAM organization or a set-associative RAM–RAM organization requires a detailed investigation of all of the design issues, and may be strongly influenced by low-level circuit issues such as novel ways to build power-efficient sense-amplifiers or CAM hit detectors.

Exploiting sequential accesses to save power and to increase performance is always a good idea. Typical dynamic execution statistics from the ARM show that 75% of all accesses are sequential, and since sequential accesses are fundamentally easier to deal with, this seems to be a statistic that should not be overlooked. Where power-efficiency is paramount, it may be worth sacrificing performance by making nonsequential accesses take two clock cycles; this will only reduce performance by about 25% and may reduce the cache power requirements by a factor of two or three.

An interesting question for research into low power is to ask whether the best cache organization for power-efficiency is necessarily the same as the best organization for high performance.

12.1.6 | ARM710T MMU

The ARM710T memory management unit implements the ARM memory management architecture described in Section 11.6 on page 258 using the system control coprocessor described in Section 11.5 on page 256.

The translation look-aside buffer (TLB) is a 64-entry associative cache of recently used translations which accelerates the translation process by removing the need for the 2-stage table look-up in a high proportion of accesses.

12.1.7 | ARM710T Write Buffer

The write buffer holds four addresses and eight data words. The memory management unit defines which addresses are bufferable. Each address may be associated with any number of the data words, so the write buffer may hold one word (or byte) of data to write to one address and seven words to write to another address, or two blocks of four words to write to different addresses, and so on. The data words associated with a particular address are written to sequential memory locations starting at that address.

(Clearly multiple data words associated with one address are generated principally by store multiple register instructions, the only other potential source being a data transfer from an external coprocessor.)

The mapping is illustrated in Figure 12.3, which shows the first address mapping six data words and the second and third addresses mapping one data word each. The fourth address is currently unused. The write buffer becomes full either when all four addresses are used or when all eight data words are full.

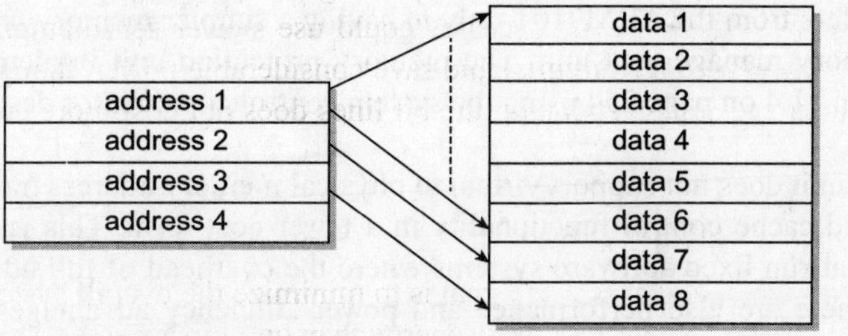

Figure 12.3 Write buffer mapping example

The processor can write into the buffer at the fast (cache) clock speed and continue executing instructions from the cache while the write buffer stores the data to memory at the memory clock rate. The processor is therefore fully decoupled from the memory speed so long as the instructions and data it needs are in the cache and the write buffer is not full when it comes to perform a write operation. The write buffer gives a performance benefit of around 15% for a modest hardware cost.

The principal drawback of the write buffer is that it is not possible to recover from external memory faults caused by buffered writes since the processor state is not recoverable. The processor can still support virtual memory since translation faults are detected in the on-chip MMU, so the exception is raised before the data gets to the write buffer. But, for example, a memory error correction scheme based on software error recovery cannot be supported if buffered writes are enabled.

12.1.8 | ARM710T Silicon

The characteristics of an ARM710T implemented on a 0.35 μm CMOS process are summarized in Table 12.1.

Table 12.1 ARM710T characteristics

Process	0.35 μm	**Transistors**	N/A	**MIPS**	53
Metal layers	3	**Core area**	11.7 mm²	**Power**	240 mW
Vdd	3.3 V	**Clock**	0–59 MHz	**MIPS/W**	220

12.1.9 | ARM720T

The ARM720T is very similar to the ARM710T with the following extensions:

- Virtual addresses in the bottom 32 Mbytes of the address space can be relocated to the 32 Mbyte memory area specified in the ProcessID register (CP15 register 13).
- The exception vectors can be moved from the bottom of memory to 0xffff0000, thereby preventing them from being translated by the above mechanism. This function is controlled by the 'V' bit in CP 15 register 1.

These extensions are intended to enhance the ability of the CPU core to support the Windows CE operating system. They are implemented in the CP15 MMU control registers described in Section 11.5 on page 256.

12.1.10 | ARM740T

The ARM740T differs from the ARM710T only in having a simpler memory protection unit in place of the 710T's memory management unit. The memory protection unit implements the architecture described in Section 11.4 on page 254 using the system control coprocessor described in Section 11.3 on page 253.

The protection unit does not support virtual to physical memory address translation, but provides basic protection and cache control functionality in a lower cost form. This is of benefit to embedded applications that run fixed software systems where the overhead of full address translation cannot be justified. There are also performance and power-efficiency advantages in omitting address translation hardware (where it is not needed), since a TLB miss results in several external memory accesses.

The organization of the ARM740T is illustrated in Figure 12.4.

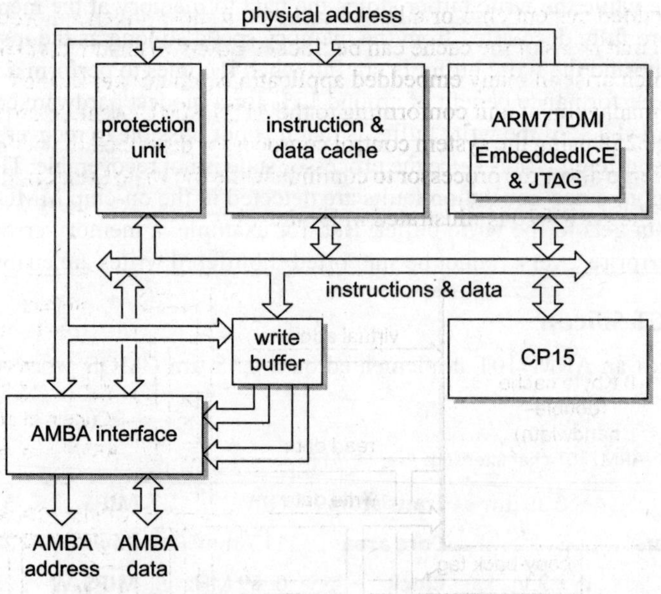

Figure 12.4 ARM740T organization

12.1.11 | ARM740T Silicon

The characteristics of an ARM740T implemented on a 0.35 μm CMOS process are summarized in Table 12.2.

As can be seen from Table 12.2, the general characteristics of the ARM740T are the same as those of the ARM710T and 720T as listed in Table 12.1. The only significant differences are the saving of just under 2 mm² of core area due to the omission of the MMU, and the reduced power consumption.

Table 12.2 ARM740T characteristics

Process	0.35 μm	**Transistors**	N/A	**MIPS**	53
Metal layers	3	**Core area**	9.8 mm²	**Power**	175 mW
Vdd	3.3 V	**Clock**	0–59 MHz	**MIPS/W**	300

12.2 | The ARM810

The ARM810 is a high-performance ARM CPU chip with an on-chip cache and memory management unit. It was the first implementation of the ARM instruction set developed by ARM Limited to use a fundamentally different pipeline structure from that used on the original ARM chip designed at Acorn Computers and carried through to ARM6 and ARM7. The ARM810 has now been superseded by the ARM9 series.

The ARM8 core is the integer processing unit used in the ARM810. It was described in Section 9.2 on page 221. The ARM810 adds the following on-chip support to the basic CPU:

- An 8 Kbyte virtually addressed unified instruction and data cache using a copy-back (or write-through, controlled by the page table entry) write strategy and offering a double-bandwidth capability as required by the ARM8 core. The cache is 64-way associative, and constructed from 1 Kbyte components to simplify the future development of a smaller cache for an embedded system chip or a larger cache on a more advanced process technology. It is designed so that areas of the cache can be 'locked down' to ensure that speed-critical sections of code, which arise in many embedded applications, do not get flushed.
- A memory management unit conforming to the ARM MMU architecture described in Section 11.6 on page 258 using the system control coprocessor described in Section 11.5 on page 256.
- A write buffer to allow the processor to continue while the write to external memory completes.

The organization of the ARM810 is illustrated in Figure 12.5.

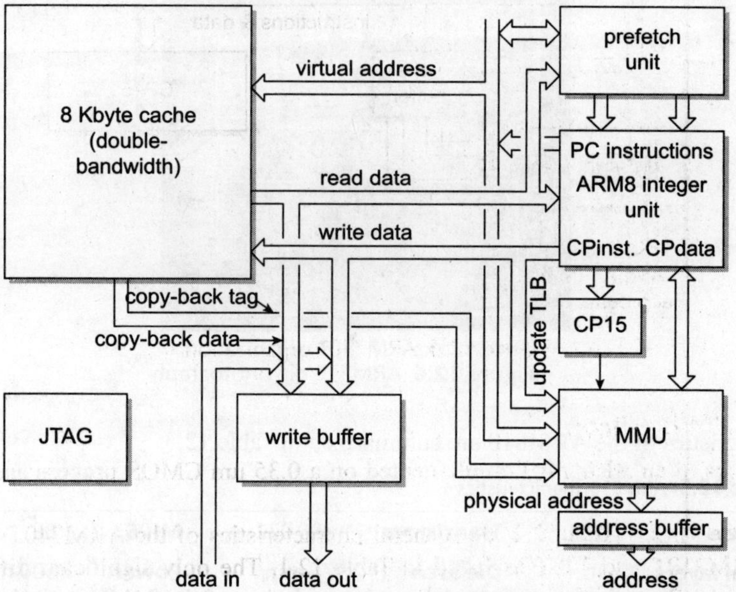

Figure 12.5 ARM810 organization

12.2.1 | Double-bandwidth Cache

The core's double-bandwidth requirement is satisfied by the cache; external memory accesses use conventional line refill and individual data transfer protocols. Double-bandwidth is available from the cache only for sequential memory accesses, so it is exploited by the prefetch unit for instruction fetches and by the core for load multiple register instructions.

Since the pipeline organization used on ARM7TDMI uses the memory interface almost every cycle, some way must be found to increase the available memory bandwidth if the CPI (the number of clocks per instruction) of the processor is to be improved. The StrongARM (described in the next section) achieves an increased bandwidth by incorporating separate instruction and data caches, thereby making double the bandwidth potentially available (though not all of this bandwidth can be used since the ARM generates instruction traffic with around twice the bandwidth of the data traffic, so the effective increase in bandwidth is approximately 50%). The ARM810 delivers an increased bandwidth by returning two sequential words per clock cycle which, since typically around 75% of an ARM's memory accesses are sequential, increases the usable bandwidth by about 60%. Although the ARM810 approach gives more bandwidth, it also creates more opportunity for conflict between instruction and data accesses; evaluating the relative merits of the two approaches is not straightforward.

As the cache uses a copy-back write strategy and is virtually addressed, evicting a dirty line requires an address translation. The mechanism used on the ARM810 is to send the virtual tag to the MMU for translation.

12.2.2 | ARM810 Silicon

A photograph of an ARM810 die is shown in Figure 12.6. The ARM8 core datapath is visible at the top of the photograph with its control logic immediately below. The MMU TLB is in the top right-hand corner and the eight 1 Kbyte cache blocks occupy the bottom area of the chip.

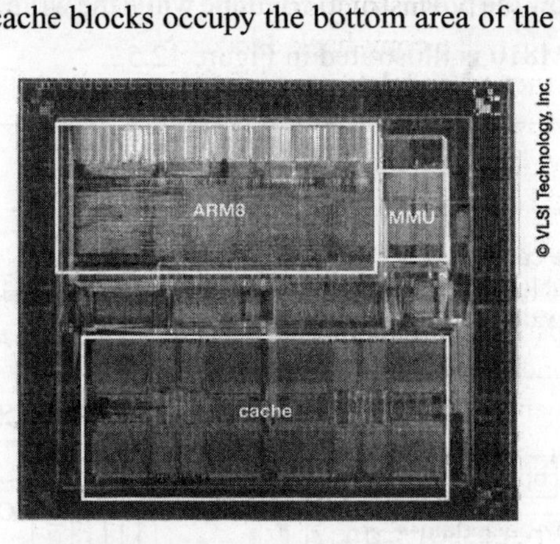

Figure 12.6 ARM810 die photograph

The characteristics of the ARM810 are summarized in Table 12.3.

Table 12.3 ARM810 characteristics

Process	0.5 µm	**Transistors**	836,022	**MIPS**	86
Metal layers	3	**Die area**	76 mm^2	**Power**	500 mW
Vdd	3.3 V	**Clock**	0–72 MHz	**MIPS/W**	172

12.3 | The StrongARM SA-110

The StrongARM CPU was developed by Digital Equipment Corporation in collaboration with ARM Limited. It was the first ARM processor to use a *modified-Harvard* (separate instruction and data cache) architecture.

The SA-110 is now manufactured by Intel Corporation following their take-over of Digital Semiconductor in 1998.

12.3.1 | Digital Alpha Background

Digital were, perhaps, best known in the microprocessor business for their range of 'Alpha' microprocessors which are 64-bit RISC processors that operate at very high clock rates. The ability to sustain these clock frequencies is a result of advanced CMOS process technology, carefully balanced pipeline design, a very thoroughly engineered clocking scheme and in-house design tools that give unusually good control of all these factors.

The same approach has been applied to the design of StrongARM, with the added objective of achieving exceptional power-efficiency.

12.3.2 | StrongARM Organization

The organization of StrongARM is shown in Figure 12.7. Its main features are:

- A 5-stage pipeline with register forwarding.
- Single-cycle execution of all common instructions except 64-bit multiplies, multiple register transfers and the swap memory and register instruction.
- A 16 Kbyte 32-way associative instruction cache with 32-byte line.
- A 16 Kbyte 32-way associative copy-back data cache with 32-byte line.
- Separate 32-entry instruction and data translation look-aside buffers.
- An 8-entry write buffer with up to 16 bytes per entry.
- Pseudo-static operation with low power consumption.

The processor uses system control coprocessor 15 to manage the on-chip MMU and cache resources, and incorporates JTAG boundary scan test circuitry for testing printed circuit board connectivity (the JTAG 'in-test', for in-circuit testing of the device itself, is not supported).

The first StrongARM chips are implemented on Digital's 0.35 μm CMOS process, using three layers of metal. They use around 2.5 million transistors on a 50 mm^2 die (which is very small for a processor of this performance) and deliver 200 to 250 Dhrystone MIPS with a 160 to 200 MHz clock, dissipating half to just under one watt using a 1.65 V to 2 V supply.

12.3.3 | The StrongARM Processor Core

The processor core employs a 'classic' 5-stage pipeline with full bypassing (register forwarding) and hardware interlocks. The ARM instruction set requires some instruction decoding to take place before the register bank read accesses can begin, and it also requires a shift operation in series with the ALU, but both of these additional logic functions are fitted within their respective pipeline stages and do not add to the pipeline depth. The pipeline stages are:

1. Instruction fetch (from the instruction cache).
2. Instruction decode and register read; branch target calculation and execution.
3. Shift and ALU operation, including data transfer memory address calculation.

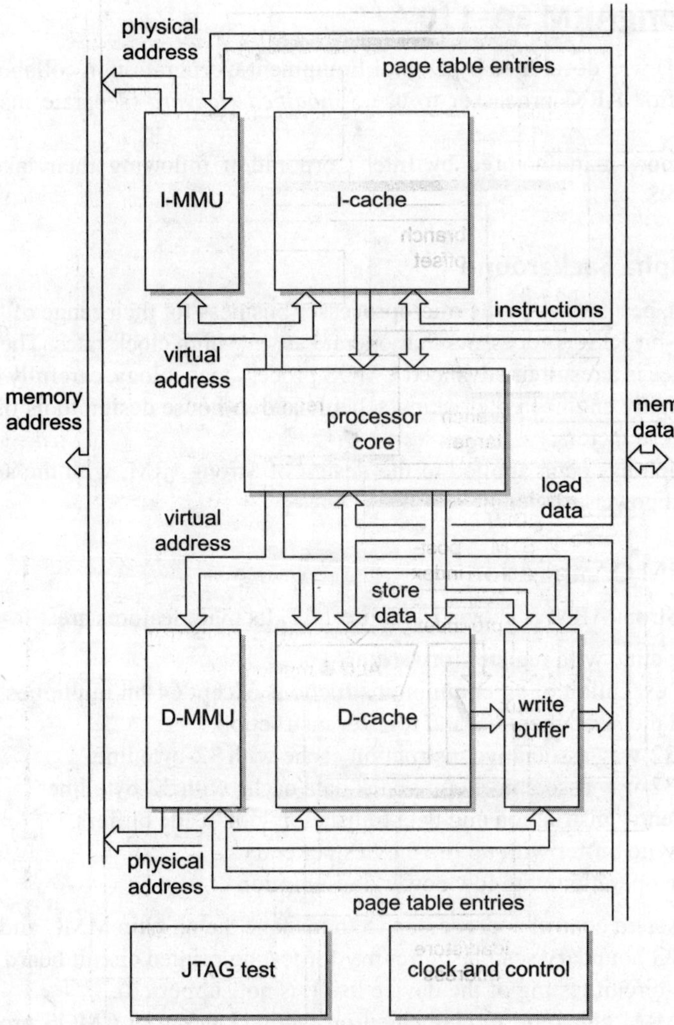

Figure 12.7 StrongARM organization

4. Data cache access.
5. Result write-back to register file.

The organization of the major pipeline components is illustrated in Figure 12.8. The shaded bars delimit the pipeline stages and data which passes across these bars will be latched at the crossing point. Data which feeds around the end of a bar is being passed back or forward across pipeline stages, for example:

- The register forwarding paths which pass intermediate results on to following instructions to avoid a register interlock stall caused by a read-after-write hazard.
- The PC path which forwards pc + 4 from the fetch stage of the *next* instruction, giving pc + 8 for the current instruction, to be used as r15 and in the branch target calculation.

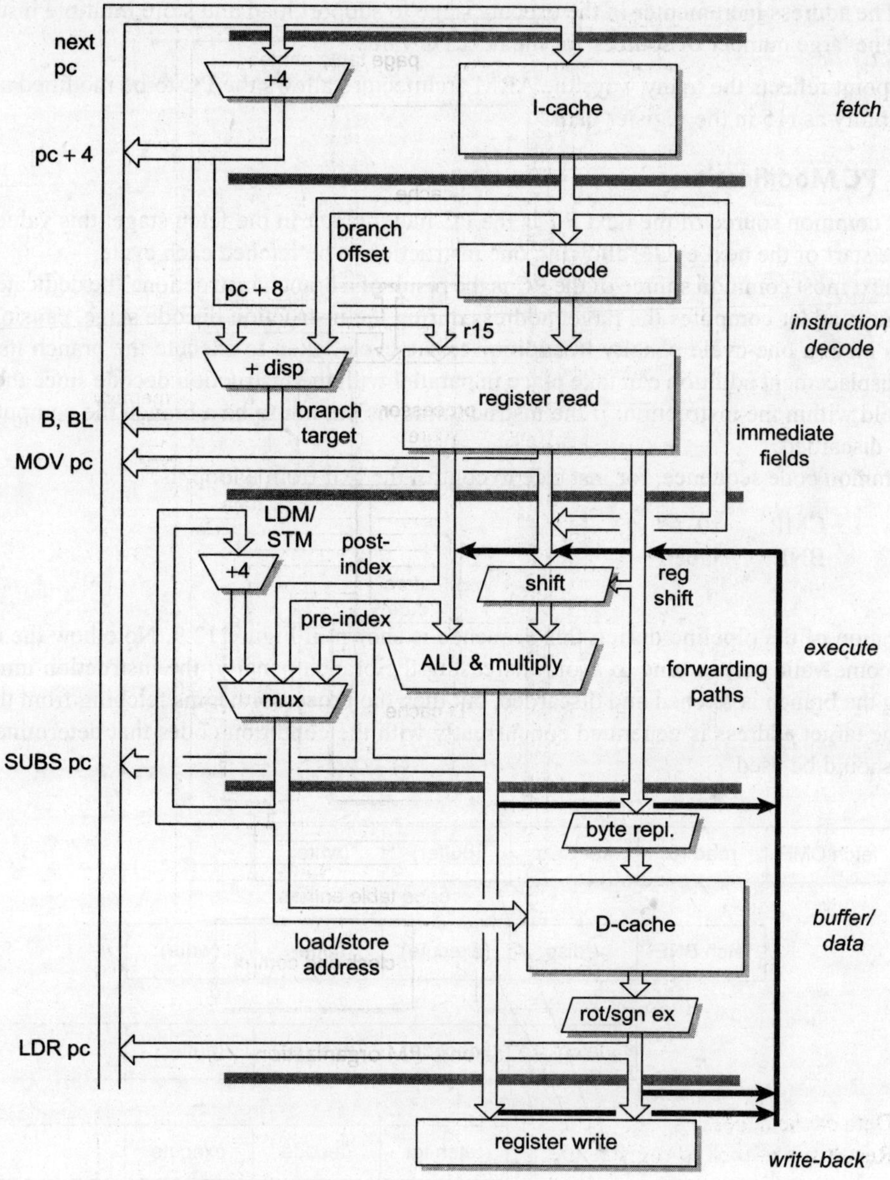

Figure 12.8 StrongARM core pipeline organization

12.3.4 | Pipeline Features

Of particular note in this pipeline structure are:

- The need for three register read ports to enable register-controlled shifts and store with base plus index addressing to issue in one cycle.
- The need for two register write ports to allow load with auto-index to issue in one cycle.

- The address incrementer in the execute stage to support load and store multiple instructions.
- The large number of sources for the next PC value.

This last point reflects the many ways the ARM architecture allows the PC to be modified as a result of its visibility as r15 in the register bank.

12.3.5 | PC Modification

The most common source of the next PC is the PC incrementer in the fetch stage; this value is available at the start of the next cycle, allowing one instruction to be fetched each cycle.

The next most common source of the PC is the result of a branch instruction. The dedicated branch displacement adder computes the target address during the instruction decode stage, causing a taken branch to incur a one-cycle penalty in addition to the cycle taken to execute the branch itself. Note that the displacement addition can take place in parallel with the instruction decode since the offset is a fixed field within the instruction; if the instruction turns out not to be a branch the computed target is simply discarded.

A common code sequence, for instance to control the exit from a loop, is:

```
CMP     r0, #0
BNE     label
..
```

The operation of the pipeline during this sequence is shown in Figure 12.9. Note how the condition codes become valid just in time to avoid increasing the branch penalty; the instruction immediately following the branch is fetched and discarded, but then the processor begins fetching from the branch target. The target address is generated concurrently with the condition codes that determine whether or not it should be used.

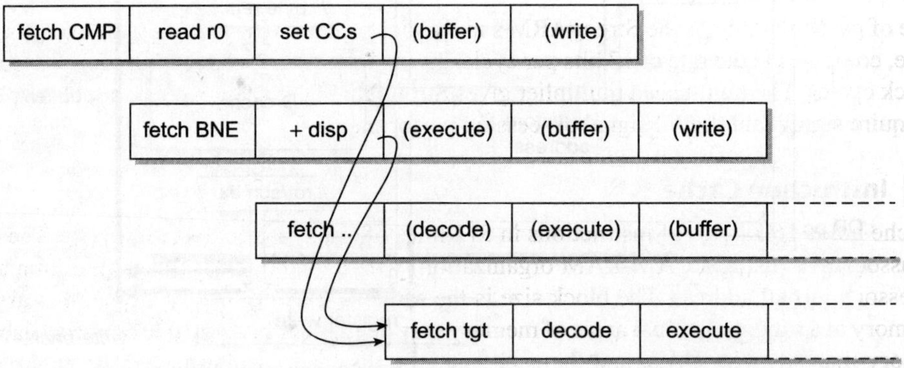

Figure 12.9 StrongARM loop test pipeline behaviour

The same one cycle penalty applies to branch and link instructions which take the branch in the same way but use the execute and write stages to compute pc + 4 and write it to rl4, the link register. It also applies to the normal subroutine return instruction, MOV pc, l r, where the target address comes from the register file rather than from the branch displacement adder, but it is still available at the end of the decode stage.

If the return address must be computed, for example when returning from an exception, there is a two-cycle penalty since the ALU result is only available at the end of the execute stage, and where the PC is loaded from memory (from a jump table, or subroutine return from stack) there is a three-cycle penalty.

12.3.6 | Forwarding Paths

The execution pipeline includes three forwarding paths to each register operand to avoid stalls when read-after-write hazards occur. Values are forwarded from:

1. the ALU result;
2. data loaded from the data cache;
3. the buffered ALU result.

These paths remove all data-dependency stalls except when a loaded data value is used by the following instruction, in which case a single cycle stall is required.

12.3.7 | Abort Recovery

It might seem that one of these paths could be avoided if the ALU result were written into the register file in the following stage rather than buffering it and delaying the write to the last stage. The merit of the delayed scheme is that data aborts can occur during the data cache access, perhaps requiring remedial action to recover the base register value (for instance when the base register is overwritten in a load multiple sequence before the fault is generated). This scheme not only allows recovery but supports the cleanest recovery mechanism, leaving the base register value as it was at the start of the instruction and removing the need for the exception handler to undo any auto-indexing.

12.3.8 | Multiplier

A feature of particular note is the StrongARM's multiplication unit which, despite the processor's high clock rate, computes at the rate of 12 bits per cycle, giving the product of two 32-bit operands in one to three clock cycles. The high-speed multiplier gives StrongARM considerable potential in applications which require significant digital signal processing performance.

12.3.9 | Instruction Cache

The I-cache holds 16 Kbytes of instructions in 512 lines of eight instructions (32 bytes). The cache is 32-way associative (using a CAM-RAM organization) with a cyclic replacement algorithm and uses the processor's virtual address. The block size is the same as the line size, so whole lines are loaded from memory at a time. Individual areas of memory may be marked as cacheable or uncacheable using the memory management tables, and the cache may be disabled and flushed (in its entirety) under software control.

12.3.10 | Data Cache

The data cache uses a similar organization to the instruction cache but with added functions to cope with data stores (instructions are read-only). It has a capacity of 16 Kbytes with 512 32-byte lines arranged as a 32-way virtually addressed associative cache with cyclic replacement. The block size is also 32 bytes. The cache may be disabled by software and individual regions of memory may be made uncacheable. (Making I/O regions uncacheable is usually a good idea.)

The data cache uses a copy-back write strategy, and has two dirty bits per line so that when a line is evicted from the cache all, half or none of it is written to memory. The use of two dirty bits rather than one reduces memory traffic since the 'half dirty' case is quite common. The cache stores a copy of the physical address with each line for use when the line is written back to memory, and evicted lines are placed into the write buffer.

Since the cache uses a copy-back write strategy, it is sometimes necessary to cause all dirty lines to be written back to memory. On StrongARM this is achieved using software to load new data into every line, causing dirty lines to be evicted.

12.3.11 | Synonyms

As with any virtually addressed cache, care must be taken to ensure that all cacheable physical memory locations have unique virtual addresses that map to them. When two different virtual addresses map to the same physical location the virtual addresses are **synonyms;** where synonyms exist, neither virtual address should be cacheable.

12.3.12 | Cache Consistency

The separate instruction and data caches create the potential for the two caches to have inconsistent copies of the same physical memory location. Whenever a region of memory is treated as (writeable) data at one time and as executable instructions at another, great care must be taken to avoid inconsistencies.

A common example of this situation is when a program is loaded (or copied from one memory location to another) and then executed. During the load phase the program is treated as data and passes through the data cache. When it is executed it is loaded into the instruction cache (which may have copies of previous instructions from the same addresses). To ensure correct operation:

1. The load phase should be completed.
2. The entire data cache should be 'cleaned' (by loading new data into every line as described above) or, where the addresses of the affected cache lines are known, these lines may be explicitly cleaned and flushed.
3. The instruction cache should be flushed (to remove obsolete instructions).

Alternative solutions might involve making certain regions of memory uncacheable during the load phase.

Note that this is not a problem for literals (data items included in the instruction stream) which are quite common in ARM code. Although a block of memory may be loaded into both caches since it contains a mixture of instructions and literals, so long as individual words (or bytes) are treated consistently as *either* instructions *or* data, there will be no problem. It is even acceptable for the program to change the value of a literal (though this is rarely used and is probably bad practice) so long as it does not affect the values of instructions which may be in the instruction cache. It is better practice, however, to avoid literals altogether and to keep data in data areas that are separate from code areas which contain instructions.

12.3.13 | Compiler Issues

The separation of the instruction and data caches should be observed by the compiler, which should pool constants across compiler units rather than placing them at the end of each routine. This minimizes the pollution of the data cache with instructions and of the instruction cache with data.

12.3.14 | The Write Buffer

The write buffer smooths out small peaks in the write data bandwidth, decoupling the processor from stalls caused by the memory bus saturating. A large peak that causes the buffer to fill will stall the processor. Independent writes to the same 16-byte area are merged within the write buffer, though only to the last address written into the buffer. The buffer stores up to eight addresses (each address aligned to a 16-byte boundary), copying the virtual address for use when merging writes and the physical address to address the external memory, and up to 16 bytes of data for each address (so each address can handle a dirty half-line or up to four registers from a single store multiple).

The write buffer may be disabled by software, and individual memory regions may be marked as bufferable or unbufferable using the MMU page tables. All cacheable regions are bufferable (evicted cache lines are written through the write buffer) but uncacheable regions may be bufferable or unbufferable. Normally the I/O region is unbufferable. An unbuffered write will wait for the write buffer to empty before it is written to memory.

Data reads that miss the data cache are checked against entries in the write buffer to ensure consistency, but instruction reads are not checked against the write buffer. Whenever memory locations which have been used as data are to be used as instructions a special instruction should be used to ensure that the write buffer has drained.

12.3.15 | MMU Organization

StrongARM incorporates the standard ARM memory management architecture, using separate translation look-aside buffers (TLBs) for instructions and data. Each TLB has 32 translation entries arranged as a fully associative cache with cyclic replacement. A TLB miss invokes table-walking hardware to fetch the translation and access permission information from main memory.

12.3.16 | StrongARM Silicon

A photograph of a StrongARM die is shown in Figure 12.10 with an overlay indicating the major functional areas. The die area is, not surprisingly, dominated by the instruction cache (ICACHE) and the data cache (DCACHE). Each cache has its own MMU (IMMU and DMMU). The processor core

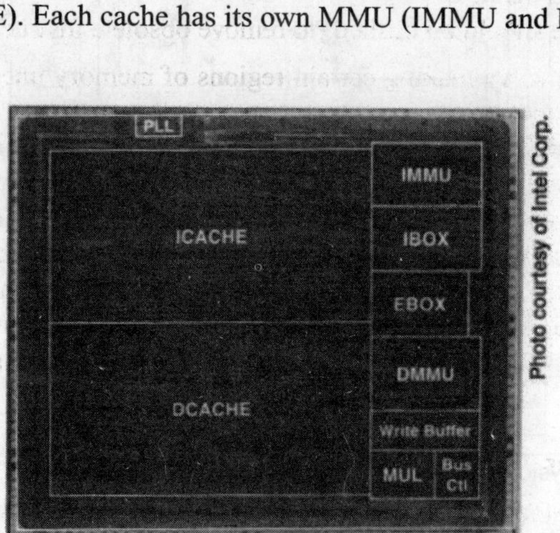

Figure 12.10 StrongARM die photograph

has the instruction issue unit (IBOX) and the execution unit (EBOX) with high-speed multiplication hardware (MUL). The write buffer and external bus controller complete the processor logic.

The high-frequency on-chip clock is generated by a phase-locked loop (PLL) from an external 3.68 MHz clock input.

The characteristics of the StrongARM are summarized in Table 12.4.

Table 12.4 StrongARM characteristics

Process	0.35 μm	**Transistors**	2,500,000	**MIPS**	115/268
Metal layers	3	**Die area**	50 mm²	**Power**	300/1000 mW
Vdd	1.65/2 V	**Clock**	100/233 MHz	**MIPS/W**	380/268

12.4 | The ARM920T and ARM940T

The ARM920T and ARM940T are based upon the ARM9TDMI processor core (see Section 9.3 on page 224), to which instruction and data caches have been added. The instruction and data ports are merged via an AMBA bus master unit, and a write buffer and memory management unit (ARM920T) or memory protection unit (ARM940T) are also incorporated.

12.4.1 | ARM920T

The overall organization of the ARM920T is illustrated in Figure 12.11.

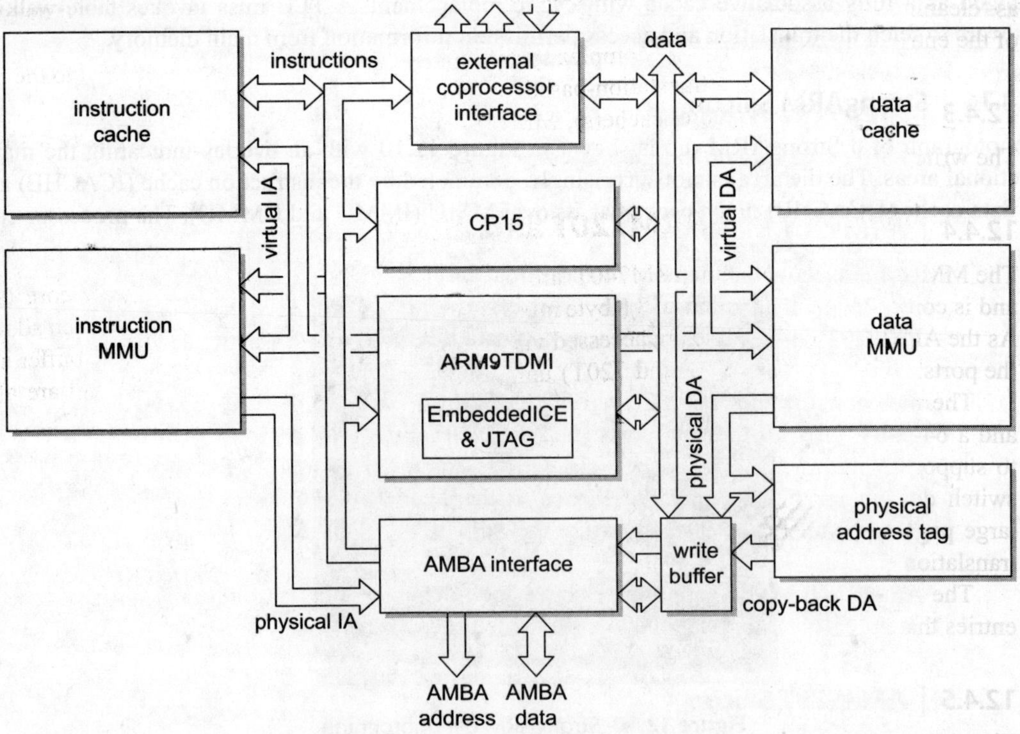

Figure 12.11 ARM920T organization

12.4.2 | ARM920T Caches

The instruction and data caches are both 16 Kbytes in size and are built using a segmented CAM-RAM organization to give 64-way associativity. Each cache comprises eight segments of 64 lines, the required segment being addressed by A[7:5]. They have 8-word (32 byte) lines and support lock-down in units of 256 bytes (corresponding to one line in each segment). The replacement strategy is pseudo-random or round-robin, and is determined by the 'RR' bit (bit 14) in CP15 register 1. A complete 8-word line is reloaded on a cache miss.

The instruction cache is read-only. The data cache supports a copy-back write strategy, and each line has one valid bit, two dirty bits and a write-back bit. The write-back bit duplicates information usually found in the translation system, and enables the cache to implement a write operation as write-through or copy-back without reference to the MMU. When a cache line is replaced any dirty data is sent to the write buffer, and this may amount to zero, four or eight words depending on the two dirty bits. The data cache allocates space only on a read miss, not on a write miss.

As the data cache is accessed using virtual addresses, there is a problem whenever dirty data has to be written back to main memory since this action requires the physical address. The ARM810 solves this by passing the virtual address back to the MMU for translation, but of course there is no guarantee that the necessary translation entry is still in the TLB. The whole process can therefore be quite time consuming. The ARM920T avoids this problem by having a second tag store that is used to hold the physical address for each line in the cache. A cache line flush does not then need to involve the MMU and can always proceed without delay to transfer the dirty data to the write buffer.

The ARM920T can force dirty cache lines to be flushed back to main memory (a process known as 'cleaning') using either the cache index or the memory address. It is therefore possible to clean all of the entries corresponding to a particular memory area.

12.4.3 | ARM920T Write Buffer

The write buffer will hold up to four addresses and 16 data words.

12.4.4 | ARM920T MMU

The MMU implements the memory management architecture described in Section 11.6 on page 258 and is controlled by the system control coprocessor, CP15, as described in Section 11.5 on page 256. As the ARM920T has separate instruction and data memory ports it has two MMUs, one for each of the ports.

The memory management hardware includes a 64-entry TLB for the instruction memory port and a 64-entry TLB for the data port. The ARM920T includes the ProcessID logic that is required to support Windows CE. The caches and MMUs come after the ProcessID insertion, so a context switch doesn't invalidate either the caches or the TLBs. In addition to supporting the 64 Kbyte large pages and the 4 Kbyte small pages, the ARM920T MMU also supports 1 Kbyte 'tiny' page translation.

The ARM920T MMU supports selective lock-down for TLB entries, ensuring that translation entries that are critical, for example to a real-time process, cannot be ejected.

12.4.5 | ARM920T Silicon

The characteristics of the ARM920T are summarized in Table 12.5.

Table 12.5 ARM920T characteristics

Process	0.25 μm	**Transistors**	2,500,000	**MIPS**	220
Metal layers	4	**Core area**	23–25 mm²	**Power**	560 mW
Vdd	2.5 V	**Clock**	0–200 MHz	**MIPS/W**	390

12.4.6 | ARM940T

The ARM940T is another CPU core based on the ARM9TDMI integer core. It is simpler than the ARM920T as it does not support virtual to physical address translation. The organization of the ARM940T is shown in Figure 12.12.

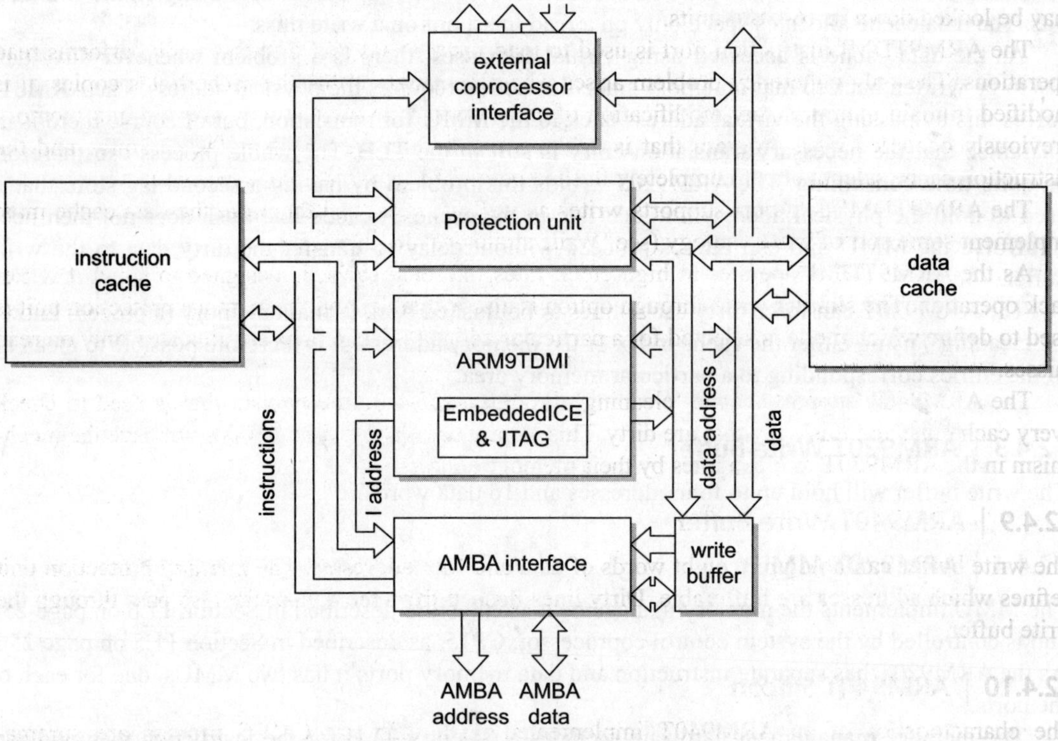

Figure 12.12 ARM940T organization

12.4.7 | Memory Protection Unit

The memory protection unit implements the architecture described in Section 11.4 on page 254. As the ARM940T has separate instruction and data memory ports it has two protection units, one for each of the ports.

This configuration has no virtual to physical address translation mechanism. Many embedded systems do not require address translation, and as a full MMU requires significant silicon area, its omission when it is not required represents a significant cost saving. The AMBA interface and absence of address translation hardware both indicate the expectation that the application will be in embedded systems with other AMBA macrocells on the same chip.

12.4.8 | ARM940T Caches

Both instruction and data caches have a size of 4 Kbytes and comprise four 1 Kbyte segments, each of which uses a fully associative CAM-RAM structure. (For an explanation of these cache terms see Section 10.3 on page 233.) They have a quad-word line structure, and always load a complete line on a cache miss if the address is cacheable as indicated by the memory protection unit.

The caches support lock-down, which means that sections of the cache can be loaded and then the contents protected from being flushed. Locked-down sections of the cache are clearly unavailable for further general-purpose cache use, but the ability to guarantee that certain critical code sections will always be found in the cache may be more important than getting the best cache hit rate. The caches may be locked down in 16-word units.

The ARM9TDMI instruction port is used to load instructions and therefore only performs read operations. The only coherency problem arises when the program that the cache holds copies of is modified in main memory. Any modification of code (such as loading a new program into memory previously occupied by a program that is no longer required) must be handled carefully, and the instruction cache selectively or completely flushed before the new program is executed.

The ARM9TDMI data port supports writes as well as reads, and therefore the data cache must implement some sort of write strategy (see 'Write strategies' on page 238).

As the ARM9TDMI operates at high clock rates, the data cache is designed to support write-back operation. The simpler write-through option is also available, and the memory protection unit is used to define which mode is selected for a particular address. Cache lines are allocated only on read misses.

The ARM940T supports cache 'cleaning' through a software mechanism that is used to check every cache line and flush any that are dirty. This clearly takes some time. It does not have the mechanism in the ARM920T to clean lines by their memory address.

12.4.9 | ARM940T Write Buffer

The write buffer can hold up to eight words of data and four addresses. The memory protection unit defines which addresses are bufferable. Dirty lines flushed from the data cache also pass through the write buffer.

12.4.10 | ARM940T Silicon

The characteristics of an ARM940T implemented on a 0.25 μm CMOS process are summarized in Table 12.6 and a plot of the layout is shown in Figure 12.13. It can be seen that the complete CPU core occupies a relatively small proportion of the area of a low-cost system-on-chip design.

Table 12.6 ARM940T characteristics

Process	0.25 μm	**Transistors**	802,000	**MIPS**	220
Metal layers	3	**Core area**	8.1 mm^2	**Power**	385 mW
Vdd	2.5 V	**Clock**	0–200 MHz	**MIPS/W**	570

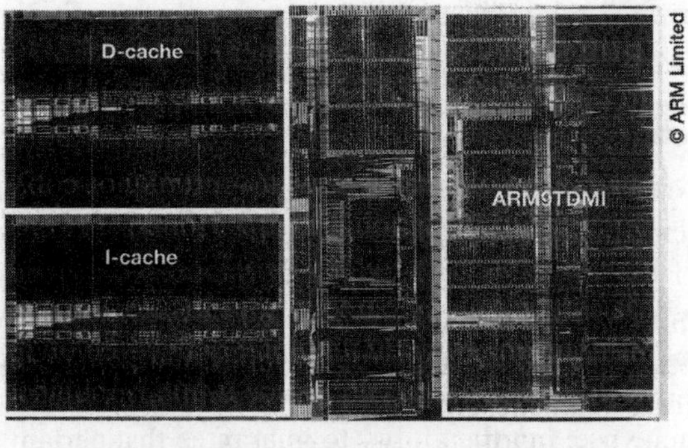

Figure 12.13 ARM940T CPU core plot.

12.5 | The ARM946E-S and ARM966E-S

The ARM946E-S and ARM966E-S are synthesizable CPU cores based upon the ARM9E-S integer core. (See 'ARM9E-S' on page 227.)

Both CPU cores have AMBA AHB interfaces and can be synthesized with an embedded trace macrocell as described in Section 8.8 on page 204. They are intended for embedded applications and do not have address translation hardware.

12.5.1 | ARM946E-S Cache

The ARM946E-S has a 4-way set-associative cache. The set-associative organization was chosen over the CAM-RAM organization used in the ARM920T and ARM940T because it is easier to construct a set-associative cache with synthesizable RAM structures available in standard ASIC libraries. Synthesizing CAM–RAM cache structures is still difficult for most design systems.

The instruction and data caches can each be from 4 Kbytes to 64 Kbytes in size, and the two caches need not be the same size as each other. Both use an 8-word line, support lock-down, and employ a software-selectable replacement algorithm which may be pseudo-random or round-robin. The write strategy is also software selectable between write-through and copy-back.

The ARM946E-S incorporates memory protection units and has an overall organization similar to the ARM940T (shown in Figure 12.12).

12.5.2 | ARM966E-S Memory

The ARM966E-S does not employ caches. Instead, the synthesized macrocell incorporates tightly coupled SRAM mapped to fixed memory addresses. These memories can be a range of sizes. One memory is connected only to the data port, whereas the second memory is connected to both ports. Generally the second memory is used by the instruction port, but data port access is important for two reasons:

- Constants (such as addresses) embedded in code must be read through the data port.
- There must be a mechanism for initializing the instruction memory before it can be used. The instruction port is read-only and therefore cannot be used to initialize the instruction memory.

The ARM966E-S also incorporates a write buffer to optimize the use of the AMBA AHB bandwidth and supports the connection of on-chip coprocessors.

12.5.3 | Soft IP

These synthesizable CPU cores address the strong market demand for high-performance processors that can readily be resynthesized on new process technologies. They represent an alternative to the 'hard' macrocells that have been the usual delivery mechanism for ARM technology.

12.6 | The ARM1020E

The ARM1020E CPU is based around the ARM10TDMI core described in Section 9.4 on page 227. It implements ARM architecture version v5TE which includes the Thumb instruction set and the signal processing instruction set extensions described in Section 8.9 on page 206.

The organization of the ARM1020E is very similar to that of the ARM920T shown in Figure 12.11, the differences being the size of the cache and the bus widths. The only difference of substance (at the level of detail shown in this figure) is the use of two AMBA AHB bus master request-grant handshakes for the instruction and data sides, whereas the ARM920T arbitrates these internally to form a single external request-grant interface.

12.6.1 | ARM1020E Caches

The ARM1020E incorporates a 32 Kbyte instruction cache and a 32 Kbyte data cache. Both caches are 64-way associative and use a segmented CAM–RAM structure. They have a 32-byte line size. Both caches use either a pseudo-random or a round-robin replacement algorithm and support lock-down.

In order to satisfy the ARMl0TDMI's bandwidth requirements both caches have a 64-bit data bus; the instruction cache can supply two instructions per cycle, and the data cache can supply two words of data during each cycle of a load multiple or write two words of data during each cycle of a store multiple.

The instruction cache is read-only. The data cache employs a copy-back write strategy and has one valid, one dirty and one write-back bit per line. When a line is replaced in the cache it may result in zero or eight words being written back to main memory, depending on the state of the dirty bit. The full eight-word cast-out process can be implemented in four memory cycles due to the 64-bit memory data bus.

The write-back bit duplicates information usually found in the translation system, and enables the cache to implement a write operation as write-through or copy-back without reference to the MMU.

12.6.2 | Hit-under-miss Buffer

The ARM1020E also supports 'hit-under-miss' operation. This means that if one data reference causes a cache miss, the cache can continue to satisfy subsequent data references (provided that they don't also miss) while it is fetching the line containing the missing data.

12.6.3 | ARM1020E Write Buffer

The write buffer comprises eight slots each capable of holding an address and a 64-bit data double-word. A separate four-slot write buffer is used to handle cache cast-outs to ensure that there is no conflict in the main write buffer between cast-outs and hit-under-miss write traffic.

12.6.4 | ARM1020E MMU

The memory management systems is based upon two 64-entry translation lookaside buffers, one for each cache. The TLBs also support selective lock-down to ensure that translation entries for critical real-time code sections do not get ejected.

12.6.5 | ARM1020E Bus Interface

The external memory bus interface is AMBA AHB compliant (see Section 8.2 on page 187). The ARM1020E has separate AMBA AHB interfaces for the instruction and data memories. Each interface makes its own requests to the bus arbiter, though they share the 32-bit address and 64-bit unidirectional read and write data bus interfaces.

12.6.6 | ARM1020E Silicon

The target characteristics for an ARM1020E running at 1.5 V on 0.18 μm CMOS are summarized in Table 12.7. The CPU will run at supply voltages down to 1.2 V for improved power-efficiency.

Table 12.7 ARM1020E target characteristics

Process	0.18 μm	**Transistors**	7,000,000	**MIPS**	500
Metal layers	5	**Core area**	12 mm^2	**Power**	400 mW
Vdd	1.5 V	**Clock**	0–400 MHz	**MIPS/W**	1,250

12.6.7 | ARM10200

The ARM10200 is a reference chip design based upon the ARM1020E CPU core, to which the following additions have been made:

- a VFP10 vector floating point unit;
- a high-performance synchronous DRAM interface;
- a phase-locked loop circuit to generate the high-speed CPU clock.

The ARM10200 is intended to be used for the evaluation of the ARM1020E CPU core and to support benchmarking and system prototyping activities.

12.6.8 | VFP10

High-performance vector floating-point support is provided for the ARM10TDMI through the accompanying VFP 10 floating-point coprocessor. The VFP 10 incorporates a 5-stage load/store pipeline and a 7-stage execution pipeline and supports single- and double-precision IEEE 754 floating-point arithmetic (see Section 6.3 on page 137). It is capable of issuing a floating-point multiply-accumulate operation at a rate of one per clock cycle. It exploits the 64-bit data memory interface of the ARM10TDMI to load or store one double-precision value or two single-precision values in a clock cycle. Both the arithmetic and load/store instructions include 'vector' variants that perform the same operation on a set of registers, and since vector operations and vector load/stores can run concurrently, a peak throughput of 800 MFLOPS (at 400 MHz) is achievable.

12.6.9 | ARM10200 Silicon

A plot of the 0.25 μm ARM10200 silicon is shown in Figure 12.14. This first version of the chip has a fully synthesized VFP10 core and the cache was designed using generic design rules. The 0.18 μm

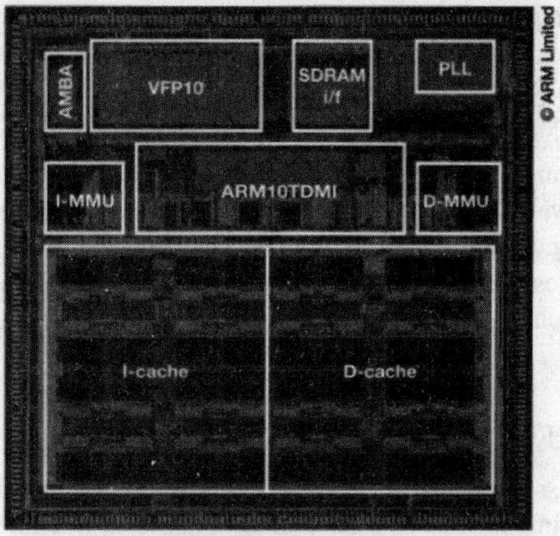

Figure 12.14 ARM10200 chip plot

version of the chip will incorporate a VFP10 core with a manually laid-out custom datapath and synthesized control, and the caches will use more process-specific design rules that will significantly reduce their relative size.

12.7 | Discussion

The ARM CPU cores described in this chapter highlight a number of important aspects of the development of high-performance low-power processor subsystems.

The issues relating to the design of the processor core itself were discussed in Chapter 9 and summarized in Section 9.5 on page 229. Here we are concerned with the other components that are intimately connected to the processor core and are critical to its ability to realize its intrinsic performance potential.

12.7.1 | Memory Bandwidth

The performance of a processor is ultimately limited by the bandwidth of its associated memory system. The ARM CPU core family demonstrates how a cache memory system can be optimized to different performance points:

- The ARM7TDMI is designed to waste very few memory cycles. It requires a memory that can supply a word of data in every clock cycle. As it employs a von Neumann architecture (that is, it has a single memory port used for both instruction and data transfers), a unified cache can support its memory bandwidth requirements. The ARM710T, 720T and 740T all include such a cache.
- The ARM9TDMI requires more than one word of data per clock cycle and employs a Harvard architecture (separate instruction and data memory ports) to achieve this. Separate caches (and memory management units) can satisfy its needs. The ARM920T and 940T incorporate separate 32-bit caches.

- The ARM10TDMI requires more than one instruction per clock cycle as it attempts to predict and remove branches before they enter the execution unit. It also transfers two data words per cycle during load and store multiple instructions. It therefore requires separate caches each wider than 32 bits, such as the 64-bit caches in the ARM1020E.

The separate caches used on the ARM9 and ARM10 series of CPUs can lead to coherency problems which are left to software to resolve. Alternative ways to provide the necessary bandwidth are illustrated by the double-bandwidth cache of the ARM810 and the dual-ported local memory on the AMULET3H subsystem (described in Section 14.6 on page 335). Both of these approaches use a unified memory model which simplifies software design but at the cost of somewhat more complex hardware.

12.7.2 | Cache Associativity

The relative merits of set-associative RAM–RAM caches and fully associative CAM-RAM caches have been discussed at length in this chapter and in Chapter 10. The earliest ARM CPU designs adopted the segmented CAM–RAM structure for a combination of performance and power-efficiency reasons. The ARM7 series of CPUs switched to a 4-way set-associative RAM–RAM organization principally because RAM is smaller than CAM (it requires about half the layout area per bit) and is more generally available in the standard design libraries of the many target processes that the ARM must address. The later ARM8, ARM9 and ARM10 CPUs have reverted to the segmented CAM–RAM organization, at least in part to facilitate the support of cache lock-down (discussed further in Example 12.1).

12.7.3 | Cache Write Strategy

Write-through caches are the simplest to design, and they cope well when the processor clock rate is a small multiple of the main memory cycle rate. Once the processor clock rises to ten or more times the memory cycle rate, the write data traffic generated by data store instructions will begin to saturate the external memory bus and the processor will frequently be stalled waiting for write cycles to complete. The only way around this problem is to use a cache strategy that does not result in all writes passing to main memory, for example by implementing a copy-back cache.

Current main memory will typically cycle at around 10 MHz, so the ARM7 series of CPUs can operate satisfactorily at 60 MHz with a write-through cache. The ARM810 is borderline at its first design clock rate, but had it not been superseded by the ARM9 series it would have been taken to higher clock rates and was therefore designed with a copy-back cache. Caches for the ARM9 and ARM10 must employ a copy-back strategy if their performance is not to be compromised.

12.7.4 | Cache Line Length

Longer cache lines reduce the size of the tag store (for a given data store size), reduce the cache miss rate and increase the miss cost (the time taken to load a cache line). The ARM CPU cores all use either a quad-word (16-byte) or an 8-word (32-byte) line, the smaller size being preferred for the smaller caches and embedded code and the larger size for larger caches and general-purpose code. The 64-bit buses used on the ARM1020E allow a 32-byte cache line to be loaded and flushed in the same number of memory cycles as a 16-byte line requires with a 32-bit bus.

12.7.5 | Memory Management

The ARM MMU is a sophisticated unit that occupies a similar silicon area to the processor core itself. Where its functionality is needed it must be included. Any general-purpose system where the mix of application code is unknown at design time probably requires this functionality. Embedded systems running known application code can be designed to work without memory management, and it is hard to justify the cost of the MMU for such systems.

The ARM CPU cores have evolved into two distinct series, one with the full MMU for general-purpose applications and one with the much simpler memory protection unit for fixed-program embedded systems. The ARM740T and ARM940T are examples of the latter, while the general-purpose CPUs include versions that support Windows CE (ARM720T, ARM920T and ARM1020E) and those that do not (ARM710T and ARM810).

The latest development in the memory management architecture is the support for TLB lock-down in the ARM810, ARM920T and ARM1020E. This has a similar role to cache lock-down: it can be used to ensure that critical real-time code runs as efficiently as possible.

12.8 | Example and Exercises

EXAMPLE 12.1

Why is a segmented associative cache better suited to support lock-down than a set-associative cache?

Early ARM CPUs, such as the ARM3 whose cache was studied in Section 10.4 on page 239, used highly associative caches with a CAM–RAM structure. The ARM700 series of CPUs abandoned CAM–RAM caches in favour of RAM–RAM set-associative caches because the RAM tag store uses less die area than the equivalent CAM tag store. Later ARM CPUs, from the ARM810 onwards, have reverted to a CAM–RAM cache, at least in part because of the need to support partial cache lock-down.

The reason why a CAM–RAM cache provides better support for lock-down is simply to do with its level of associativity. The cache locations that a particular memory location can map into are determined by decoding some of its address bits. In a direct-mapped cache there is only one cache location, a 2-way set-associative cache offers a choice of two possible locations, 4-way offers four, and so on.

In the ARM CPUs that support it, lock-down operates by reducing the range of this choice. With a 4-way set-associative cache it is practical to lock down a quarter of the cache (leaving a 3-way cache), half of the cache (2-way), or three-quarters of the cache (leaving a direct-mapped cache). This is a coarse granularity and is inefficient if, for example, all that need be locked down is memory to hold a small interrupt handler.

The CAM–RAM caches typically offer 64-way associativity, enabling the cache to be locked-down in units of 1/64 of the total cache, which is a much finer granularity.

Exercise 12.1.1

Discuss the impact of the following cache features on performance and power dissipation:

1. Increasing associativity by splitting the tag and data RAMs into multiple blocks which perform parallel look-ups.
2. Serializing the tag and data RAM accesses.
3. Exploiting sequential access patterns to bypass the tag look-up and to optimize the data RAM access mechanism.
4. Including separate data and instruction caches (as on StrongARM).

Exercise 12.1.2

Explain why an on-chip write buffer cannot be used with an off-chip memory management unit.

Exercise 12.1.3

Cache coherence is an important issue and many solutions have been proposed and used in different processors. How is cache coherence ensured in ARM? Will this solution hold even if the processor is a multi core one?

13

Embedded ARM Applications

SUMMARY OF CHAPTER CONTENTS

Increasingly the trend in embedded system design is to integrate all the major system functions apart from some memory components into a single chip. The benefits in terms of component costs, reliability and power-efficiency are considerable. The development that makes this possible is the advance in semiconductor process technology which now allows chips incorporating millions of transistors to be built cheaply, and within a few years will allow tens of millions of transistors on a chip.

So, the era of complex systems on a single chip is upon us. The ARM has played a leading role in the opening of this era since its very small core size leaves more silicon resources available for the rest of the system functions. In this chapter we look at several examples of ARM-based 'systems on chips', but we are, in fact, only scratching the surface of this domain. The next few years will see a flood of embedded applications, many of which will be based around ARM processor cores.

Designing a 32-bit computer system is a complex undertaking. Designing one on a single chip where it must be 'right first time' is still very challenging. There is no formula for success, but there are many very powerful design tools available to assist the designer. As in most engineering endeavours, one can only get so far by studying the problem and the experiences of others. Understanding an existing design is far easier than creating a new one. Developing a new system on a chip is one of today's greatest challenges in digital electronics.

13.1 | The VLSI Ruby II Advanced Communication Processor

VLSI Technology, Inc., were the first ARM semiconductor partner and were instrumental, along with Acorn Computers Limited and Apple Computer, Inc., in setting up ARM Limited as a separate company. Their relationship with the ARM predates the existence of ARM Limited, since they fabricated the very first ARM processors in 1985 and licensed the technology from Acorn Computers in 1987.

VLSI have manufactured many standard ARM-based chips for Acorn Computers and produced ARM610 chips for Apple Newtons. They have also produced several ARM-based designs for customer-specific products and a number which they have made available as standard parts. The Ruby II chip is one such standard part which is intended for use in portable communications devices.

13.1.1 | Ruby II Organization

The organization of Ruby II is illustrated in Figure 13.1. The chip is based around an ARM core and includes 2 Kbytes of fast (zero wait state) on-chip SRAM. Critical routines can be loaded into the RAM under application control to get the best performance and minimum power consumption. There is a set of peripheral modules which share a number of pins, including a PCMCIA interface, four byte-wide parallel interfaces and two UARTs. A mode select block controls which combination of these interfaces is available at any time, and byte-wide FIFO buffers decouple the processor from having to respond to every byte which is transferred.

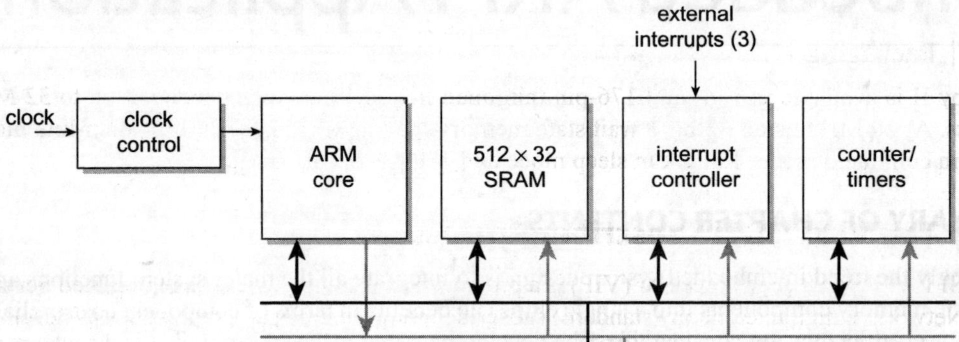

Figure 13.1 Ruby II advanced communication controller organization

A synchronous communications controller module supports a range of standard serial communication protocols, and a serial controller module provides a software-controlled data port which can be used to implement various serial control protocols such as the I²C bus defined by Philips which enables a range of serial devices such as battery-backed RAM, real-time clock, E²PROM and audio codecs to be connected.

The external bus interface supports devices with 8-, 16- and 32-bit data buses and has flexible wait state generation. The counter-timer block has three 8-bit counters connected to a 24-bit prescaler, and an interrupt controller gives programmable control of all on- and off-chip interrupt sources. The chip has four power-management modes:

1. On-line – all circuits are clocked at full speed.
2. Command – the ARM core runs with 1 to 64 wait states but all other circuitry runs at full speed. An interrupt switches the system into on-line mode immediately.
3. Sleep – all circuitry is stopped apart from the timers and oscillators. Particular interrupts return the system to on-line mode.
4. Stopped – all circuits (including the oscillators) are stopped. Particular interrupts return the system to on-line mode.

13.1.2 | Packaging

The Ruby II is available in 144- and 176-pin thin quad flat packs and can operate at up to 32 MHz at 5 volts. At 20 MHz using 32-bit 1 wait state memory the chip consumes 30 mA in on-line mode, 7.9 mA in command mode, 1.5 mA in sleep mode and 150 µA in stop mode.

13.2 | The VLSI ISDN Subscriber Processor

The VLSI ISDN Subscriber Processor (VIP) is a programmable engine for **ISDN** (Integrated Services Digital Network; a digital telephony standard) subscriber communications. The design was developed by Hagenuk GmbH for use in their ISDN product range and subsequently licensed back to VLSI Technology for sale as an **ASSP** (Application Specific Standard Part). It incorporates most of the circuitry required to implement a full-feature ISDN terminal, supporting voice, data and video services down the same digital line. The sort of applications it is targeted at include:

- ISDN terminal equipment, such as domestic and digital PABX telephones, H.320 videophones and integrated PC communications.
- ISDN to **DECT** (Digital European Cordless Telephone) controllers, allowing a number of cordless telephones to link to each other and to an ISDN line for domestic and business use.
- ISDN to PCMCIA communication cards.

The VIP chip incorporates the specialized interfaces required to connect to the ISDN SO-interface, support for telephony interfaces such as a numeric keypad, a number display, a microphone and an earphone, digital links for external signal processors or codecs, and power management features such as a programmable clock and an analogue to digital converter to monitor the battery state.

The ARM6 core performs general control and ISDN protocol functions. A 3 Kbyte on-chip RAM operates without wait states at the full processor clock rate of 36.864 MHz. Critical code routines can be loaded into this RAM as required, for example, the signal processing routines required to support hands-free operation.

13.2.1 | VIP Organization

The organization of the VIP chip is illustrated in Figure 13.2 and a typical system configuration is shown in Figure 13.3.

13.2.2 | Memory Interface

The external memory interface supports 8-, 16- and 32-bit off-chip static RAMs and ROMs and 16- and 32-bit dynamic RAMs. The addressable memory is divided into four ranges, each of which

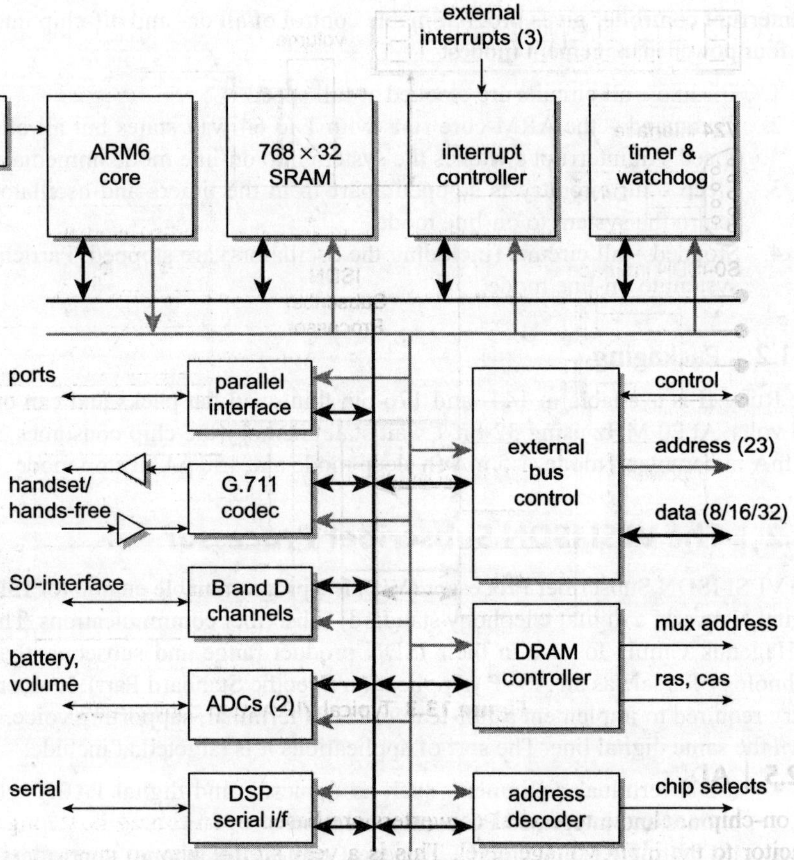

Figure 13.2 VIP organization

operates with a programmable number of wait states (where the minimum is one wait state giving a 54 ns access time).

13.2.3 | S0-Interface

The on-chip ISDN S0-interface allows connection to an S0-interface bus via isolating transformers and surge protection. The on-chip functions include a phase-locked loop for data and clock recovery, framing, and low-level protocols. The 192 kbit/s raw data rate includes two 64 kbit/s B channels and one 16 kbit/s D channel. In telephony applications the B channels carry 8-bit speech samples at an 8 kHz sample rate and the D channel is used for control purposes.

13.2.4 | Codec

The G.711 codec includes an on-chip analogue front end that allows direct connection to both a telephone handset and a hands-free microphone and speaker. The input and output channels have independently programmable gains. The amplification stages have power-down modes to save power when they are inactive.

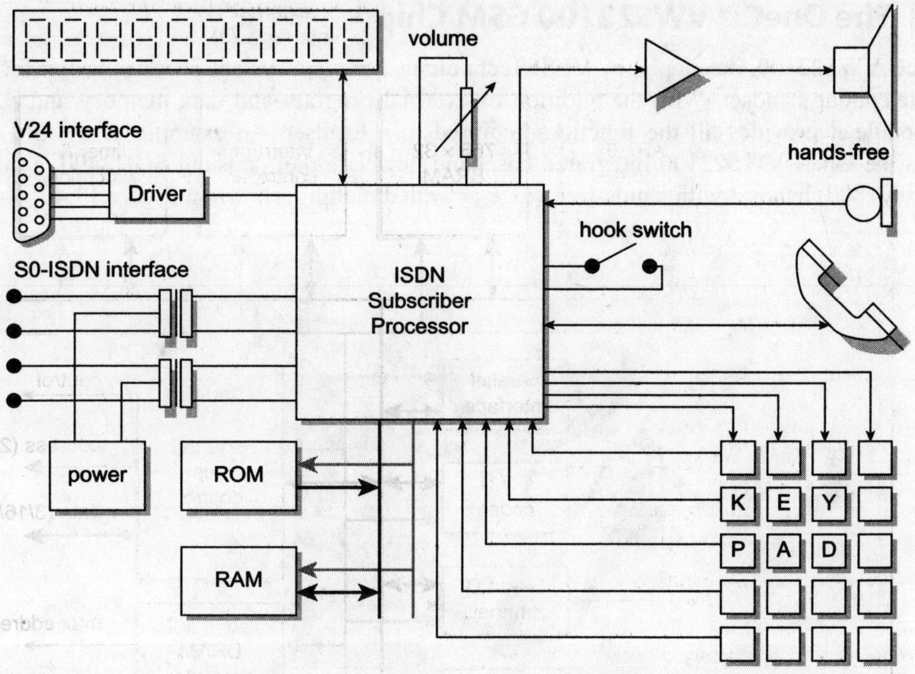

Figure 13.3 Typical VIP system configuration

13.2.5 | ADCs

The on-chip analogue to digital converters are based upon timing how long it takes to discharge a capacitor to the input voltage level. This is a very simple way to measure slowly varying voltages, requiring little more than an on-chip comparator, an output to charge the capacitor at the start of the conversion and a means of measuring the time from the start of the conversion to the point where the comparator switches. Typical uses would be to measure the voltage from a volume control potentiometer or to check the battery voltage in a portable application.

13.2.6 | Keypad Interface

The keyboard interface uses parallel output ports to strobe the columns of the keypad and paralel input ports with internal pull-down resistors to sense the rows. An OR gate on the inputs can generate an interrupt. If all the column outputs are active, any key press will generate an interrupt whereupon the ARM can activate individual columns and sense individual rows to determine the particular key pressed.

13.2.7 | Clocks and Timers

The chip has two clock sources. Normal operation is at 36.864 MHz, with 460.8 kHz used during power-down. A watchdog timer resets the CPU if there is no activity for 1.28 seconds, and a 2.5 ms timer interrupts the processor from sleep mode for DRAM refresh and multitasking purposes.

13.3 | The OneC™ VWS22100 GSM Chip

The OneC VWS22100, developed by VLSI Technology, Inc., is a system-on-chip design for a GSM mobile telephone handset. With the addition of external program and data memory and a suitable radio module it provides all the functions required in a handset. An example of a GSM handset that uses the OneC VWS22100 integrated baseband device is the Samsung SGH2400, a dual-band (GSM 900/1800) handset with hands-free voice-activated dialling, shown in Figure 13.4.

Figure 13.4 Samsung's SGH2400 GSM handset uses the OneC VWS22100

13.3.1 | VWS22100 Organization

The system architecture of the OneC VWS22100 is typical of a controller used in today's mobile phone handsets, incorporating an ARM7TDMI core as a general-purpose controller handling the user interface and certain GSM protocol layers and a DSP core to handle the baseband signal processing aided by some special-purpose signal processing hardware blocks. It is illustrated in Figure 13.5.

13.3.2 | DSP Subsystem

The DSP subsystem (shown in the shaded rectangle in Figure 13.5) is based around the 16-bit Oak DSP core. It performs all the real-time signal processing functions which include:

- voice coding;
- equalization;
- channel coding;
- echo cancellation;
- noise suppression;
- voice recognition;
- data compression.

13.3.3 | ARM7TDMI Subsystem

The ARM7TDMI core is responsible for the system control functions which include:

- the user interface software;
- the GSM protocol stack;

- power management;
- driving the peripheral interfaces;
- running some data applications.

13.3.4 | Duty Allocation

The split of tasks between the ARM and Oak cores can be illustrated by examining some of the details in Figure 13.5.

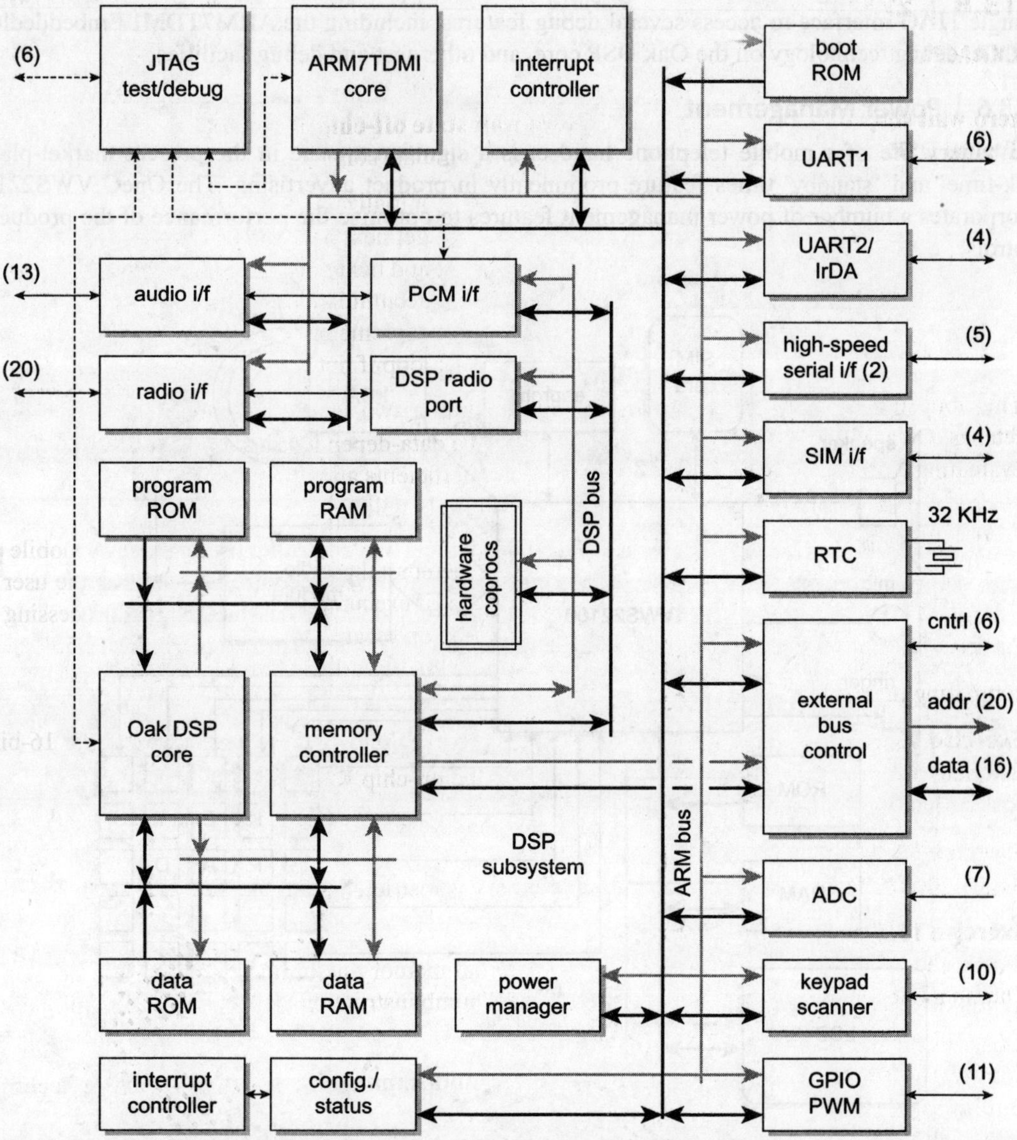

Figure 13.5 OneC VWS22100 GSM chip organization

The audio and radio interfaces (on the left of the figure) are connected to both processing systems. The ARM system sets the gains of the amplifiers, controlling the radio transmission power level and the frequency synthesizers, causing the ringer to inform the user of an incoming call, and so on.

The data streams, which include the encoded voice data and the symbols transmitted and received over the radio link, pass directly between the Oak system and the peripheral interfaces.

13.3.5 | On-chip Debug

There are two heterogeneous processing systems on the chip. The on-chip debug hardware employs a single JTAG interface to access several debug features, including the ARM7TDMI EmbeddedICE module, debug technology on the Oak DSP core, and other test and debug facilities.

13.3.6 | Power Management

The battery life of a mobile telephone handset is a significant issue in the present market-place; 'talk-time' and 'standby' times feature prominently in product advertising. The OneC VWS22100 incorporates a number of power management features to optimize the performance of the product it controls:

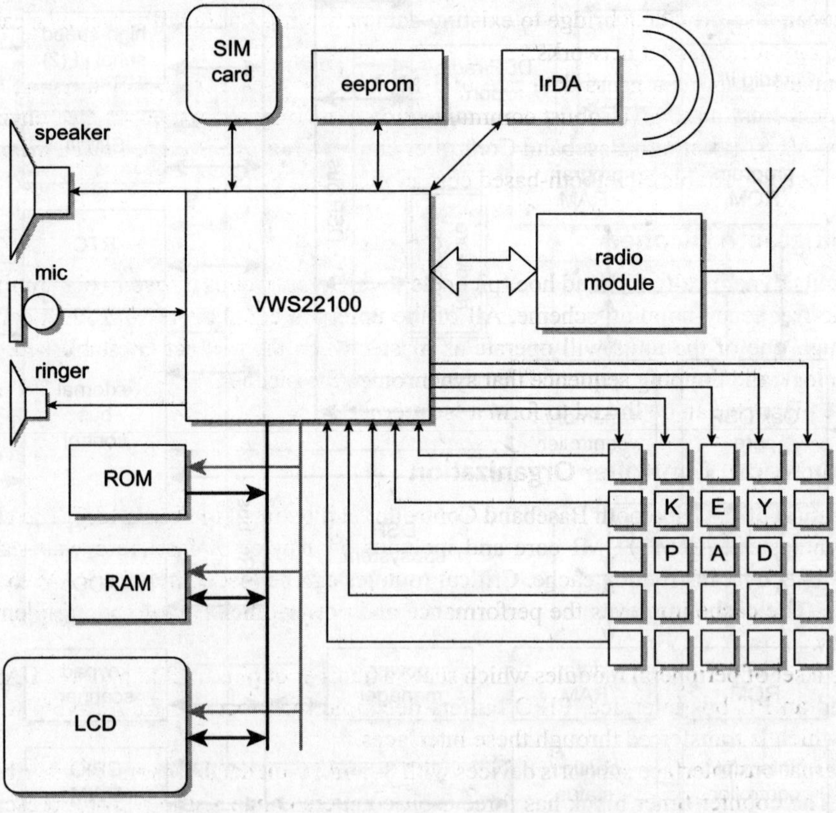

Figure 13.6 Typical GSM handset architecture

- global and selective power-down modes;
- the ability to slow down the system clock in idle mode;
- the analogue circuits also can operate at reduced power;
- the on-chip pulse-width modulation outputs control battery charging;
- the on-chip analogue-to-digital converters (ADCs) provide for the monitoring of the temperature and battery voltage to give optimum operation.

13.3.7 | GSM Handset

The typical hardware architecture of a GSM cellular telephone handset based around the OneC VWS22100 is illustrated in Figure 13.6.

13.4 | The Ericsson-VLSI Bluetooth Baseband Controller

Bluetooth is a de-facto standard for wireless data communication for the 2.4 GHz band developed by a consortium of companies including Ericsson, IBM, Intel, Nokia and Toshiba. The standard is intended to support short-range communication (from 10 cm to 10 m range) in a manner similar to that currently achieved with infrared communication using the IrDA standard, but avoiding the line-of-sight, alignment, and mutual interference restrictions of IrDA. Using radio communication, Bluetooth is intended to support laptop to cellular telephone, printer, PDA, desktop, fax machines, keyboards, and so on, and it can also provide a bridge to existing data networks. As such it serves as a cable replacement technology for personal networks.

The standard supports a gross data rate of 1 Mbit/s, and uses a frequency hopping scheme and forward error correction to give robust communication in a noisy and uncoordinated environment. The Ericsson-VLSI Bluetooth Baseband Controller chip is a jointly developed standard part which is intended for use in portable Bluetooth-based communication devices.

13.4.1 | Bluetooth 'piconet'

Bluetooth units dynamically form ad hoc 'piconets', which are groups of two to eight units that operate the same frequency-hopping scheme. All of the units are equal peers with identical implementations, though one of the units will operate as master when the piconet is established. The master defines the clock and hopping sequence that synchronize the piconet.

Multiple piconets can be linked to form a 'scatternet'.

13.4.2 | Bluetooth Controller Organization

The organization of the Bluetooth Baseband Controller is illustrated in Figure 13.7. The chip is based around a synthesized ARM7TDMI core and includes 64 Kbytes of fast (zero wait state) on-chip SRAM and a 4K byte instruction cache. Critical routines can be loaded into the RAM to get the best performance. The cache improves the performance and power-efficiency of code resident in the off-chip memory.

There is a set of peripheral modules which share a number of pins, including three UARTs, a USB interface and an I^2C-bus interface. FIFO buffers decouple the processor from having to respond to every byte which is transferred through these interfaces.

The external bus interface supports devices with 8- and 16-bit databuses and has flexible wait state generation. The counter timer block has three 8-bit counters connected to a 24-bit prescaler, and an interrupt controller gives control of all on- and off-chip interrupt sources.

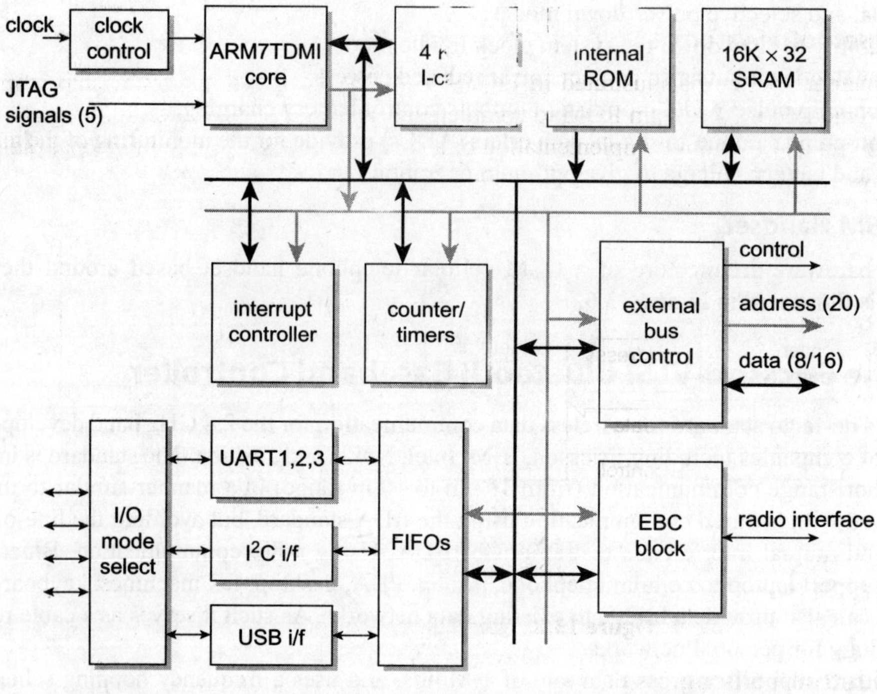

Figure 13.7 Ericsson-VLSI Bluetooth Baseband Controller organization

13.4.3 | Ericsson Bluetooth Core

The Bluetooth Baseband Controller includes a power-optimized hardware block, the Ericsson Bluetooth Core (EBC), which handles all the Link Controller functionality within the Bluetooth specification and includes the interface logic to a Bluetooth radio implementation. The EBC performs all the packet-handling functions for point-to-point, multislot and point-to-multipoint communications.

The baseband protocol uses a combination of circuit and packet switching. Slots can be reserved for synchronous channels, for example to support voice transmission.

13.4.4 | Power Management

The chip has four power management modes:

- On-line: all blocks are clocked at their normal speed. The ARM7TDMI core clock is between 13 and 40 MHz, depending on the application. At the maximum data transfer rate the current consumption is around 30 mA.
- Command: The ARM7TDMI clock is slowed by the insertion of wait states.
- Sleep: The ARM7TDMI clock is stopped, as are the clocks to a programmable subset of the other blocks. The current drawn in this mode is around 0.3 mA.
- Stopped: The clock oscillator is turned off.

13.4.5 Bluetooth System

A typical Bluetooth system is illustrated in Figure 13.8. The baseband controller chip requires an external radio module and program ROM to complete the system. The high level of integration leads to a very compact and economic implementation of a sophisticated and highly functional radio communication system.

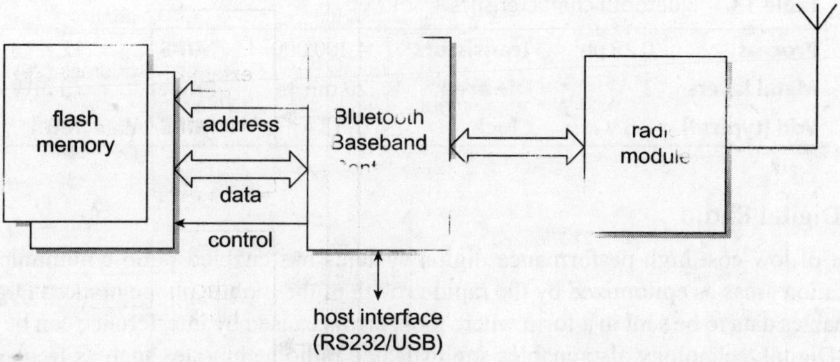

Figure 13.8 Typical Bluetooth application

13.4.6 | Bluetooth Silicon

A photograph of a Bluetooth die is shown in Figure 13.9. The die area is dominated by the 64 Kbyte SRAM, with the synthesized EBC (in the bottom right-hand quadrant) being the second largest block.

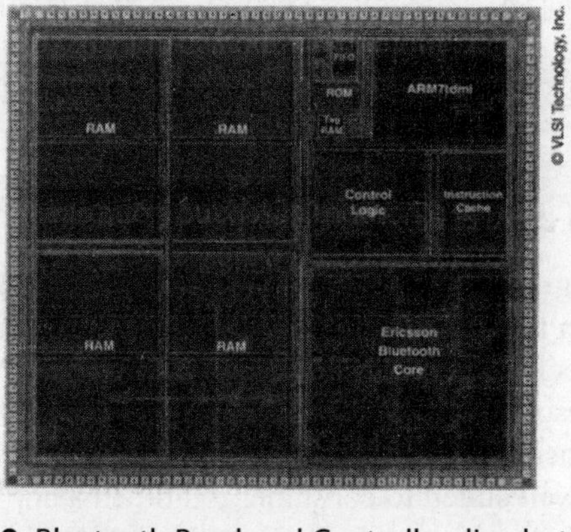

Figure 13.9 Bluetooth Baseband Controller die photograph

The synthesized ARM7TDMI core in the top-right corner of the chip has far less visible structure than the ARM7TDMI hard macrocell shown Figure 9.4 on page 220. This is because the hard macrocell was laid out by hand and manual designers use very regular datapath structures to give dense layout and to minimize the number of different cells that must be created. Synthesized cells use less dense and less regular structures. The advantage of the synthesized core is that it can be ported to a new CMOS process much more rapidly.

The characteristics of the Bluetooth core are summarized in Table 13.1. The processor is capable of operating at up to 39 MHz, but the data shown in the table are representative of a typical GSM application. The chip I/Os operate at 3.3 V, but the core logic typically operates at 2.5 V.

Table 13.1 Bluetooth characteristics

Process	0.25 μn	**Transistors**	4,300,000	**MIPS**	12
Metal layers	3	**Die area**	20 mm^2	**Power**	75 mW
Vdd (typical)	2.5 V	**Clock**	0–13 MHz	**MIPS/W**	160

13.4.7 | Digital Radio

The advent of low-cost high-performance digital systems has enabled radio communication to find new application areas as epitomized by the rapid growth of the mobile phone market. Digital communication enables data to be sent in a form where most errors caused by interference can be detected and corrected. Digital technology also enables sophisticated radio techniques such as frequency hopping to be controlled, further reducing the effects of interference.

Bluetooth extends this advantage to much smaller communication networks and points to a future where not only the individual but also all of their personal data appliances will be invisibly connected to each other and to global networks.

13.4.8 | Bluetooth System-on-chip

The Bluetooth application area has become a focus for activities aimed at integrating digital and radio functions onto a single CMOS chip. The typical application shown in Figure 13.8 can then be implemented on a single chip.

The EBC block is also available as licensable intellectual property for use in other AMBA-based designs.

13.5 | The ARM7500 and ARM7500FE

The ARM7500 is a highly integrated single-chip computer which combines the major components of the Acorn Risc PC (apart from the memory) onto a single chip. It was the first such system chip to employ as its processor macrocell a full ARM CPU, including cache and memory management, rather than just a basic integer processor core. The ARM7500FE adds the FPA10 floating-point coprocessor as an on-chip macrocell, and incorporates a number of other minor changes.

Both of these devices are well suited to consumer multimedia applications such as set-top boxes, Internet appliances and games consoles, but have many other potential application areas.

The principal macrocells on the ARM7500 and ARM7500FE chips are:

- the ARM CPU core;
- the FPA10 floating-point coprocessor (on the ARM7500FE only);
- the video and sound macrocell;
- the memory and I/O controller.

13.5.1 | The ARM CPU Core

The ARM CPU core contains most of the functionality of the ARM710 CPU, the only compromise to allow room for the other macrocells being a reduction in the size of the cache from 8 Kbytes to 4 Kbytes.

The CPU is based around the ARM7 integer core (a forerunner of the ARM7TDMI, without Thumb and embedded debug support), with a 4 Kbyte 4-way set-associative mixed instruction and data cache, a memory management unit based on a 2-level page table with a 64-entry translation look-aside buffer and a write buffer.

13.5.2 | The FPA10 Floating-point Unit

The FPA10 was described in some detail in Section 6.4 on page 141. It provides a significant enhancement of the ability of the system to handle floating-point data types (which, without the coprocessor, would be handled using the ARM floating-point library routines). The floating point performance is up to 6 MFLOPS (measured using the Lin-pack benchmark running double-precision floating point code) at 40 MHz.

13.5.3 | The Video and Sound Macrocell

The video controller can generate displays using a pixel clock of up to 120 MHz (which is generated by a simple off-chip voltage controlled oscillator using an on-chip phase comparator). It includes a 256-entry colour palette with on-chip 8-bit digital-to-analogue converters for each of the red, green and blue outputs and additional control bits for external mixing and fading. A separate hardware cursor is supported, and the output can drive a high-resolution colour monitor or a single- or double-panel grey-scale or colour liquid crystal display. The display timing is fully programmable.

The ARM7500 sound system can generate eight independent channels of 8-bit (logarithmic) analogue stereo sound, played through an on-chip exponential digital-to-analogue converter. Alternatively, 16-bit sound samples can be generated through a serial digital channel and an external CD-quality digital-to-analogue converter. The ARM7500FE only supports the latter 16-bit sound system.

The data channels for the video, cursor and sound streams are generated using the DMA controllers in the memory and I/O controller.

13.5.4 | The Memory and I/O Controller

The memory controller supports the direct connection of up to four banks of DRAM and two banks of ROM. Each bank can be programmed to be 16 or 32 bits wide and the memory controller will make double accesses for 32-bit quantities in 16-bit banks.

The DRAM controller uses page mode accesses for sequential cycles in bursts of up to 256 transfers and supports a range of DRAM refresh modes, and the ROM controller also supports burst-mode where suitable devices are used. Three DMA controllers handle data streams for the video, cursor and sound channels.

The I/O controller manages a 16-bit off-chip I/O bus (which is expandable to 32 bits using external buffers) and a number of on-chip interfaces. The off-chip bus supports simple peripheral devices, intelligent peripheral modules, PC-style peripherals and an interface for PCMCIA cards.

The on-chip interfaces include four analogue comparators which can be used to support four analogue input channels, two serial ports intended for keyboards and/or mice, counter-timers, eight general-purpose open-drain I/O lines and a programmable interrupt controller. Power management facilities are also available.

13.5.5 | System Diagram

There are many variations on how these chips could be used, but a typical system organization is illustrated in Figure 13.10.

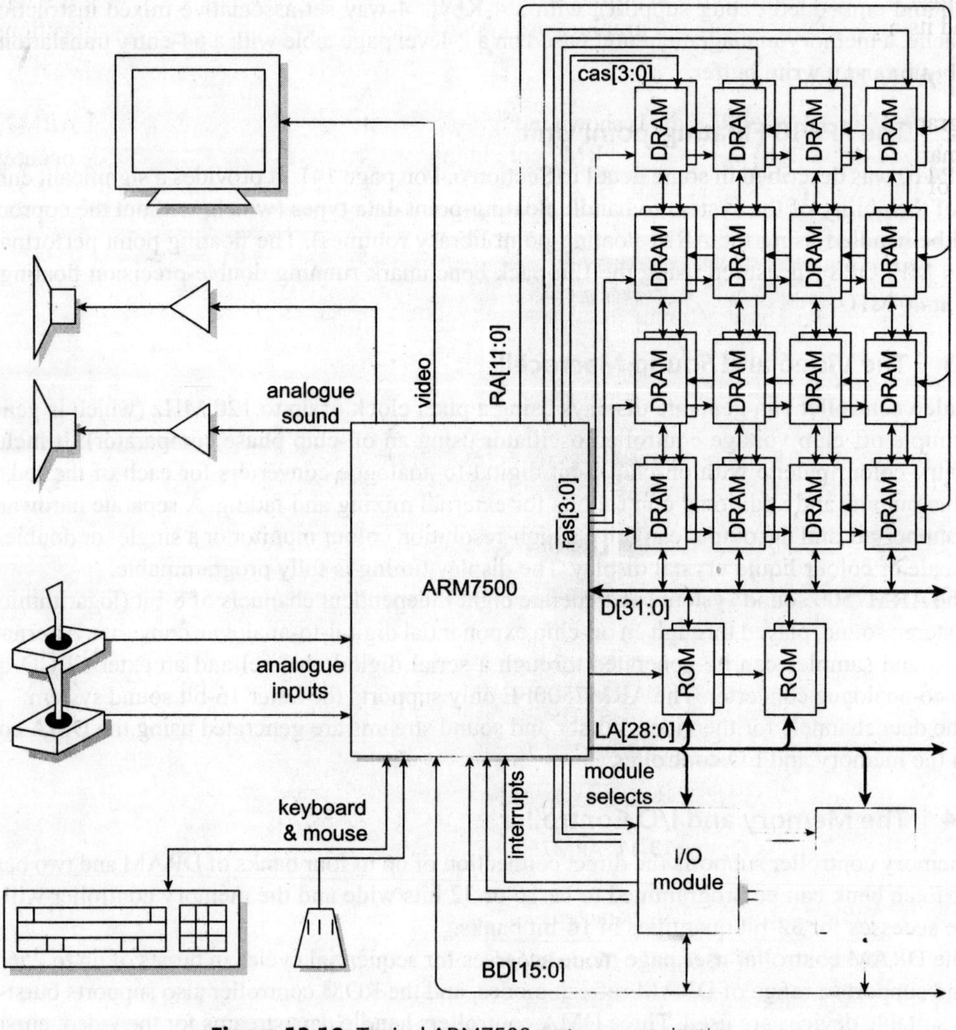

Figure 13.10 Typical ARM7500 system organization

13.5.6 | Applications

The ARM7500 has been used in low-cost versions of the Acorn Risc PC and in the Online Media interactive video set-top box. Its principal limitation compared with the original Risc PC chip set is restricting the video data stream to normal DRAM, whereas high-resolution displays on the standard Risc PC use VRAM. This precludes the use of large numbers of colours on displays with high resolutions, but with LCD displays or monitors of television, VGA or super-VGA resolution the restriction is not apparent. It is only at resolutions of 1,280 × 1,024 and above that the number of colours become restricted because of the bandwidth limitations of standard DRAM.

Since interactive video and games machines use TV quality displays, and portable computers use liquid crystal displays at VGA (640 × 480 pixel) resolution, the ARM7500 is ideally suited to these applications. Its high integration and power-saving features make it suitable for hand-held test equipment, and its high quality sound and graphics are good characteristics for multimedia applications.

13.5.7 | ARM7500 Silicon

A photograph of an ARM7500FE die is shown in Figure 13.11 and the characteristics of the ARM7500 are summarized in Table 13.2. Note the ARM7 core in the upper left-hand corner of the die occupying only 5% of the die area.

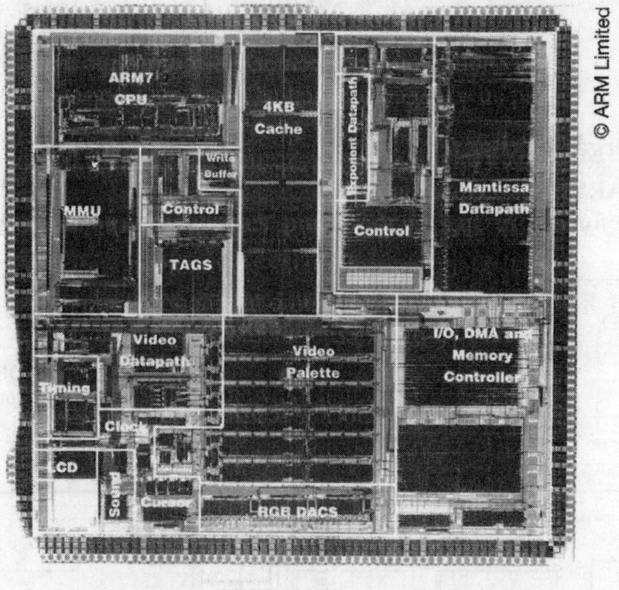

Figure 13.11 ARM7500FE die photograph

Table 13.2 ARM7500 characteristics

Process	0.6 µm	**Transistors**	550,000	**MIPS**	30
Metal layers	2	**Die area**	70 mm²	**Power**	690 mW
Vdd	5 V	**Clock**	0–33 MHz	**MIPS/W**	43

13.6 | The ARM7100

The ARM7100 is a highly integrated microcontroller suited to a range of mobile applications such as smart mobile phones and palm-top computers. It is the basis of the Psion Series 5 range of palm-top computers.

A photograph of the Psion Series 5MX (which uses a later version of the 7100 with a modified architecture and a more advanced process technology) is shown in Figure 13.12.

Figure 13.12 The Psion Series 5MX

13.6.1 | ARM7100 Organization

The organization of the ARM7100 is illustrated in Figure 13.13. The ARM710a CPU incorporates an ARM7 processor core (a forerunner of the ARM7TDMI, without Thumb support), an ARM memory

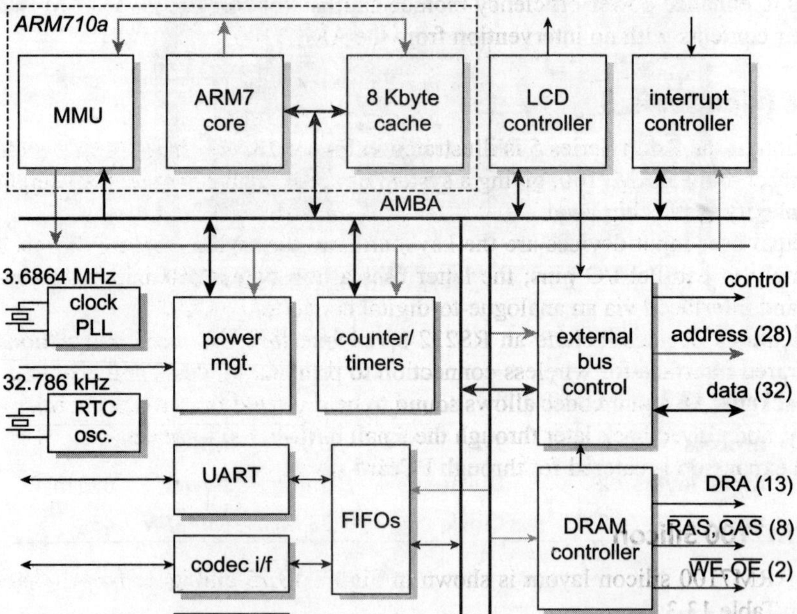

Figure 13.13 ARM7100 organization

management unit, an 8 Kbyte 4-way associative quad-word line cache and a 4-address 8-data word write buffer. The use of a cache memory in this class of product is primarily to improve power-efficiency, which it does by reducing the number of off-chip memory accesses. The incorporation of a memory management unit is required to support the class of operating system required to run the general-purpose application mix.

The system-on-chip organization is based around the AMBA bus. The peripherals include an LCD controller, serial and parallel I/O ports, an interrupt controller, and a 32-bit external bus interface to give efficient access to off-chip ROM, RAM and DRAM. A DRAM controller provides the necessary multiplexed address and control signals needed by this type of memory.

13.6.2 | Power Management

The ARM7100 is intended for use in battery-powered portable equipment where it is expected to deliver high performance in response to user input, but to operate at very low power consumption levels when awaiting user input. To address these requirements the chip has three levels of power management:

- in full operational mode the ARM CPU delivers around 14 MIPS while consuming 24 mA at 3.0 V;
- in idle mode with the CPU stopped but other systems running it consumes 33 mW;
- in standby mode, with only the 32 kHz clock running, it consumes 33 μW.

Other features to enhance power-efficiency include support for self-refresh DRAM memories which will retain their contents with no intervention from the ARM7100.

13.6.3 | The Psion Series 5

The organization of the Psion Series 5 is illustrated in Figure 13.14. This shows how the various user interfaces connect to the ARM7100, giving a system of considerable architectural sophistication with minimal complexity at the chip level.

The principal user input devices are the keyboard and the stylus pointing device. The former is connected simply to parallel I/O pins; the latter uses a transparent digitizing tablet overlaid on the LCD display and interfaced via an analogue-to-digital converter (ADC).

Communications devices include an RS232 serial interface for wired connection and an IrDA compliant infrared interface for wireless connection to printers, modems and host PCs (for software loading and backup). An audio codec allows sound to be digitized from a built-in microphone, stored in the memory, and played back later through the small built-in loud-speaker.

Hardware expansion is catered for through PCcard slots.

13.6.4 | ARM7100 Silicon

A plot of the ARM7100 silicon layout is shown in Figure 13.15 and its principal characteristics are summarized in Table 13.3.

It can be seen from Figure 13.15 that the silicon area is dominated by the CPU core which occupies all but the leftmost quarter of the chip core area. The 8 Kbyte cache RAM occupies the lower half of the CPU core area, with the cache tag store above it to the left, the MMU above that, and the ARM7 core at the top right. All of the peripherals and the AMBA bus are in the leftmost quarter.

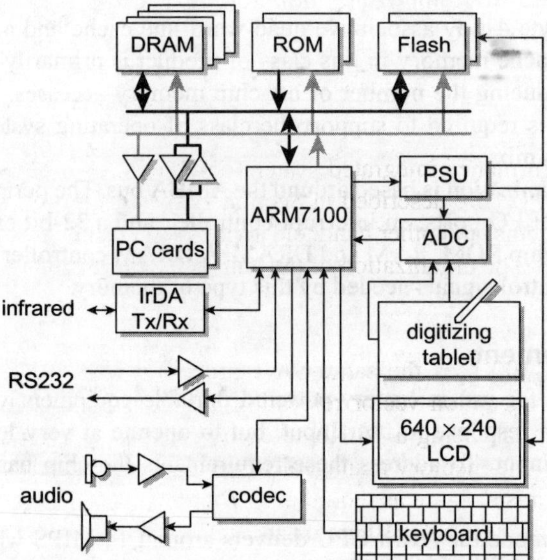

Figure 13.14 The Psion Series 5 hardware organization

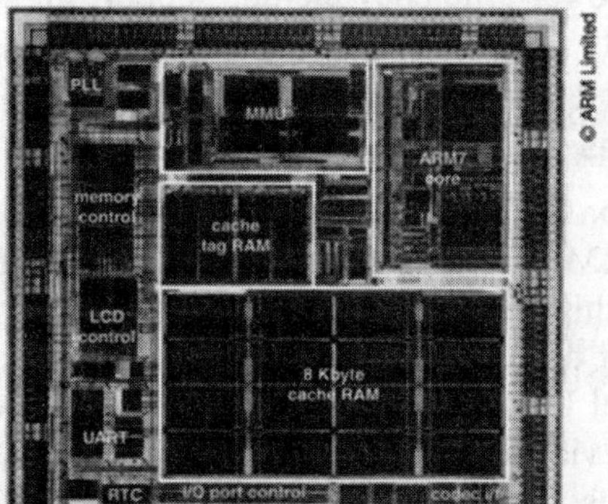

Figure 13.15 ARM7100 die plot

Table 13.3 ARM7100 characteristics

Process	0.6 μm	**Transistors**	N/A	**MIPS**	14
Metal layers	2	**Die area**	N/A mm²	**Power**	24 mW
Vdd	3.0 V	**Clock**	18.432 MHz	**MIPS/W**	580

13.6.5 | Comparison with ARM7500FE

The balance here is different from the ARM7500FE (see Figure 13.11). The high-speed colour look-up table required to drive a CRT monitor on the ARM7500FE occupies more area than does the LCD controller on the ARM7100, and the floating-point hardware on the ARM7500FE also occupies a considerable area. To compensate the ARM7500FE has a half-size cache, but it still occupies a greater area.

13.7 | The SA-1100

The SA-1100 is a high-performance integrated system-on-chip based around a modified version of the SA-110 StrongARM CPU core described in Section 12.3 on page 279. It is intended for use in mobile phone handsets, modems, and other handheld applications that require high performance with minimal power consumption. The organization of the chip is illustrated in Figure 13.16.

13.7.1 | CPU Core

The CPU core on the SA-1100 uses the same SA-1 processor core as the SA-110 with a small modification to support the exception vector relocation mechanism required by Windows CE. The instruction cache is also similar, being a 16 Kbyte cache using a 32–way associative CAM–RAM structure with 8-word lines. The memory management systems are unchanged apart from the inclusion of the ProcessID mechanism, again as required by Windows CE.

The major differences from the SA-110 are on the data cache side, where the original 16 Kbyte cache has been replaced by an 8 Kbyte 32-way associative cache in parallel with a 512 byte 2-way set-associative cache. The memory management tables are used to determine which data cache a particular memory location should be mapped into (if any). The objective of the second 'mini-cache' is to allow large data structures to be cached without causing major pollution of the main data cache.

The other difference on the data cache side is the addition of a read buffer. This unit can be used to pre-load data before the processor requests it so that when it is requested it is available with much reduced latency. The read buffer is software controlled via coprocessor registers.

The final extension to the CPU core is the addition of hardware breakpoint and watchpoint registers, again programmed via coprocessor registers.

13.7.2 | Memory Controller

The memory controller supports up to four banks of 32-bit off-chip DRAM, which may be conventional or of the 'extended data out' (EDO) variety. ROM, flash memory and SRAM are also supported.

Further memory expansion is supported through the PCMCIA interface (which requires some external 'glue' logic), where two card slots are supported.

13.7.3 | System Control

The on-chip system control functions include:

- a reset controller;
- a power management controller that handles low-battery warnings and switches the system between its various operating modes;
- an operating system timer block that supports general timing and watchdog functions;
- an interrupt controller;
- a real-time clock that runs from a 32 KHz crystal source;
- 28 general-purpose I/O pins.

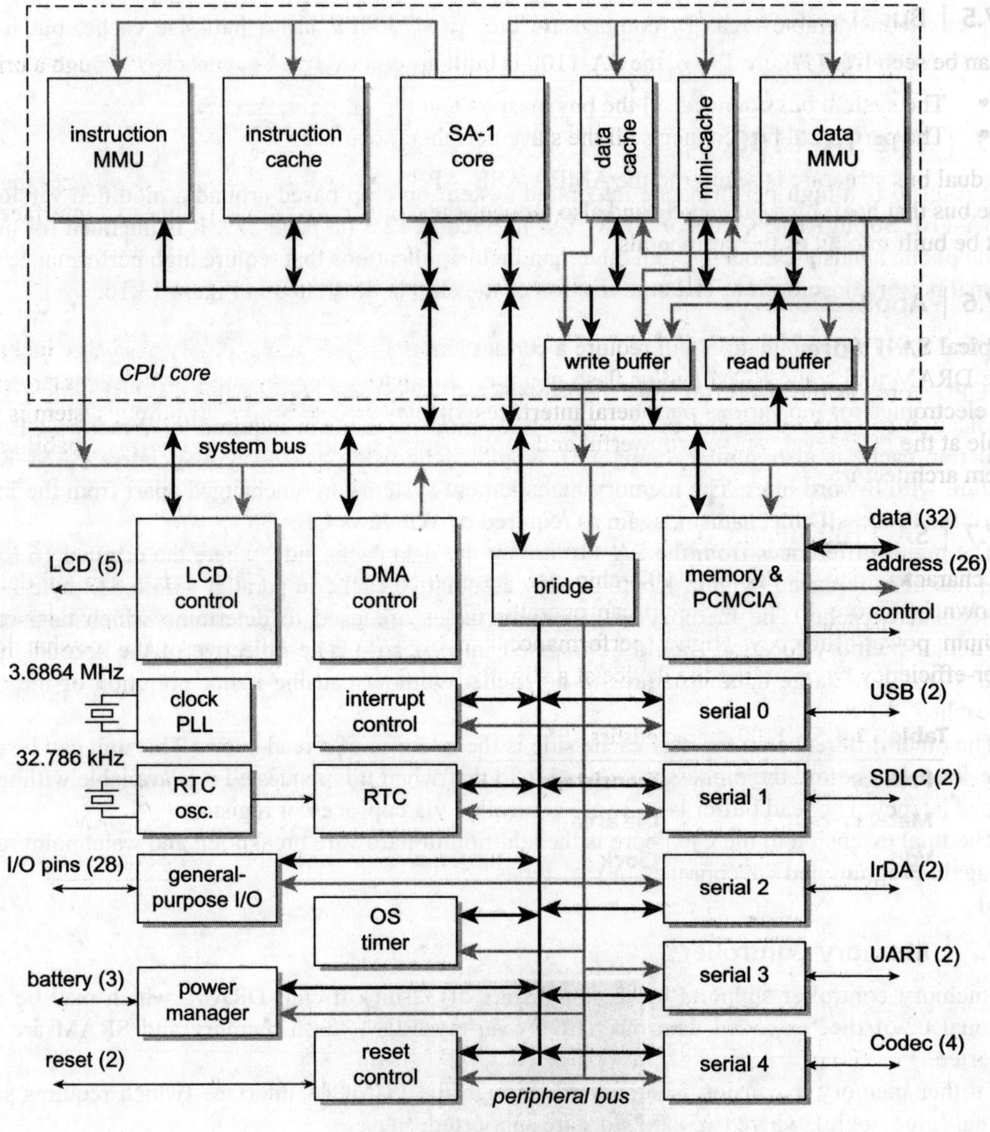

Figure 13.16 SA-1100 organization

13.7.4 | Peripherals

The peripheral subsystem includes an LCD controller and specialized serial ports for USB, SDLC, IrDA, codec and standard UART functions. A 6-channel DMA controller releases the CPU from straightforward data transfer responsibilities.

13.7.5 | Bus Structure

As can be seen from Figure 13.16, the SA-1100 is built around two buses connected through a bridge:

- The system bus connects all the bus masters and the off-chip memory.
- The peripheral bus connects all the slave peripheral devices.

This dual bus structure is similar to the AMBA ASB-APB (or AHB-APB) split. It minimizes the size of the bus that has a high duty cycle and also reduces the complexity and cost of the bus interface that must be built into all of the peripherals.

13.7.6 | Applications

A typical SA-1100 application will require a certain amount of off-chip memory, probably including some DRAM and some ROM and/or flash memory. All that is then required is the necessary interface electronics for the various peripheral interfaces, display, and so on. The resulting system is very simple at the PCB level, yet very powerful and sophisticated in terms of its processing capability and system architecture.

13.7.7 | SA-1100 Silicon

The characteristics of the SA-1100 chip are summarized in Table 13.4 and a plot of the die is shown in Figure 13.17. The chip can operate with a power supply voltage as low as 1.5 V for optimum power-efficiency. Higher performance can be achieved at the cost of somewhat lower power-efficiency by operating the device at a slightly higher supply voltage.

Table 13.4 SA-1100 characteristics

Process	0.35 μm	**Transistors**	2,500,000	**MIPS**	220/250
Metal layers	3	**Die area**	75 mm^2	**Power**	330/550 mW
Vdd	1.5/2 V	**Clock**	190/220 MHz	**MIPS/W**	665/450

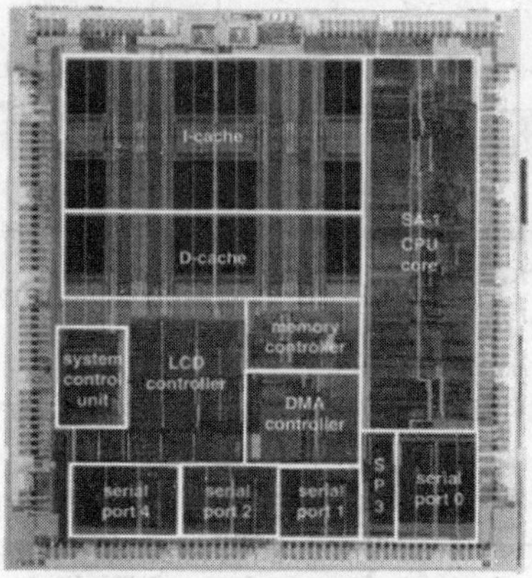

Photo courtesy of Intel Corp.

Figure 13.17 SA–1100 die plot

13.8 | Examples and Exercises

EXAMPLE 13.1

Estimate the performance improvement which results from running a critical DSP routine in zero wait state on-chip RAM instead of two wait state off-chip RAM.

Typical DSP routines are dominated by multiply-accumulate computations. A code sequence might be:

```
                ..                    ; initialize
LOOP    LDR     r0, [r3], #4          ; get next data value
        LDR     rl, [r4], #4          ; and next coefficient
        MLA     r5, r0, rl, r5        ; accumulate next term
        SUBS    r2, r2, #1            ; decrement loop counter
        BNE     LOOP                  ; loop if not finished
```

This loop requires seven instruction fetches (including two in the branch shadow) and two data fetches. On a standard ARM core the multiply takes a data-dependent number of computation cycles, evaluating two bits per cycle. If we assume 16-bit coefficients and order the multiplication so that the coefficient determines the number of cycles, the multiply will require eight internal cycles. Each load also requires an internal cycle.

If the data and coefficients are always in on-chip memory, the loop takes 19 clock cycles if executed from on-chip RAM, with 14 additional wait state cycles if executed from two wait state off-chip RAM. The use of on-chip RAM therefore speeds the loop up by around 75%.

Note that this speed-up is a lot less than the factor three that might be expected from simply comparing memory access speeds.

Exercise 13.1.1

Estimate the power saving that results from using the on-chip RAM. (Assume that on-chip accesses cost 2 nJ and off-chip accesses 10 nJ.)

Exercise 13.1.2

Repeat the estimates assuming the external memory is restricted to 16 bits wide.

Exercise 13.1.3

Repeat the estimates for both 32- and 16-bit external memory assuming that the processor supports Thumb mode (and the program is rewritten to use Thumb instructions) and high-speed multiplication.

EXAMPLE 13.2

Survey the designs presented in this chapter and summarize the power-saving techniques employed on the system chips described here.

Firstly, all the system chips display a high level of integration which saves power whenever two modules on the same chip exchange data.

All the chips are based around an ARM core which is, itself, very power-efficient.

Though none of the chips has enough on-chip memory to remove the need for off-chip memory completely, several have a few kilobytes of on-chip RAM which can be loaded with critical routines to save power (and improve performance).

Several of the chips incorporate clock control circuitry which reduces the clock frequency (or stops the clock altogether) when the chip is not fully loaded, and switches the clock to individual modules off when they are inactive.

The chips are mainly based upon static or pseudo-static CMOS technology where, with a little care, digital circuits only consume power when they switch. Some of the chips also incorporate analogue functions which require continuous bias currents, so these circuits can usually be powered down when they are inactive.

Exercise 13.2.1

In what context does a watch dog timer find use in embedded systems? How exactly does it work?

Exercise 13.2.2

What is the function of the 'real time counter' used as a module in almost all ARM microcontrollers?

Exercise 13.2.3

The ARM7500 has an on-chip cache, AMULET2e (see Section 14.4 on page 330) has on-chip memory which can be configured either as a cache or as directly addressed memory, and Ruby II and VIP simply have directly addressed on-chip memory. Explain the difference between on-chip RAM and an on-chip cache and explain why the designers of these chips made the choices that they did.

14

The AMULET Asynchronous ARM Processors

SUMMARY OF CHAPTER CONTENTS

The AMULET processor cores are fully asynchronous implementations of the ARM architecture, which means that they are self-timed and operate without any externally supplied clock.

Self-timed digital systems have potential advantages in the areas of power-efficiency and electromagnetic compatibility (EMC), but they require a radical redesign of the system architecture if the asynchronous timing framework is to be fully exploited, and designers need to learn a new mind set if they are to work in this style. Support for self-timed design from the tools industry is also lacking.

The AMULET processor cores are research prototypes, developed at the University of Manchester in England, and their commercial future is not yet clear. There is insufficient space in this book to present complete descriptions of them, but they are outlined here since they represent another, very different way to implement the ARM instruction set. See the 'Bibliography' on page 355 for references where further details on AMULET1 and AMULET2e may be found. Fuller details on AMULET3 will be published in due course.

The latest self-timed core, AMULET3, incorporates most of the features found in the clocked ARM cores, including support for the Thumb instruction set, debug hardware, an on-chip macrocell bus which supports system-on-chip modular design, and so on. It brings the asynchronous technology up to the point where it is ready to enter commercial use, and the next few years will tell if this technology has a role to play in the future of the ARM architecture.

14.1 | Self-timed Design

Today, and for the past quarter of a century, virtually all digital design has been based around the use of a global 'clock' signal which controls the operation of all of the components of the system. Complex systems may use multiple clocks, but then each clocked domain is designed as a synchronous subsystem, and the interfaces between the different domains have to be designed very carefully to ensure reliable operation.

Clocks have not always been so dominant. Many of the earliest computers employed control circuits which used local information to control local activity. However, such 'asynchronous' design styles fell out of favour when highly productive design methodologies based around the use of a central clock were developed to match the demands of an industry with access to integrated circuit technologies which offered rapidly increasing transistor resources.

14.1.1 | Clock Problems

Recently, however, clocked design styles have begun to run into practical problems:

- Ever-increasing clock frequencies mean that maintaining global synchrony is getting harder; **clock skew** (the difference in the clock timing at different points on the chip) compromises performance and can ultimately lead to circuit malfunction.
- High clock rates also lead to excessive **power consumption.** The clock distribution network can be responsible for a significant fraction of the total chip power consumption. Although clock-gating techniques can give a degree of control over the activity of the clock net, this is usually coarse-grained and can adversely affect clock skew.
- Global synchrony maximizes supply current transients, causing **electromagnetic interference**. EMC (Electromagnetic compatibility) legislation is becoming more stringent, and increasing clock rates make compliance ever more challenging.

14.1.2 | Motivation for Self-timed Design

For these reasons, asynchronous design techniques have recently attracted renewed interest as they address the above problems as follows:

- There is no problem with **clock skew** because there is no clock.
- An asynchronous design only causes transitions in the circuit in response to a request to carry out useful work, avoiding the continuous drain caused by the clock signal and the overhead of complex power management systems. It can switch instantaneously between zero power dissipation and maximum performance. Since many embedded applications have rapidly varying workloads, an asynchronous processor appears to offer the potential of significant **power savings**.
- Asynchronous circuits emit less **electromagnetic radiation** owing to their less coherent internal activity.

In addition, an asynchronous circuit has the potential to deliver typical rather than worst-case performance since its timing adjusts to actual conditions whereas a clocked circuit must be toleranced for worst-case conditions.

The AMULET series of asynchronous microprocessors was developed at the University of Manchester, in England, as one aspect of the growing global research into asynchronous design. There are other examples of asynchronous microprocessor developed elsewhere which support other instruction set architectures, but only the AMULET processors implement the ARM instruction set.

14.1.3 | Self-timed Signalling

Asynchronous design is a complex discipline with many different facets and many different approaches. It is outside the scope of this book to offer any general introduction to asynchronous design, but a few basic concepts should enable the reader to come to grips with the most important features of the AMULET cores. The foremost of these concepts is the idea of asynchronous communication. How is the flow of data controlled in the absence of any reference clock?

The AMULET designs both use forms of the *Request-Acknowledge* handshake to control the flow of data. The sequence of actions comprising the communication of data from the *Sender* to the *Receiver* is as follows:

1. The Sender places a valid data value onto a bus.
2. The Sender then issues a *Request* event.
3. The Receiver accepts the data when it is ready to do so.
4. The Receiver issues an *Acknowledge* event to the Sender.
5. The Sender may then remove the data from the bus and begin the next communication when it is ready to do so.

The data is passed along the bus using a conventional binary encoding, but there are two ways Request and Acknowledge events may be signalled:

14.1.4 | Transition Signaling

- AMULET1 uses transition encoding where a change in level (either high to low or low to high) signals an event; this is illustrated in Figure 14.1.

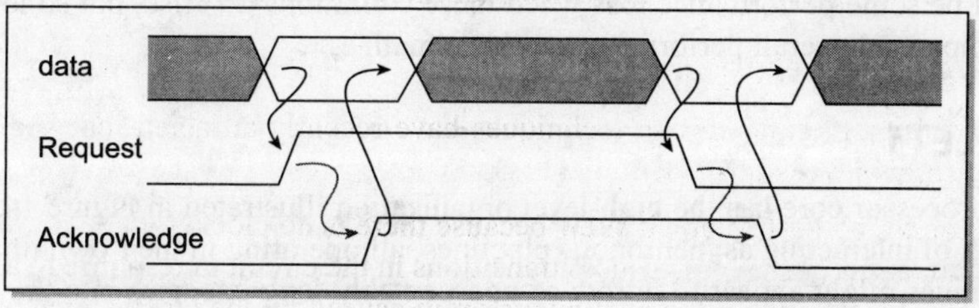

Figure 14.1 Transition-signalling communication protocol

14.1.5 | Level Signalling

- AMULET2 and AMULET3 use level encoding where a rising edge signals an event and a return-to-zero phase must occur before the next event can be signalled; this is illustrated in Figure 14.2.

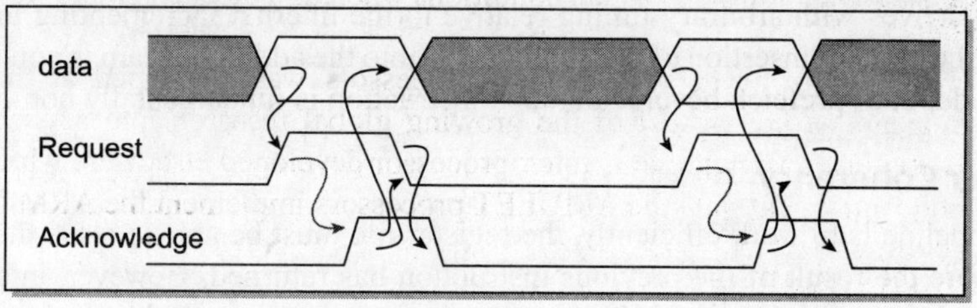

Figure 14.2 Level-signalling communication protocol

Transition signalling was used on AMULET1 since it is conceptually cleaner; every transition has a role and its timing is therefore determined by the circuit's function. It also uses the minimum number of transitions, and should therefore be power-efficient. However, the CMOS circuits used to implement transition control are relatively slow and inefficient, so AMULET2 and AMULET3 use level signalling which employs circuits which are faster and more power-efficient despite using twice the number of transitions, but leave somewhat arbitrary decisions to be taken about the timing of the recovery (return-to-zero) phases in the protocol.

14.1.6 | Self-timed Pipelines

An asynchronous pipelined processing unit can be constructed using self-timing techniques to allow for the processing delay in each stage and one of the above protocols to send the result to the next stage. When the circuit is correctly designed variable processing and external delays can be accommodated; all that matters is the local sequencing of events (though long delays will, of course, lead to low performance).

Unlike a clocked pipeline, where the whole pipeline must always be clocked at a rate determined by the slowest stage under worst-case environmental (voltage and temperature) conditions and assuming worst-case data, an asynchronous pipeline will operate at a variable rate determined by current conditions. It is possible to allow rare worst-case conditions to cause a processing unit to take a little longer. There will be some performance loss when these conditions do arise, but so long as they are rare enough the impact on overall performance will be small.

14.2 | AMULET1

The AMULET1 processor core has the high-level organization illustrated in Figure 14.3. The design is based upon a set of interacting asynchronous pipelines, all operating in their own time at their own speed. These pipelines might appear to introduce unacceptably long latencies into the processor but, unlike a synchronous pipeline, an asynchronous pipeline can have a very low latency.

The operation of the processor begins with the address interface issuing instruction fetch requests to the memory. The address interface has an autonomous address incrementer which enables it to prefetch instructions as far ahead as the capacities of the various pipeline buffers allow.

14.2.1 | Address Non-determinism

Instructions that need to generate a new memory address, such as data transfer instructions and unpredicted branches, calculate the new address in the execution pipeline and then send it to the address interface. Since it arrives with arbitrary timing relative to the internal incrementing loop within the address interface, the point of insertion of the new address into the address stream is non-deterministic, so the processor's depth of prefetch beyond a branch instruction is fundamentally non-deterministic.

14.2.2 | Register Coherency

If the execution pipeline is to work efficiently, the register file must be able to issue the operands for an instruction before the result of the previous instruction has returned. However, in some cases an operand may depend on a preceding result (this is a *read-after-write* hazard), in which case the register file cannot issue the operand until the result has returned unless there is a forwarding mechanism to supply the correct value further down the pipeline.

The register forwarding mechanism used on many RISC processors (including ARM8 and StrongARM) is based upon the characteristics of a synchronous pipeline since it involves comparing

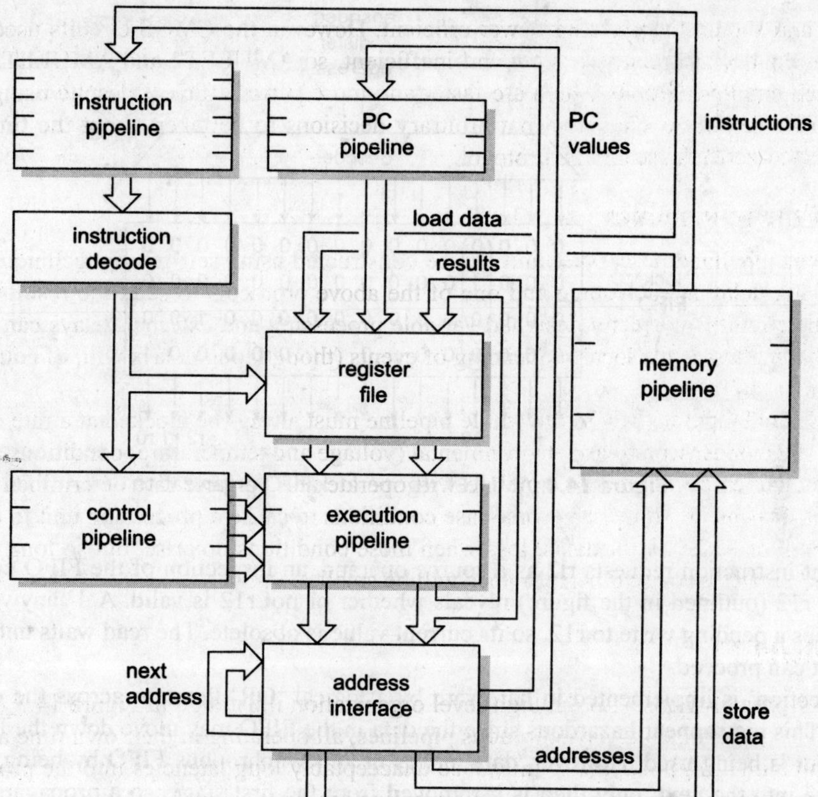

Figure 14.3 AMULET1 internal organization

the source operand register number in one pipeline stage with the destination register number in another stage. In an asynchronous pipeline the stages are all moving at different times and such a comparison can only be made by introducing explicit synchronization between the stages concerned, thereby losing most of the benefits of asynchronous operation.

14.2.3 | Register Locking

On AMULET1 register coherency is achieved through a novel form of register locking, based on a register lock FIFO (first-in-first-out queue). The destination register numbers are stored, in decoded form, in a FIFO, until the associated result is returned from the execution or memory pipeline to the register bank.

The organization of the lock FIFO is illustrated in Figure 14.4. Each stage of the FIFO holds a '1' in the position corresponding to the destination register. In this figure the FIFO controls 16 registers (in AMULET1 the FIFO has a column for each physical register, including the ARM banked registers) and is shown in a state where the first result to arrive will be written into r0, the second into r2, the third into r12 and the fourth FIFO stage is empty.

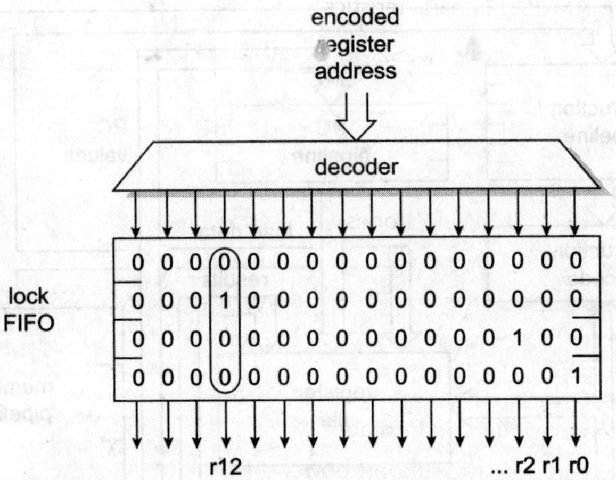

Figure 14.4 AMULET register lock FIFO organization

If a subsequent instruction requests r12 as a source operand, an inspection of the FIFO column corresponding to r12 (outlined in the figure) reveals whether or not r12 is valid. A '1' anywhere in the column signifies a pending write to r12, so its current value is obsolete. The read waits until the '1' is cleared, then it can proceed.

The 'inspection' is implemented in hardware by a logical 'OR' function across the column for each register. This may appear hazardous since the data in the FIFO may move down the FIFO while the 'OR' output is being used. However, data moves in an asynchronous FIFO by being duplicated from one stage into the next, only then is it removed from the first stage, so a propagating '1' will appear alternately in one or two positions and it will never disappear completely. The 'OR' output will therefore be stable even though the data is moving.

AMULET1 depends entirely on the register locking mechanism to maintain register coherency, and as a result the execution pipeline is stalled quite frequently in typical code. (Register dependencies between consecutive instructions are common in typical code since the compiler makes no attempt to avoid them because standard ARM processors are insensitive to such dependencies.)

14.2.4 | AMULET1 Performance

AMULET1 was developed to demonstrate the feasibility of designing a fully asynchronous implementation of a commercial microprocessor architecture. The prototype chips were functional and ran test programs generated using standard ARM development tools. The performance of the prototypes is summarized in Table 14.1, which shows the characteristics of the devices manufactured on two different process technologies by European Silicon Systems (ES2) and GEC Plessey Semiconductors (GPS). The layout of the 1 μm AMULET1 core is shown in Figure 14.5. The performance figures, based on the Dhrystone benchmark, show a performance which is of the same order as, but certainly no better than, an ARM6 processor built on the same process technology. However, AMULET1 was built primarily to demonstrate the feasibility of self-timed design, which it manifestly does.

Table 14.1 AMULET1 characteristics

	AMULET1/ES2	AMULET1/GPS	ARM6
Process	1 μm	0.7 μm	1 μm
Area (mm²)	5.5 × 4.1	3.9 × 2.9	4.1 × 2.7
Transistors	58,374	58,374	33,494
Performance	20.5 kDhrystones	~40 kDhrystones[a]	31 kDhrystones
Multiplier	5.3 ns/bit	3 ns/bit	25 ns/bit
Conditions	5 V, 20°C	5 V, 20°C	5 V, 20 MHz
Power	152 mW	N/A[b]	148 mW
MIPS/W	77	N/A	120

a. Estimated maximum performance.

b. The GPS part does not support power measurement.

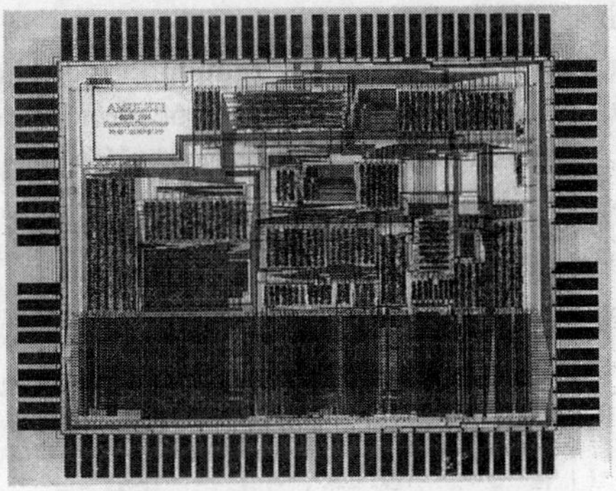

Figure 14.5 AMULET1 die plot

14.3 | AMULET2

AMULET2 is the second-generation asynchronous ARM processor. It employs an organization which is very similar to that used in AMULET1, as illustrated in Figure 14.3. As described earlier, the two-phase (transition) signalling used on AMULET1 was abandoned in favour of four-phase (level) signalling. In addition, a number of organizational features were added to enhance performance.

14.3.1 | AMULET2 Register Forwarding

AMULET2 employs the same register-locking mechanism as AMULET1, but in order to reduce the performance loss due to register dependency stalls, it also incorporates forwarding mechanisms to handle common cases. The bypass mechanisms used in clocked processor pipelines are inapplicable to asynchronous pipelines, so novel techniques are required. The two techniques used on AMULET2 are:

- A *last result* register. The instruction decoder keeps a record of the destination of the result from the execution pipeline, and if the immediately following instruction uses this register as a source operand the register read phase is bypassed and the value is collected from the last result register.

- A *last loaded data* register. The instruction decoder keeps a record of the destination of the last data item loaded from memory, and whenever this register is used as a source operand the register read phase is bypassed and the value is picked up directly from the last loaded data register. A mechanism similar to the lock FIFO serves as a guard on the register to ensure that the correct value is collected.

Both these mechanisms rely on the required result being available; where there is some uncertainty (for example when the result is produced by an instruction which is conditionally executed) the instruction decoder can fall back on the locking mechanism, exploiting the ability of the asynchronous organization to cope with variable delays in the supply of the operands.

14.3.2 | AMULET2 Jump Trace Buffer

AMULET1 prefetches instructions sequentially from the current PC value and all deviations from sequential execution must be issued as corrections from the execution pipeline to the address interface. Every time the PC has to be corrected performance is lost and energy is wasted in prefetching instructions that are then discarded.

AMULET2 attempts to reduce this inefficiency by remembering where branches were previously taken and guessing that control will subsequently follow the same path. The organization of the jump trace buffer is shown in Figure 14.6; it is similar to that used on the MU5 mainframe computer developed at the University of Manchester between 1969 and 1974 (which also operated with asynchronous control).

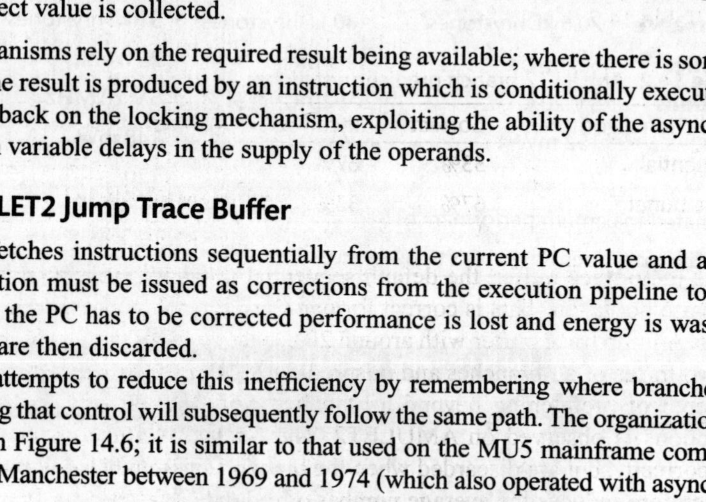

Figure 14.6 The AMULET2 jump trace buffer

The buffer caches the program counters and targets of recently taken branch instructions, and whenever it spots an instruction fetch from an address that it has stored it modifies the predicted control flow from sequential to the previous branch target. If this prediction turns out to be correct, exactly the right instruction sequence is fetched from memory; if it turns out to be wrong and the branch should not have been taken, the branch is executed as an 'unbranch' instruction to return to the previous sequential flow.

14.3.3 | Branch Statistics

The effectiveness of the jump trace buffer depends on the statistics of typical branch behaviour. Typical figures are shown in Table 14.2.

Table 14.2 AMULET2 branch prediction statistics

Prediction algorithm	Correct	Incorrect	Redundant fetches
Sequential	33%	67%	2 per branch (ave.)
Trace buffer	67%	33%	1 per branch (ave.)

In the absence of the jump trace buffer, the default sequential fetch pattern is equivalent to predicting that all branches are not taken. This is correct for one-third of all branches, and incorrect for the remaining two-thirds. A jump trace buffer with around 20 entries reverses these proportions, correctly predicting around two-thirds of all branches and mispredicting or failing to predict around one-third.

Although the depth of prefetching beyond a branch is non-deterministic, a prefetch depth of around three instructions is observed on AMULET2. The fetched instructions are used when the branch is predicted correctly, but are discarded when the branch is mispredicted or not predicted. The jump trace buffer therefore reduces the average number of redundant fetches per branch from two to one. Since branches occur around once every five instructions in typical code, the jump trace buffer may be expected to reduce the instruction fetch bandwidth by around 20% and the total memory bandwidth by 10% to 15%.

Where the system performance is limited by the available memory bandwidth, this saving translates directly into improved performance; in any case it represents a power saving due to the elimination of redundant activity.

14.3.4 | 'Halt'

Unlike some other microprocessors, the ARM does not have an explicit 'Halt' instruction. Instead, when a program can find no more useful work to do it usually enters an idle loop, executing:

```
B    .    ;  loop until interrupted
```

Here the '.' denotes the current PC, so the branch target is the branch instruction itself, and the program sits in this single instruction loop until an interrupt causes it to do something else.

Clearly the processor is doing no useful work while in this idle loop, so any power it uses is wasted. AMULET2 detects the opcode corresponding to a branch which loops to itself and uses this to stall a signal at one point in the asynchronous control network. This stall rapidly propagates throughout the control, bringing the processor to an inactive, zero power state. An active interrupt request releases the stall, enabling the processor to resume normal throughput immediately.

AMULET2 can therefore switch between zero power and maximum throughput states at a very high rate and with no software overhead; indeed, much existing ARM code will give optimum power-efficiency using this scheme even though it was not written with the scheme in mind. This makes the processor very applicable to low-power applications with bursty real-time load characteristics.

14.4 | AMULET2e

AMULET2e is an AMULET2 processor core (see Section 14.3) combined with 4 Kbytes of memory, which can be configured either as a cache or a fixed RAM area, and a flexible memory interface (the *funnel)* which allows 8-, 16- or 32-bit external devices to be connected directly, including memories built from DRAM. The internal organization of AMULET2e is illustrated in Figure 14.7.

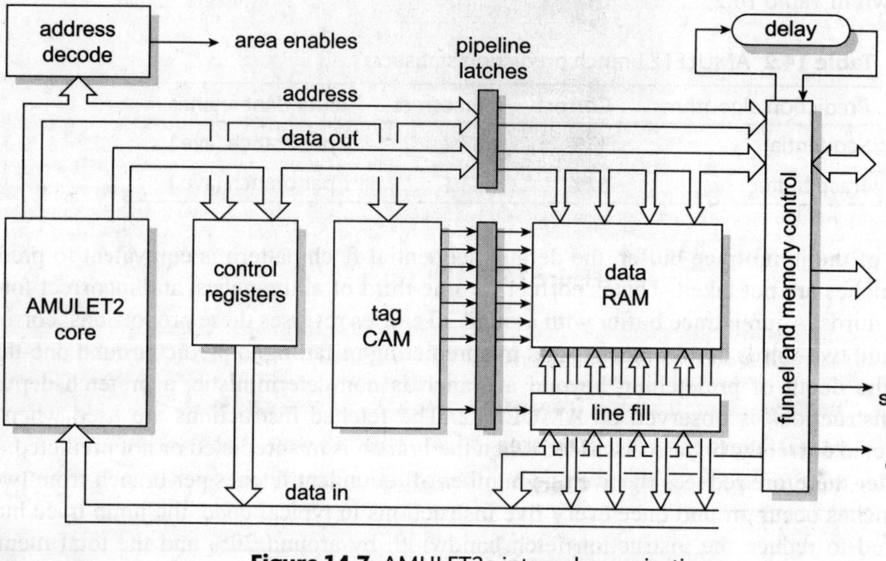

Figure 14.7 AMULET2e internal organization

14.4.1 | AMULET2e Cache

The cache comprises four 1 Kbyte blocks, each of which is a fully associative random replacement store with a quad-word line and block size. A pipeline register between the CAM and the RAM sections allows a following access to begin its CAM look-up while the previous access completes within the RAM; this exploits the ability of the AMULET2 core to issue multiple memory requests before the data is returned from the first. Sequential accesses are detected and bypass the CAM look-up, thereby saving power and improving performance.

Cache line fetches are non-blocking, accessing the addressed item first and then allowing the processor to continue while the rest of the line is fetched. The line fetch automaton continues loading the line fetch buffer while the processor accesses the cache. There is an additional CAM entry that identifies references to the data which is stored in the line fetch buffer. Indeed this data remains in the line fetch buffer where it can be accessed on equal terms to data in the cache until the next cache miss, whereupon the whole buffer is copied into the cache while the new data is loaded from external memory into the line fetch buffer.

14.4.2 | AMULET2e Silicon

A plot of the AMULET2e die is shown in Figure 14.8 and the characteristics of the device are summarized in Table 14.3. The AMULET2 core uses 93,000 transistors, the cache 328,000 and the remainder are in the control logic and pads.

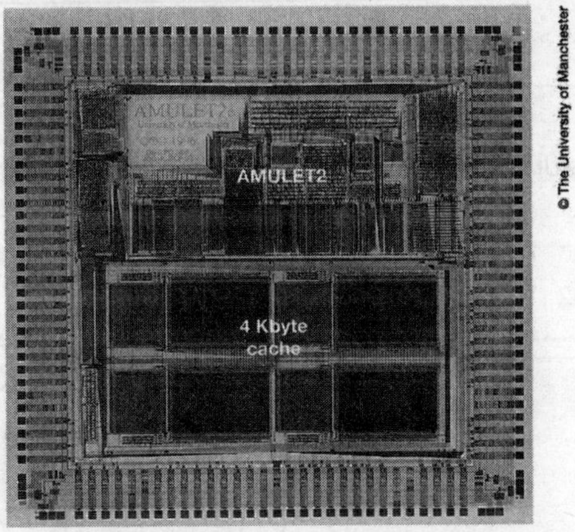

Figure 14.8 AMULET2e die plot

Table 14.3 AMULET2e characteristics

Process	0.5 μm	**Transistors**	454,000	**MIPS**	40
Metal layers	3	**Die area**	41 mm^2	**Power**	140 mW
Vdd	3.3 V	**Clock**	none	**MIPS/W**	285

14.4.3 | Timing Reference

The absence of a reference clock in an asynchronous system makes timing memory accesses an issue that requires careful consideration. The solution incorporated into AMULET2e uses a single external reference delay connected directly to the chip and configuration registers, loaded at start-up, which specify the organization and timing properties of each memory region. The reference delay could, for example, reflect the external SRAM access time, so the RAM will be configured to take one reference delay. The slower ROM may be configured to take several reference delays. (Note that the reference delay is only used for off-chip timing; all on-chip delays are self-timed.)

14.4.4 | AMULET2e Systems

AMULET2e has been configured to make building small systems as straightforward as possible. As an example, Figure 14.9 shows a test card incorporating AMULET2e. The only components, apart from AMULET2e itself, are four SRAM chips, one ROM chip, a UART and an RS232 line interface. The UART uses a crystal oscillator to control its bit rate, but all the system timing functions are controlled by AMULET2e.

The ROM contains the standard ARM 'Angel' code and the host computer at the other end of the RS232 serial line runs the ARM development tools. This system demonstrates that using an asynchronous processor need be no more difficult than using a clocked processor provided that the memory interface has been carefully thought out.

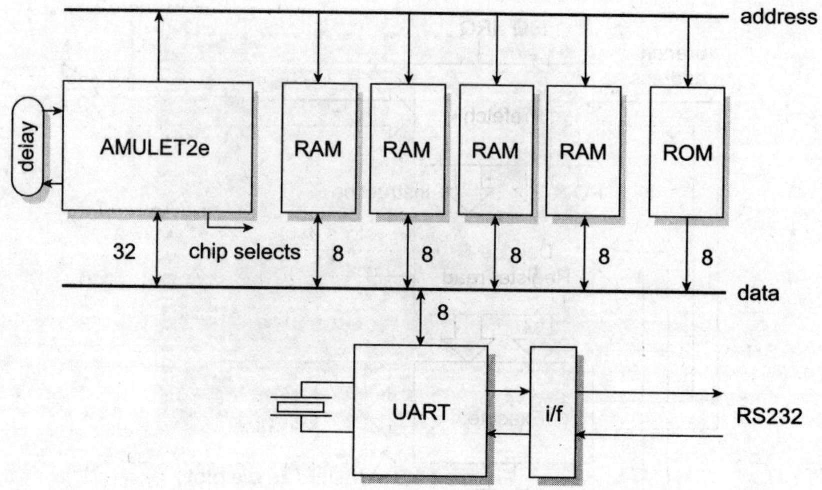

Figure 14.9 AMULET2e test card organization

14.5 | AMULET3

AMULET3 is being developed to establish the commercial viability of asynchronous design. Like its predecessors, AMULET3 is a full-functionality ARM-compatible microprocessor with support for interrupts and memory faults. AMULET1 and AMULET2 implemented the ARM6 architecture (ARM architecture version 3G). AMULET3 supports ARM architecture version 4T, including the 16-bit Thumb instruction set.

14.5.1 | Performance Objective

The objective of the AMULET3 project was to produce an asynchronous implementation of ARM architecture v4T which is competitive in terms of power-efficiency and performance with the ARM9TDMI. This implies a performance target of over 100 MIPS (measured using Dhrystone 2.1) on a 0.35 μm process, compared to the 40 MIPS delivered by AMULET2e on a 0.5 μm process.

Increasing the performance by more than a factor of two requires a radical change to the core organization. As with a clocked processor, the basic approach is based on a combination of increasing the cycle rate of the processor pipeline and decreasing the average number of cycles per instruction. Here, however, the 'cycles' are not defined by an external clock and are not of fixed duration.

14.5.2 | AMULET3 Core Organization

The organization of AMULET3 is illustrated in Figure 14.10. The six principal pipeline stages are as follows:

- the instruction prefetch unit, which includes a branch target buffer;
- the instruction decode, register read and forwarding stage;
- the execute stage, which includes the shifter, multiplier and ALU;
- the data memory interface;
- the reorder buffer;
- the register result write-back stage.

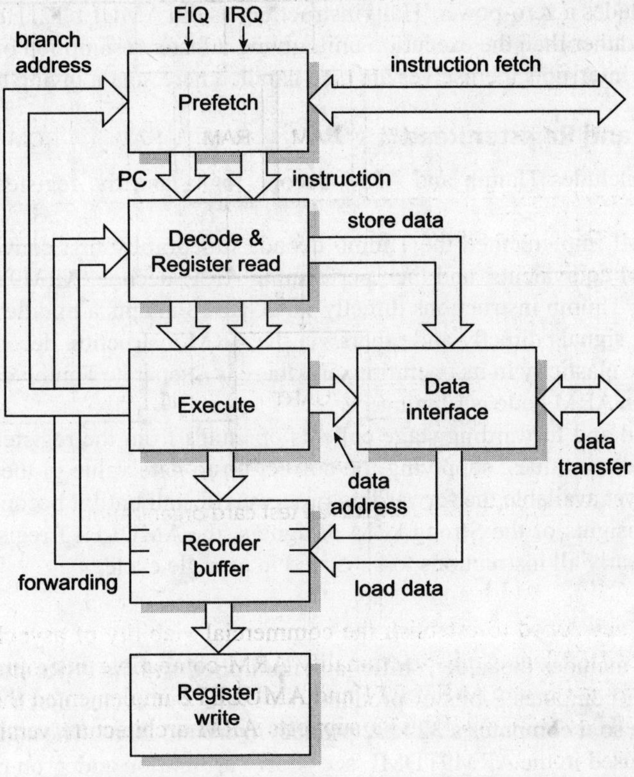

Figure 14.10 AMULET3 core organization

The core employs a Harvard architecture (separate instruction and data memory ports) which provides the higher memory bandwidth required to support higher performance. Only those instructions that require data memory access (loads and stores) pass through the data memory, so the pipeline depth is greater for these instructions than, for example, for simple data processing instructions.

Further details on each of the pipeline stages are given below.

14.5.3 | Instruction Prefetch Unit

The prefetch unit operates autonomously, fetching 32-bit (one ARM or two Thumb) instruction packets from memory whenever it has room to store them.

It incorporates a branch prediction unit that is similar to the jump trace buffer used in AMULET2, but has extensions to support branch prediction in Thumb code. A two- instruction Thumb packet may contain zero, one or two branch instructions, and the branch predictor must handle all of these cases. When executing Thumb code the 16-entry branch prediction unit works in two 8-entry halves, with branches at even half-word addresses being stored in one half and branches at odd half-word addresses in the other. A packet with a branch in each half word may 'hit' in both halves, whereupon the target of the first instruction (at the even address) takes priority.

AMULET3 includes a zero-power 'Halt' instruction, as did AMULET2. Here the halt takes effect in the prefetch unit rather than the execution unit, giving a faster resumption of full throughput when an interrupt occurs. Interrupts themselves are also handled here, again giving reduced latency.

14.5.4 | Decode and Register Read

The decode stage includes Thumb and ARM decode logic, and the register read and forwarding mechanisms.

The ARM7TDMI implemented the Thumb decode function by first converting Thumb instructions into their ARM equivalents, and then performing ARM decode. ARM9TDMI reduced decode latency by decoding Thumb instructions directly. AMULET3 adopts a middle way, decoding certain time-critical control signals directly and others via the ARM instruction decoder. The asynchronous pipeline allows some elasticity in its operation, and there is a separate Thumb decode stage that effectively collapses when ARM code is running.

The register read and forwarding stage collects operands from the register file and searches the reorder buffer for newer values, supplying the correct up-to-date value to the execution unit. If the correct value is not yet available the forwarding process will stall until it becomes available.

Following the insights of the StrongARM designers, the AMULET3 register file has three read ports. This allows nearly all instructions to be issued in a single cycle.

14.5.5 | Execute

The execution stage includes the adder, shifter and multiplier, and the PSRs also fit logically into this stage. The multiplier computes 8 bits of product in a cycle, but cycles much faster than the typical processor cycle time so it computes a 32×32 product in around 20 ns. The adder uses the carry arbitration scheme also used in the ARM9TDMI (see 'Carry arbitration adder' on page 78).

14.5.6 | Data Memory Interface

The data memory interface operates as a separate pipeline stage in load and store instructions but is bypassed by other types of instruction. A load that addresses a slow memory location will therefore not hold up other instructions in the pipeline, provided that they do not use the loaded value.

14.5.7 | Reorder Buffer

The reorder buffer accepts results from the execution unit and the data memory interface in the order that they become available and stores them until they can be written back to the register file in program order. Once a result is in the reorder buffer it is available for forwarding to any instruction that needs it.

The structure used to achieve this functionality is illustrated in Figure 14.11. The buffer has four 'slots', and a slot is allocated to each result produced by an instruction when that instruction is issued. (Slots are also allocated to 'store' instructions so that memory faults can be handled correctly.) As soon as the result is available it is moved into its slot.

Forwarding from the reorder buffer requires a search of the buffer contents. Conditional ARM instructions may or may not return valid results to the buffer; multiple instructions may use the same destination register. Identifying the most up-to-date value for a particular register potentially requires waiting for a result to become available in a slot, seeing that it is invalid, and then (worst case) searching all the other slots in series. This case is rare, though, and is easily accommodated by the asynchronous timing framework.

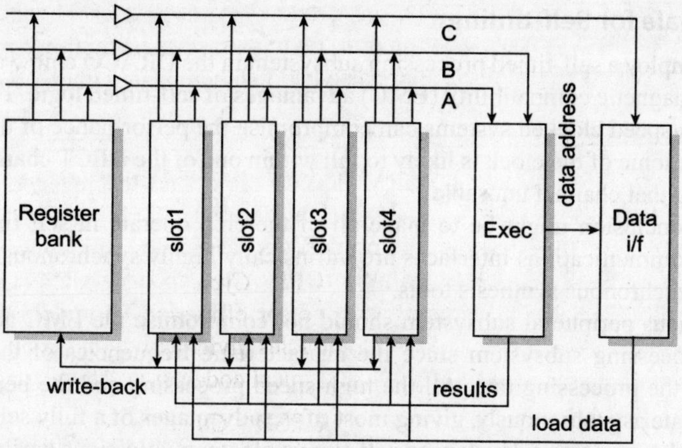

Figure 14.11 The AMULET3 reorder buffer organization

14.5.8 | Register Write

The write-back stream delivered by the reorder buffer is in program order, so this stage of the pipeline simply delivers values to the register file, checking each one for validity and looking for any memory faults. If a fault is detected an exception is raised and subsequent results are discarded until the exception handling mechanism has activated.

14.5.9 | AMULET3 Performance

The performance characteristics of AMULET3 are summarized in Table 14.4. It can be seen that the objective of achieving comparability with the ARM9TDMI on the same process has been met.

AMULET3 has been used as the processing core in the DRACO telecommunications controller; this is the subject of the next section.

Table 14.4 AMULET3 characteristics

Process	0.35 µm	**Transistors**	113,000	**MIPS**	120
Metal layers	3	**Core area**	3 mm²	**Power**	154 mW
Vdd	3.3 V	**Clock**	none	**MIPS/W**	780

14.6 | The DRACO Telecommunications Controller

The DRACO (DECT Radio Communications Controller) chip is the first commercial design based on AMULET technology; it uses the AMULET3H self-timed processing subsystem described later in this section as its compute and control engine.

DRACO was developed in collaboration between Hagenuk GmbH (who designed the clocked telecommunications peripherals) and the University of Manchester (who were responsible for the AMULET3H subsystem) with funding from the European Union.

14.6.1 | Rationale for Self-timing

The decision to employ a self-timed processing subsystem in the DRACO chip was influenced primarily by the electromagnetic compatibility (EMC) advantages of self-timed logic. The radio interference generated by high-speed clocked systems can compromise the performance of the DECT radio communication; a harmonic of the clock is likely to fall within one of the DECT channel frequency bands, possibly rendering that channel unusable.

The logical conclusion might be to make all of the chip operate in self-timed logic. However, many of the telecommunications interfaces are intrinsically highly synchronous and are much easier to design using synchronous synthesis tools.

The synchronous peripheral subsystem should not compromise the EMC advantages offered by the self-timed processing subsystem since the characteristic frequencies of the peripherals are all much lower than the processing rate. All the high-speed processing and the heavily loaded external memory bus operate asynchronously, giving most of the advantages of a fully self-timed system without incurring the design cost of developing self-timed telecommunications peripherals.

14.6.2 | DRACO Functions

The DRACO chip includes the following functions in the synchronous peripheral subsystem:

- an ISDN controller with a 16 Kbit/s HDLC controller and transformerless analogue ISDN interfaces;
- a DECT radio interface baseband controller and analogue interface to the DECT radio subsystem;
- a DECT encryption engine;
- a four-channel full-duplex ADPCM/PCM conversion signal processor;
- 8 Kbytes of shared RAM used for buffer space by the DECT controller;
- a telecommunications codec with an analogue front-end for speech input and output which could alternatively be used for an analogue telecommunications port;
- two high-speed UARTs with an IrDA interface that can be used by either UART;
- an interrupt controller;
- counter-timers and a watchdog timer;
- a 2 Mbit/s IOM2 highway controller with programmable switching functionality;
- an I^2C interface;
- an analogue-to-digital converter (ADC) interface;
- 65 flexible I/O ports including an 8-bit parallel port with handshake capability;
- 2 general-purpose pulse-width modulation controllers;
- an on-chip clock oscillator produces 36.864 MHz, and on-chip phase-locked loops produce the 12.288 MHz master clock required by the ISDN interface and the 13.824 MHz master clock required by the DECT controller;
- an ISDN-DECT synchronizer phase-locked loop avoids bit loss in data transfers between the ISDN and DECT clock domains;
- the clock system has power-down features.

In addition, the self-timed AMULET3H processing subsystem incorporates:

- a 100 MIPS AMULET3 32-bit processor that implements ARM architecture v4T (including the Thumb 16-bit compressed instruction set) with debug hardware;
- 8 Kbytes of dual-port high-speed RAM (local to the processor);

- a self-timed on-chip bus with a bridge to the synchronous on-chip bus that connects the synchronous peripherals;
- a 32-channel DMA controller;
- 16 Kbytes of ROM holding standard telecommunications application software;
- an asynchronous event-driven load module that holds the processor in zero-power wait mode while an analogue-to-digital conversion completes, thereby synchronizing the software to external data rates;
- a programmable external memory interface that supports the direct connection of SRAM, DRAM and flash memory;
- an on-chip reference delay line calibrated by software to control off-chip memory access timings.

14.6.3 | AMULET3H

AMULET3H is a subsystem based around an AMULET3 core that forms an asynchronous 'island' at the heart of the DRACO telecommunications controller in which it is interfaced to a range of synchronous peripheral controllers. To reap the benefits of asynchronous operation the core must have access to some memory that operates asynchronously, and there are significant electromagnetic compatibility benefits in having off-chip memory also operate asynchronously.

14.6.4 | MARBLE On-chip Bus

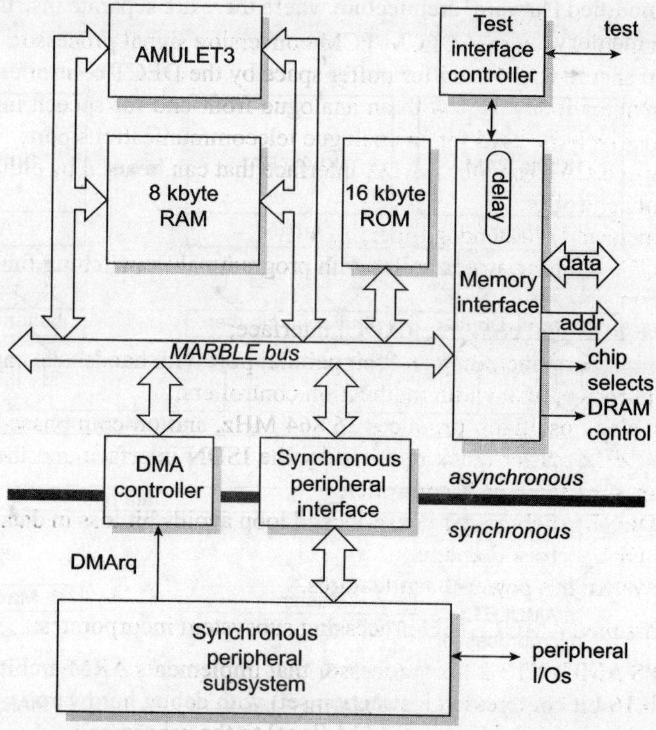

Figure 14.12 The AMULET3H asynchronous subsystem

The organization of the asynchronous subsystem is illustrated in Figure 14.12. The AMULET3 core is connected directly to a dual-ported RAM (discussed further below) and then to the MARBLE on-chip bus. MARBLE is similar in concept to ARM's AMBA bus, the major difference being that it does not use a clock signal. Its transfer mechanism is based around a split transaction primitive.

System components other than the local RAM are accessed via the MARBLE bus. These include on-chip ROM, a DMA controller, a bridge to the synchronous bus where the application-specific peripheral controllers reside, and an interface to external memory.

14.6.5 | External Memory Interface

The external memory interface presents a conventional set of signals for off-chip devices. It is similar to the AMULET2e interface (see Section 14.4), being highly configurable and using a reference delay to time external accesses.

Instead of using an off-chip reference delay, however, AMULET3H has an on-chip delay which can be calibrated by software against a timing reference, perhaps using a timer/counter in the synchronous peripheral subsystem for this purpose.

Off-chip DRAM is supported directly, as are conventional ROM, SRAM and memory-mapped peripheral devices.

14.6.6 | AMULET3H Memory Organization

The AMULET3 processor core has separate address and data buses for instruction and data memory accesses. This would normally require separate instruction and data memories; RISC systems frequently employ a 'modified Harvard' architecture where there are separate instruction and data caches with a unified main memory.

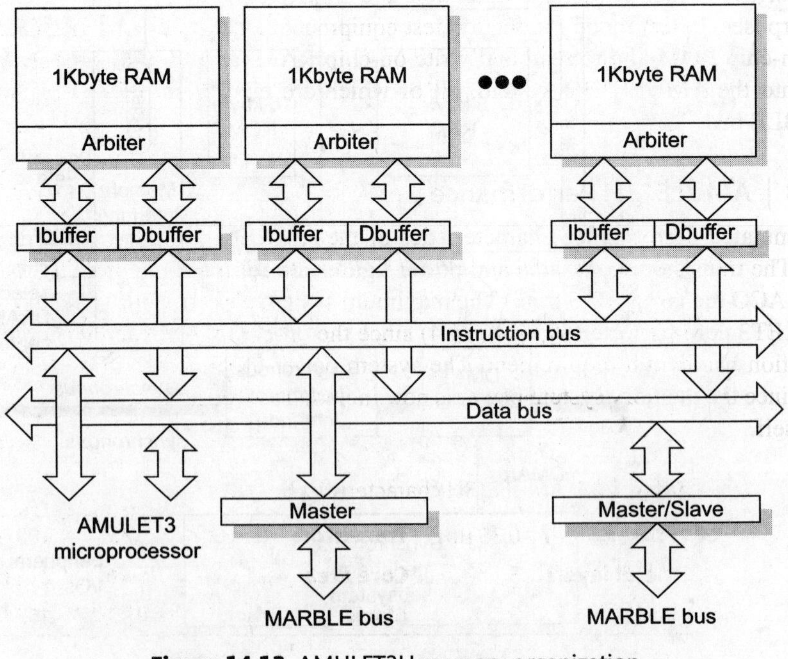

Figure 14.13 AMULET3H memory organization

The AMULET3H controller employs direct-mapped RAM rather than cache memory as this is more cost-effective and has more deterministic behaviour for realtime applications. It also avoids separate instruction and data memories (and the associated difficulties of keeping them coherent) through the use of a dual-ported memory structure (see Figure 14.13). Dual-porting the memory at the individual bit level would be too costly, so instead the memory is divided into eight 1 Kbyte blocks, each of which has two ports which are arbitrated internally. When concurrent data and instruction accesses are to different RAM blocks, each can proceed unimpeded by the other; when they happen to conflict on the same block, one access will suffer a delay while it waits for the other to complete.

Conflicts (and average memory access times) are further reduced by including separate quad-word instruction and data buffers in each RAM block. Each access to a block first checks to see whether the required data is in the buffer. Only if it is not must the RAM be interrogated, with a risk of conflict. Simulations suggest that about 60% of instruction fetches may be satisfied from within these buffers and many short, time-critical loops will run entirely from them.

These buffers, in effect, form simple 128-byte first-level caches in front of the RAM blocks. This is a particularly apt analogy when it is observed that the avoidance of the RAM array results in a faster read cycle, an occurrence which is accepted automatically by the asynchronous pipeline.

14.6.7 | Test Interface Controller

AMULET3H is being developed for commercial use and must therefore be testable in production. There are many features in the design to ensure that this is possible, the most visible of which is the test interface controller (see Figure 14.12). This extension to the external memory interface logic follows the example set by AMBA (see "Test interface" on page 189) in enabling the external memory interface, which in normal operation is a MARBLE slave, to become a MARBLE master for test purposes. In test mode production test equipment can become a MARBLE master, allowing it to read on-chip ROM and to read and write on-chip RAM, and to access the many other test facilities built into the AMULET3H system, all of which are controlled via test registers connected to the MARBLE bus.

14.6.8 | AMULET3H Performance

The simulated performance characteristics of the AMULET3H subsystem are summarized in Table 14.5. (The transistor count, area and power figures are for the asynchronous subsystem only. Overall the DRACO die is 7.8 × 7.3 mm.) The maximum system performance is slightly lower than that of the AMULET3 core (reported in Table 14.4) since the on-chip RAM cannot supply the processor's peak instruction bandwidth requirement. The system power-efficiency is lower than that of the processor alone since the memory system power is now included as well as the power consumed by the processor core itself.

Table 14.5 AMULET3H characteristics

Process	0.35 μm	**Transistors**	825,000	**MIPS**	100
Metal layers	3	**Core area**	21 mm^2	**Power**	215 mW
Vdd	3.3 V	**Clock**	none	**MIPS/W**	465

It can be seen that the AMULET3H subsystem is competitive with the equivalent clocked ARM systems in terms of performance and power-efficiency. It has the advantages of better electromagnetic interference and system power management properties. Against these advantages must be weighed the present shortcomings in the available tool support for asynchronous design.

14.6.9 | DRACO Applications

The DRACO chip can be used in a number of telecommunications applications. A typical application is a combined ISDN terminal and DECT base-station which would enable a number of users to communicate with each other using cordless DECT handsets and to connect to the telecommunications network via the ISDN line or a cordless ISDN network terminator. The principal target market for the chip is in cordless DECT data applications.

14.6.10 | DRACO Silicon

A plot of the DRACO silicon layout is shown in Figure 14.14. The AMULET3H asynchronous subsystem occupies the bottom half of the core area; the synchronous telecommunications peripherals occupy the top half. First silicon was fabricated early in 2000.

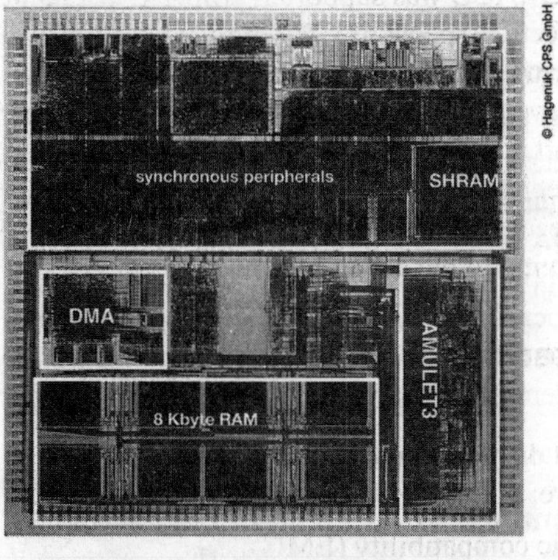

Figure 14.14 DRACO die plot

14.7 | A self-timed Future?

Although AMULET3 will be used commercially the AMULET programme has, so far, been primarily of a research nature, and there is no immediate prospect of the AMULET cores replacing the clocked ARM cores in widespread use. However, there is a resurgence of world-wide interest in the potential of asynchronous design styles to save power, to improve electromagnetic compatibility, and to offer a more modular approach to the design of computing hardware.

The power savings which result from removing the global clock, leaving each subsystem to perform its own timing functions whenever it has useful work to perform, are clear in theory but there are few demonstrations that the benefits can be realized in practice with circuits of sufficient complexity to be commercially interesting. The AMULET research is aimed directly at adding to the body of convincing demonstrations of the merits of asynchronous technology.

An obstacle to the widespread adoption of self-timed design styles is the knowledge-base of the existing design community. Most IC designers have been trained to have a strong aversion to asynchronous circuits because of the difficulties that were experienced by the designers of some early asynchronous computers. These difficulties resulted from an undisciplined approach to self-timed design, and modern developments offer asynchronous design frameworks which overcome most of the problems inherent in what is, admittedly, a more anarchic approach to logic design than that offered within the clocked framework.

The next few years will tell whether or not AMULET and similar developments around the world can demonstrate the sort of advantages that will cause designers to throw away most of their past education and learn a new way to perform their duties.

14.7.1 | AMULET Support

AMULET1 was developed using European Community funding within the Open Microprocessor systems Initiative- Microprocessor Architecture Project (OMI-MAP). AMULET2 was developed within the Open Microprocessor systems Initiative - Deeply Embedded ARM (OMI-DE/ARM) project. The development of AMULET3 and DRACO was supported primarily within the European Union funded OMI-DE2 and OMI-ATOM projects. Aspects of the work have benefited from support from the UK government through the Engineering and Physical Sciences Research Council (EPSRC) in the form of PhD studentships and the tools development funded under ROPA grant GR/K61913.

The work also received support in various forms from ARM Limited, GEC Plessey Semiconductors (now part of MITEL) and VLSI Technology, Inc. Tools from Compass Design Automation (now part of Avant!) were important to the success of both projects, and TimeMill from EPIC Design Technology, Inc. (now part of Synopsys) was vital to the accurate modelling of AMULET2 and AMULET3.

14.8 | Example and Exercises

EXAMPLE 14.1

Summarize the advantages and disadvantages of self-timed design.

The advantages discussed here are:

- improved electromagnetic compatibility (EMC);
- improved power-efficiency;
- improved design modularity;
- the removal of the clock-skew problem;
- the potential for typical rather than worst-case performance.

The disadvantages are:

- the unavailability of design tools for self-timed design;
- the lack of designer experience;
- an aversion to self-timed techniques has been encouraged in design education;
- there is a lack of commercial-scale demonstrations of the above-claimed advantages.

In general it is still a high-risk option to pursue a self-timed solution to a design problem, and the lack of tools can make it very labour-intensive.

Exercise 14.1.1

Estimate the effect on the performance of both clocked and self-timed processors of memory conflicts when the processor core has separate instruction and data ports both of which are connected to a single dual-port memory. Assume the memory is constructed from eight arbitrated segments similar to the AMULET3H memory but without the line buffers (see "AMULET3H memory organization" on page 338).

You can assume that the processor fetches instructions continuously and requires about one data memory access for every two instructions. The instruction and data accesses from the clocked processor will be synchronized (by the clock!), so every time contention arises one of the two accesses will be stalled for one cycle. The asynchronous processor has no such sychronization so the two accesses have random relative timing and the stall will be for whatever proportion of the first contending access time remains when the second contending access is requested.

Exercise 14.1.2

Estimate the effect on performance of the instruction and data line buffers in the AMULET3H memory system. Make the same assumptions as in the previous exercise.

Appendix: Computer Logic

Computer Logic

Computer design is based upon Boolean logic where a signal on a wire has one of two values: **true** or **false**. Typically a voltage near ground represents 'false' and one near the supply voltage represents 'true'; however, any representation that can reliably reflect two different states can be used. 'True' is sometimes called logic '1' and 'false' logic '0'.

Logic Gates

A logic gate produces a function of one or more logic inputs. A 2-input 'AND' gate, for example, produces a 'true' output if the first input is 'true' AND the second input is 'true'. Since each input is either 'true' or 'false', there are only four possible input combinations, and the complete functionality of the gate can be expressed in a **truth table** as shown in Figure A.1, which also shows the logic symbol for an AND gate. An AND gate can be extended to more than two inputs (though current CMOS technology limits the practical **fan-in** to four inputs, reducing to three inputs on some sub-micron process technologies). The output is a '1' when all the inputs are '1', and the output is '0' when at least one input is '0'.

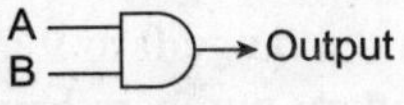

Logic symbol

A	B	Output
0	0	0
0	1	0
1	0	0
1	1	1

Truth table

Figure A.1 The logic symbol and truth table for an AND gate

An OR gate is defined similarly, giving a '0' when all the inputs are '0' and a '1' when at least one input is a '1'. The logic symbol and truth table for a 2-input OR gate are shown in Figure A.2.

A vital logic component is the inverter. This has one input and produces the opposite output. Its logic function is NOT. The output is false ('0') if the input is true ('1') and vice versa. An AND gate with an inverter on the output is a NAND (NOT AND) gate, and an OR gate with an inverter on the output is a NOR (NOT OR) gate. Inversion is often denoted by a circular 'bubble' on the input or output of a gate.

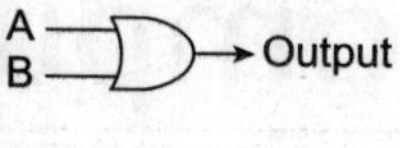

Logic symbol

A	B	Output
0	0	0
0	1	1
1	0	1
1	1	1

Truth table

Figure A.2 The logic symbol and truth table for an OR gate

In fact conventional simple CMOS gates are inherently inverting, so NAND is simpler than AND, the latter being formed by adding an inverter to the former, and similarly OR gates are formed from NOR gates by adding inverters.

Boolean Algebra

All logic circuits can be constructed using only 2-input NAND gates. This stems from the rules of Boolean algebra. First, observe that if both inputs of a NAND gate are connected to the same signal, the output is the inverse of the input, so we have an inverter. Next, connect an inverter to each input of a NAND gate. A brief examination of the truth table reveals that the resulting circuit performs the OR function.

Often logic equations are written using the notation of conventional arithmetic, using '·' for AND and '+' for OR. Thus '*A* AND (*B* OR *C*)' is written '$A{\cdot}(B + C)$'. Logical inversion is denoted by an overbar: '*A* NAND *B*' is written '$\overline{A \cdot B}$'. This notation is very convenient provided that the context makes it clear that an equation is a Boolean logic equation where $1 + 1 = 1$.

Binary Numbers

Numbers are usually represented in computers in binary notation (there is a more complete discussion of data types and number representation in Section 6.2 on page 132). Here, instead of using the familiar base 10 number notation where each digit is in the range 0 to 9 and positions have values which scale by powers of 10 (units, tens, hundreds,...), binary numbers have digits which are either 0 or 1 and positions have values that scale by powers of 2 (units, twos, fours, eights, sixteens,...). Since each binary digit **(bit)** is restricted to one of two values it can be represented by a Boolean value, and the complete binary number is represented by an ordered set of Boolean values.

Binary Addition

The sum of two single-bit binary numbers can be formed using the logic gates we have met already. If both bits are zero the sum is zero; the sum of a one and a zero is one, but the sum of two ones is two, which is represented in binary notation by the two bits '10'. An adder for two single-bit inputs must therefore have two output bits: a **sum** bit with the same weight as the input bits and a **carry** bit which has twice that weight.

If the inputs are *A* and *B*, the sum and carry are formed as follows:

$$sum = A \cdot \overline{B} + \overline{A} \cdot B \qquad \text{Equation 18}$$

$$carry = A \cdot B \qquad \text{Equation 19}$$

The sum function arises frequently in digital logic and is called the **exclusive OR** or XOR function. It is 'exclusive' because it is true if *A* is true, or *B* is true, but not if they are both true. It has its own logic symbol which is shown in Figure A.3 along with a (non-obvious) implementation which uses four NAND gates.

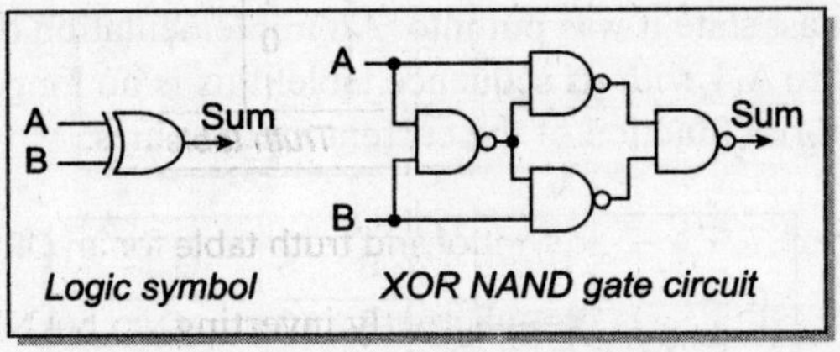

Figure A.3 The logic symbol and NAND circuit for an XOR gate

An adder for *N*-bit binary numbers can be constructed from single-bit adders, but all bits except the first may have to accept a carry input from the next lower stage. Each bit of the adder produces a sum and a carry-out from the inputs and the carry-in:

$$sum_i = A_i \cdot \overline{B}_i \cdot \overline{C}_{i-1} + \overline{A}_i \cdot B_i \cdot \overline{C}_{i-1} + \overline{A}_i \cdot \overline{B}_i \cdot C_{i-1} + A_i \cdot B_i \cdot C_{i-1} \qquad \text{Equation 20}$$

$$C_i = A_i \cdot B_i + A_i \cdot C_{i-1} + B_i \cdot C_{i-1} \qquad \text{Equation 21}$$

Here the equations apply for $i = 1$ to N and C_0 is zero.

Multiplexers

A common requirement in a processor implementation is to select the source of an operand from a number of alternative inputs on a cycle-by-cycle basis. The logic component that performs this function is a **multiplexer** (or simply a **'mux'**). A 2-input multiplexer has a Boolean *select* input (S) and two binary input values A_i and B_i, where $1 \le i \le N$ and N is the number of bits in each binary value. When S is zero, the output Z_i should equal A_i and when S is one Z_i should equal B_i. This is a straightforward logic function:

$$Z_i = \overline{S} \cdot A_i + S \cdot B_i \qquad \text{Equation 22}$$

Clocks

Almost all processors are controlled by a free-running timing reference signal called a **clock**. (But not quite all; see Chapter 14 on page 321 for details of the AMULET processor cores that operate without any external timing reference signal). The clock controls the state changes within the processor.

Generally, all the state is held within **registers**. During the clock cycle **combinatorial** logic (logic whose outputs depend only on the current input values) works out the next state values using Boolean logic gates as described above. At the end of the clock cycle the active clock edge causes all the registers to switch simultaneously to the next state. For maximum performance the clock frequency is set at the highest rate at which all the combinatorial logic can be guaranteed to complete, under worst-case conditions, in time for the next active clock edge.

Sequential Circuits

A register stores the state between active clock edges and changes its contents on the active edge. It is a **sequential** logic circuit; its outputs depend not only on the current input values, but also on how they have changed in the past.

The simplest sequential circuit is the R-S (**Reset-Set**) flip-flop. This is a circuit whose output is set high whenever the *Set* input is active and is reset low whenever the *Reset* input is active. If both inputs are active at the same time the flip-flop behaviour depends on the implementation; if both are inactive the flip-flop *remembers* the last state it was put into. An implementation of an R-S flip-flop using two NOR gates is shown in Figure A.4 with its sequence table; this is no longer a simple truth table since the output is not a combinatorial function of the current input values.

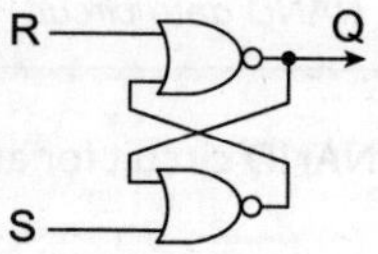

Circuit

R	S	Q_{t+1}
0	0	Q_t
0	1	1
1	0	0
1	1	undefined

Sequence table

Figure A.4 An R-S flip-flop circuit and sequence table

Transparent Latches

A transparent (or **D-type**) latch has a data input (*D*) and an enable signal (*En*); the output follows the *D* input whenever *En* is high, but remains constant at whatever value applied just before *En* went low while *En* stays low. This can be constructed from an R-S flip-flop by generating *R* and *S* from *D* and *En* as shown in Figure A.5.

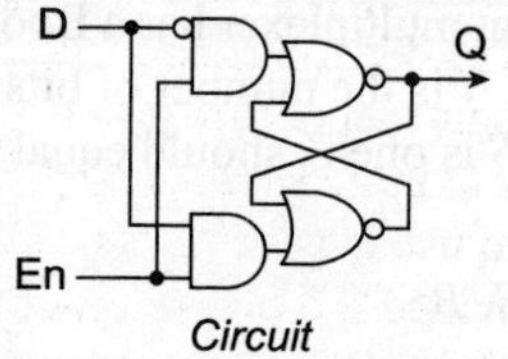

Circuit

En	D	Q_{t+1}
0	0	Q_t
0	1	Q_t
1	0	0
1	1	1

Sequence table

Figure A.5 A D-type transparent latch circuit and sequence table

In principle it should be possible to build any sequential circuit using a D-type latch provided the combinatorial logic between stages is slow enough. Applying a very short positive pulse to *En* will let the next state data through the latch and then hold it before the combinatorial logic has time to respond to the new values. However, in practice this turns out to be a very hard way to build a reliable circuit.

Edge-triggered Latches

There are various ways to build more reliable latching circuits, most of which require each signal to pass through two transparent latches per clock cycle. In the simplest of these, the second latch is placed in series with the first and operates with the inverse enable function. At all times, one latch or the other is holding and the other is transparent. On one clock edge, where the first latch goes opaque and the second goes transparent, the input data value propagates through to the output. It is then held through the full cycle until the same edge in the following cycle. This is therefore an **edge-triggered**

latch; its logic symbol, circuit and sequence table are shown in Figure A.6. (In the table an 'x' in an input column indicates that the input has no effect on the output.)

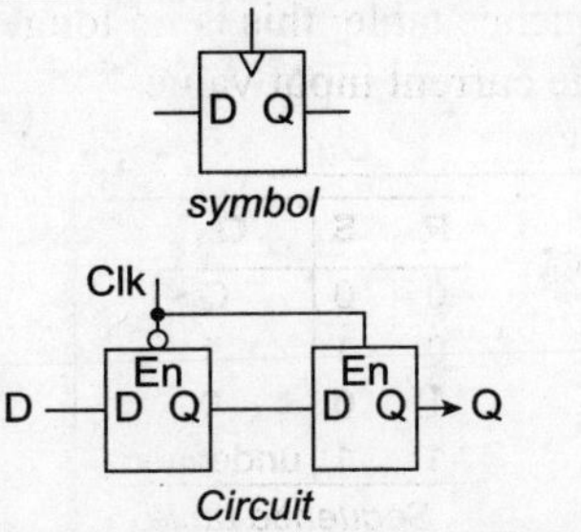

Clk	D	Q_{t+1}
0	x	Q_t
1	x	Q_t
↑	0	0
↑	1	1
↓	x	Q_t

Sequence table

Figure A.6 A D-type edge-triggered latch symbol, circuit and sequence table

Edge-triggered latches require very careful design, since they are not simply combinatorial logic circuits and their function depends critically on the dynamic properties of the circuit elements. If constructed, as suggested above, from two transparent latches in series, there are various *race conditions* which must be avoided. But, with good tools, reliable latches can be designed, and once a reliable latch is available, sequential circuits of arbitrary complexity can be constructed.

Registers

A set of edge-triggered (or equivalent) latches which jointly store the state of a binary value through a clock cycle is termed a **register**. A flexible form of register is connected to a free-running clock and has a 'clock enable' control input so that control logic can decide on a cycle-by-cycle basis whether or not to update the register's contents. A simple way to build such a register is to add a gate on the common clock line to the edge-triggered latches. If we use negative-edge triggered latches, an AND gate will remove the entire high-going clock pulse provided the enable input is low before the clock goes high and stays low until the clock has gone low again. (These are the **set-up** and **hold** conditions for the enable input.) If the enable is, itself, produced from a similar register running off the same clock, it will meet these constraints. The register circuit is shown in Figure A.7.

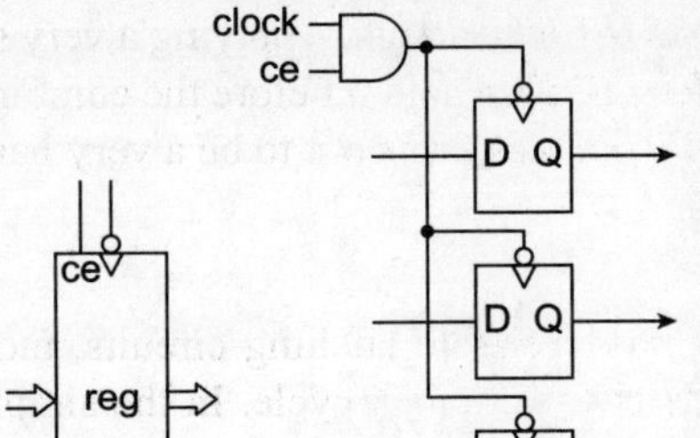

Figure A.7 A register with a clock enable control signal

Glossary

ACM *Association for Computing Machinery*; the American association for computing professionals.

Acorn Computers Limited The UK company where the *ARM* processor was developed between 1983 and 1985. Acorn also developed the *BBC* microcomputer, which established the wide spread educational use of computers in the UK, and the Archimedes range of ARM-based computers which followed the BBC micro into the schools market.

ADC *Analogue to Digital Converter*; an electronic circuit that takes an input which may vary continuously within a specified range and converts it into an n-bit binary number that approximates the input to one of 2^n discrete values within that range.

ALU *Arithmetic-Logic Unit*; the component in a processor that performs the arithmetic (addition, subtraction, and sometimes including multiplication and division) and logic (shift, bit-wise AND, and so on) operations.

AMBA *Advanced Microcontroller Bus Architecture*; an open standard for an on-chip bus which connects the various modules used to build a complex embedded system chip.

AMULET *Asynchronous Microprocessor Using Low-Energy Technology*; this term is used to describe the prototype asynchronous implementations of the *ARM* architecture developed at the University of Manchester.

ANSI *American National Standards Institute*; the American standards body that has defined many useful conventions which are widely used in computing, for example *ASCII* and ANSI standard C.

APCS *ARM Procedure Call Standard*; a calling convention defined by ARM Limited to allow procedures generated by different compilers (or written in assembly language) to call each other.

ARM Formerly *Advanced RISC Machine* (and before that *Acorn RISC Machine*), but the acronym expansion has now been formally abandoned; a 32-bit microprocessor based on *RISC* design principles.

ARM Limited The company spun out from Acorn in 1990 to develop the ARM technology. Based in Cambridge, England, but with design and sales activities in several world regions.

ASCII *American Standard for Computer Information Interchange*; a standard way to represent printable and print control characters in 7-bit binary numbers (often extended to 8-bit fields in today's computers).

ASIC *Application-Specific Integrated Circuit*; a *VLSI* device designed for a particular application, usually for a particular customer.

ASSP *Application-Specific Standard Part*; a *VLSI* device designed for a particular application that is sold as a standard component by the semiconductor manufacturer. Often the chip will have been developed as an *ASIC*, but then in response to market demand the manufacturer will have come to an agreement with the original customer to make the chip available to other customers.

BBC The *British Broadcasting Corporation*; the UK public service radio and television broadcasting company. The BBC is funded mainly through licence fees which are a compulsory feature of television ownership in the UK. Their charter includes a duty to educate the public, and in 1982 they produced a popular series called 'The Computer Programme' based around the BBC micro which was commissioned for the series.

BCD *Binary Coded Decimal*; a way to represent a number by encoding each decimal digit as its binary equivalent.

BCS The *British Computer Society*; the UK association for computing professionals.

C The *C* programming language, widely used for general-purpose and embedded system development.

CAM *Content Addressable Memory*; this is memory which contains a number of different data items and is accessed by presenting a data value which is compared with all the stored items to see if there is a match. If there is a match, the address of the matched location is output; otherwise the CAM signals a 'miss'. It is also described as *associative memory*, and is an important component of an associative cache or *TLB*.

CISC *Complex Instruction Set Computer*; a term created at the same time as *RISC* to describe earlier architectures that do not have the characteristics of RISCs. Typically a CISC has a variable instruction length minicomputer-style instruction set with many addressing modes, memory-to-memory operations and support for many data types.

CMOS *Complementary Metal Oxide Semiconductor*; the predominant technology used for modern integrated circuits, CMOS combines *NMOS* and *PMOS* field-effect transistors on the same chip. This gives the technology active signal drive in both directions, hence fast switching, and near zero power dissipation when it is not switching.

Codec *Coder-decoder*; an electronic system that converts an input (for example an analogue speech signal) into a digitally encoded form and can also reverse this conversion. The same term can also be used for a *compressor-decompressor.*

CPI *Cycles Per Instruction*; a measure of processor efficiency based on the number of clock cycles divided by the number of instructions in a typical code sequence.

CPSR *Current Program Status Register*; an *ARM* register which contains the condition code bits, interrupt disable flags and processor operating mode bits.

CPU The *Central Processing Unit*; a term used somewhat imprecisely to refer to the processor in a computer. It might be just the integer core, or it might include the on-chip *MMU* and cache, and possibly the main memory as well. In this book its use is restricted to those processor cores that include cache memory, and it is used to describe the system comprising the processor, cache and MMU (if present).

DAC *Digital-to-Analogue Converter*; an electronic circuit that converts a digital signal, usually presented in binary form on *n* wires, into an analogue signal presented as one of 2^n values on a single wire.

DECT *Digital European Cordless Telephone*; a European standard for cordless telephones where speech is transferred in digital form between the handset and a local base-station through a radio link.

DRAM *Dynamic Random Access Memory*; the lowest price per bit form of *RAM*, used as the main memory in most computer systems. The data is stored as charge on a capacitor and leaks away in a few milliseconds (hence *dynamic*); to store for longer periods the DRAM must be *refreshed* periodically, which means it must be read while it is still valid and then rewritten to restore the full charge.

DSP *Digital Signal Processor*; a programmable processor whose organization is optimized towards processing continuous streams of digital data. This should be contrasted with a general-purpose processor such as the *ARM* that is optimized for control (decision making) operations.

EDO *Extended Data Out*; a particular interface standard for *DRAM* memory that allows high-performance memory systems to be built.

EEPROM (also E^2PROM.) *Electrically Erasable and Programmable Read Only Memory*; a *ROM* that can be programmed and erased by applying suitable electrical signals. Similar to *flash* memory, but uses a different technology and is generally less flexible than flash.

EPLD *Electrically-Programmable Logic Device*; a general-purpose logic chip which has a large number of gates whose connectivity is defined by the state of on-chip memory cells. These cells may be reprogrammed to change the logic function of the device. (See also *FPGA*, which is a generic configurable device.)

EPROM *Electrically-Programmable Read Only Memory*; a *ROM* which can be programmed by applying suitable electrical signals. Usually it can be erased using an ultra-violet light source and reprogrammed many times.

Flash A form of electrically programmable read only memory that can be erased and reprogrammed electronically. It is widely used to store infrequently changing programs and data in portable systems, and increasingly used as a form of non-volatile file store.

FPA *Floating-Point Accelerator*; additional hardware to speed up floating-point operations, for example, the ARM FPA 10.

FPASC *Floating-Point Accelerator Support Code*; the software that is run in an *ARM* system which includes an FPA 10 floating-point accelerator. The FPA 10 implements a subset of the ARM floating-point instruction set in hardware, and requires the FPASC to handle the remaining instructions.

FPE *Floating-Point Emulator*; the software which is run in an *ARM* system which does not include an FPA 10 floating-point accelerator to support the ARM floating-point instruction set.

FPGA *Field-Programmable Gate Array*; a general-purpose logic chip which has a large number of gates whose connectivity is defined by the state of programmable on-chip components such as anti-fuses or memory cells. (See also *EPLD*.)

FPSR *Floating-Point Status Register*, a user-visible register in the *ARM* floating-point architecture which controls various options and indicates error conditions.

FPU *Floating-Point Unit*; the component in a processor that carries out the floating-point operations.

FSM *Finite State Machine*; a sequential digital circuit that has an internal state and whose outputs and next state are combinatorial logic functions of its inputs and current state.

GSM *Global System for Mobile communications*; a digital standard for mobile telephony used throughout Europe and Asia and in other world regions.

IC *Integrated Circuit*; a semiconductor device where several (up to several million) transistors have been printed during the same manufacturing process. An IC is sometimes referred to as a 'chip'.

IDE *Integrated Drive Electronics*; an interface for a hard disk drive where all the intelligence is in the drive electronics and the host computer interface comprises a data bus and a few address lines.

IEE The *Institution of Electrical Engineers;* the UK professional association for electronics (and electrical) engineers. The IEE sponsors colloquia and publishes journals in the computing area.

IEEE The *Institute of Electrical and Electronics Engineers, Inc.*; the American professional association for electronics and electrical engineers. Membership is not restricted to US nationals, and the IEEE is very active in sponsoring international conferences and publishing journals in the computing area, often in collaboration with the *ACM*.

I²C *Inter-IC*; a serial bus standard used to connect *IC*s together on a printed circuit board. It is particularly useful for connecting small *CMOS RAMs* and *RTC* chips that are powered up even when the rest of the system is switched off.

I/O *Input/Output*; the activity of transferring data between the computer and its environment through a peripheral device.

IrDA *Infra-red Data Association*; an organization established to standardize infra-red communication protocols across the industry, the acronym is frequently applied to a system interface that complies with the resulting standards.

ISDN *Integrated Services Digital Network*; an international standard for digital telephony where speech is sent as a 64 Kbit/s data stream. The standard also defines control protocols.

JTAG *Joint Test Action Group*; the committee which defined the test standard based on a serial interface which is used on many ARM chips.

LCD *Liquid Crystal Display*; the display technology favoured for most portable applications such as lap-top computers and *PDA*s due to its low weight and power consumption.

LRU *Least-Recently Used*; this term describes an algorithm for choosing which value in an associative cache or *TLB* to evict in order to make room for a new value.

MFLOPS *Millions of Floating-Point Operations Per Second*; a measure of the performance of a computer when executing floating-point operations.

MIPS *Millions of Instructions Per Second*; a measure of the rate at which a processor can execute its own instructions. Since different instruction sets have different semantic content per instruction, comparing two processors on the basis of their native MIPS rating is meaningless. Benchmark programs attempt to provide a basis for valid comparison, and 'Dhrystone MIPS' is a normalized rating that is (arguably) more valid.

MMU *Memory Management Unit*; the part of the processor that translates the virtual address into the physical address, using page tables in memory. It includes the table-walking hardware and the *TLB*.

Modem *Modulator-demodulator*; an electronic system or subsystem that converts digital data into a form that can be sent (for example) over a conventional voice telephone connection, and can recover digital data from a similar received audio signal. Simple modems use one audio frequency for a 0 and a different frequency for a 1, but today's high-speed modems use much more sophisticated modulation techniques.

NMOS *N-type Metal Oxide Semiconductor*; a semiconductor technology that pre-dates *CMOS* that was used to build some 8- and 16-bit microprocessors. It supports a logic family with active pull-down and passive pull-up outputs, and gates with a low output draw current even when not switching. NMOS transistors are used, with *PMOS* transistors, to form CMOS. NMOS transistors are more effective than PMOS transistors, which is why NMOS superseded PMOS as the technology of choice for microprocessors, but the combination of the two in CMOS, though more complex to manufacture, is greatly superior to either in both speed and power-efficiency.

OS *Operating System*; the central code in a system that manages the application code, handling scheduling, resource allocation, protection, and so on.

PC *Program Counter*; the register in a processor that holds the address of the next instruction to be fetched. Usually the context should differentiate this use from the next.

PC *Personal Computer*; although apparently generic, this term is now used to refer to desktop computers which are compatible with the IBM PC, which means, *inter alia,* that they use a processor with the Intel x86 instruction set architecture.

PCMCIA *Personal Computer Memory Card International Association*; the organization responsible for a physical form and interface standard for cards which plug into *PCs* (and other portable equipment). Despite the name, the standard is not limited to memory cards; various peripheral interface cards are also conformant. PCMCIA cards are often referred to simply as 'PC-cards'.

PDA *Personal Digital Assistant*; a term first coined to describe the Apple Newton, but now applied to any palmtop computer.

PLA *Programmable Logic Array;* a pseudo-regular structure on an integrated circuit that implements a complex multi-output combinatorial logic function.

PLL *Phase-Locked Loop;* a circuit used to generate a clock signal using another clock signal as a reference.

PMOS *P-type Metal Oxide Semiconductor*; a semiconductor technology that pre-dates *CMOS* and *NMOS* that was used to build early 4-bit microprocessors. It supports a logic family with active pull-up and passive pull-down outputs, and gates with a high output draw current even when not switching. PMOS transistors are used, with NMOS transistors, to form CMOS.

PSR *Program Status Register*; the register in a processor that holds various bits of information such as the condition codes, the interrupt disable bits and the operating mode bits. The *ARM* has a *CPSR* (Current Program Status Register), and an *SPSR* (Saved Program Status Register) for each non-user mode.

PSU *Power Supply Unit*; the electronics that provides the regulated supply voltage(s) required by the system, usually using a mains electricity or battery power source.

RAM *Random Access Memory*; a misnomer, since *ROM* is also random access, RAM is used to refer to the readwrite memory used to store programs and data in a computer; the term is also used to describe the semiconductor components used to build this memory and also used in structures such as caches and *TLBs*.

RISC *Reduced Instruction Set Computer*; a processor with an architecture with certain characteristics based on ideas expounded around 1980 by Patterson (U.C. Berkeley), Ditzel (Bell Laboratories) and Hennessy (Stanford University).

ROM *Read-Only Memory*; the fixed program store in a computer, also used to describe the semiconductor devices which may be used in this role. Contrast with *RAM*.

RS232 A particular standard for asynchronous serial communications, enabling the connection of modems, printers, and communication with other machines.

RTC *Real-Time Clock*; a clock source which allows a computer to work out the time of day, date, and so on. Normally this is a small battery-backed system with a low frequency crystal oscillator which runs all the time, even when the computer itself is turned off.

RTL *Register Transfer Level*; an abstract view of a hardware system such as a processor where multi-bit values are viewed as flowing between registers along buses.

RTOS *Real-Time Operating System*; an operating system that supports programs that must satisfy external timing constraints. These are often small (a few kilobytes) and well suited to use in embedded systems.

SDLC *Synchronous Data Link Controller*; a peripheral that connects a computer to a clocked serial interface and supports one or more standard protocols.

SoC *System-on-Chip*; a single integrated circuit that incorporates all of the functionality of an electronic system, including the processor, memory and peripherals. At the time of writing most SoCs still require off-chip memory resources in addition to their on-chip memory, but all other system components are on chip.

SPSR *Saved Program Status Register*; an *ARM* register used to save the values of the *CPSR* when an exception occurs.

SRAM *Static Random Access Memory*; more expensive than *DRAM*, this form of *RAM* holds its data in flip-flops which do not require refreshing. SRAM has a lower access time than DRAM and can retain its contents indefinitely with almost no power dissipation. It is used for most RAM functions on processor chips, such as cache and *TLB* memory, and may be used for the main memory in some smaller embedded systems.

TLB *Translation Look-aside Buffer*; a cache of recently used page table entries which avoids the overhead of page table walking on every memory access.

UART *Universal Asynchronous Receiver/Transmitter*; a peripheral device that interfaces a serial line (typically with an *RS232* signalling protocol) to a processor bus.

USB *Universal Serial Bus*; a standard interface on more recent *PC*s that supports the connection of various peripherals. It uses a high-speed serial protocol and an electrical interface that allows devices to be connected and disconnected while the machine is running (that is, it is 'hot-pluggable').

VHDL *VHSIC Hardware Description Language* (where VHSIC expands to *Very High-Speed Integrated Circuit*); a standard language for describing hardware at a behavioural or structural level which is supported by most semiconductor design tool companies.

VLSI *Very Large Scale Integration*; the process of putting a lot of transistors onto a single chip. There was an attempt to categorize chip transistor counts as SSI, MSI, LSI (Small, Medium and Large Scale Integration), VLSI, and so on, on the basis of orders of magnitude, but process technology advanced faster than new terms could be coined. The next term, ULSI (Ultra Large Scale Integration) never gained widespread use, and would probably now be obsolete anyway.

VLSI Technology, Inc. VLSI Technology, Inc., sometimes abbreviated to just *VLSI*, manufactured the first ARM chips designed at Acorn Computers and, with Acorn and Apple, established ARM Limited as a separate company in 1990. VLSI was the first ARM semiconductor partner and manufactures a range of ARM-based CPUs and system chips. It is now owned by Philips Semiconductors.

VM *Virtual Memory*; the address space that the program runs in which is mapped to physical memory by the *MMU*. The virtual space may be larger than the physical space, and parts of the virtual space may be paged out onto a hard disk or may not exist anywhere.

VRAM *Video Random Access Memory*; a form of *DRAM* with on-chip shift registers to give high-bandwidth access to sequential data for generating video displays.

Bibliography

ARM texts

- http://www.arm.com/

  Datasheets on the ARM processors and other relevant material are available over the Internet from ARM's World Wide Web site.

- Jaggar (ed.), 'ARM Architectural Reference Manual', Prentice Hall. ISBN 0-13-736299-4.

  A reference book with details of the ARM and Thumb instruction set, the memory management architecture, and so on. Known in the ARM community as the 'ARM ARM'.

Thumb

- Segars, Clarke and Goudge, 'Embedded Control Problems, Thumb, and the ARM7TDMI', *IEEE Micro,* **15** (5), October 1995, pages 22–30.

  A paper describing the philosophy and performance of the Thumb instruction set.

RISC architecture

- Patterson and Ditzel, 'The Case for the Reduced Instruction Set Computer', ACM SIGARCH *Computer Architecture News,* **8** (6), October 1980, pages 25–33.

  The seminal paper that questioned the trend towards ever-increasing complexity in processor design.

- Katevenis, *Reduced Instruction Set Computer Architectures for VLSI,* MIT Press, Cambridge, MA, USA, 1985. ISBN 0-262-11103-9.

  A detailed account of the Berkeley RISC designs and an ACM Doctoral Dissertation Award winner.

- Hennessy and Patterson, *Computer Architecture–A Quantitative Approach,* 2nd edition, Morgan Kaufrnann, San Francisco, CA, USA, 1990. ISBN 1-55860-329-8.

  This is the authoritative text on mainstream RISC design, written by the two people with primary responsibility for making RISC happen.

- Patterson and Hennessy, *Computer Organization and Design–The Hardware/Software Interface,* Morgan Kaufrnann, San Francisco, CA, USA, 1994. ISBN 1-55860-281-X.

  Following the considerable success of *Computer Architecture–A Quantitative Approach* by the same authors (but in a different order!), this book goes into the basics in rather more detail.

CMOS design

- Weste and Eshraighan, *Principles of CMOS VLSI Design, A Systems Perspective,* 2nd edition, Addison-Wesley, Reading, MA, USA, 1993. ISBN 0-201-53376-6.

  This is an authoritative text on transistor-level CMOS design, covering physical layout, circuits and systems issues.

Self-timed logic

- 'Proceedings ofthe IEEE', **87** (2), February 1999, ISSN 0018-9219.

  This special issue on asynchronous design contains background material and details on several complex asynchronous designs, including AMULET2e.

- http://www.cs.man.ac.uk/async/

  The asynchronous logic home pages contain tutorial material and links to most of the groups active in asynchronous logic research world-wide.

Endianness

- Cohen, 'On Holy Wars and a Plea for Peace', *Computer,* **14** (10), October 1981, IEEE Computer Society Press, pages 48–54.

  The article which raised the issue of big- and little-endian byte ordering and established the endian terminology by analogy with *Gulliver's Travels.*

Clanguage

- Kernighan and Ritchie, *The C Programming Language,* 2nd edition, Prentice Hall, Englewood Cliffs, NJ, USA, 1988. ISBN 0-13-110362-8.

  This is a standard reference book for C; note that the second edition covers ANSI standard C which the first edition did not.

- Koenig, *C Traps and Pitfalls,* Addison-Wesley, Reading, MA, USA, 1989. ISBN 0-201-17928-8.

  A text describing how to avoid the standard pitfalls in C programming; useful for C programmers at all levels of experience.

Index